MONSOON

MW00831255

The Dhufar revolution in Oman (1965–1976) was the longest-running major armed struggle in the history of the Arabian Peninsula, Britain's last classic colonial war in the region, and one of the highlights of the Cold War in the Middle East. *Monsoon Revolution* retrieves the political, social, and cultural history of that remarkable process. Relying upon a wide range of untapped Arab and British archival and oral sources, it revises the modern political history of Oman by revealing the centrality of popular movements in shaping events and outcomes. The ties that bound transnational anti-colonial networks are explored, and Dhufar is revealed to be an ideal vantage point from which to demonstrate the centrality of South-South connections in modern Arab history.

Abdel Razzaq Takriti is Associate Professor and Arab-American Educational Foundation Chair in Modern Arab History at the University of Houston. He holds a DPhil from St Antony's College, Oxford and was a Junior Research Fellow at St Edmund Hall, Oxford. He won the MESA Malcolm Kerr Dissertation Award and the BRISMES Leigh Douglas Memorial Prize for this work.

OXFORD HISTORICAL MONOGRAPHS

Editors

P. CLAVIN   L.GOLDMAN   J. INNES   R. SERVICE
P. A. SLACK   B. WARD-PERKINS   J. L. WATTS

Monsoon Revolution

Republicans, Sultans, and Empires in Oman, 1965–1976

ABDEL RAZZAQ TAKRITI

OXFORD
UNIVERSITY PRESS

OXFORD

UNIVERSITY PRESS

Great Clarendon Street, Oxford, OX2 6DP,
United Kingdom

Oxford University Press is a department of the University of Oxford.
It furthers the University's objective of excellence in research, scholarship,
and education by publishing worldwide. Oxford is a registered trade mark of
Oxford University Press in the UK and in certain other countries

First published 2013
First published in paperback 2016

Published in the United States of America by Oxford University Press
198 Madison Avenue, New York, NY 10016, United States of America

British Library Cataloguing in Publication Data

Data available

Library of Congress Cataloging in Publication Data

Data available

ISBN 978–0–19–967443–5 (Hbk.)
ISBN 978–0–19–878317–6 (Pbk.)

To the People of Oman
and
For Suha al-Nashif and Karma Nabulsi

Preface to the paperback edition

Since the publication of this book in 2013, new evidence has come to light regarding some important events discussed here. Major Ray Kane, who played a key role in carrying out the 1970 coup, generously shared with me his recently published memoirs. Accordingly, I have updated some of the narrative in Chapter 7. While the rest of the text now includes minor changes, the main empirical claims and historiographical engagements are left unaltered. This paperback edition was completed at the University of Houston and I am grateful to my colleagues for appointing me to the Arab-American Educational Foundation Chair in Modern Arab History. Last but not least, I am very thankful to Dr Hollie Thomas of Oxford University Press for her patience and support.

Houston, May 1, 2016

Acknowledgements

Writing this book has been a lesson in humility and I simply could not have done it alone. The editing process was concluded at the University of Sheffield, and I am thankful to my former colleagues there for embracing me into their scholarly community. Most of the work was completed in the beautiful surroundings of St Edmund Hall, Oxford, and I am extremely grateful to the Principal and Fellows of the College (especially Karma Nabulsi) for electing me to the SG Younis Junior Research Fellowship in Political History. In the Middle East Centre at St Antony's College particular thanks go to Eugene Rogan, who has guided this project from beginning to end, initially as my doctoral supervisor and then as the guest editor. His door was always open, his mind sympathetic and engaging, and his comments thorough and detailed. Avi Shlaim offered caring support throughout, and Michael Willis kindly granted permission for reproducing the images. Mastan Ebtehaj forgave many fines at the library, and Debbie Usher patiently hosted me for countless days in the archive.

Elsewhere in Oxford, Sudhir Hazareesingh gave me the great benefit of his love, rare intellect, and vast theoretical and empirical knowledge. He read every chapter and provided helpful comments and subtle observations, firmly and crucially intervening at the right moments. Without his careful watch this work would have been much impoverished. David Priestland was a constant intellectual presence, a true friend from whom I have learned much, and an ideal internal examiner. Charles Tripp was a fantastic external examiner and commentator on the research. Helen Lackner was her usual generous self, providing a great deal of material and answering many questions. John Wilkinson, a leading scholar of Oman, carefully read the draft monograph, shared his precious time and specialist knowledge, encouraged important changes, gave material, and saved me from crucial mistakes. Fred Lawson came to the rescue at the very end, meticulously reading the text and helping transform it from a dissertation to a book. Thanks are also owed to James Piscatori, Robert Gildea, and Andrew Kahn for their encouragement at various points.

This book has benefited from the help of other friends in different corners of the globe. In Toronto, Amir Hassanpour inspired me with his integrity, introduced me to Dhufar and its revolution, and suggested that I write on it. James Reilly and Jens Hanssen solidly grounded me in the study of Arab history in my undergraduate years, and Sam Ginden was my graduate mentor. In Beirut, Raghid al-Solh introduced me to everyone and gave me essential suggestions; Fawaz Traboulsi enthusiastically shared with me his immense personal and scholarly experience of Dhufar; Muhsin Ibrahim offered me an extremely rare interview at a busy and intense moment, and Riad al-Rayyes gifted me with books and shared with me thoughtful observations.

Help also arrived from elsewhere: Mohammad Jamal Barut gave me rare documents from his personal collection in Aleppo, Laleh Khalili shared useful notes, and Heiny Srour told me of her memories and sent me her conference papers. In Bahrain, the late Hisham al-Shehabi hosted me in his home, introduced me to his comrades, and touched me with his gentleness and fortitude. The late Abdel Rahman al-Nuaimi shared with me his rich collection gathered during his unique revolutionary life. Abdel Munim al-Shirawi gave many hours of his time, and I will always remember his invaluable assistance and his dedication to documenting the history of his generation.

Abdel Nabi al-Ikri helped in ways too numerous to count: time, interviews, suggestions, contacts, and unwavering support. Nouh gave me a profound interview and gifted me a 'return ship' to Palestine crafted with his own hands. Osama Takriti afforded me a place to stay, and my dear friend Omar al-Shehabi took me everywhere and endured many days of research in my company. Many others in Bahrain contributed to this work, but in accordance with their wishes they remain unnamed. The same goes for the remarkable Omanis who helped me during my stay in Salalah; their strength and persistence was a true inspiration.

This work would not have been appeared without the kind acceptance of the Editors of the Oxford Historical Monographs series. Joanna Innes played an essential role in expediting the publication process. My gratitude also goes to Stephanie Ireland at OUP for commissioning the book and patiently preparing it for publication, and for Cathryn Steele for her oversight of the editorial process. Emma Barber, Senior Production Editor, has been exceedingly kind, helpful, and a joy to work with. I am also very much indebted to Nicholas Bromley for his copy-edits. Michael Athanson, Deputy Map Librarian at the Bodleian Library, created the maps with precision. The staff at the British Library were extremely helpful on each of my many visits, as were the archivists at the National Archives at Kew Gardens, and Rhodes House at Oxford. Special thanks go to Afzal Hassan at Exeter's Arab World Documentation Unit for helping with the cover image.

This book drew on financial support received during the completion of the doctoral dissertation upon which it is based. First and foremost, I wish to thank Hani Kalouti, who had generously and discretely funded my education when it really mattered. His was a grand gesture that had a major impact on my life, and I shall forever remember it with heartfelt appreciation and gratitude. Suha al-Nashif worked very hard to give me vital help throughout, and I shall never forget her sacrifices. Thanks are also due to Wadham College, and especially to Ian Thompson for assisting me with a grant from the Warden's Exhibition Fund; Karma Nabulsi and Ilan Pappe for the first Edward Said and Ibrahim Abu-Lughod Scholarship; the British Society for Middle Eastern Studies for a Research Award; the Social Sciences and Humanities Research Council of Canada for a Doctoral Fellowship; the Pachachi Trustees and the Director and Fellows of the Middle East Centre at St Antony's College for the Ali Pachachi Studentship; the Council Secretariat of the University of Oxford and the Board of Management of the Beit Fund for funding two research trips; and Ismail Takriti, who gave assistance at several important moments.

Finally, this book is dedicated to Suha al-Nashif and Karma Nabulsi. My earliest inspiration and first example, Suha's generous humanity, sharp mind, and kind heart gave me strength for every step, and made everything good in my life possible, including this work. Karma Nabulsi read and commented on each individual chapter, provided essential theoretical engagement, elevated the tone of this work, and sharpened its argument. She has been my guide, mentor, and friend—a truly creative scholar who irrevocably transformed both mind and spirit. Her generous and selfless presence shaped the course of my writing journey, and I am enormously grateful to her.

Table of Contents

List of Illustrations

Abbreviations

CSAF	Commander of the Sultan's Armed Forces
DCA	Dhufari Charitable Association
DF	Dhufar Force
DLF	Dhufar Liberation Front
DR	Desert Regiment
DSO	Dhufari Soldiers' Organization
MAN	Movement of Arab Nationalists
MR	Muscat Regiment
NDFLOAG	National Democratic Front for the Liberation of the Occupied Arab Gulf
NLF	National Liberation Front
OG	Oman Gendarmerie
OLA	Oman Liberation Army
PDRY	People's Democratic Republic of Yemen
PFLO	Popular Front for the Liberation of Oman
PFLOAG	Popular Front for the Liberation of the Occupied Arab Gulf; or
PFLOAG	Popular Front for the Liberation of Oman and the Arab Gulf
PR	Political Resident in the Persian Gulf
PRM	Popular Revolutionary Movement
SAF	Sultan's Armed Forces
SOAF	Sultan of Oman's Air Force
TOS	Trucial Oman Scouts
UAR	United Arab Republic
YAR	Yemen Arab Republic

Introduction

In the winter of 1965, a group of young Dhufari men assembled in Basra. Arriving from all corners of the Gulf, their rendezvous point was the Caravan, one of the many unassuming hotels dotted across the port city. A few days after their arrival, they were discreetly contacted by Iraqi military intelligence officers, who took them north to Baghdad's Mansuriya camp. There, they underwent a month and a half of training in guerrilla warfare, automatic weapons, rocket launchers, land mines, wireless communication, and destroying military installations. In total, 140 fighters took the course, which was given in three consecutive sessions between December 1964 and the first months of 1965. The fighters had been brought together by a determination to overthrow the Sultan and expel the British, forming the military nucleus of the newly created Dhufar Liberation Front (DLF).[1]

Over the following months, the fighters made their way back to Dhufar, then a dependency of the Sultanate of Muscat and Oman. By 9 June 1965, a fiery communiqué announced the launch of armed struggle. The text was replete with the language of Arab nationalism and anti-colonialism, of freedom and liberation:

> Oh Arab People of Dhufar, a revolutionary vanguard from amongst your ranks has emerged, believing in God and in the homeland. Taking the freedom of the homeland as its principle, it has raised the banner of liberation from the rule of the tyrannical Al Bu Said Sultans whose Sultanate has been connected with the columns of British colonialist invasion.[2]

Such terms seem hardly remarkable for the high age of pan-Arabism and tricontinentalism.[3] They were nonetheless novel entries into the vocabulary

---

[1] FO1016/782, 'Capture of Launch with Arms for Dhufar', 8 June 1965.

[2] Dhufar Liberation Front, 'Bayan I'lan al Kifah al Mussalah,' 9 June 1965 in Al-Jabha al-Sha'biya. *Wathaiq al Nidal al Watani: 1965–1974*. Beirut: Dar Al Talia'a, 1974, p.9.

[3] For the use of 'tricontinentalism' to refer to the liberation movements of Africa, Asia and Latin America see Robert Young, *Postcolonialism: An Historical Introduction*, Oxford: Blackwell, 2001, p.5.

of Dhufar, a territory that had hitherto seemed distant from regional political intrigues. Sparsely populated and severely underdeveloped, Dhufar was a small forgotten corner in a part of the world consumed by the grand struggles for independence, state building, unity, development, and Palestine. Yet, in spite of its quintessential peripherality, it gave birth to the most significant internal threat to the modern Gulf state structure. The insurrectionary words of the 1965 communiqué translated into a decade long struggle against both the Sultans and the British, placing Dhufar on the map of third world revolutions.

One of the factors that facilitated the struggle was the monsoon. That phenomenon has an almost miraculous impact on Dhufar, endowing it with a 'cloud forest' that rises sharply out of the seemingly endless expanse of the Arabian Desert. It was in the wooded highlands that the revolutionaries largely operated, sheltered from detection by the lush trees; and it was during the monsoon that they launched most of their offensive operations, enveloped by the thick mist descending upon the territory. Like the monsoon, the revolution sustained by these fighters made a profound, if temporary, impact on their homeland, rendering its striking mountains and coasts more fertile with ideas, events, and possibilities than before or after.

This book offers a study of that revolution and its absolutist opponents, focusing on the armed struggle conducted in the period 1965–76. In doing so, it pursues three purposes: historical retrieval; revision; and contextualization. Drawing on a wide range of archival and oral sources, it aims to protect the memory of a pivotal episode in Arab revolutionary history and its participants from 'the enormous condescension of posterity'.[4] This connects the book to a broader revisionist aim: to contribute, however modestly, to the project of re-writing the history of Arab revolutions and revolutionaries in a way that frees them from their current imprisonment in colonial accounts, counterinsurgency studies, official histories, and contemporary auto-critiques. Since the 1960s, such an effort has been undertaken with regard to several revolutions across the world, but its application to the Arab world has been extremely limited—and, in the case of the Gulf, almost entirely absent.

The second objective of this book is to consider the Dhufar revolution not just as an episode of Omani history, but to re-read Omani history in its light. As it stands today, Omani history is dominated by the figure of the Sultan. Official and colonial accounts tell a story of a 'medieval' nation that

---

[4] To borrow E.P. Thompson's famous expression in *The Making of the English Working Class*. London: Penguin, 1991, p.12.

underwent a 'modern' renaissance on the initiative of a reforming and enlightened Sultan, Qaboos bin Said. An emerging critical literature has begun to question this particular narrative.[5] This has greatly contributed to our understanding of Omani history, but the Sultan is still at the centre of the story, absolutely dominating the historiography as much as he now controls the country. This work seeks to shift the focus from the ruler to the people who made this history themselves. It examines how Omani women and men, through the difficult craft of popular mobilization, created their own history and forced through the economic transformation of their country. Simultaneously, it examines the political limitations of this process, analysing the causes for the failure of revolutionary or reformist alternatives to achieve a permanent presence. The principal explanation that it offers to account for this phenomenon is British colonial ascendancy, which was the essential factor in anchoring absolutism. This explanation is also a contribution to the broader literature, tracing the role of the colonial past in shaping contemporary autocratic regimes.[6]

A third ambition of the book is to integrate revolutionary and Omani history into the greater narrative of which they were a small but essential constituent part. This is the story of the struggle between imperial and popular sovereignties and the larger battle between monarchical regimes and republican movements in the Arab world and beyond during the period under consideration. In this vein, significant strands of the Omani past belong to the realm of the 'Bandung spirit' and the tricontinental era, reflecting a shift in modern Arab political and intellectual history. Up to the first half of the twentieth century, movements and intellectual currents of the Arab 'liberal age' had their gaze fixed on Europe, taking their cue from such diverse sources as the French revolution, German romanticism, and the Italian *Carbonari*. A shift occurred in the revolutionary age of the 1960s, and South-South connections began playing a much more important role. The new sources of inspiration for thought and practice

---

[5] Allan and Rigsbee have emphasized the continuities between the Qaboos and Said bin Taimur eras; Owtram has focused on the imperial role in the Sultanate; while Valeri has scrutinized the Qaboos regime from the perspective of nation building and legitimization. See C. Allen and W. Rigsbee, *Oman Under Qaboos: From Coup to Constitution, 1970–1996*, London: Frank Cass, 2002; F. Owtram, *A Modern History of Oman: Formation of the State since 1920*, London: I.B. Tauris, 2004; Marc Valeri, *Oman: Politics and Society in the Qaboos State*, London: Hurst and Company, 2009.

[6] See for example Mahmoud Mamdani, *Citizen and Subject: Contemporary Africa and the Legacy of Late Colonialism*, Princeton: Princeton University Press, 1996, and Joseph Massad, *Colonial Effects: The Making of National Identity in Jordan*, New York: Columbia University Press, 1998.

were Cuba, Vietnam and China, as well as Arab arenas such as Algeria and Palestine. In examining this transnational dimension, this book will outline the ways in which Omani revolutionary movements were intimately connected to wider Arab and international currents. Regionally they belonged to a network that raised the banner of the struggle against 'Zionism, Imperialism and Arab reactionary regimes'. Internationally, they were part of a global community of revolution that boasted its own practices, literatures, modes of expression, ideologies and signs. In similar ways, the monarchical opponents of the revolutionaries belonged to regional, international, political, cultural, military, and economic networks that will also be explored.

The three aims of historical retrieval, revision, and contextualization will be pursued through an account of the birth and development of a revolutionary movement, the transformation of a princely state into an absolutist monarchy, and the clash between these two forces in the context of a longstanding struggle between a fading British empire and its local opponents. This narrative is connected by a single analytical thread: the contrasting visions of sovereignty expressed by revolution and absolutism. Borrowing from Karma Nabulsi's enabling conceptualization tracing the practices of war within particular traditions, the ways in which a local Arabist republican tradition clashed with its Anglo-Sultanic martialist opposite are illustrated.[7] The former was rooted in a notion of anticolonial popular sovereignty, representing a quest for citizenship; the latter exemplified imperial sovereignty and its local monarchic manifestation, imposing subjecthood and pursuing the Hobbesian 'commonwealth by acquisition'.

In narrating and analysing the story of Omani revolution and absolutism, a plethora of Arab personal collections and unpublished papers were consulted, and lengthy interviews were undertaken in Oman, Bahrain, and Lebanon. These materials are detailed in the bibliography. Unfortunately, the official revolutionary archives based in Aden were lost during the Yemeni civil war of 1994. Nevertheless, former PFLOAG revolutionaries have responded to this loss by gathering and digitalizing a significant amount of unpublished papers. These, along with the publications, newspapers, and pamphlets of the revolution, have provided a very rich source of both insight and information.

Most of the leading positions in the Sultanate administration, intelligence, and army in the period concerned were staffed by Britons, and the archival collections in the United Kingdom offer the largest and most

---

[7] See Karma Nabulsi, *Traditions of War: Occupation, Resistance, and the Law,* Oxford: Oxford University Press, 2005.

comprehensive resource on Omani absolutism, as well as on imperial policy. They also include a wealth of intelligence reports and assessments detailing the activities of the revolutionaries. These documents were approached with care, constantly read against, and counterbalanced as much as possible with revolutionary accounts and sources. Some British materials were extremely difficult to find. In particular, the sources on the July 1970 coup continue to be suppressed, and access to them is still denied to the public by the Foreign Office. It took seven years of careful searching to find the relevant collection of papers. They were tucked away in a seemingly unrelated Ministry of Defence file, having escaped the watchful eyes of official censors.

CONCEPTUALIZING OMANI REVOLUTION AND ABSOLUTISM

Revolution and absolutism, the central concepts with which this book is concerned, appear to be straightforward and transparent, describing, respectively, an historical process and a form of rule. However, these simple abstractions signify complex realities and accordingly require critical unpacking. Although it is one of the most dynamic words available, 'revolution' is often viewed from a static lens, describing a moment when a particular order is completely overthrown. In this understanding, the term suggests a beginning leading to an end, an act defined only by its climax. The focus is upon the criterion of success: a process that leads to the overthrow of an order is a revolution; processes that fail to do so are given lesser designations—'rebellion', 'revolt', 'uprising', 'insurrection'. Yet such a view gives rise to several historiographical problems. Like all 'performance-based' measures, it reduces entire processes to their end result. Concerned with judgements of 'success' or 'failure', it overlooks substantive elements.

Accordingly, there is a need to challenge influential definitions, such as Charles Tilly's, which posits that a revolution combines a 'revolutionary situation' with a 'revolutionary outcome'. According to this view: 'A revolutionary *situation*...entails multiple sovereignty: two or more blocks make effective, incompatible claims to control the state, or to be the state.' As for a revolutionary outcome, 'it occurs with transfer of state power from those who held it before the start of multiple sovereignty to a new coalition—which may, of course, include some elements of the old ruling coalition'.[8] By this definition, Dhufar had a revolutionary situation, but

---

[8] Charles Tilly, *European Revolutions, 1492–1992*, Oxford: Blackwell, 1995, pp.10–14. Italics in the original.

not a revolutionary outcome. However, once one shifts focus from the final outcome to the actual process, another picture emerges. For eleven years in Dhufar a substantial percentage of the population lived independently of the Anglo-Sultanic authorities, controlled a large territory, created their own institutions, instituted social reforms, and implemented radical change. The generation living in Dhufar at the time experienced these events as a revolution, and indeed it touched every civic, social, economic, and intellectual facet of their lives.

So comprehensive were the transformations that took place that it would be both insufficient and inaccurate to describe this period in Dhufar solely as a revolutionary situation. Changes included: the creation of an entirely new civic space under a unified revolutionary authority; the abolition of slavery; the introduction—for the first time since the arrival of Islam—of new supra-tribal identities; the suppression of sheikhs; the rise of members from lower tribes and slave backgrounds into positions of leadership; the arrival of reading, writing, and contemporary medicine; the introduction of new crops; the spread of modern ideologies; the Arabization and Omanization, from below, of Dhufari identity, language and culture; and, above all, the waging of a protracted armed struggle. Moreover, although the *ancien regime* of the Sultanate was never destroyed, a temporary transfer of power occurred in large sectors of the Dhufari highlands, territories that the revolutionaries called the liberated areas.

Another concern here is the definition of the state. Central to Tilly's definition of revolution is the idea that 'whatever else they involve, revolutions include forcible transfers of power over states'.[9] However, such state-centrism effectively denies the relevance of the revolutionary category to several non-European peoples. In places like Oman, revolution preceded the creation of the formal state and, indeed, one of the revolution's aims was to create an independent republic in place of a monarchic-tribal order that revolved around a British-maintained ruler. Although the ruler remained, and his rule was upgraded to an absolutist level, the nature and practices of his administration were enormously altered so as to contain those revolutionary pressures. In other words, the very creation of the state was profoundly shaped by the revolution, which acted as the historical engine of change in Oman.

At any rate, historians have written extensively of revolutions that are deemed to have 'failed'. They have long described the European events of 1848 as 'revolutions', in spite of their eventual outcomes. They have painstakingly documented the Caribbean revolutions in the late eighteenth and

---

[9] Tilly, *European Revolutions*, p.5.

early nineteenth centuries, highlighting the profound and lasting nature of the events that took place, regardless of defeats in such places as Guadelope. Likewise, they have referred to a Chilean 'revolution from below' during the Allende years, in spite of Pinochet's quick seizure of power. Equally, they have written about the Spanish revolution, which never entailed a full republican claim to power and culminated in the establishment of Franco's regime and its hold on the state and its institutions for decades.[10]

In choosing to define the events in Dhufar between 1965 and 1976 as a revolution, this book is already in line with the predominant—although by no means uncontested—terminological practice in the Arabic. However, it diverges from the majority of English works that have been published on Dhufar which, with a few exceptions, have avoided the term 'revolution', relying instead upon such terms as 'insurgency', 'rebellion', 'war', and 'campaign'. Accordingly, there is a large conceptual gap between the Arabic and English works, and writings from the former colonies and the metropolises. This gap can be explained with reference to the work of Raymond Williams, who notes that, since the eighteenth century, there existed:

> … a new climate of political thought, in which the adequacy of a political system rather than loyalty to a particular sovereign was more and more taken as a real issue, revolution was obviously preferred to rebellion, by anyone who supported independent change. There is a surviving significance in this, in our own time. Rebellion is still ordinarily used by a dominant power and its friends, until (or even after) it has to admit that what has been taking place—with its own independent cause and loyalties—is a revolution.[11]

Such an acknowledgement has never been accorded to the Dhufar revolution in the literature in English. In Arabic, the term *Thawrat Dhufar* was adopted as the events themselves were unfolding. The revolutionaries and their sympathizers across the Arab world did not use this solely for the purposes of description: they also used it for a legitimization of the enterprise. In contrast, the Sultanate and its supporters deployed a different and more denigrating term, *tamarrud*, signifying a treacherous mutiny against the legitimate authority. The political potency of these terms can

---

[10] Laurent Dubois, *A Colony of Citizens: Revolutions and Slave Emancipation in the French Caribbean, 1787–1804*, Chapel Hill: University of North Carolina Press, 2004; Robert Evans and Hartmut Von Strandmann, *The Revolutions in Europe, 1848–1849: From Reform to Reaction*, Oxford: OUP, 2002; Peter Winn, *Weavers of Revolution: The Yarur Workers and Chile's Road to Socialism*, Oxford: OUP, 1989.

[11] Raymond Williams, *Keywords: A Vocabulary of Culture and Society*, Glasgow: Fontana/Croom Helm, 1976, p.228.

still be seen in recent debates within the Arab press, where the past is instrumentalized for the sake of present concerns.[12] As with many other revolutions, the memory of Dhufar is held hostage by current agendas: disillusioned Arab intellectuals see it as a distant reminder of a misguided youth; loyalist writers present it as an international communist conspiracy that was defeated by a glorious Sultan; reformists as an opportunity that was missed due to the mistakes of ultra-leftism; finally, current Dhufari separatists see it as a code for their own repressed aspirations. All of these approaches to Dhufar illustrate the challenges in setting out an account of a counter-order at a time when the order against which it battled has so comprehensively prevailed.

In describing the creation of the currently prevailing order in Oman, this book has relied upon the term 'absolutism', which was carefully chosen over other terms, such as 'despotism' and 'tyranny'. Absolutism, it must be emphasized, is a recent phenomenon in Omani history, Qaboos being the first monarch to exercise absolute rule. His father could be persuasively defined as a tyrant, if applying the virtue-based Aristotlean definition of tyranny as 'monarchy with a view to the advantage of the monarch' as opposed to the 'common good'.[13] He could certainly be described as a despot, in accordance with Montesquieu's procedural-based view of despotism as a rule that is arbitrary, and where there are no 'fundamental laws' and 'no depository of laws'.[14]

Qaboos may share these characteristics with his father. However, his regime is singular in its absolutist character. Absolutism can encompass either classical tyranny or enlightenment notions of despotism. However, unlike these terms, which signify the quality of domination, it also stands for the centralization of domination and its spread by military and bureaucratic institutions which are themselves entirely controlled by the monarch. Moreover, absolutism as a term avoids reproducing Orientalist discourse. For centuries, the notion of 'Oriental Despotism' was prevalent in European thought. In an effort to confront growing absolutism at home, enlightenment philosophers counterpoised 'civilised' Europe to the 'barbaric' and 'enslaved' East.[15] In the discussions of the political systems that the book sets out to explore, the perpetuation of such mischaracterizations is consciously avoided. Rather than being a primordial

---

[12] For a recent controversy see: Abbas Baydoun, 'Al-Bahr Sahra'a Oman wal Makan Usturatuha', *As-Safir*, 14/02/2009, and 'Takfi, 'Ibara Wahidah', *As-Safir*, 18/03/2009.

[13] Aristotle, *The Politics*, Chicago: University of Chicago Press, 1985, Book 3, Chapter 7, p.96.

[14] Montesquieu, *The Spirit of the Laws*, Cambridge: CUP, 1989, p.19.

[15] Alan Grosrichard, *The Sultan's Court: European Fantasies of the East*, London: Verso, 1998.

oriental phenomenon, Omani absolutism was a recent outcome of a series of historical contests over the character and location of sovereign terminal political authority.

These contests were by no means of solely local relevance. Indeed, at its peak, the Dhufar revolution held a broader meaning that is difficult to appreciate today. Its significance was captured in a 1975 *New Left Review* editorial:

> The war in the southern, Dhofar, province of the Sultanate of Oman has now been in progress for over ten years. Following the Portuguese retreat from Africa and the defeat of US imperialism in Indochina it is the only revolutionary war of any significant military dimensions taking place in the world today.[16]

One of the closing chapters of the classical age of anti-colonialism, Dhufar carried the 'Bandung spirit' and the vision of the Havana tricontinental. It is my hope that this book would contribute, even in a small way, to an appreciation of that struggle and the world to which it belonged.

---

[16] 'Introduction—British Troops in Oman', *New Left Review*, I/92, July/August, 1975.

1

Imperial Sovereignty in Omani History

Twentieth-century Arab history was marked by the question of sovereignty, by territorial divisions, and by the nature of the states ruling over them—all were subjected to intense contestation.

Outstanding issues included the location of terminal authority, the extent of the sovereigns' territory, the limits to their rule, the structure of the order that they reigned over, and their relationships with imperial powers. Similar questions were posed in every land but the outcome of the struggles they unleashed varied widely, even within closely connected geographic units. In Oman, the last contest over sovereignty took place in 1965–76 between the imperially backed Sultanate and the Dhufari revolutionary movement. The features of that contest were shaped by geographic and political processes unfolding over the course of the previous century and a half. The British imperial role in determining the outcome of these processes was decisive, leading to remarkable structural transformations within the Omani geographic and political spheres.

In the pre-British era, the political order was shaped by local dynamics revolving around three polycentric sites of authority: the tribes; the Imamate; and the ruling dynasties. The tribal system tended to polarize around moiety divisions that emerged out of periods of internal conflict. The most recent division between the Ghafiri and Hinawi factions arose in the course of a civil war that engulfed Oman in the early eighteenth century. Connected to this political division, there existed a supra-tribal institution embodied in the Ibadhi Imamate, which has periodically manifested itself from the eighth to the mid-twentieth century. The ideology of the Imamate was premised on the rejection of the *jababira*, rulers who forcefully imposed their individual will upon the community. Its central axiom was that 'there is no rule other than God's' and that submission was exclusively reserved for him.[1]

Sovereignty was esteemed as a divine attribute, with any human attempt to mirror it an abomination; even the leader of the Imamate did not possess it. At least in theory, the Imam was elected by the scholars and notables, and given allegiance by the community as a whole. His primary role

---

[1] See J. C. Wilkinson's classic study *The Imamate Tradition of Oman*, Cambridge: Cambridge University Press, 1987.

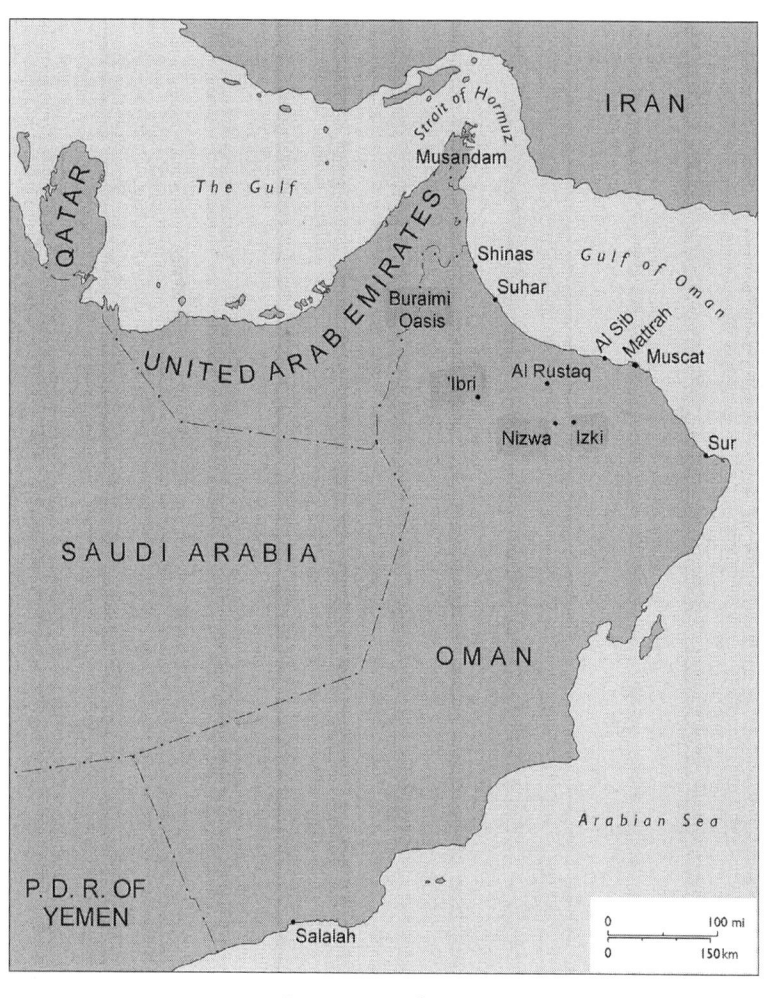

Fig. 1. Map of Oman

was to administer the law for the benefit of all.[2] The limitations upon him were numerous, clear and distinct. He was not to impose more than the religiously decreed taxes, or live in opulence, or maintain a standing army. Expected to adhere to a strict moral code, he was not to be 'jealous, or vindictive or miserly, or overzealous, or wasteful or perfidious'.[3] These austere financial, military, judicial, and moral bounds rendered the merger of central power and doctrinal fidelity untenable. Accordingly, the Imamate tended to morph regularly into dynasty.

Nevertheless, in a land divided by powerful centrifugal forces but united by an explicitly anti-despotic religious ideology, no ruler (except for the present Sultan) has historically managed to attain a monopoly over violence, political power, or rent. As elsewhere, despotism was dynasty's temptation, but the material means for its attainment were unavailable and communal vigilance against it was considerable. Even dynastic founding fathers and the strongest amongst their progeny were not powerful enough to rule arbitrarily. Respect was due to religion, established property relations and the tribal system. Nor was sovereignty, in its absolutist sense as *summa potestas*, sought or attained. The most that could be achieved was control over some major towns and forts and the successful accumulation of customs from coastal trade.

In a strictly geographic sense, the extent of dynastic control was extremely limited. Most of the land was divided into tribal territories in which sheikhs were the predominant figures. These leaders could even project power beyond their immediate domains, especially if they were acknowledged as paramount sheikhs (*tamimas*) or if they managed to form tribal Princedoms (*Imaras*). The boundaries of the relationship between dynasts and sheikhs were in a state of constant flux, further blurred by the Ghafiri–Hinawi moiety division. Most rulers acquired the backing of one faction and the hostility of the other; the two rarely united in their support for a ruler or joined in struggle against them. As such, tribal factionalism was both the grace of dynasty and the cause of its perpetual instability.

THE ARRIVAL OF BRITISH IMPERIALISM

Following the British arrival, relations between tribal, Imamate, and dynastic political structures were gradually transformed. Dynastic rulers

---

[2] For a summary of the theory of the Imamate written by one of its leading twentieth-century intellectuals see Mohammad bin Abdullah (Abu Bashir) Al-Salimi, *Nahdat al-A'yan Bi-'Hurriyat 'Oman*, Cairo: Dar al-Kitab al-'Arabi, 1961, p.140.

[3] Hussein Ghubash, *Oman—The Islamic Democratic Tradition*, London and New York: Routledge, 2006, p.35.

progressively came to depend on foreign patronage as their basis of power, and this distorted established patterns of interaction with other local actors. The British interest in Oman began in the context of inter-imperialist rivalry. During the French revolutionary wars, Britain succeeded in pressuring Sayid Sultan bin Ahmad (r.1792–1804) to sign the *qulanameh* of 1798, the first Anglo-Arab agreement in modern history.[4] The agreement bound the ruler of Muscat 'to the British side in the Anglo-French contest, excluding the French from his territories during its continuance, and granting the British a right to settle at Bandar 'Abbas, which he held on lease from Persia'.[5]

Relations with the British reached unprecedented levels under the long reign of Sayid Said bin Sultan (r.1806–1856). Large-scale military cooperation began when Said gathered his troops in support of the British forces that ravaged the Gulf in September 1809 under the pretext of combating the 'piracy' of the Qassimis of Sharjah and Ras al-Khaimah. The greatest classical Omani historian Abdullah al-Salimi described this collusion in the following terms:

> [Said] sought support from the Christians [i.e. the British] in his war against the people of Sharjah in the north [the Qawasim] and he defeated his enemies with their aid. This call for help was the initial excuse with which the Christians intervened in the kingdoms of the Omani Muslims. Thus, they remained a bane upon his [Said's] progeny and an illness in his Kingdom, displaying friendship but harbouring enmity. For, the worst enemy is one who comes to you in the image of a friend, revealing amity but wishing your ruin.[6]

This was just the first of several campaigns, notable amongst which were the British attacks against the Bani Bu Ali, Said's most powerful local opponents. Although the first expedition against the rebellious tribal confederation was defeated in 1820, a second successful campaign was launched in 1821 so as to 'vindicate the national character' of the British Empire, and to consolidate the rule of its local ally.[7]

---

[4] For the full text of the agreement see C.U. Aitchison, *A Collection of Treaties, Engagements, and Sanads Relating to India and Neighbouring Countries*, 3rd Edition, Vol. XI, Calcutta, 1892, pp.54–5.

[5] John Gordon Lorimer, *Gazetteer of the Persian Gulf, 'Oman, And Central Arabia*, Volume I, Historical, Part 1, Calcutta: Superintendent Government Printing, India, 1915, Westmead and Shannon: Greg International Publishers and Irish University Press, 1970, p.17.

[6] Abdullah Ibn Humaid Al-Salimi, *Tuhfat al A'yan bi-Sirat Ahl 'Uman*, Part 2. Cairo: Dar al-Kitab al-'Arabi, 1961, p.198.

[7] George Percy Badger,, 'Introduction and Analysis' in Humayd Ibn Ruzayq, *History of the Imams and Seyyids of Oman*, New York: Burt Franklin Publishers, n.d., p.172.

Undoubtedly, such support was invaluable to Britain's 'old and faithful ally' (as Sayid Said came to be referred to).[8] Yet, in the very process of accepting British offerings and appealing for help, Said placed himself in a position of intractable dependency. His power was progressively alienated from its roots. Previously emanating from fluid Omani dynamics and relations, it now derived from a constant, but severely limiting, source: imperial backing. His death in 1856 signalled a century of political crisis, foreign rule and economic decline from which the Omani coast and interior did not recover for well over a century. Said's two sons, Majid and Thuwayni, openly fought for the throne, and the British intervened, assuming their role as the ultimate arbiters of Omani political power. In 1861, they announced the 'Caning Award', which gave Muscat to Thuwayni and Zanzibar to Majid in 1861.[9] The revenue from Zanzibar was double that accrued from Muscat, and an annual subsidy was established to compensate Muscat for its huge loss of income. The subsidy came to be given directly by the British authorities in India, anchoring Muscati political and economic dependence on the Raj.

THE IMPOSITION OF IMPERIAL SOVEREIGNTY

Thereafter, imperial sovereignty was imposed in three phases: the Raj phase (1861–1954), during which the coast of Oman was gradually controlled and Dhufar was annexed; the Oil phase (1954–1965), over the course of which the Omani interior was subdued and the Imamate and its al-Jabal al-Akhdar rebellion suppressed; and, finally, the Revolutionary phase (1965–1976), whose peak was the confrontation between imperial sovereignty and the revolution in Dhufar. The structure, nature, and *raison d'être* of the Omani state cannot be understood without reference to these three phases, during which the contemporary absolutist Sultanate acquired its essential features.

In the non-specialist literature, the current Omani Sultanic state is often presented as an ancient institution with a continuous history.[10] This

---

[8] See [I.O.] *Enclos. to Bombay Sec. Letter*, vol. 43, enclose. to Sec. Letter 29 of 30 March 1842, Maddock to Willoughby, Fort William, 28 February 1842 (No. 110 Sec. Dep.). Quoted in J.B. Kelly, *Britain and the Persian Gulf, 1795–1880*, Oxford: Clarendon Press, 1968, p.449.

[9] John Peterson, *Oman in the Twentieth Century: Political Foundations of an Emerging State*, London: Croom Helm, 1978, p.28.

[10] For example, see Ilyia Harik, 'The Origins of the Arab State System', in Giacomo Luciani (ed.), *The Arab State*, London: Routledge, 1990, pp.7–8; George Joffe, 'Concepts of Sovereignty in the Gulf Region', in Richard Schofield, *Territorial Foundation of the Gulf States*, London: UCL Press, 1994, p.83.

arises out of confusing the concepts of state and dynasty. This confusion and the accompanying impulse to refer to 'the state' as a constant must be resisted. In Oman, dynastic states have historically corresponded to a diverse range of social bases, acquired different powers, and established their political presence in uneven ways. The pre-colonial idea of the state (the classical *dawla*) was nearly synonymous with dynasty. This notion has a long and continuous application in Oman. However, whereas dynastic structures had long existed, the bureaucratic monarchical state that claims a monopoly on violence was a novel creation. The material process of establishing that state did not begin in earnest until the mid-twentieth century. Nevertheless, the discursive foundations for it go back a century earlier, beginning with the adoption of the title 'Sultanate'.

Although there had long been monarchical dynasties in the pre-colonial era, they were never referred to as Sultanates. The title 'Sultan of Muscat' (also known at the time as the 'Sultan of Muscat and Oman') was introduced by the British as part of the Canning Award of 1861. The Sayids (Lords) of the Al Bu Sa'id dynasty thus assumed, under colonial patronage, a new identity twinning a monarchical sovereign rank with a geographical designation. The significance of such a linguistic shift was classically explained by Rousseau:

> … [the ancients] only calling themselves Kings of the Persians, of the Scythians, of the Macedonians, seem to have looked upon themselves as chiefs of men rather than as masters of the country. Present-day monarchs more shrewdly call themselves Kings of France, of Spain, of England etc. By thus holding the land, they are quite sure of holding its inhabitants.[11]

In spite of its political connotations, the new title did not reflect the realities of the time, the Sultans having no hold over most of the land or the inhabitants. If anything, they reigned over progressively shrinking domains, increasing strife, empty coffers and declining legitimacy.

Politically, the areas under the Sultans' control were integrated into a British global system, acting as a 'frontier of the Raj'.[12] Multiple layers of British policy determination affected the Gulf region, of which the Sultanate was a major part, reflecting the priorities of three tiers of imperial administration:

> Whitehall officials tended to think of the Persian Gulf in terms of empire-wide communications, power balances among the European great powers,

---

[11] Jean-Jacques Rousseau, *The Social Contract and Other Later Political Writings*, Cambridge CUP, 1997, p.56.

[12] James Onley, *The Arabian Frontier of the British Raj: Merchants, Rulers, and the British in the Nineteenth Century Gulf*, Oxford: OUP, 2008.

and as a field in which Western 'civilisation' might be extended. Anglo-Indian authorities in Calcutta and Bombay viewed the Gulf mainly in the light of Indian frontier politics... Finally, Britain's on-the-spot representatives in the Gulf concerned themselves mainly with day-to-day conditions, specific disorders or problems, treaty clauses, and individual personalities.[13]

Regardless of its causes, British imperialism dominated Muscat. Undoubtedly, there was strong resistance from the interior. From the 1840s onwards, attempts had been made to re-establish the Imamate (the institution carrying the highest form of legitimacy in Oman), finally succeeding in 1868. However, this Imamate was overthrown three years later by the British-backed Sultan Turki bin Said (r.1871–1888).

Besides Imamate resistance, there were occasional Sultanic attempts at independence, but such challenges to Britain incurred severe punishment. The last of these attempts resulted in the 'Masqat Crisis' of 1898–99.[14] Sultan Faisal bin Turki (r. 1888–1913) planned to reduce his dependence on Britain, and he therefore granted a lease allowing for the establishment of a French coaling station on Muscati territory. In response, Lord Curzon, the foremost proponent of a 'British Monroe Doctrine' in the Gulf, authorized severe action on the grounds that 'defiance by the Sultan of the British power could not be permitted'.[15] The Sultan was threatened with the destruction of his palace and armed forces if he did not change course. Under heavy duress, he capitulated, yielding to all British demands and was forced to publicize this submission in a humiliating public Durbar.[16]

Theoretically, the British continued to proclaim the Sultan's independence, but this was nothing more than an inconvenience caused by inter-imperialist rivalry. Indeed, in 1890, the Government of India sought to turn Muscat and Oman into a protectorate. However, it confronted an obstacle in the form of an 1862 Anglo-French agreement to respect the independence of the Muscati Sultans. Nevertheless, this legal independence did not amount to political, let alone economic, autonomy. The British referred to the Sultan as a sovereign but he did not enjoy the attributes of sovereignty. One of these essential attributes— according to both European and Arab philosophers—is terminal authority. As noted by Ibn Khaldun:

> Kingship is not held by every *assabiya* [solidarity network]. It is held by one that subjugates the flock, gathers taxes, commands armies, protects frontiers

---

[13] R.G. Landen, *Oman Since 1856: Disruptive Modernization in a Traditional Arab Society*, Princeton, New Jersey: Princeton University Press, 1967, p.171.

[14] Landen, *Oman Since 1856*, p.249.

[15] Lorimer, *Gazetteer of the Persian Gulf*, pp.556–9.

[16] Briton Cooper Busch, *Britain and the Persian Gulf, 1894–1914*, Berkeley and Los Angeles: University of California Press, 1967, p.77.

and does not have above him a more powerful hand...He whose *assabiya* falls short of exaltation over all other *assabiyas*, lacks the ability to beat all hands, and has above him the rule of another is deficient and incomplete in his kingship...The latter type of kingship is often found in vast states, where there are Kings ruling their people in peripheral lands while owing their obedience to the state that empowered them.[17]

Sultanic sovereignty was in fact none other than the extension of 'imperial sovereignty'. This concept has been used in myriad ways to explain such themes as spatial history, geographies of domination, or the complex dynamics governing imperial networks.[18] Here, however, the concept is deployed in a more limited political sense, defined as a dominant foreign power investing local authority in an indigenous body of its choosing, while retaining a degree of control over that body. Rather than signifying the suzerain relationship between empire and vassal (expressed in the word 'suzerainty'), the term refers to the role of empire in shaping local sovereignty arrangements. As such, it is oriented towards understanding the process that has been identified by Sugata Bose as the colonial replacement of a concept of 'layered and shared sovereignty that had characterized Indian and Indian Ocean polities of the pre-colonial era' with an imported notion of 'unitary sovereignty'.[19]

ESTABLISHING THE COMMONWEALTH BY ACQUISITION

Up to the second half of the twentieth century, imperial sovereignty was only imposed on the Omani coast. In other parts of the country, polycentric notions and practices of political authority continued to prevail. The imperial interest was to control the coast and to contain (as opposed to govern) the interior. As such, the Sultan was not given the tools—military and financial power—to dominate the interior, and was effectively made a ruler of a princely state under the supervision of the Government of India. In 1896, the Secretary of the India Office Political and Secret Department noted that

---

[17] Ibn Khaldun, 'Fi Haqiqat al-Mulk Wa-Asnafih', *Al-Muqadima*, p.188.

[18] For legal and socio-economic uses, see Lauren Benton, 'Empires of Exception: History, Law, and the Problem of Imperial Sovereignty', *Quaderni di Relazioni Internazionali*, Vol.54, 2007. Ward, Kerry, *Networks of Empire: Forced Migration in the Durch East India Company*, Cambridge: CUP, 2009.

[19] Sugata Bose, *A Hundred Horizons: The Indian Ocean in the Age of Global Empire*, Cambridge and London: Harvard University Press, 2006, p.43.

... the authority of the Sultan is quite rotten beyond Muscat and Mattrah where our gunboats protect him against deserved rebellion ... Yet the fiction of keeping the Sultan's rule is to us useful as keeping off Foreign Powers from some 600 miles of the coast. But how long can we keep the fiction going, when the Sultan is afraid to go 10 miles from his capital?[20]

Until the end of the Raj, the British did not go beyond supporting the fiction of the Sultan's rule and the minimal form of governance required to sustain it.

This changed after the Second World War. Gradually, a severely overstretched and economically undermined Britain was beginning to come to terms with two needs: reducing imperial commitments to the minimum, and acquiring oil to the maximum. In the long run, Britain had to leave the Gulf. In the short term it had to make sure that its domestic network of rulers could lay claim to oil reserves and defined territories, thus surviving its departure. The latter task was complicated by an essential factor: the rise of new regional and international forces. Some of these were competitive friends, like the United States and Saudi Arabia, who had no qualms about clashing with Britain over territory and oil, even if that threatened to destabilize its protectorates and realms of influence. Then there was the local giant, Iran, whose awakening from an uneasy sleep was simply a matter of time. There were also the potential contenders, the Communist bloc countries who were currently far from the scene, but could arrive at any moment. Above all, there was the rising enemy of empire, President Gamal Abdel Nasser, and a range of anti-colonial networks spreading across the region.

Accordingly, there were two forms of threat to the British imperial system in the Gulf: challenges from current and potential allies who wanted a slice of the map; and contestations from genuine radicals who sought to redefine regional geography. Occasionally, degrees of collusion could occur across these camps. Britain, for instance, suffered from the short-lived Saudi-Egyptian alliance and the American response to Suez. But the long-term interest—at least on the Anglo-American level—lay in suppressing non-aligned or Eastern-oriented alternatives, especially in the context of the global Cold War.

The location of the contest between Britain and its various challengers was the local Gulf governing structures. In the 1950s, none of the regional entities (with the significant exceptions of Kuwait and Bahrain) could be called a state, having no effective monopoly on violence or extensive bureaucracies. The greatest threat to these vulnerable structures was the

---

[20] Quoted in Busch, *Britain and the Persian Gulf*, pp.59–60.

fard al jala'a (imposing withdrawal) war launched by Nasser and carried by movements in various forms across the region. Ever since it was waged on a regional level in 1956, the British knew that the ride was getting rough. In a 1957 assessment of their position, Selwyn Lloyd noted: 'pan-Arabism at present led by Egypt has spread to many parts of the Gulf and can hardly be prevented from eventually spreading to the whole'. Nevertheless, he argued that, although change was inevitable, its pace and character must be strictly controlled:

> … we have no choice at the present time save to adopt a temporising policy. If change becomes inevitable we should endeavour to ensure that its purpose and the way it takes place should as far as possible be in accordance with our interests. It is particularly important that any liberalisation of the regimes designed to meet genuine grievances or to mollify reformist elements shall not go so far as to cripple the powers of the Ruling Families or compel them to bow to nationalist demands at the expense of their own attachment to us.[21]

Again and again, the overall thrust was on imperial sovereignty, the empire determining the location of terminal authority in the Gulf. The challenge was to ensure that the sovereigns could still be rulers with an 'attachment to us'. 'Liberalisation', in other words the establishment of representative government, had to be limited in accordance with imperial requirements. Power had to remain in the hands of the ruling tribal regimes, and until that was assured, the possibility of British withdrawal was off the table.

In containing the rising anti-colonial trend, the ultimate challenge for Britain was creating the local state under the sovereignty of its chosen rulers. This process has generally been depicted with reference to the notions of 'modernisation' and 'development'. These are inaccurate descriptions with reference to the Omani case, even if the long-questioned strict dichotomy between the 'modern' and the 'traditional' is to be accepted in the first place. Although the structures that were being created could be seen as partially modern in military, bureaucratic and economic regards, the process was far from developmental in its political substance, initially taking the form of limited princely despotism under Said bin Taimur, and culminating in comprehensive monarchic absolutism under Qaboos. In essence, British policy was centred upon establishing a Hobbesian 'commonwealth by acquisition'. Such a commonwealth arises when 'the sovereign power is acquired by force; and it is acquired when men singly (or many together by plurality of voices) for fear of death or bonds do authorize

---

[21] CAB/129/87, 'Persian Gulf: Memorandum by the Secretary of State for Foreign Affairs', 7 June 1957.

all the actions of that man or assembly that hath their lives and liberty in his power'.[22] In the Hobbesian vision, a ruler achieving ascendancy by these means would still attain all the rights of sovereignty:

> His power cannot, without his consent, be transferred to another; he cannot forfeit it; he cannot be accused by any of his subjects of injury; he cannot be punished by them; he is judge of what is necessary for peace, and judge of doctrines; he is sole legislator, and supreme judge of controversies, and of times and occasions of war and peace; to him it belongeth to choose magistrates, counsellors, commanders, and all other officers and ministers, and to determine of rewards and punishments, honour and order.[23]

This *pericope* from *Leviathan* reads like a partial list of the rights that were eventually acquired by the Sultan with British planning and implementation. These rights were by no means traditional. In fact, they were anti-traditional, clashing with ancient doctrines of the Ibadhi Imamate.

The destruction of the Imamate structure was the first major step in creating the Sultanic commonwealth by acquisition. Under the Raj, British policy was to contain the Imamate. This was achieved by the means of the Sib agreement of 1920, signed between the British Political Agent in Muscat and tribal representatives of the Imamate. In accordance with this agreement, the Omani interior was held by the Imamate, while the coastal strip was controlled by the Sultanate. Three decades later, and after the realization that oil lay in Imamate-controlled territories, the British endeavoured to acquire the interior for the Sultan, and to unify it with the coast under a Sultanic state. Following on earlier regional precedents, such as the Jordanian one, the most important instrument in the project of local state building was the army.[24]

The history of the Sultan's army can be read as a series of responses to imperial crises. Until 1921, the Sultans of Muscat did not have an army, relying on tribal levies and gendarmes (mainly East African slaves and Baluchi and Yemeni mercenaries). In times of crisis, they were directly protected by the British government of India. It was following one such crisis that the British decided to establish a Muscati army in order to reduce expenses and pressures on their troops. The crisis began with the election of Imam Salim al-Kharusi in May 1913. This was the first time an Imam had been elected since 1868, and it was expected that the restored Imamate would take over Muscat and effectively destroy the Sul-

---

[22] Thomas Hobbes, *Leviathan*, Cambridge and Indianapolis: Hackett Publishing, 1994, Part 2, Chapter xx, 1, p.127.

[23] Hobbes, *Leviathan*, p.128.

[24] For the significance of the military in the creation of the Jordanian state and national identity, see Joseph Massad, *Colonial Effects*, New York: Columbia University Press, 1998.

tanate. To prevent this from happening, Indian Army troops were sent to Muscat, defeating the forces of the Imamate in 1915, and remaining for five years thereafter. In order to allow for their withdrawal, a permanent local force, the Muscat Levy Corps (which later became the Muscat Infantry) was established, mostly staffed by Baluchi mercenaries and commanded by a British Captain.[25] Accordingly, the Sultan's earliest regular force acquired its first role: containing local threats, especially those coming from the interior.

The second role, expansion, came in the context of the 'oil game'. Imperial sovereignty had to be extended in light of the oil operations that were planned in the Omani and Dhufari interiors and in the Buraimi oasis. In 1937, the Sultan signed an agreement—carefully crafted and tailored to British needs—giving an oil concession in all of these areas to the Iraq Petroleum Company (IPC). The advent of the Second World War delayed prospecting efforts, but the oil question resurfaced with force following the end of the war. Imperial interest lay in ensuring that all potential oil areas were in British hands, protected from any incursion by Saudi Arabia and its American-owned oil company, ARAMCO. As early as 1949, following an official tour of the Gulf, the head of the Eastern Department at the Foreign Office reported:

> The possibility of finding oil in large quantities in an area in which it could be brought to the sea east or south of the narrows at the Straits of Hormuz has a strategic interest which is fairly obvious. It is therefore greatly in the interest of H.M. Government that the oil company's operations should be facilitated. Moreover, if the Sultan does not extend his authority in the interior some of the tribes will probably tend to give their allegiance to Ibn Saud. If his claims to the territory were established this would mean that the oil resources would automatically pass to the Arabian American company.[26]

Thus, the Batinah Force was formed in 1953, mostly staffed by members of the Hawasinah client tribe, for the purpose of extending the Sultan's authority over the promising areas on the northern frontiers. Next, the Muscat and Oman Field Force (MOFF) was founded in 1954 in order to expand into the interior and allow oil excavations there. It was funded by IPC money under the supervision of the British Foreign Office. Finally, in 1955, the Sultan created the Dhufar Force to protect operations in that territory. The context in which these units—the genesis of the SAF—were

---

[25] John Peterson, *Oman's Insurgencies*, London: Saqi, 2007, pp.40–9.

[26] 'Annex 1: Memorandum by B.A.B. Burrows dated 8.6.1949', in Bernard Burrows, *Footnotes in the Sand: The Gulf in Transition, 1953–1958*, Salisbury: Michael Russell, 1990, p.155.

created reveals the extent to which the military was directly shaped by material interests.

The death of Imam Mohammad al-Khalili on 3 May 1954 was a turning point in the history of Sultanic expansionism. Under al-Khalili, a *modus vivendi* was maintained between Sultanate and Imamate, each retaining their territories in accordance with the Sib Agreement. However, Sultan Said bin Taimur and the British saw the death of the Imam as affording them an opportunity for further expansion. Fearing incursions into his territory, the new Imam, Ghalib al-Hina'i, with the help of his brother Talib, established relations with Saudi Arabia and initiated an outward-looking foreign policy. This was certainly wise on his part. For, in January 1955, Anthony Eden, Britain's Foreign Secretary, submitted a memorandum to the Cabinet emphasizing the need to back the Sultan's military efforts against the Imamate. Eden explained that Central Oman was inhabited by tribes friendly to the Sultan, but 'just beyond their tribal lands are pro-Saudi factions and a religious dignitary, known as the Imam, who disputes the Sultan's claim to Central Oman and who is being encouraged by the Saudis to make trouble'.[27]

In this context, the Sultan's forces had to be strengthened: 'I am sure that we must help the Sultan, by all means at our disposal, to strengthen his forces both in Central Oman and in Dhofar and speed is essential'. Acting on his certainty, Eden asked the Cabinet to approve giving limited air support, arms, and equipment to the Sultan. His request was granted in January 1955 in a fascinating meeting—whose highlight was a lament at the upcoming Bandung Afro-Asian Conference as 'an unfortunate initiative... [that] seemed likely to result in resolutions deprecating colonialism and urging prohibition of all further development of thermo-nuclear weapons'.[28]

While furnishing the means for expansionism in Imamate territories, Britain was also attentive to the Buraimi Oasis. That collection of villages was suspected to have oil (although it eventually proved not to contain any worthwhile reserves). It further had a great deal of strategic significance, 'lying at the intersection of transport routes in the East of the Arabian Peninsula'.[29] In July 1954, Britain agreed to submit the Buraimi dispute with Saudi Arabia for international arbitration. By October 1955, the British were fully convinced that they were going to lose the case. Failing to achieve its objectives diplomatically, Britain turned to violence. The new

[27] CAB/129/73, 'Muscat and Oman: Assistance to the Sultan', 12 January 1955.
[28] CAB/128/28, 'Conclusions of a Meeting of the Cabinet', 13 January 1955.
[29] Mohammad bin Abdullah (Abu Bashir) Al-Salimi, *Nahdat al-A'yan Bi-'Hurriyat 'Oman*, Cairo: Dar al-Kitab al-'Arabi, 1961, p.46.

Foreign Secretary, Harold Macmillan, told the Cabinet: 'arbitration having failed, I doubt whether we can safely entrust the matter to any other form of international decision or negotiation...the only safe course now is to rely on a position of strength'. He explained that this 'involves re-occupying those parts of the disputed area to which we consider our claim really sound and which are vital to our interests and those of our client Rulers [the Sheikh of Abu Dhabi and the Sultan]'. Such a forceful course of action, Macmillan insisted, was well within the bounds of established British practice in the area: 'This is the method we adopted earlier in the year in dealing with the Aden Protectorates and Muscat frontier with Saudi Arabia.'[30] Macmillan's policy was subsequently adopted and the Saudi garrison in Buraimi was expelled by a British operation on 26 October 1955. The expansionist role was concluded three weeks later with the full takeover of the Imamate territories. Faced with force he could not match, Imam Ghalib left his capital, Nizwa, on the night of 14 December 1955.[31]

This was by no means the end of the story. In the context of the regional clash between the forces of colonialism and anti-colonialism, and the competition for territory and oil between the American-backed Saudis and Britain's Sultanic vassal, there was bound to be an Imamate comeback. The Imamate already had contacts with Nasser's Egypt. In early November 1954, the Imam's brother, Talib, headed to Cairo and held extensive meetings with Fathi al-Deeb, the head of the Egyptian Bureau for Arab Liberation Movements. Based on this contact, Egypt smuggled its military attaché in Jeddah, Ali Khashabah, into Omani territory to examine the situation in March 1955. Upon his return, he recommended that Egypt support the Imamate's capacity for self-defence in five respects: providing guerrilla warfare training to Omani youth; preparing a detailed plan for the clandestine delivery of supplies; coordinating with the Saudis on the question of supporting the Imamate; launching a media campaign highlighting the British colonial role in Oman on Cairo's *Sawt al Arab* radio; and providing diplomatic support within the Arab League. The decision to help the Imamate in these ways was formally adopted in mid-June 1955 by a Revolutionary Council meeting chaired by Nasser.[32]

Actual supplies were sent long after the Egyptian decision, delayed by the run-up to the Suez war, but they arrived in due time to start a revolt against the forces of the Sultan. Substantial Saudi support was also given and the

[30] CAB/129/78, 'Buraimi', 15 October 1955.
[31] John Peterson, *Oman in the Twentieth Century: Political Foundations of an Emerging State*, London: Croom Helm, 1978, p.77.
[32] Al-Deeb, Fathi, *Abdel Nasser wa Tahrir al-Mashriq al 'Arabi: Shahadat Fathi al-Deeb*, Cairo: Markaz al-Dirasat al Istratijya wal Siyassiya bil Ahram, 2000, pp.204–23.

Imamate's Oman Liberation Army (OLA) established its main base in al-Dammam. In May 1957, the OLA finally began to operate in the interior. In response, and for the first time in their history, the Sultan's forces had acquired the function of suppressing a major organized revolt. They failed to fulfil that task and, by July, the Imamate fighters had succeeded in expelling the Sultanic presence from the interior. In response to their effective revolt, named after al-Jabal al-Akhdar (the Green Mountain), direct British intervention occurred.

The Cabinet discussions from the period reveal that the Macmillan government was unhappy with this direct involvement and that it only pursued it after substantial hesitation. After all, Britain had been chastized following Suez. Nasser had put the waning empire on the defensive, and direct colonial action was liable to further increase tension, harm Britain's international image, and weaken its future in the region. Moreover, there was a great deal of sensitivity towards Saudi Arabia, as any action seen to be hostile towards it was likely to solicit American criticism.[33] This necessitated a major reorganization of the Sultan's forces, so that they could assume their role as a proxy force that could control the population of the interior and prevent the outbreak of rebellion following the eventual withdrawal of British troops. On 25 July 1958, this resulted in an 'Exchange of Letters between the Government of the United Kingdom and the Sultan of Muscat and Oman' in which the terms of British assistance were officially stipulated.[34] In return for strengthening the authority of their client, the British secured an extended long lease of Massirah Island, which had assumed enormous significance for their Indian Ocean military and communications network. Such imperial considerations merged with oil politics, leading to the effective birth of the Sultan's Armed Forces (SAF).

At this stage, the SAF played a supporting rather than a principal role, too weak to counter the al-Jabal al-Akhdar revolt on its own. That task was mainly carried out by British units, concluded in January 1959 by an SAS division that landed in Oman right after conducting operations against the revolutionaries in Malaya.[35] With this intervention, the Sultan's authority was extended fully over the Omani interior. The Imamate and its forces remained in exile, recognized by Arab states but unable to regain its territories. Following this domestication of the Omani centre, future challenges to the Sultan came from the periphery: the dependency of Dhufar.

---

[33] See CAB/128/31, 'Conclusions of a Meeting of the Cabinet', 18 July 1957; CAB/128/31, 'Conclusions of a Meeting of the Cabinet', 23 July 1957; and CAB/128/32, 'Conclusions of a Meeting of the Cabinet', 14 January 1958.

[34] Francis Owtram, *A Modern History of Oman: Formation of the State since 1920*, London: I.B. Tauris, 2004, p.103.

[35] For a personal account by the Commander of the SAF at the time see David Smiley (with Peter Kemp), *Arabian Assignment*, Barnsley: Cooper, 1975.

2

Dhufari Politics, Society, and Economy

Today, Dhufar is the southernmost province of Oman. However, it had its own separate historical trajectory up to its 1879 annexation by the Sultans of Muscat in the context of Anglo-Ottoman rivalry. Historically, the territory's precarious tribal balance of power, rough terrain, geographic isolation, sparse population and limited resources rendered it as immune to foreign rule as to central authority.[1] Dhufar's coast occasionally fell under Yemeni influence, had briefly been visited by Ya'ariba troops, and suffered a temporary occupation by Sayid Sa'id bin Sultan in 1829. Nevertheless, Dhufar was effectively independent for most of its history; the highlands were governed tribally while the coastal plain was precariously controlled by a non-tribal, and usually foreign, ruler. The last of these rulers was Fadhl bin Alawi al-Hussaini, who ruled Dhufar as an Ottoman dependency.

Fadhl came from a hugely respected Indian family of Hadhrami Sayids, the Tangals, whose 'religious knowledge in itself was sufficient to endow them with sanctity and authority' amongst the peasants in Malabar. As was shown in a classic study by K.N. Pannikar, he was a 'traditional intellectual' who played a crucial role in the Mappila Uprising of 1852.[2] Following the uprising, he was banished from India for alleged implication in the murder of the Collector of Calicut, and was hosted by the Ottoman government under the condition—insisted upon by Britain—that he was not to leave its territories.[3] He subsequently lived in Mecca, where he consolidated his Ottoman connections and his reputation for religious knowledge. Based on the standing he had attained, he was approached by Dhufari pilgrims and invited to govern their politically fragmented territory. He arrived in Salalah in late 1875, strongly backed

---

[1] See Jorg Janzen, *Nomads in the Sultanate of Oman: Tradition and Development in Dhofar,* Boulder and London: Westview Press, 1986, p.45.

[2] K.N. Pannikar, *Against Lord and State: Religion and Peasant Uprisings in Malabar, 1836–1921,* Delhi: OUP, 1989, p.65.

[3] 'Introduction' in *Records of Oman, 1867–1947, Vol.5,* Farnham Common, Buckinghamshire: Archive Editions, 1988, p.3.

by the Qarra, the largest tribal grouping in the territory. British officials were alarmed at the fact that a leader so disinclined to accept their colonialism was now based at a maritime frontier of the subcontinent. Characterizing him as 'a dangerous fanatic' who bitterly hated the British, their concerns were furthered by the fact that he ruled in the name of the Sublime Porte at a time when British–Ottoman rivalry in the Arabian Peninsula was at its peak.[4]

With Fadhl in power, Britain's classic strategy of warding off Ottoman claims through signing treaties with local rulers was inapplicable. The option of annexation was equally off the table: always haunted by economies, the Government of India was thoroughly committed to the principle of indirect rule in the Peninsula. Furthermore, despite its hostility to the Ottoman regional presence, Britain had little interest in impoliticly pressuring the Porte at a time when it was involved in a painful war with Russia. Thus, the suggestion of the Political Resident at Aden of dispatching a cruiser to Salalah and twisting the arm of the Porte to dissociate itself from Sayid Fadhl was duly shelved.[5]

In the meantime, more favourable alternatives were emerging. Sultan Turki of Muscat had his eyes on Dhufar and was already making a politically opportune claim on it. One of the arguments on which he based his claim was that he had been visited upon his accession by a Dhufari notable, and that his predecessors had supposedly received a Dhufari 'deputation' in 1856 and again in 1866.[6] Another argument was that Dhufar had always been a dependency of Muscat. In a letter to the Sharif of Mecca, he explained that 'Dhufar has been a dependency of ours as it had been under the Portuguese when they were in this country, and under the Ya'ariba during their reign, and afterwards under our ancestors...'[7] Although the Government of India was 'not convinced of the Omani Sultan's title to the district', it was inclined to back this claim.[8]

According to Lorimer's *Gazetteer*, the magnum opus of British imperial knowledge in the Gulf, Turki was 'from the beginning a *persona grata* with the British government and their agents'.[9] As was mentioned in the previ-

---

[4] Sayid Fadhl signed his letters with the following words: 'From the Government of Dhufar, the dependency of the Supreme Empire': J.B. Kelly, *Britain and the Persian Gulf 1795–1880*, Oxford: Clarendon Press, 1968, p.773.

[5] Kelly, *Britain and the Persian Gulf*, p.774.

[6] Lorimer, *Gazetteer of the Persian Gulf, Oman, and Central Arabia*, p.590.

[7] Sultan Turki of Muscat to Sharif Awan al-Rafiq of Mecca, 1300 Hijri (AD 1883), RO1867–1947, Vol.5.

[8] Lorimer, *Gazetteer of the Persian Gulf, Oman, and Central Arabia*, p.591.

[9] Lorimer, *Gazetteer of the Persian Gulf, Oman, and Central Arabia*, p.499.

ous chapter, the Sultan was economically and politically reliant upon Britain and installed in accordance with its wishes. Moreover, he was personally known to the Indian authorities, having resided for two years in the Bombay Residency. His occupation of Dhufar could not harm imperial regional policy. For the British, Dhufar was one more territory on the map, one more frontier to be secured. For Turki, it was a colony to be acquired at a time when British limitations abroad coincided with political degradation and economic depression at home.

Lacking large-scale agricultural resources or trading potential, Dhufar had a wretched subsistence economy—based on herding and frankincense gathering—that could not sustain a large population, let alone an ambitious ruler. Taxation was synonymous with hunger and suffering and the tribal organization of society offered a vehicle for resisting the taxmen. Even a man who commanded religious authority, like Sayid Fadhl, could not overturn this reality. In his efforts to centralize, he reportedly imposed a 5 per cent levy on all imports and exports, and this was a cause for alienation. Furthermore, the local basis of Fadhl's power was the support of Qarra highlanders and this upset the tribal balance with the coastal sections of the Al-Kathir tribal confederation. Accordingly, the Kathiris led a revolt against his rule in early 1879, besieging him and his followers for no less than twenty days, after which he surrendered and agreed to leave the territory, going to Mukallah, and eventually to Istanbul. He was never to see the territory again, living in the Ottoman capital for the rest of his life. There, he and his sons became a fixture of Arab exile high society, joined by the likes of Sharif Hussein bin Ali of Mecca; Sayid Mohammad Abul Huda al-Sayadi, Naqeeb of Allepo; and Sheikh Mohammad Thafer al-Naqshabandi, Murshid to his Sultanic Majesty.[10] He also established a presence at the court, becoming one of the 'Arab divines' collected by Sultan Abdulhamid from various mystical orders.[11]

Subsequent to the deposition of Sayid Fadhl, a senior Kathiri Sheikh, Awadh bin Abdallah, set sail for Muscat at the head of a deputation. He met Sultan Turki and appealed for his support is 'restoring order', effectively inviting him to extend his rule to Dhufar. There can be little doubt that this was a tribal manoeuvre, directed at strengthening Sheikh Awadh's tribal section, and augmenting his position within it. As noted at the time by the British Political Agent in Muscat:

[10] Abdullah ibn al-Hussein, *Muthakarat Al-Malik Abdullah*, Amman: al-Matba'a Al Hashimya, 1970, p.24.
[11] Albert Hourani, *Arabic Thought in the Liberal Age, 1798–1939*, Cambridge: Cambridge University Press, 2002 (1962), p.107.

The leader of the deputation from Dhofar, Awadh bin Abdulla has promised his entire support to Seyyid Torkee's officers and he will be sure to give it as his own authority will be certainly increased by his alliance with them. But as Awadh is only one of several quasi independent Sheykhs who are very jealous of each other, it is possible there may become differences among them about the reception of the new Walee.[12]

This action on the part of Sheikh Awadh followed a well-established pattern within Dhufari politics. The degree of tribal division, and the lack of a social basis for an internal centripetal mechanism, ensured that appeals to external powers were a common occurrence. This was especially the case during episodes in which the delicate tribal balance was upset. The expulsion of Sayid Fadhl was one such episode, and the coastal Kathiris may well have feared that they could be subjected to Qarra reprisals if the political vacuum were not filled by a foreign ruler allied to them.

Sultan Turki was only too pleased to exploit this situation, appointing one of his officers, Sulaiman bin Suwailem as a Wali, and arranging for him to accompany the Kathiri deputation on their journey back to their country. On 28 February 1879, Sultan Turki mobilized armed support for the new Wali, loading two *Baghla* sailing vessels with a hundred men and sending them off to Dhufar.[13] Britain did not orchestrate this course of action but it certainly did not object to it. The Foreign Department of the Government of India saw 'at present no occasion to interfere with His Highness' proceedings so far as they are directed to the acquisition of control over Dhofar'.[14]

From then on, the Sultans of Muscat established their authority over the Dhufari coast. By holding the Salalah plain, they were able to impose taxes on the highlands, which were organically dependent on trade with the coast. Oppressive rule, excessive taxation, lack of sensitivity to the needs of Dhufari society, and local Sheikhly ambition led to several tribal uprisings. The first had occurred shortly after the Sultanic takeover of Dhufar. On 18 December 1880, the Sultan received word of the seizure and imprisonment of his Acting Wali, and the killing of three of his men. Ironically, this act was carried out by Sheikh Awadh bin Abdallah, the same man who overthrew Sayyid Fadhl and invited the Sultan to Dhufar in the first place.[15] In order to suppress this rebellion, Sultan Turki sent

[12] S.B. Miles (PA and Consul Muscat) to E.C. Ross (PR in the Persian Gulf, Bushire), 27 February 1879, in *RO1867–1947, Vol.5*, p.16.
[13] S.B. Miles (PA and Consul Muscat) to E.C. Ross (PR in the Persian Gulf, Bushire), 27 February 1879, in *RO1867–1947, Vol.5*, p.16.
[14] A.C. Lyall (Secretary of the Government of India, Simla) to E.C. Ross (PR in the Persian Gulf, Bushire), 25 August 1879, in *RO1867–1947, Vol.5*, p.26.
[15] S.B. Miles (PA and Consul Muscat) to E.C. Ross (PR in the Persian Gulf, Bushire), 20 December 1880, in *RO1867–1947, Vol.5*, p.33.

180 men aboard his yacht *Dar al-Salaam* but the party found that the Sultan's men had already regained control over Salalah.[16]

Up to this point, it may appear that the annexation of Dhufar was a local matter, irrelevant to imperial policy. However, subsequent events show that Britain played a crucial role in cementing the Sultanic hold over the territory. This took the form of preventing Sayid Fadhl and his Ottoman backers from regaining the territory, and of militarily interven-ing to maintain the Sultan's rule when necessary. Indeed, Sayid Fadhl had never given up his claim, and he mobilized the Ottoman regional net-work of governors to press his cause, effectively threatening Muscat in the name of the Sublime Porte. In a letter to Sultan Turki, Awn al-Rafiq, the Sharif of Mecca, warned that the entry of Muscati forces into Dhufar was 'a result of the attempt of some corrupters' to implicate the Sultan in their crimes, and that 'this harms the honour of the Most Sublime State and yours, for his Excellency Sayid Fadhl Pasha is one of the Most Sublime State's Ministers, and he is one of your friends and a neighbour of yours'. On a cautionary note, Sharif Awn told Turki:

> It is our belief that those acts were not intentional on your part and that they do not derive from underestimating the Most Sublime State. Therefore, moved by our amity and loyalty to you, we urge you to inform those present in Dhufar from your side that they should hand over the territory to the representatives of Sayid Fadhl upon their arrival there...This would illustrate your good will towards the Most Sublime State and secure its forgiveness.[17]

A few months before, Sayid Fadhl wrote in a similar vein, emphasizing his status as a representative of the Sublime Porte and reproaching Turki for his actions:

> No kingdom is free of tumults and conflict between corrupting subjects and their rulers, as you have yourself experienced before. So do not view us as weak and look upon us not with contempt. Rather, follow the righteous path of your forefathers, which was praised amongst the Arabs, and do not think that we would ever leave our kingdoms and the lands of our ancestors so long as we shall live.[18]

More interestingly, Sayid Fadhl implicitly recognized that the British representatives were the effective kingmakers in the region, suggesting to

---

[16] S.B. Miles (PA and Consul Muscat) to E.C. Ross (PR in the Persian Gulf, Bushire), 7 February 1881, in *RO1867–1947, Vol.5*, p.34.

[17] Sharif Awan al-Rafiq to Sultan Turki, 21 Rajab 1300 (8 June 1883) in *RO1867–1947, Vol.5*, p.43.

[18] Fadhl bin Alawi to Turki bin Said, 3 Jumada al Awwal, 1300 (11 March 1883) in *RO1867–1947, Vol.5*, p.37.

Turki that he should not assume that they would support him to the detriment of Fadhl:

> To those from your side who say that the Consul of the State of the English in Muscat helps Turki, we say that this is the case in your domains, and the thought should not cross your mind that he would support you in aggression over our lands. For, the State of the English is a great Kingdom and not a small Princedom... I am one of their friends now... and I am of greater benefit to them than you are...[19]

The Government of India clearly did not share this view. Exercising its imperial sovereignty, it reserved Dhufar for Turki, and prevented Fadhl and his Ottoman suzerains from retaking it. Thus, in mid-January 1886, the British stopped a steamer docked in Aden from heading to Dhufar. The ship was carrying Fadhl's son Mohammad, one hundred men, and an arsenal of weapons. The Political Agent Muscat advised that this party's 'presence at Dhofar would be prejudicial to us' and the ship was accordingly searched, and the weapons it was carrying were confiscated. Mohammad subsequently declared himself 'an Officer of the Turkish government sent specially to rule Dhofar under the Porte' but this did not get him very far with the British authorities.[20]

In subsequent years, Fadhl continued to try to regain Dhufar, backed— at least verbally—by the Ottoman authorities. For instance, the Wali of Basra wrote to Turki on behalf of the Ottoman Ministry of the Interior, demanding that Turki reverse his policies.[21] However, Turki took no notice—he did not even honour this letter with a reply. He understood very well that Britain was the only empire that mattered to him. Ten years later, having failed to achieve anything through asserting Ottoman power, Fadhl sought to appeal to the British. In 1894, he contacted the British Ambassador in Istanbul and asked to be allowed to return under British protection, promising complete adherence to British economic and political requirements. Of course, there was no interest in accepting this offer, for Britain already had a local client in place who was acting in accordance with all its wishes. Instead of serving Fadhl's cause, this desperate attempt led to Britain heightening its surveillance over his activities in Cairo, Jeddah, and Aden, advising the Sultan to consolidate his presence in Dhufar.[22]

---

[19] Fadhl bin Alawi to Turki bin Said, 3 Jumada al Awwal, 1300 (11 March 1883) in *RO1867–1947, Vol.5*, p.37.

[20] Political Agent Muscat to Political Resident Persian Gulf, 18 January 1886; Political Resident Aden to Chief Secretary Bombay, 20 January 1886, *RO1867–1947, Vol.5*, pp.71–3.

[21] Hussein Ali Rida Pasha of Basra to Turki bin Said, 20 Rajab, 1303 (26 April 1886). *RO1867–1947, Vol.5*, p.76.

[22] 'Introduction' in *Records of Oman, 1867–1947, Vol.5*, p.8.

So tight was the British naval grip over the region that external threats, such as the Ottoman one exemplified by Fadhl, were all relatively easy to frustrate. The only serious challenges were internal, posed by the Dhufaris themselves. On 13 January 1888, the Sultan sent a detachment of 200 men led by his sons Faisal and Fahd to suppress a local rebellion. Five leading Dhufari sheikhs accused of correspondence with Sayid Fadhl and the Chief of Shihr were arrested, humiliatingly placed in irons and taken to Muscat. Similar local revolts occurred regularly in the following years, challenging the authority of the Sultan's hugely unpopular Wali, Suleiman bin Suwaliem. These culminated in a major uprising led by the Al-Kathir tribe, lasting for 18 months between 1895 and 1897. This was suppressed by means of direct British intervention, carried out by the Indian Government vessel *Lawrence* and H.M.S. *Cossack*:

> In January 1897 the Sultan, being at length convinced of his own inability to recover Dhufar, solicited the assistance of a British man-of-war and accepted the conditions upon which the British Government were now willing to grant it: these were pardon, after full submission for the rebels; the appointment of a Wali acceptable to the local Sheikhs; and the discontinuance of extra-taxation.[23]

Over the following decades, knowledge of British support for the Sultan helped anchor his local position. Whenever a crisis occurred, Britain imposed the Sultan on the local population, but also sought to ensure that Dhufaris remained pacified by the removal of economic and social grievances. This imperial trend of simultaneously upholding political autocracy and encouraging economic amelioration, of suppressing political rights by means of armed intervention and economic reform, was deployed as late as the Dhufari revolution of 1965–76.

In spite of attempts at local pacification, the position of the Sultans in Dhufar continued to be precarious during the first quarter of the twentieth century. In February 1907, the long-serving and much-hated Wali, Sulaiman bin Suwailem, was assassinated in the Sharqiya region of northern Oman. Shortly thereafter, an uprising took place against his deputy, a Nubian slave named Bakhit. The latter's men had been accused of murdering Sheikh La'ait of the Al-Kathir, and the afflicted tribe responded by killing three of them and appealing for protection to the ruler of Mukalla in neighbouring Yemen. Responding in January 1908, Sultan Faisal despatched a force led by his son Taimur to restore control over Dhufar. In the tradition of his forefathers, he took a further precaution, requesting help from the British. Accordingly, H.M.S. *Perseus* sailed to lend 'moral

---

[23] Lorimer, *Gazetteer of the Persian Gulf, Oman, and Central Arabia*, p.597.

support'. By the time it had arrived, the Sultan's men had already completed their task, but its presence undoubtedly played the usual function of parading strength for the benefit of potentially rebellious subjects.[24]

This incident illustrates the limited courses of action available to the various actors in Dhufar. On their own initiative, the two largest local tribal confederations—the Qarra and the Kathir—could pose a temporary threat to the Sultan's authority. However, they were then likely to be confronted with non-Dhufari troops sent from abroad, as well as opposition from smaller loyalist coastal tribes such as the Shanafir of al-Hafa, or from larger tribal opponents who were susceptible to forming alliances of opportunity with the ruler. Support from a regional authority, be it Ottoman or Yemeni, was one way of improving a rebellious tribe's chances of success, but such help was not guaranteed. More importantly, it could always be trumped by the card of British backing. In case of initial Sultanic failure, the overwhelming military might of his imperial backers was a solid guarantee of eventual success. However, this success could not last if the Sultans did not adhere to the economic and social requisites for maintaining the local tribal balance. Lacking the resources to forcibly dominate, or the legitimacy to establish a peaceful hegemony, the Sultan's representatives were likely to be attacked whenever they attempted to impose excessive taxation or unwarranted social control.

This was a conclusion that had been arrived at during the reign of Sultan Taimur. Prior to his ascension to the throne in 1913, Dhufar had been ruled by two unpopular governors: Sulaiman bin Suwailem and Bakhit al-Nubi. Owing to their respective quests for local control, they suffered from multiple rebellions and were forcibly reinstalled against local wishes. Things began to change following the 1907–1908 rebellion. Although Bakhit continued to be Wali until his removal in 1915, he seemed to have taken a tamer approach and this was certainly the policy of his successors, Abdallah bin Sulaiman al-Harithi (appointed in 1915) and Saoud bin Ali bin Badr (appointed in 1923). Thus, by 1923, the Political Agent Muscat could recommend adding the following words to the official *Gazetteer of the Persian Gulf*:

> The country [i.e., Salalah and Mirbat] at this time appeared both peaceful and prosperous. Opinion was unanimous that the population had increased in the last fifteen years, and the towns showed a considerable increase of substantial buildings ... This state of affairs is probably due to the policy of non-interference, based on complete impotence, pursued by the Muscat

[24] Wingate (PA Muscat) to Knox (PR Bushire), 'History of Dhufar', 4 May 1923, *RO1867–1947, Vol. 5*, p.76, p.113.

local representatives. Very little revenue is collected, and that only from the sea customs and the lands in the immediate vicinity of Dhufar proper and it no more suffices for the very modest establishment the Wali keeps up.[25]

The structure of Dhufar's economy and society could not sustain a more elaborate or potent form of central administration without causing grave hardship and, eventually, rebellion. Unsurprisingly then, Sultan Taimur's general absence of ambition, lack of interest, and overall passivity served Muscati rule well in that territory. British representatives were aware of the situation and encouraged its maintenance, having no developmental aspirations or requirements in what was seen as no more than a frontier buffer zone inhabited by 'wild tribesmen':

> The country runs itself on the tribal system, with the occasional raids and murders that this system entails, but in the absence of the danger of foreign invasion it may be asserted without hesitation that it is the most suitable one in the present condition of the country. The existence of the Muscat Government exercises a mild moral restraint on the extreme forms of inter-tribal warfare...and as long as it maintains its present policy and continues to extract the minimum revenue and to entertain visiting sheikhs, there is no valid reason why the Sultan should not be able to retain his suzerainty.[26]

One of the factors that aided in the maintenance of a policy of general non-interference was the enormous distance that separated Dhufar from Oman. A vast inhospitable desert lay between the two areas, and they were almost solely connected by sea. Dhufar was even more isolated during the monsoon period, the raging waves of the Indian Ocean rendering navigation along its shoreline perilously unsafe. Along with the cool misty monsoon weather, this was one of the factors that encouraged Sultan Taimur to spend some of his summers in Dhufar. There, far away from visiting Omani Sheikhs loaded with monetary requests, he could save considerable amounts of money. By means of conveyance on a British military or commercial ship, even his travel costs could be significantly reduced. The fort in Salalah, Al-Hisn, offered comfortable and pleasant accommodation, and was effectively 'a small village' that could house the Sultanic retinue.[27]

---

[25] Wingate (PA Muscat) to Knox (PR Bushire). 'History of Dhufar' 4 May 1923, *RO1867–1947, Vol. 5*, p.76, p.114.

[26] Wingate (PA Muscat) to Knox (PR Bushire). 'History of Dhufar' 4 May 1923, *RO1867–1947, Vol. 5*, p.76, p.115.

[27] Wingate (PA Muscat) to Knox (PR Bushire), 'History of Dhufar', 4 May 1923, *RO1867–1947, Vol. 5*, p.111.

Still, the Sultan generally preferred the more expensive option of staying in India, where he lived for most of the year, generally ignoring Muscat, Oman, and Dhufar. In 1920, he asked for the Viceroy's permission to abdicate, but his proposal was 'not entertained'.[28] Later that year, he was forced to make a commitment to the Government of India that he would spend at least three months each year in Muscat. He could not always honour this commitment. Besides hating his capital, he was generally depressed by the fact that he was rendered so impotent by British financial and military control of his affairs. On the whole, he was patronized, denied free will, and subjected to reward and punishment as his imperial overlords saw fit. In April 1931, he received a letter telling him that the 'Government of India cannot but view with grave displeasure your failure to adhere to your undertaking to spend three months of every year in Muscat and your refusal last November to meet the Political Resident at Muscat...' Although he was informed that the 'Government of India are willing to overlook your Highness's absence from Muscat this winter', the Sultan's annual allowance from Britain was cut by half, and he was further told that '[s]hould your highness persist in your determination to stay away from Muscat...it may become necessary further to reduce your allowance next year'.[29] By 17 November 1931, he was finally able to abdicate, requesting that the Political Resident in the Persian Gulf 'convey to the Government our determination to abdicate from our Sultanate and we have from today taken off our hand from all the ruling rights, and we have made our successor our son Saiyid Saeed bin Saiyid Taimur as Sultan of our Government'.[30]

On 9 January 1932, the British Government recognized Said bin Taimur as the new Sultan of Muscat and Oman, and he proclaimed his ascension to the throne on 10 February 1932. In the classic ceremonial fashion of the Raj, the closest thing to a coronation was a formal Durbar held on 3 March 1932 so as to mark the Political Resident's delivery to the Sultan of the 'Kharita from his Excellency the Viceroy and Governor General of India'. Three British ships docked in Muscat harbour and a salute of 31 guns was fired in honour of the Viceroy, followed by a salute of 21 guns in honour of the Sultan. The ceremony took place in the Sultan's palace. To his right were seated the Political Resident and several

---

[28] Deputy Foreign Secretary, Government of India. 'Brief Note on the Position of the Sultan of Muscat', 18 August 1920, *RO1867–1947, Vol. 3*, p.183.

[29] Political Agent and Consul (Muscat) to His Highness Sir Saiyid Taimur bin Faisal, 22 April 1931, *RO1867–1947, Vol.3*, p.397.

[30] Sultan Taimur bin Faisal to Colonel H.V. Biscoe (PR Bushire), *RO1867–1947, Vol.3*, p.418.

Naval, Army and RAF officers. The dignitaries of Muscat, who were seated opposite the Sultan and the British, were addressed by the Political Resident, and then by the Sultan.[31] Whereas the natives were expected to stand during the Sultan's address, the British officers continued to sit down. Of course, the function of such ceremonies was to remind the local ruler and the native population of their exact position in the imperial hierarchy. As befitted the occasion, the ceremony concluded with the Sultan asking the Political Resident to 'convey to His Majesty the King-Emperor his thanks for the recognition accorded to him, and to His Excellency the Viceroy his thanks for the congratulations contained in his Kharita'.[32]

DHUFAR UNDER SAID BIN TAIMUR

Thus, Sultan Said had his colonial initiation, and a new era in the histories of Muscat, Oman, and Dhufar effectively began. Inheriting a weak administration characterized by political detachment and crippled by massive debts, the twenty-two-year-old was determined to balance finances and re-establish Sultanic authority. From the vantage point of British Raj politics, he was an ideal ruler: loyal to Britain in all affairs foreign, and personally domineering in all matters local. Resolute, obsessive, and controlling, he began to intervene in the plethora of affairs that his father had long ignored, seeking to re-build the princely state, to fill its coffers, and to regain the respect of local subjects and British overlords. Unsurprisingly then, his arrival signalled the end of the policy of non-interference in Dhufar.

Sultan Said took a personal interest in Dhufar and began to spend every summer there, intervening directly in the affairs of the territory. During the first ten years of his reign, he effectively transformed the relationship between Muscati rulers and Dhufar. On the personal level, he established a strong local connection, marrying a Dhufari woman from the most powerful section of the largest local tribe, the Ma'ashanis of the Qarra. He also spent every summer in the territory, and it was not uncommon for him to be in residence there for the whole year. The Sultan directed affairs from his seaside palace, protecting himself from any potential tribal raids through generous expenditure on arms and defensive

[31] H.V. Biscoe (PR Bushire) to the Foreign Secretary to the Government of India (New Delhi), 26 March 1938. *RO1867–1947, Vol.3*, p.459.
[32] H.V. Biscoe (PR Bushire) to the Foreign Secretary to the Government of India (New Delhi). 26 March 1938. *RO1867–1947, Vol.3*, p.459.

fortifications around Salalah town. He reinforced his position by raising a standing force of 200 partially trained men, mostly former slaves of East African descent. These were made mobile through the purchase of ponies and two light trucks, and were well equipped with modern rifles. Such a force was superior to any potential local competitor. Dhufaris, be they tribesmen or townsfolk, were poorly armed, and the former 'were too divided to be formidable'.[33]

This military superiority formed the basis for enforcing a degree of economic control that was unprecedented in the recent history of the territory. Unlike his predecessors, Sultan Said was able to establish an efficient regime of revenue extraction. Local produce was subject to an annual levy, payable in kind. Gold ornaments were directly taxed and customs duties were more effectively collected.[34] One of the factors that facilitated the success of Sultanic tax policies was that trade was limited to a few markets in the coastal settlements of Salalah, Mirbat and Taqa, and could thus be easily monitored and controlled.[35] In a sense, this factor had always been present, and was used to the advantage of previous rulers with varying degrees of success. However, Sultan Said managed to monitor the flow of goods as never before. He further developed new avenues for generating personal wealth, dominating shipping, owning and operating the largest dhow in Mirbat port. He was the largest retailer, controlling the state shop and importing all goods sold in it with the help of his Indian partners. He further benefited from Second World War contracts, supplying all materials for the construction of a new RAF airport in Salalah. Last but not least, the Sultan acquired large tracts of land, claiming ownership of 'all lands not proved to be in a possession of another'. He thus quickly became the foremost agriculturalist in the territory, and was the only one to employ modern methods. He let some of the newly irrigated plots he owned, acquiring up to 25 per cent of the produce.[36]

Dhufar was accordingly treated as a private estate, heavily exploited by its ruler. Lacking industry or special trade significance, it was an agrarian territory, economically divided into four zones: the perennially irrigated coastal plain; the southerly inclined moist highlands; the northern side of the water-shed, located between the moist highlands and the desert; and

[33] C.N. Jackson, 'A Note on the Dhufar Province, Southern Arabia', Kuwait, 23 June 1943, *RO1867–1947, Vol.5*, p.127.
[34] C.N. Jackson, 'A Note on the Dhufar Province, Southern Arabia', Kuwait, 23 June 1943, *RO1867–1947, Vol.5*, p.131.
[35] Jorg Janzen, *Nomads in the Sultanate of Oman: Tradition and Development in Dhofar*, Boulder and London: Westview Press, p.49.
[36] C.N. Jackson, 'A Note on the Dhufar Province, Southern Arabia', Kuwait, 23 June 1943, *RO1867–1947, Vol. 5*, p.130.

the northern desert areas known as the Najd. The coastal plain roughly extended over 140,000 acres, an estimated 90,000 of which were flat lands. These were covered by a thin layer of soil of poor to average fertility and underlain by limestone. Rainfall on the plain averaged six inches, sufficient for thin strands of herbage to grow and to thicken significantly as the plain met the mountain range. Historically, acacia scrub and trees covered substantial parts, but the trees surrounding Salalah were deliberately destroyed so as to enhance the Sultan's military control, removing potential cover for any raiding party. The excesses of fuel cutters ensured that the remaining trees did not survive.[37]

The destruction of natural vegetation by no means meant that the plain was barren. Indeed, several crops were grown including sweet potatoes, coconuts, sorghum, eleusine, lucerne, wheat, sugar cane and cotton. By 1947, 1,200 acres of the lands were irrigated using the waters of 200 shallow wells, and 280 acres were supplied by the five permanent springs, whose supplies were improved in the 1940s by Pradham Singh, the State Engineer.[38] The Sultan used two of these springs, Rizat and Hamran, to maintain the lushness of his own private gardens. These gardens, especially the one at Ma'moura, took up the best soil, producing an ample amount of bananas, figs, limes, and other fruits and vegetables.[39]

Such items, of course, mainly grew on the plain. Soaring above were 520,000 acres of territory stretched over the southerly inclined escarpment and mountains. In the most favoured parts of this area rainfall averaged over 30 inches, a thick mist offering cover throughout the monsoon. In this part of Dhufar, whose ecosystem is described by hydrologists as a 'seasonal cloud forest', the uplands offered rich pasture for cattle for part of the year, while the steeper scrub areas below provided for a considerable number of camels and goats.[40] Beyond these richer areas lay the northerly slopes, beginning at that point where the Al Qatn heights descend into the Qarn Shaiba drainage, causing a remarkable change in vegetation. Here the grass grew shorter and the earth revealed tufted patches of bareness, offering approximately 700,000 acres of seasonal short grass grazing land. North of these areas, Frankincense and Myrrh trees grew, supplying Dhufar with its most prized export and a magical reputation steeped in

---

[37] CO/725/101/3. B.J. Hartley, 'A Preliminary Survey of the Land Resources of the Dhufar Province, Sultanate of Muscat and Oman', November 1947.

[38] The springs were Rizat (Arzat), Sahalnaut, Jirziz, Hamran, and Tabraq.

[39] CO/725/101/3. B.J. Hartley, 'A Preliminary Survey of the Land Resources of the Dhufar Province, Sultanate of Muscat and Oman', November 1947.

[40] Anke Hildebrant, 'Ecohydrology of a Seasonal Cloud Forest in Dhofar', PhD Thesis in Hydrology, Massachusetts Institute of Technology, June 2005, p.22.

the annals of antiquity. With little warning, this landscape descended into desert, where only camels and goats could be pastured.[41]

With this unique topography in mind, it was unsurprising that there were three major population clusters in Dhufar: highlanders; desert dwellers; and coastal town inhabitants and villagers. In 1977, when the first rough census was produced by a British SAS officer, only an estimated 67,200 people were spread across the highlands, deserts, and coastal towns and villages of Dhufar (See Appendix I). The largest population centre, Salalah, only had 35,000 inhabitants, in itself a substantial rise from the 7,500 that it was thought to house up until 1970. The economic activities of this tiny population were severely limited, their character and division determined by geographical location, seasonal fluctuations, tribal belonging, caste, and gender.

The highland economy was centred on three animals: cows; camels; and goats. Sheep were noticeably rare, the severe humidity as well as the scrubs and the grass being inimical to their health and afflicting flocks with tick-borne ailments and intestinal parasites. This explained the fact, unusual for the Arabian Peninsula, that the most important activity was cattle husbandry. Each cow produced an estimated 20 pounds of clarified butter fat (ghee) annually, and this was an essential good for local consumption as well as export. Accordingly, the grazing of cows determined the seasonal movement and whereabouts of most inhabitants. Dhufari cows are unhumped and small, rarely growing above four feet high. On average, each cow-herding family owned ten. By the mid-1970s, the total cattle population was thought to amount to 50,000 head.[42] Due to the endemic persistence of Foot and Mouth disease as well as a lack of advanced agricultural knowledge, milk output tended to be poor. Whereas vigorous culling of less productive cattle was practised in neighbouring areas such as Yemen, Dhufaris tended to be less selective, possibly due to the greater availability of fodder in their lands.

The highlands did not provide year-round resources to sustain the cows. Although Dhufar was one of the only corners of the Arabian Peninsula to receive some of the spoils of the Indian Ocean monsoon (lasting from mid-June to mid-September), the seasonal grass was not enough to feed the cows for more than a few months.[43] Accordingly, the population practised a quarterly rotational grazing cycle. Most highlanders had two

---

[41] CO/725/101/3. B.J. Hartley. 'A Preliminary Survey of the Land Resources of the Dhufar Province, Sultanate of Muscat and Oman', November 1947.

[42] MEC-Sichel 2/4, 'Development Priorities in Dhofar,' n.d *c.*1977, p.2.

[43] CO/725/101/3. B.J. Hartley, 'A Preliminary Survey of the Land Resources of the Dhufar Province, Sultanate of Muscat and Oman', November 1947.

villages and two homes: one permanent; the other temporary. Clustered in the permanent villages were up to fifty families, living in houses made of a thick stone wall that was approximately three feet high, sheltered by a roof made of branches and thatch. Such villages were mostly located in the highlands, although they could be occasionally found lower down on the Salalah plain, known locally as the *Jarbaib*. They were inhabited during the monsoon and winter. In the post-monsoon and the summer periods, dwellers generally moved to temporary settlements located on the hilltops. Houses there were built of light sticks, straw, and such material as old garments supported by branches in clusters.[44]

The best time for grazing was mid-September to mid-December when the Jabal was covered with post-monsoon lush grass growing 3 to 4 feet high. During that time, the highlanders tended to move from the permanent villages to the temporary ones. Between mid-December and mid-March (the winter season), they generally returned to their main village sites. Initially, they grazed their cows in proximate grounds, but whenever a herd ate up an area, it was taken beyond it, grazing further and further away from the village as each week passed. By mid-March, the temperatures rose significantly and the grass supply surrounding the permanent villages was consumed. In search of cooler temperatures and better pasture, the cow-herding population generally relocated once again to their elevated temporary homes. To supplement the diet of the cows, the women collected hay during that period, using it as fodder. This was not enough to feed the herds, and they were further supplied with dried sardines (*ooma*) imported from coastal fishermen. As such, the highlands were severely dependent on the coast, especially during the dry summer months, and any interruption to the sardine supply caused cows to die and humans to starve. This precarious seasonal state of affairs continued until the return of the monsoon season in mid-June. At that point, highlanders could feel more secure, returning to their permanent villages, hoping for a season of plenty and completing the population movement cycle.[45]

Besides the cow economy, there existed a major network of production centred upon camels. Camel herding families also had a seasonal dwelling cycle. Generally taking shelter in tents, they tended to inhabit the Salalah plain during the monsoon or, in the case of herders belonging to the Amri tribe, the northern edge of the Jabal. This was to avoid the conditions prevailing in more elevated areas during that season, rendering the high

---

[44] MEC-Sichel 1, 'Sultanate of Oman Demographic Survey: Dhofar 1977', pp.1–7.
[45] MEC-Sichel 1, 'Sultanate of Oman Demographic Survey: Dhofar 1977', pp.6–7.

ground too slippery for camels and the *wadi* bottoms intolerably infested with biting flies. With the onset of winter and the marked decline of biting fly numbers, camel herding families moved to the *wadis*, where they could find adequate grazing ground and protection from wind chill. Finally, during the summer, they often moved camp, grazing their camels on the upper slopes of the *wadis*.[46]

The third most important animals in Dhufar were goats, providing a supplementary source of milk. Goat keepers tended to live in caves for most of the year and they did not need to abandon the highlands during the monsoon. This was due to the sturdy and sure-footed nature of their animals, able to graze on the *wadi* sides without slipping on the sticky soil of the mountains. Their cave houses included separate accommodation for animals, clearly delineated sleeping and cooking areas, as well as rock and wattle shelves built into the walls. The interiors of the caves were occasionally adorned with charcoal drawings, and their mouths were blocked off with branches.[47]

Each highland tribe in Dhufar included cow, camel, and goat herding families. These were distributed unevenly amongst the tribal sub-sections. The Jabali tribe with the largest number of people and owning the most animals was the Qarra. This was a loose structure divided into major sub-tribes, which included, from largest to smallest, the houses of al-Ma'ashani, al-Amri, Tabawk, Ja'boob, Kashawb, Qatn, and Said.[48] While they identified themselves as an Arabic tribe, the Qarra spoke a distinct Southern Arabian tongue called Shahri.[49] The second largest and strongest tribe in the highlands was the Al-Kathir. Although many of its men and women were to be found along the coast or in the Najd desert, it had a presence on the Jabal through such subsections as the Bait Ali bin Badr and the Bait Amr Bin-Mohammad.[50] Another major grouping on the Jabal was the Shahra. This was the oldest group to inhabit the area, but it was weakened and reduced to subordinate status by the Qarra. Accordingly, Shahra sections were spread around the territory, living on the lands owned by the various Qarra and Kathiri families. For instance, the Zawaamir and Hadyaan were Shahra families living in Bait Qatn lands in Jarbaib and

[46] MEC-Sichel 1, 'Sultanate of Oman Demographic Survey: Dhofar 1977', p.9.

[47] MEC-Sichel 1, 'Sultanate of Oman Demographic Survey: Dhofar 1977', p.10.

[48] By the late 1970s, the Ma'ashanis included 783 families, the Bait al-Amri 697 families, the Bait Tabawk 336 families, the Bait Ja'boob 314 families, the Bait Kashawb 308 families, the Bait Qatn 202 families, and the Bait Said 183 families.

[49] For one of the earliest discussions of this language in English, see Bertram Thomas, 'Four Strange Tongues from South Arabia, the Hadara Group', *Proceedings of the British Academy, Vol XXIII*, London: Humphrey Milford Amen House, 1939.

[50] Numbering 314 and 50 families respectively by the late 1970s.

South Nahiz.[51] Besides these tribes, the highlands also included a scatter-
ing of Mahris.[52]

By regional standards, Dhufari tribes had a severely splintered nature,
rendering them vulnerable to external powers such as the Muscati Sultanate. For instance, the Ma'ashanis were divided into four sub-tribes (Bait
Izam, Bait Aliti, Bait Akineen, and Bait Erdahayl), which in turn branched
out into 15 minor sections. Even more splintered were the Amris, who
were distributed among 12 sub-tribes.[53] Tribal subsections typically
included a large number of cattle breeding families, a smaller number of
camel owners, and a few goat herders.[54] Of course, not all members of
these families were solely engaged in herding. Incense collection was an
extremely important supplementary income-generating activity and
Kathiri Bedouin, in particular, tended to possess a number of trees holding the precious substance, living as they did in drier areas conducive to
frankincense tree growth. Incisions were made into the trunks of the trees
during the summer season, and they were collected some weeks later.[55]
This activity was labour intensive and required remarkable patience. As
the Omani historian Mohammad al-Salimi notes:

> Collectors beat the tree trunk with an iron rod until its milk begins to flow
> and hardens. Leaving it for a month, they come back to it, hitting the
> outside layer for ten days, after which they retire to their homes. Ten days
> later, they return to the mountain and spend five months gathering the
> incense.[56]

Although the frankincense trade was historically the most important, it
witnessed a substantial decline during the twentieth century. Dhufar was
gradually overtaken by Somalia as the major international exporter of this
prized commodity.

In addition to farming, animal produce, and the collection of frankincense, fishing played an important role in Dhufari life. This was an activity

---

[51] MEC-Sichel 1. 'Sultanate of Oman Demographic Survey: Dhofar 1977', p.21.

[52] MEC-Sichel 2/2. Tribal Information: 'Distribution of Mahri in Dhofar'. In the late
1970s, Mahri numbers were estimated to be 320 in the Eastern Jabal and 150 in the Central Jabal.

[53] These were: Aar; Hawto; Amr bin Kashawb; Izam; Mahawnt; Beinteen; Timoon; Ali
bin Qatn; Mahadan; Ashilgawt; Zeedi bin Aat; and Salaama. See MEC-Sichel 1, 'Sultanate
of Oman Demographic Survey: Dhofar 1977', p.26.

[54] For example, the Bait Qatn included 165 cattle breeding families, 34 camel owning
families, and 3 goat herding families, while the Bait Ali bin Badr had 202 cattle breeding
families, 77 camel owning families, and 35 goat herding families.

[55] Walter Dostal, 'Two South Arabian Tribes: Al-Qara and Al-Harasis', *Arabian Studies
II,* Middle East Centre, University of Cambridge, 1975, p.37.

[56] Mohammad bin Abdullah Al-Salimi (Abu Bashir), *Nahdat al-A'yan Bi-'Hurriyat
'Oman,* Cairo: Dar al-Kitab al-'Arabi, 1961, p.54.

carried out by the lower caste of the *baharra,* who made use of the immense shoals of sardines that visited nearby waters in the winter. In the 1940s, up to ten thousand bags of sardines were caught in Salalah alone, not to mention the smaller catches in other coastal towns. These were then dried and sold to local merchants in exchange for clothes, food, and other items. The coastal merchants in turn bartered the sardines with the highlanders in exchange for cow milk. Barter was generally the preferred method of purchase across the territory, although the Maria Theresa Dollar was beginning to circulate much more than before. Advancing the sardines in the autumn, the merchants moved, along with their families, to the cow pastures during the monsoon summer months, collecting their milk and overseeing its production into ghee butter, as well as gathering cow hides. The merchants exported the ghee butter and hides, as well as incense, to India, importing in return rice and other essential goods.[57] They also received some supplies of honey, coming from a strain of non-aggressive bee that was unique to Dhufar, typically nesting in holes along the wadi sides. In each area, one man would be assigned the role of honey collector. His role would be to climb up to nests, or to be lowered down to them on a rope, smoking the bees out with a smouldering cloth and removing their combs.[58]

The mountain may have literally been the land of milk and honey, but it did not endow its inhabitants with the pre-requisites of self-sufficiency. By holding the coast, the Sultan shackled Dhufaris with dependency, effectively controlling the exchange cycle of all goods. The degree of leverage he held over the highlanders, despite the lack of armed presence in their territories, can hardly be exaggerated. The flow of trade was not just a prerequisite of prosperity but of actual survival. Lack of dried sardines meant that cows could not be adequately fed, their milk production fell significantly, and the population starved as a result. Sometimes, this condition was caused by Sultanic policy, the 'sardine blockade' constituting the traditional 'means of repression by the state against any tendency to rebel on the part of the nomadic tribes'.[59] Alternatively, hunger resulted from natural causes. For instance, the meagreness of the sardine catch in 1942 caused it to be a year of genuine destitution for the highlanders. Being an agent of local extraction rather than spending, the Sultan did not aid them, despite having adequate reserves to buy food. The only

---

[57] C.N. Jackson, 'A Note on the Dhufar Province, Southern Arabia', Kuwait, 23 June 1943, *RO1867–1947, Vol. 5*, p.128.
[58] Alan Berkeley, 'Beekeeping in Dhofar', in MEC-Sichel 1.
[59] Janzen, *Nomads in the Sultanate of Oman,* p.49.

recourse left for the highlanders was to work for the British who were building RAF aerodromes in Salalah.[60]

Ironically, while this project benefited the highlanders in the short run, it caused them greater destitution in the future. Indeed, the airbase eventually became the strongest instrument in sustaining Sultanic control. From it, rebellious groups could be bombed, and through it the Sultan could be much better connected with the outside world, receiving military and civil supplies. This was of course a purpose that it acquired at a later stage. Initially, it was developed as a station in the empire-wide network of routes established by the British Overseas Airways Corporation. It then became an RAF emergency landing ground as part of the Aden–Karachi link. Finally, it was used during the war by the RAF and the United States Army Air Corps for protecting reinforcement convoys to India and for transporting eastbound personnel and freight. To these ends, it provided 'a good airfield suitable for the largest aircraft, ancillary buildings and accommodation for the permanent staff and for 100 men in transit'.[61]

With the creation of RAF Salalah, the Sultan was no longer dependent on the sea for transportation. This coincided with further advances in his communication network, brought about by the extension of a line from Muscat to Dhufar by Cable and Wireless Limited, and the installation of a wireless transmitter and receiver in al-Hisn palace.[62] Although the Sultan was keen to be better connected and to utilize modern technologies for consolidating his power, he sought to isolate Dhufaris as much as possible. His main purpose was to protect an economic system that ensured him maximal personal profit with minimal social spending, and to insulate Dhufar from any external influences that could shake the foundations of his rule. After financing his forces, paying his administrators, and filling his coffers, little was left to improve the economic condition of the local population. Accordingly, 'the economic system of Dhofar was first and foremost geared to the extraction of revenue, with little or no service in return by the state'.[63]

With regard to health, hardly any investment was made, and the British did not help. In 1942, the Sultan asked the Government of India if a sub-surgeon could be provided in Salalah. He was informed that 'civilian doctors are unobtainable these days, and that while it may be possible to

---

[60] Janzen, *Nomads in the Sultanate of Oman,* p.128.
[61] Janzen, *Nomads in the Sultanate of Oman,* p.132.
[62] J.B. Howes (Political Agent Muscat) to Political Resident Bahrain, 28 October 1941, *RO1867–1947, Vol.5,* p.121.
[63] Janzen, *Nomads in the Sultanate of Oman,* p.49.

get one released from the military, the charges would be very heavy and unless your Highness is particularly anxious to have a man there would be a great deal of reluctance to release even one doctor from essential military duties'.[64] Thus, the people of Dhufar lived without any encounter with modern medicine, relying instead on traditional remedies and rituals. Eventually, an Iranian medic established a basic dispensary in Salalah, but he could hardly offer expert advice. As for education, the Sultan did not believe it to be necessary for local Dhufaris, merely creating one traditional primary school, exclusively reserved for the benefit of his retinue. At the height of its operations, this school had 150 boys, catered for in the Al-Hisn district near the Sultan's palace.[65]

As early as 1947, an expert agricultural survey was produced for the Sultan, including various recommendations for improving rural production. The surveyor, B.J. Hartley, noted that Dhufar offered 'considerable scope for agricultural development'. This required time and a good deal of expenditure. However, the suggested investments were all 'considered necessary' and undertaking them promised to 'help the people of the Province to improve their condition and move forward with an economy which will conserve and develop some of the natural resources with which the province is favoured'.[66] Alas, the Sultan was not prepared to spend on anything that was not going to yield him profit directly. Although unfortunate for his subjects, this policy made him very wealthy. His growing treasury was 'buttressed by the possession of possibly three fifths of the currency in the Province, over the expenditure of which the strictest control' was maintained.[67] The British more than matched the Sultan in their lack of interest in development. In 1960, they even rejected an application for a small development loan to finance some projects in Dhufar. Of course, these projects were ultimately geared to serving the economic interests of the Sultan but they may have had a trickle-down effect that would have helped the local population.[68]

Oil prospecting work began in Dhufar in 1955, carried out by Dhufar City Services, a company set up by Wendell Phillips, an American who had befriended the Sultan. The company failed to find any major fields,

[64] Political Agent Muscat to Assistant Political Agent Salalah, 27 November 1942, *RO1867–1947, Vol.5*, p.124.

[65] MEC-Sichel, Box 3/1/5, 'Civil Aid Department-Southern Region', 29 September 1977.

[66] CO/725/101/3, B.J. Hartley, 'A Preliminary Survey of the Land Resources of the Dhufar Province, Sultanate of Muscat and Oman', November 1947.

[67] Jorg Janzen, *Nomads in the Sultanate of Oman* p.130.

[68] Middleton (British Residency Bahrain) to Phillips (CG Muscat), 29 December 1960, *RO-1961*, p.3.

and it was taken over by John Mecom, a Texan investor who bought a 60 per cent share in January 1962. The arrival of the prospectors brought about some changes in Dhufar, and the oil company vehicles and its foreign employees began to venture deep into the territory, creating some of the first roads. But the possibility of oil did not bring out the promise of change. The Sultan, backed by his reactionary colonial adviser, Major Chauncy, continued to insist on maintaining a Raj style of administration. The archives abound with evidence attesting to this fact. For instance, in 1965, and in the context of a discussion with the British Consul General on the changes to be undertaken after the oil revenues begin to flow, the Sultan maintained the position that 'there is no desire for change'. In the words of the Consul:

> On education, he sees perhaps one more primary school somewhere. He will not want teachers from any Arab country, except possibly the Sudan. This circumscribed and conservative attitude is all-pervading in the oil development context and the least I would say is that things are going to get appreciably worse before they get better.[69]

The Sultan's position on local employment and involvement in state structures was equally conservative. He repeatedly informed his British backers that if the oil were to flow, he would not be interested in 'delegating work and training his own people to govern', and that 'there was nobody he could trust except the British'.[70]

Although they were aware of the political difficulties that this attitude could cause, the British vigorously supported the Sultan. Their views are reflected in a dispatch submitted by Bernard Burrows, British Political Resident in Bahrain to the Marquess of Salisbury. Upon visiting Dhufar on 29 August 1953, Burrows reported the following:

> The Sultan's rule in Dhufar is essentially autocratic. It is in fact run not so much as part of the state but as a private domain or fief of which he is the personal owner as well as sovereign. It is impossible to say on such short acquaintance how these conditions are appreciated by the inhabitants. The Sultan's rule is, at least on occasion, harsh. I understand he has cut off the water supply of a village in order to provide greater supplies for his own gardens.[71]

---

[69] J.F.S. Phillips (British Consulate General, Muscat) to Arabian Department, 17 March 1962, *RO-1962*, p.703.
[70] J.F.S. Phillips (British Consulate General, Muscat) to Arabian Department, 17 March 1962, *RO-1962*, p.703.
[71] CO 1015/695, PR Bahrain (Burrows) to Principal Secretary of State for Foreign Affairs (Marquess of Salisbury), 8 September 1953.

Even more worryingly, Said deviated from tried and tested 'traditional' Arab politics in British-controlled domains:

> ... [He] did not aspire to the authority of the traditional Arab leader, based on the open exercise of superior personality in surroundings of *apparent* democracy, and his relations with his subjects were more those of master to serf than of leader to follower.[72]

Burrows did not take issue with sovereignty being vested in the person of the Sultan, nor did he view autocracy as the problem *per se*. If anything, the maintenance of both monarchical sovereignty and autocratic rule were essential, for it was only natural for the native 'followers' to have an individual ruler to 'lead' them. What was lamentable in the case of Said bin Taimur was that he based his rule solely on coercion despite the alienation of the Dhufari population. The potential pitfalls of this approach did not escape Burrows and other imperial administrators of the new generation of the post-Raj era. Concerned as they were with strengthening the regime, they displayed an intuitive grasp of the Weberian maxim that 'an order which is adhered to from motives of pure expediency is generally much less stable than one upheld on a purely customary basis through the fact that corresponding behaviour has become habitual'.[73]

In the eyes of British modernists, so-called 'traditional Arab' leadership was clearly preferable to Said's feudal-like lordship, for habitual followers were more loyal than oppressed serfs. The crux of the problem was not the lack of a distribution of power but rather the insufficiency of the means of upholding it: the Sultan's methods were deemed to be inadequately oriented to generating loyalty in an age of transformation. For the Sultan's subjects to willingly follow him, he needed to create the appearance of consultation, the semblance of participation, while actually exercising his 'superior personality' and taking the final decisions. Undoubtedly, the 'surroundings of apparent democracy' that Burrows had in mind were those of the *majalis*, the rulers' councils that were common in other parts of the Gulf. Advantageously for Britain and the rulers connected to it, the *majlis* was not an abstracted space of collective inclusion (such as a parliament for example): it was a grounded physical space, constrained by actual and symbolic walls. It was a place of rigid particularity—action and discourse took place on behalf of delineated units (such as the tribes and the merchants), precluding the potential rise of universal notions that

---

[72] CO 1015/695. PR Bahrain (Burrows) to Principal Secretary of State for Foreign Affairs (Marquess of Salisbury), 8 September 1953. Emphasis added.

[73] Max Weber, *The Theory of Social and Economic Organisation*, trans. A.M. Henderson and Talcott Parsons, New York: The Free Press of Glencoe, 1947, p.125.

could dangerously encompass the entirety of a population in a given territory (especially 'the people'). It was a system held together by a chain of leadership, linking tribes, tribal coalitions, ruling families, rulers, Political Agents, Political Residents, and ultimately Whitehall.

In Dhufar, not only was the *majlis* system absent and the population entirely excluded from any form of political involvement, but they were also subjected to the rule of a foreign Sultan who had imposed a wide array of petty restrictions that aroused substantial resentment. He severely restricted travel, limited the spread of such objects as radios and spectacles, and inflicted harsh punishments. In the light of these policies, the judgement of a prominent scholar that 'Said bin Taimur was one of the nastiest rulers the world has seen for a long time' seems difficult to fault.[74] Yet there were limits to Said's oppression, with local resistance taking very elaborate forms in the highlands. The forms that this resistance took correspond to a global pattern. Like other hill peoples, Dhufari highlanders engaged in a 'deliberate and reactive statelessness'. Whereas such statelessness could not take place on the coast, it flourished in the mountains. Indeed, the highlanders' aforementioned political, social, and economic patterns could be analysed as acts of resistance to state incursion. This allows us to follow James Scott in reconsidering the whole notion of 'primitiveness' amongst mountain peoples:

> Virtually everything about these people's livelihoods, social organisation, ideologies, and (more controversially) even their largely oral cultures, can be read as strategic positionings to keep the state at arm's length…Pastoralism, foraging, shifting cultivation, and segmentary lineage systems are often a 'secondary adaptation', a kind of 'self-barbarisation' adopted by peoples whose location, subsistence, and social structure are adapted to state evasion. For those living in the shadow of states, such evasion is also perfectly compatible with derivative, imitative, and parasitic state forms in the hills…[75]

Like others across the world—'Gypsies, Cossacks…the Marsh Arabs, San-Bushmen, and so on'—Dhufaris engaged in such state evasion for centuries. However, the advent of the oil age changed the rules of the game. The state began gradually to expand into tribal zones for prospecting purposes, and this disturbed the balance that had prevailed before.

---

[74] Fred Halliday, *Arabia Without Sultans*, London: Saqi Books, 2nd edition 1999, p.275.
[75] James Scott, *The Art of Not Being Governed: An Anarchist History of Upland Southeast Asia*. New Heaven: Yale University Press, 2009. p.x. I am very grateful to Sudhir Hazareesingh for pointing out the global pattern to which the resistances of Dhufari highlanders correspond.

Likewise, economic migration began to occur, with Dhufari youth travelling in secrecy to surrounding Gulf countries in search of work. The experiences of these young men and their political responses to the Sultan's regime will be traced in detail in the next chapter. Suffice to note here that they were no longer content with state evasion, seeking instead the overthrow of the regime and takeover of the state.

3

A Struggle for Sovereignty

In the beginning there was dispersion and economic exile. Since the 1940s, poverty at home had compelled young Dhufaris to seek employment abroad.[1] This trend was accelerated by a severe drought from which their families suffered in the late 1950s.[2] They spread out across the Gulf, working in the expanding oil companies and the emerging local armies and security forces. This had broad effects, two of which are of particular importance: exposure to new paradigms of political thought, and experience of wide-scale political action. These effects cannot be understood in isolation from the context in which these Dhufaris lived, especially in Kuwait, the birthplace of their revolutionary movement.

Kuwait was the most economically and politically dynamic territory in the Gulf region in the 1950s. The state and the economy were growing with the help of oil revenues, and this gave Dhufaris their first experience of economic modernization. Political movements were also developing. The largest by far was the Movement of Arab Nationalists (MAN). The Gulf headquarters of the MAN was founded by Kuwait's first physician, Dr Ahmad al-Khatib. In 1942, al-Khatib was given a scholarship to attend the American University in Beirut. There, he attended the lectures of Constantine Zureiq and became active in Arab nationalist circles. The 1948 loss of Palestine—designated 'al-Nakba' (the catastrophe) in Arabic— had a profound impact on him and he was marked by his experiences as a volunteer in Ain al-Hilweh refugee camp.[3]

Al-Khatib's closest friends were George Habash and Wadie Haddad, Palestinians who had lost all their income and were forced to share his pocket money. The three youths were filled with frustration 'at the Zionists, the countries that supported them, and the Arab parties and countries

---

[1] J.E. Peterson, 'Oman's Diverse Society: Southern Oman', *Middle East Journal*, Volume 58, no.2, Spring 2004, p.266.
[2] Carol Riphenburg, *Oman: Political Development in a Changing World*, London: Praeger, 1998, p.48.
[3] Ahmad al-Khatib, *Al-Kuwait, Min al-Imara ila al-Dawla: Thikrayat al- 'Amal al Wa'tani wal 'Qawmi*, 2nd edition, Beirut: al-Markaz al-Tha'qafi al-'Arabi, 2007, p.76.

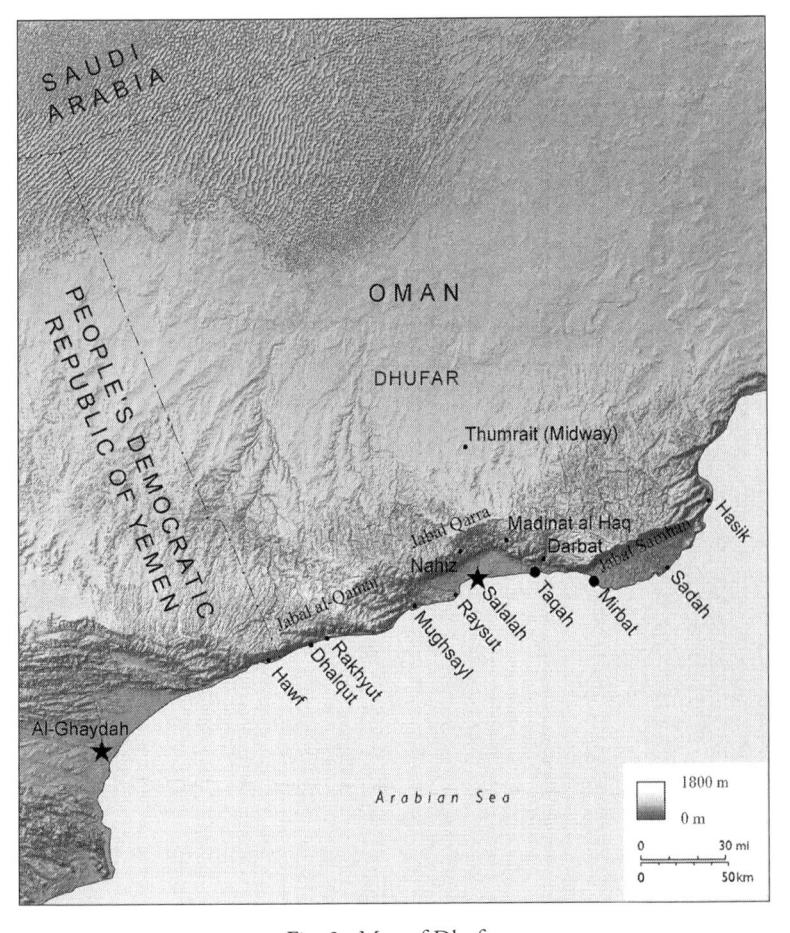

Fig. 2. Map of Dhufar

that failed the Palestinians'.[4] Along with other members of Zureiq's circle, they began to strategize for their response to the Nakba. That response was shaped by the vision propagated in Zureiq's influential work, *Ma'ana al-Nakba* ('The Meaning of Catastrophe'). Zureiq argued that the twin challenges of Zionism and imperialism could not be addressed except through a united, modern nation state that can achieve the transformation of society from the 'medieval era' to 'modernity'. Achieving that goal would require the initiative of a select creative group of Arab youth 'organized and united through political parties and cohesive organizations, committed to a common and pure doctrine and bound by concrete and true loyalty'.[5] The notion of a *Tali'a*, a transformative vanguard that champions the people, was thus firmly established in the minds of al-Khatib and his friends from the beginning.

Following his return to Kuwait, al-Khatib energetically began to organize and recruit Arab nationalists into the embryo group that was later named the MAN. In the wake of Gamal Abdel Nasser's stance against the Baghdad pact and the nationalization of the Suez Canal, they gravitated towards Nasserism, eventually becoming the main arm of its popular policy in the Gulf. During the events of 1956, Al-Khatib and his group organized the largest marches in Kuwaiti history. They were even joined by the Chief of Police, Jasim al-'Qatami, who had resigned along with thirteen of his officers after being ordered to attack the demonstrators.[6] Pictures of Nasser were hung everywhere, and messages were sent to him and read on Cairo's *Sawt al-Arab* radio station. There were boycotts of French and British goods, huge fundraisers for Egypt, a popular strike and explosions in the Al-Ahmadi oil fields.[7] Elsewhere in the region, there were also mass popular actions. In Qatar, there was a general strike.[8] In Bahrain, several British buildings were burnt and mass demonstrations occurred.[9] Across the Gulf, support for Nasserism was in clear evidence.

Like everyone around them, Dhufari workers were influenced by the revolutionary moment of 1956. They too had been listening to the broadcasts of Cairo's *Sawt al-Arab*, and were affected by the popular mobilization

---

[4] al-Khatib, *Al-Kuwait, Min al-Imara ila al-Dawla: Thikrayat al-'Amal al Watani wal 'Qawmi*, p.77.

[5] Constantine Zureiq, *Ma'ana al-Nakba*, Beirut: Dar al-'Ilm lil Malayaeen, 1948, p.55.

[6] Miriam Joyce, *Kuwait, 1945–1996: An Anglo-American Perspective*, London: Frank Cass, 1998, p.43.

[7] Al-Mdairis, *al-Mujtama' al-Madani wal 'Haraka al-Wat'aniya fil Kuwait*, Kuwait: Dar Qirtas, 2000, pp.26–31.

[8] Nour el Din bin-Al 'Habeeb Hejlawi, *Ta'thir al Fikr al Nas'iri 'ala al-Khaleej al-'Arabi, 1952–1971*, Beirut: Markaz Dirasat al-Wih'da al-'Arabiyya, 2003, pp.195–8.

[9] Hejlawi, *Ta'thir al Fikr al Nas'iri 'ala al-Khaleej al-'Arabi, 1952–1971*, pp.189–94.

in the aftermath of Suez.[10] Nasserism's appeal did not just lie in the liberationist nature of its discourse, but in the seriousness of its policies. Behind it lay the heavy weight of Egypt, the most populous and influential of all Arab countries. Like all grand visions, it was at once romantic and concrete, providing inspiration as well as actual results, such as the defeat of the tripartite aggression.[11]

The traditional view of Nasserism has focused on three of its elements: pan-Arabism; anti-colonialism; and revolutionary socialism.[12] However, a fourth aspect that requires emphasis is that of republicanism. Nasser had a classically Jacobin republican understanding of the question of representation, believing that in the Egyptian context, the will of the people could only be genuinely represented by a revolutionary state that works for their interest, and with their popular backing.[13] He propagated republican principles, foremost amongst which is *Siyadat al Sha'ab*, popular sovereignty. That principle is found across his *oeuvre* and especially in his speeches, the main medium through which his ideas were carried in the Gulf. Nasser explicitly tied the three questions of unity, self-determination, and economic development with the removal of monarchy. When he made his historic announcement of the nationalization of the Suez Canal, widely listened to across the Gulf, he represented monarchy as a form of domestic exploitation that was eradicated by the revolution.[14] Republican principles were even more clearly articulated in the speech celebrating the

---

[10] Interview F.

[11] The focus here is on the articulation and reception of Nasserism as opposed to its motivation. The latter is a question that has been debated widely. For a sympathetic study that focuses on the role of principles in Nasserist foreign policy, see Mohammad Al-Sayyed Saleem, *Al Ta'hlil al-Siyassi al-Nassiri: Dirasa fil 'Akaaed wal Siyassa al-Kharijiya*, Beirut: Markaz Dirasat al-Wih'da al-'Arabiyya, 1983. For a harsh assessment that views Nasser as manipulating Arab sentiments to further Egyptian hegemony, see Tawfig Hassou, *The Struggle for the Arab World: Egypt's Nasser and the Arab League*, London and Boston: KPI, 1985. For a discussion that situates Nasser's policy in the context of the emergence of a Westphalian Arab regional system, see Fred Lawson, *Constructing International Relations in the Arab World*, Stanford: Stanford University Press, 2006.

[12] Perhaps the most renowned discussion of these three elements in the English academic literature is found in Malcolm Kerr, *The Arab Cold War, 1958–1964: A Study of Ideology in Politics*, London: Oxford University Press and the Royal Institute of International Affairs, 1965, pp. 1–9. Other accounts have viewed Nasser in terms of the broader notion of populism. See, for example, Ali al-Dein Hilal, 'Ta'tawur Al-Ideologiyya al Rasmiya fi Misr: Al-Dimuqratiya wal Ishtirakya,' in *Misr: Min al-Thawra ila al-Rida*, Beirut: Dar al-Tali'a, 1981. Elie Podeh and Onn Winckler, 'Nasserism as a Form of Populism', in Elie Podeh and Onn Winckler (eds.), *Rethinking Nasserism: Revolution and Historical Memory in Modern Egypt*, Gainesville, FL: University Press of Florida, 2004.

[13] For the characteristics of Jacobinism, see Sudhir Hazareesingh (ed.), *The Jacobin Legacy in Modern France: Essays in Honour of Vincent Wright*, Oxford: OUP, 2002, p.6.

[14] Nasser, '4th Anniversary of the Revolution Speech.' 26 July 1956: <http://www.nasser.org>

adoption of the 1956 constitution: 'Citizens: today, popular sovereignty prevails, not the sovereignty of the princes or the rulers…'[15]

Following the end of his brief *entente* with Saudi Arabia, and especially in the wake of the 1962 revolution in Yemen, Nasser's republican discourse was increasingly directed towards the rest of the Arab world. Monarchs were represented as 'traitors' to the Arab nation, 'agents of colonialism,' and 'enemies of unity',[16] Moreover, Nasser's discourse was now focused on the extension of republicanism to the Arabian Peninsula:

> We are the ones who have launched the revolution so that we could be rid of the likes of [king] Saud, and so that we could be rid of feudalism and despotism. We are the ones who have launched the revolution so that our fate could be in our own hands. Should we stand silent and watch reaction defeat the revolution in Yemen?[17]

Nasser's republicanism was intimately tied to anti-colonialism. His slogan: 'let British colonialism pick up its stick and leave the entirety of the Arabian Peninsula', was complemented by his declaration that 'colonialism does not just lie in military bases, it resides in the palaces of the Kings and the Sultans'. That vision had a special appeal for Dhufaris, for whom the connection between Al Bu Sai'd dominance and British imperial presence was unmistakable. Events such as the 1958 Iraqi revolution only seemed to vindicate it.

The Omani Sultan, Said bin Taimur, was meanwhile swimming against the tide of his age. He was enthusiastically cheering for Britain in 1956, going 'so far as to criticise the British for doing too little, too late to curb Egyptian aggression in the Middle East'.[18] Britain's dominance made him secure but it also exposed him to growing scrutiny. In the past, Britain could support him quietly, protected by the utter isolation of South East Arabia and the weakness of the surrounding powers. But, in the age of mass-communication, every act was suddenly open to condemnation. When Britain assembled the SAS and its troops in Oman and bombed the Jabal al-Akhdar, *Sawt al-Arab* announced its activities on its radio waves, and newspapers described them in print. The voice of the Imamate leaders was widely transmitted, recounting the feats of their movement and its attacks on British troops.

---

[15] Nasser, 'Address at Republic Square', 16 January 1956: <http://www.nasser.org>
[16] Nasser, '6th Anniversary of the Victory Address', 23 December 1962: <http://www.nasser.org>
[17] Nasser, '6th Anniversary of the Victory Address': <http://www.nasser.org>
[18] Uzi Rabi, *The Emergence of States in a Tribal Society*, Brighton: Sussex Academic Press, 2006, p.98. In contrast, Britain was widely criticized in Muscat society. See Neil Innes, *Minister in Oman: A Personal Narrative*, Cambridge: Oleander Press, 1987, p.204.

For Dhufaris, the al-Jabal al-Akhdar rebellion hit close to home. Its enemies, the Sultan and the British, also ruled over their own lands. Thus, along with constant exposure to Nasserist discourse, the rebellion played an important role in mobilizing migrant Dhufari youth in the Gulf.[19] Even before the Jabal al-Akhdar events began, they were lifted by the rising tide of pan-Arabism and 'warmed up' by the Suez events and the Tripartite Aggression of 1956, forming several loose groupings in the late 1950s. These mainly emerged in Kuwait and Saudi Arabia, but also amongst the ranks of young men serving in the police and armed forces in Qatar, Bahrain and Sharjah. They tended to be localized and small, their growth facilitated by the tight-knit nature of Dhufari gatherings, which were, in the habit of migrant communities, clustered around known neighbourhoods. Secrecy was of paramount importance and members swore an oath to it over the Quran, for there was much fear at the time. Towards the end of 1958 and the beginning of 1959, links were established among the Dhufari formations which gradually took a more solid form. Yet they were not 'organized' in the strict sense of the term, as they lacked charters, political programmes, or cadre registers. Instead, they were networks of youths who shared a common opposition to the injustice suffered under the Sultans.[20]

The idea of overthrowing the Sultanic regime began to spread but there was still no clear vision as to how that objective was to be achieved. Some advocated a coup-based approach and tried to enlist in the Dhufar Force (DF). Seeking recruitment, they wrote letters to Captain St John Armitage (DF Commander, 1955–1959) but their applications were rejected. With the option of a military coup proving untenable, the idea of armed struggle as the only path available gained widespread currency.[21] Armed struggle was being conducted by the Imamate forces. On an even grander scale, it was adopted by the fighters in Algeria, in the face of the imperial prowess of France. These examples gave Dhufaris hope. And so the Dhufari Charitable Association (DCA), the first non-tribal political grouping in Dhufari history, was formed in 1958.[22] On the surface, the DCA collected donations for such activities as building mosques and supporting students. In reality, it was a front for recruiting the youth and raising funds for weapons.[23]

[19] Falah Al-Mdairis, 'The Arab Nationalist Movement in Kuwait from its Origins to 1970', unpublished DPhil Thesis, University of Oxford, 1987, p.314.

[20] Interview F.

[21] Interview F.

[22] Al-Mdairis, 'The Arab Nationalist Movement in Kuwait', p.314.

[23] Al-Jabha al-Shabiya, *Wathaiq' al-Ni'dal al-Wat'ani, 1965–1974*, Beirut: Dar Al-Tali'a, 1974, p.6.

Such mobilization could hardly have occurred without the experience of collective migration. Away from home, a common Dhufari identity—as well as the feeling of belonging to a wider Arab nation—waxed. Regardless of their tribal affiliation, any Dhufari could join the DCA, and dozens did, forming branches in Kuwait and the other Gulf countries. On the one hand, the DCA reflected a longstanding desire for Dhufari independence; a desire manifested in numerous tribal rebellions since the Al Bu Said annexation of the territory in 1879.[24] On the other hand, it was an organization infused with the popular discourse of Nasserism. These seemingly contradictory features coexisted without tension at this stage, the DCA simultaneously committed to the notion of 'Dhufar for the Dhufaris' and supporting the wider vision of pan-Arabism. Dhufari independence countered an oppressive Sultan, while Nasserism confronted the British presence that was keeping him in power.

At the time, it was only natural for the DCA to seek cooperation with the forces of the Omani Imamate rebels. Such cooperation would represent unity in a struggle against the regime and allow access to considerable diplomatic and military resources. Muhammad Ahmad al-Ghassani, a leader of the DCA and an employee of the Kuwait Oil Company, thus went to Damascus at the head of a delegation towards the end of 1958. He initiated contact with exiled Imamate leaders and held talks with Sheikh Salih bin Issa al-Harithi. Recalling their meeting, he explains:

> We showed our readiness to participate in the Green Mountain Revolution... It was agreed with the Imamate to send some... [volunteers] to gain military training in Damascus and the first Mission was from the Dhufari Charitable Association in Kuwait.[25]

Yet, the Dhufaris waited for weeks without any sign of genuine cooperation. It was during this period of disappointed anticipation that the most important meeting in the early history of Dhufari politics occurred. Attending the February 1959 celebrations of the first anniversary of the United Arab Republic (UAR), al-Ghassani encountered George Habash. The commanding Palestinian revolutionary discussed with al-Ghassani the Movement of Arab Nationalists and its principles. The latter was clearly impressed and upon his return to Kuwait, he established contact with Ahmad al-Khatib.[26] From that moment on, the fortunes of the

---

[24] J.G. Lorimer, *Gazetteer of the Persian Gulf, 'Oman, And Central Arabia*, Volume I, Historical, Part 1. Westmead: Greg International, 1970, p.592.
[25] Quoted in Al-Mdairis, 'The Arab Nationalist Movement in Kuwait', p.315.
[26] Al-Mdairis, 'The Arab Nationalist Movement in Kuwait', p.316.

Dhufari movement were closely tied to those of a wider pan-Arabist revolutionary network.

After an initial phase of Dhufari recruitment into the MAN, a formal meeting was conducted between it and the DCA. It was agreed that the DCA in Kuwait would be dissolved and absorbed into the Movement. Out of this merger, the Dhufaris hoped to receive military training and political support for their proposed overthrow of the Sultan. As for the MAN, this was an important step in the direction of expanding its organizational reach and revolutionary activity outside Kuwait and into the other parts of the Gulf and the Arabian Peninsula. But whereas they welcomed the young Dhufaris' commitment to Arab nationalism and their enthusiasm for action, the Kuwaiti leaders of the MAN considered that there was much to be done before they would be ready for armed struggle.[27] In their estimation, Dhufari members needed to be transformed from inexperienced political enthusiasts to organized politicized cadres. Like all its members across the Arab *Mashriq*, the Dhufaris were to be introduced into the theory of Arab nationalism, committed within an organizational hierarchy and engaged in the practices of political diffusion.

The training received by Dhufaris was much less individualized and more expedited than that of other recruits. In effect, they were treated as a special group within the MAN whose education was overseen by experienced Kuwaiti leaders.[28] For literate members, the educational programme was similar to that adopted in typical MAN cells. They were given five types of material: internal publications, including the bulletin (*al-Munadil al Thawri*) and monthly political reports; the newspapers of the Movement; publications of the Movement's committee on thought; short essays; and assigned books for close study.[29]

The books provided were divided into two kinds: classics of Arab nationalist thought and substantial publications of the Movement.[30] The classics mainly included the works of al-Husri and Zureiq. These exposed cadres to romantic theories of nationalism that emphasized 'the nation as a spiritual, living being', placing 'great emphasis on the naturalness of

---

[27] Al-Mdairis, 'The Arab Nationalist Movement in Kuwait', p.316.

[28] Al-Mdairis, 'The Arab Nationalist Movement in Kuwait', p.316. These included Sulaiman al 'Askiri, 'Abd al-'Ali Nasser, 'Ali Al-Radwan, and Sami al Munayyis.

[29] 'Ta'mim 'Hawl al Tathqif al-Dhakhili' in Hani Al-Hindi and 'Abdul Ilah Al-Nas'rawi, (eds.), *Harakat al 'Qawmiyeen al 'Arab: Nashatuha wa Ta'twuruha 'Abra Wathai'qiha, 1951–1968*, Volume 1, Part 4. Beirut: Mu'asasat al-Ab'hath al-'Arabiyya, 2004, pp.15–17.

[30] Hani Al-Hindi and 'Abdul Ilah Al-Nas'rawi,'Introduction' in *Harakat al 'Qawmiyeen al 'Arab: Nashatuha wa Ta'twuruha 'Abra Wathai'qiha, 1951–1968*, Volume 1, Part 2, Beirut: Mu'asasat al-Ab'hath al-'Arabiyya, 2002, p.12.

national existence'.[31] Such theoretical conceptions formed the basis of MAN's vision:

> We want a nationalist, united, liberated Arab society that would bring us economic justice with a socialist system that suits our needs; that would bring us political justice with a democratic system in which our liberty is realised; and that would bring social justice in all our institutions.[32]

This vision appealed to politicized Dhufaris, in spite of the fact that a significant percentage of them were not native-Arabic speakers, their mother tongue being one variant or another of Jebali or Mahri. Traditionally, local genealogies asserted Arabness in the tribal sense of the term, most Dhufaris viewing themselves as *qahtani* Arabs. More recently, adopting a modern Arab national identity had an equalizing dimension, allowing Dhufaris to assert themselves as equal compatriots with other Arabs and to integrate themselves into the broader regional struggle against colonialism. The substantive importance of this dimension can be seen in one of the few pieces of revolutionary literature dealing with the period of Dhufari exile in the Gulf. In the short story 'The Tornado', the discrimination that was suffered by Dhufari workers outside pan-Arabist circles is clearly reflected. As far as the Dhufari character in the story was concerned, even the act of paying the bill was an unpleasant experience:

> He extended his hand to pay the bill, but the [Kuwaiti] owner ignored him, busying himself with something else... So he said in a gentle voice: 'My friend, here is...' But he was interrupted with haughtiness 'Be patient, what is wrong with you foreigner'. It was as if he had been stabbed in the chest with a dagger... How strange was it that matters would be reduced to slogans, and that Europeans here were treated far better than Arabs![33]

For an oppressed population, pan-Arabist circles afforded crucial access to a universal language of rights. Arab nationalism was open enough to allow such access. Anyone identifying as an Arab was considered to be such. al-Husri urged 'pride in Arab civilization without expressing a corresponding sense of comparative racial superiority'.[34]

---

[31] William Cleveland, *The Making of an Arab Nationalist: Ottomanism and Arabism in the Life and Thought of Sati' Al-Husri*, Princeton, NJ: Princeton University Press, 1971, p.89.

[32] Al-'Hakam Darwazeh and 'Hamid Al-Jbouri, *Ma' al 'Qawmiya al-'Arabiya*, 4th edition (1960), in Al-Hindi and Al-Nas'rawi, *'Harakat al 'Qawmiyeen al 'Arab: Nashatuha wa Ta'twuruha 'Abra Wathai'qiha, 1951–1968*, p.159.

[33] al-Siraj Ahmad, 'Al-Zawba'a' in Al-Jabha al-Sha'abya li Tahreer Oman, *Tis'a Yunyu*, Year 5, No.5, June 1975, p.94.

[34] William Cleveland, *The Making of an Arab Nationalist: Ottomanism and Arabism in the Life and Thought of Sati' Al-Husri*, Princeton, NJ: Princeton University Press, 1971, p.89.

Significantly, the nationalist worldview that Dhufaris were exposed to at this stage was anti-communist. The MAN at the time advocated the 'two stages of struggle' programme, which stipulated the separation of the political and the social. Initially, political struggle would be pursued. This entailed achieving Arab unity, expelling colonialism, and liberating Palestine, and accordingly creating the Arab national society. Only then would social justice and economic equality be established within that society, namely through socialism. This was counterposed to the ideology of the Ba'ath that proposed the joining of the political and social struggles.[35] The MAN defended that separation on the basis that struggle cannot be successful if not approached in stages. Moreover, it rejected Marxism, arguing that Arab socialism would not be the outcome of class struggle but of the development of a correct national consciousness.[36] Deeply critical of Arab communist parties, the MAN viewed them as agents of foreign forces and condemned their allegedly weak stance on Palestine. Such ideas were undoubtedly transferred to Dhufari MAN cadres, especially considering the fervent anti-communism of the Kuwaiti branch at the time and the bloody struggles between the MAN and the Communists in Iraq.

On the political side of things, the activities of the Dhufari cadres were supervised by a committee of leading MAN figures. The committee had a distinguished composition, reflecting the importance that the Gulf MAN placed upon Dhufar.[37] It did not escape the Kuwaiti leaders that the territory was—along with the Yemeni south—a potential zone for confronting British imperialism and extending Nasser's battle of *fard al jala'a* (imposing withdrawal upon British and French colonialism). This was not the least due to the prevalence of a political atmosphere and a physical geography that were ideal for armed struggle. Yet, as always with the MAN, the pamphlet preceded the rifle, and political organization foreran military training. The focus was on spreading ideas, building networks, and cultivating leaders. Over the course of the fifties, the Kuwaiti branch had mastered the utilization of sports and cultural clubs and associations towards these ends. Unsurprisingly, the Dhufari branch followed suit, establishing several clubs in areas with a heavy Dhufari concentration.[38]

---

[35] Moh'ammad Jamal Barut, '*Harakat al-Qawmiyeen al-'Arab: al-Nash'a, al-Ta'tawur, al-Mas'air*, Damascus: al-Markaz al-'Arabi lil Dirasat al-Istratijya, 1997, p.92.

[36] Darwazeh and Al-Jbouri, *Ma' al 'Qawmiya al-'Arabiya*, pp.164–72.

[37] Al-Mdairis, 'The Arab Nationalist Movement in Kuwait', p.316. The committee consisted of Ahmad al-Khatib, Jasim al-Qatami, Sami al-Munayyis, and the Dhufari leader Mohammad Ahmad al-Ghassani.

[38] Al-Mdairis, 'The Arab Nationalist Movement in Kuwait', pp.316–17.

In addition to political education and organization, the MAN was concerned with raising the general educational level of Dhufaris in Kuwait. Deprived of education at home, Dhufaris had the lowest literacy level in the region. The MAN—formed by intellectuals who believed in a general Arab renaissance—was deeply sympathetic to their plight. It established the Omani Student House in al Farawaniya, catering for Omani, Dhufari and Yemeni students. This became a centre for MAN activism, influenced by leading elements such as Said Masoud. The MAN also formed The Arab Gulf Cultural Association, which granted scholarships to students from the Gulf and Yemen, supporting their primary and secondary education in Kuwait and other Arab countries.[39] This was an important vehicle for the secondary socialization of Dhufari youth and for their immersion in the intellectual and political outlook of the pan-Arabist republican tradition.

REPUBLICANS, DHUFARISTS, AND TRIBALISTS

Unsurprisingly, educated Dhufaris tended to be deeply committed to the Movement of Arab Nationalists (MAN), but the majority of the old members of the DCA were discontented with it. They had joined the MAN in the hope of receiving weapons and training but they were instead given clandestine weekly meetings and strict political guidelines and disciplinary rules. Many felt the meetings to be exhausting and boring. Whenever they demanded weapons, they received nothing but promises. After several months of belonging to the Movement, a wrangle with the leadership arose over some organizational regulations. Subsequently, several dozen Dhufari members decided to quit and revive the DCA. The split was not ideological and the issue of weapons lay at its heart. Those that remained in the MAN were sarcastically told: 'Keep waiting for the Movement! These guys are lying about the guns.'[40] For its part, the MAN did not exert any pressure on those that left; it was content to keep those members who 'showed political promise'.[41] At any rate, two Dhufari political bodies now existed in Kuwait with members spread across the rest of the Gulf. One was the MAN, firmly organized and pan-Arabist and republican in outlook. The other was the DCA, loosely structured around local demands, or what could be called Dhufarism, within a general Arabist framework.

---

[39] Al-Mdairis, 'The Arab Nationalist Movement in Kuwait', pp.316–17.
[40] Interview F.
[41] Interview F.

In the meantime, Dhufari soldiers and policemen became increasingly organized along Dhufarist lines. The majority were serving in the Trucial Oman Scouts (TOS), a force that had been established by the British in Sharjah in 1951. Beyond the boundaries of the Trucial coast, Britain deployed the TOS to aid in the suppression of the al-Jabal al-Akhdar revolt. It was in that context that Dhufaris were recruited in large numbers. The campaign was conducted in high altitudes, averaging 6,500 feet and sometimes rising to 10,000 feet. Accustomed to mountain warfare, Dhufaris were seen as ideal recruits, and the TOS instituted a policy of enlisting them.[42] They arrived at its barracks through an arduous route, sailing by dhow from Salalah to Muscat and then travelling overland to Sharjah. By 1960, there were enough of them to form a special unit, 'X' Squadron.[43] Although 'the Sultan never looked with favour on their recruitment in the T.O.S', by 1967 there were roughly 200 Dhufaris out of 1,400 rank and file serving in the force.[44]

Ironically, it was the experience of counter-revolution that prepared Dhufari soldiers for revolution. The TOS introduced them to the disciplinary techniques of organized armies and trained them in the use of weapons and artillery—skills that were tremendously valuable for the future fight in Dhufar. Like their compatriots in Kuwait they desired the overthrow of the Sultan, establishing a clandestine group sometime around 1961.[45] Similar groups were organized in the Qatar Force (1962) and the Bahrain Defence Force (1963).[46] A meeting was held among representatives of the three groups in 1964 and it was agreed to merge them into a single underground formation, the Dhufari Soldiers Organization (DSO).[47] Such was the secrecy of the DSO that, even as late as December 1967, the British were unaware of its existence.[48]

Back in Kuwait, the MAN Dhufaris were growing restless, continuously pushing the Movement towards action. Following the success of the 26 September 1962 revolution in North Yemen, a formal opportunity arose for making their case. The General Secretariat of the MAN called a meeting in Beirut to discuss the ramifications of the revolution and to consider the launch of armed struggle against the British in Aden and the

[42] Michael Mann, *The Trucial Oman Scouts: The Story of a Bedouin Force*, Wilby, Norwich: Michael Russell Publishing, 1994, p.101.

[43] Mann, *The Trucial Oman Scouts*, p.101.

[44] FCO 51/41, Balfour-Paul to Ford, 6 December 1967.

[45] Mohammad Al-Amri, *Thufar: al Thawra fil Tarikh al-Omani al Mu'asir*, Beirut: Riad el-Rayyes Books, 2005, p.63.

[46] Al-Amri, *Thufar*, p.63.

[47] Al-Amri, *Thufar*, p.63.

[48] FCO 51/41, Balfour-Paul to Ford. 6 December 1967.

Protectorates. The meeting was held in late 1962 and was attended by representatives of the branches in the newly formed Yemen Arab Republic (YAR), the Occupied Arab South (i.e., South Yemen) and the Gulf.[49] The Dhufari representative pushed for a resolution on the launch of the armed struggle against the British and the Sultan in Dhufar. He argued that the events in the YAR presented an inspiring example to all revolutionary forces in the Arabian Peninsula and that the time was ripe for action in Dhufar, especially considering the broad opposition to the Sultan and the British.

Despite receiving backing from the representatives from the YAR, the Occupied Arab South and Kuwait, the Dhufari representative was out-voted by the General Secretariat, which was of the opinion that armed struggle in Dhufar required further preparation. At that early stage, MAN leaders saw the fight in Dhufar as an extension of the fight in the Occupied Arab South. Aden was the largest British base in the Arab world, the Empire's stronghold: all eyes were upon it and most resources directed towards it. As for Dhufar, Muhsin Ibrahim's recollection sums up its position in some MAN circles: 'with so many burdens on the level of the Peninsula and the Arab homeland, one would have required a microscope to see Dhufar at that particular moment'.[50]

Although it was not its foremost regional priority, the central leadership of the MAN was undoubtedly convinced of the need for the struggle in Dhufar. As the late George Habash recounts in his memoirs:

> In Oman, there existed a tyrannical regime similar to those of the Middle Ages. How could people tolerate that oppression without revolting? That is what we used to tell our comrades when they told us of the living conditions of the people in Oman, and the head of our movement in Oman was of the opinion that armed struggle needed to be launched in the Sultanate.[51]

That said, the leadership felt overstretched and the South Yemeni revolution was born while Dhufar's was postponed. This had a dampening impact on the Dhufari branch of the MAN. Soon after the Beirut meeting, several members left without notice and set up the Socialist Advance Party (SAP).[52] The intention behind the split was to exert pressure upon the MAN to adopt armed struggle in Dhufar and to create the necessary revolutionary circumstances for it to act. Indeed, the SAP hardly differed from the MAN in ideology and practice, its members studying al-Husri's

---

[49] Al-Mdairis, 'The Arab Nationalist Movement in Kuwait', p.343.
[50] Interview A.
[51] George Habash, *Al-Thawryoona La Yamoutouna Abadan,* Beirut: Al Saqi, 2011, p.64.
[52] Al-Mdairis, 'The Arab Nationalist Movement in Kuwait', p.360. Those that left included two future notable figures: Ali Mohsen and Khaled Amin.

writings and Nasser's speeches and deploying a similar organizational model. Its attempts at fostering a revolutionary atmosphere mainly involved distributing political literature in Dhufar that promoted armed struggle. British documents record that in 1963, leaflets calling for the overthrow of the Sultan circulated in the territory under the signature of the 'Dhufar Arab Youth'.[53] The timing, content, and signature of the leaflets suggest that they were the ones distributed by the SAP. Disseminative activities aside, the SAP maintained a healthy recruitment record, reportedly involving up to 150 members. This was undoubtedly a source of concern for the MAN, which reacted by infiltrating some of its own elements into the Party. These infiltrators succeeded in engineering the dissolution of the SAP in a 1964 conference held in Kuwait.[54] Thereafter, some SAP members joined the MAN, while others went to the DCA.[55]

By then, the stream of events was already surging towards action. As early as December 1962, the runway lights, generator, and power house of RAF Salalah were sabotaged.[56] Four months later, the first shot was fired by Mussalam bin Nufl, a young Sheikh of the Mussahila section of the Al-Kathir. In April 1963, he orchestrated an attack on two vehicles belonging to the American MECOM oil company. The vehicles were held up at Akabat Hatab, and one of them was pushed over a cliff.[57] Although company personnel (an Italian and a Dhufari) were released, their escort—one of the Sultan's Gendarmes—was killed.[58] Subsequently, Bin Nufl and his associates went into hiding in the heavily wooded mountainous area of Ras Sijar.

What was the motivation behind Bin Nufl's actions? Most of the answers proposed so far have focused on personal factors. One historian echoes the popular contention that he was driven by a desire for revenge against the Sultan. He cites the fact that Bin Nufl was imprisoned twice: for playing the radio in public and for riding a bicycle at night. 'The two incidents affected him, and aroused his tribal inclinations.'[59] Alternatively, a British intelligence memorandum states that Bin Nufl was 'dismissed for quarrelsome behaviour', and that he 'probably started life as a leader of a bandit gang with no particular political aims or affiliations'.[60]

[53] FCO 51/41, 'Dhofar Liberation Front', 22 October 1967.
[54] Al-Mdairis, 'The Arab Nationalist Movement in Kuwait', p.360.
[55] Interview F.
[56] DEFE 13/779, 'History of the Dhufar Campaign', Period 1 December 1962 to 27 May 1965.
[57] DEFE 13/779, 'History of the Dhufar Campaign'.
[58] FCO 51/41. 'Dhofar Liberation Front'.
[59] Al-Amri, *Thufar,* p.62.
[60] FCO 51/41. 'Dhofar Liberation Front'.

Thus, we are readily presented with a familiar portrait that reappears in many colonial contexts: the angry tribesman driven by passion and vengeance. Yet, Bin Nufl's motives deserve further enquiry. First, he wasn't entirely lacking in political outlook or experience. In fact, he had been a cell member of the MAN who had resigned his membership due to the slow pace of action in Dhufar.[61] Secondly, oil played a central role in Bin Nufl's calculations. The MECOM oil company was operating in Kathiri tribal land and Bin Nufl was eager for the potential revenues to flow into local hands as opposed to the Sultan's locked coffers.[62]

Whatever its motivation, the importance of the April 1963 attack should not be exaggerated: it was a limited act conducted through a subsection of the Al-Kathir tribe. Equally though, its significance must not be overlooked. For a start, Bin Nufl capitalized on the event and established an alliance with the grandson of a paramount sheikh of the Bait Qatn section of the Qarra tribes, the largest in Dhufar.[63] The latter brought some recruits from his tribe. He also became one of Bin Nufl's representatives in Saudi Arabia's Eastern Province, whose responsibility was to liaise with Imam 'Ghalib and his influential brother 'Talib.[64] After the defeat of the al-Jabal al-Akhdar revolt in January 1959 and his subsequent exile, Imam Ghalib built a considerable financial and diplomatic base in the city of al-Dammam. The Imam was still involved in an effort to reverse the Sultan's usurpation of the Omani interior and revolt in Dhufar was definitely in his interest. As for Riyadh, it still had not resolved its conflict with the Sultanate over Buraimi and had old designs on Dhufar. These two material factors were crowned by King Faisal's 'strong personal dislike of the Sultan'.[65]

In this context, both the Imam and the Saudis welcomed Dhufari armed action, so long as it had purely localized ambitions. Bin Nufl held such relatively limited aims and, by the middle of 1964, he was receiving financial support and 25–30 of his men were being trained in the Imamate's Iraqi training camp near Basra.[66] As for military supplies, Bin Nufl was given a shipment of light weapons, which he transported from Saudi Arabia to Dhufar in seven trucks, accompanied by 21 Kathiris and 13 Bait Qatan men.[67] The journey was nothing less than terrifying. The route from Saudi Arabia into Dhufar ran

---

[61] Interview F.

[62] Fred Halliday, *Arabia Without Sultans*, London: Saqi Books, 1999, p.317; J.B. Kelly, *Arabia, the Gulf and the West*, London: Weidenfeld and Nicolson, 1980, p.134.

[63] J. E. Peterson, *Oman's Insurgencies: The Sultanate's Struggle for Supremacy*, London: Saqi Books, 2007, p.189.

[64] Al-Amri, *Thufar*, p.66.

[65] FCO 51/41. 'Dhofar Liberation Front'.

[66] Peterson, *Oman's Insurgencies*, p.191.

[67] Peterson, *Oman's Insurgencies*, p.190.

… across 500–600 miles of desert from Al Hasa to the Southern edge of the Rub' al Khali at Bin Hamuda on the Saudi–EAP [Eastern Aden Protectorate] border and thence into Dhufar. Most of the travelling is done by night and the crossing may take up to 18 days under conditions so severe that the trucks used are abandoned at the end of the journey.[68]

The convoy was guided by Saudis belonging to the Al Murrah tribe but, even with their help, four trucks were lost in a sandstorm and the remaining ones broke down.[69] The arms were subsequently transported on camels and transferred for hiding in caves, but Bin Nufl and his men were betrayed and some weapons were confiscated after the Wali of Dhufar was informed of their location.[70] Nevertheless, several successful mining operations were conducted between August and November 1964. In total, these resulted in the death of one of the Sultan's *'askars* and an RAF sergeant, the wounding of one *'askari* and an RAF driver, damage to an oil crane, the destruction of two RAF vehicles, and the damaging of a Dhufar Force scout car.[71]

Bin Nufl was not alone in approaching the Imamate. The MAN initiated contact with it following the establishment of the Oman Liberation Front (OLF) in September 1963.[72] On the surface, the OLF seemed to offer a potential umbrella for joint action, but Dhufari MAN members where suspicious of it. This was particularly the case with the student sector, which was being exposed to the ideas of the left wing of the MAN, clearly on the rise in the early 1960s.[73]

Abdel Aziz al-Qadi, a young leader of the Dhufari students in Cairo, was particularly committed to these radical ideas, which contrasted with the traditional nationalist positions of first-generation MAN leaders. Armed with the new language of class struggle, he wrote a letter in 19 April 1964 on behalf of the student sector in Cairo to the workers' sector in Kuwait, warning of the Imamate's pitfalls: 'We completely despaired of the Imamate group, not because of their unsuccessful experiment, but because of our realisation of the nature of those people … their loyalty to their class and their famous historical role … the role of the bourgeois and aristocratic class in any primitive society'.[74] At any rate, this warning

[68] FCO 51/41. 'Dhofar Liberation Front'.
[69] Peterson, *Oman's Insurgencies*, p.190.
[70] Peterson, *Oman's Insurgencies*, p.190.
[71] DEFE 13/779. 'History of the Dhufar Campaign'.
[72] Al-Mdairis, 'The Arab Nationalist Movement in Kuwait', p.360.
[73] Moh'ammad Jamal Barut, *'Harakat al-Qawmiyeen al-'Arab: al-Nash'a, al-Ta'tawur, al-Mas'air*. Damascus: al-Markaz al-'Arabi lil Dirasat al-Istratijya, 1997, pp.223–8.
[74] Al-Mdairis, 'The Arab Nationalist Movement in Kuwait', p.360.

proved unnecessary, as the OLF was effectively disbanded in September 1964 due to internal Imamate conflicts.[75]

TRANSNATIONAL CONSOLIDATION AND THE CREATION OF THE DHUFAR LIBERATION FRONT

The rolling events of 1963 and 1964 made the MAN and the DCA even more eager to build up their strength in Dhufar and to line up support for armed struggle. Like any two groups operating in one arena, they competed over recruits, patrons and resources, and were anxious about being undercut and marginalized. Both groups were also alarmed by the tribalists. This was even noted in a British intelligence report that arose from the interrogation of Dhufari political prisoners: 'The prisoners stated that...Bin Nufl is not the leader of the movement. They regard him as an upstart and self appointed leader whom they do not trust. They were worried that if they were delayed any longer...Mussallim [*sic*] would try and take over the movement thereby disrupting it.'[76]

Such worries pushed the MAN towards expediting the establishment of its first cells inside Dhufar.[77] In 1964, it sent several leading cadres to the territory, including Said Masoud, Said al-Ghassani, and Mohammad al-Ghassani, setting up MAN cells in the capital, Salalah, and in the second largest town, Mirbat and successfully planting a cell inside the Dhufar Force.[78] As for the DCA, it is almost certain that it had begun mass recruitment in Dhufar. One of the DCA's foremost figures was Youssef Alawi, who had cultivated good relations with Cairo (some of his revolutionary opponents later suspected him of being an Egyptian intelligence agent).[79] Egyptian support for the DCA was evident from the actions of the UAR ambassador in Kuwait, an active promoter of the Association.[80] Nevertheless, the DCA did not have a monopoly on Egypt: the MAN's Dhufari branch also had contact with officials in Cairo, benefiting from the longstanding and multi-faceted relations between the Movement and Nasser.

[75] Hashim Behbehani,. *China's Foreign Policy in the Arab World, 1955–75: Three Case Studies*, London and Boston: Kegan Paul, 1981, p.138.

[76] FO1016/782, 'Capture of Launch with Arms for Dhufar', 8 June 1965.

[77] Al-Mdairis, 'The Arab Nationalist Movement in Kuwait', p.362.

[78] Al-Mdairis, 'The Arab Nationalist Movement in Kuwait', p.362. The leader of the MAN cell in the DF was Sergeant Sai'd Muhammad Bayt-Sai'd. See Peterson, *Oman's Insurgencies*, p.203.

[79] Al-Mdairis, 'The Arab Nationalist Movement in Kuwait', p.362. Alawi later became the Sultanate's Foreign Minister.

[80] Al-Mdairis, 'The Arab Nationalist Movement in Kuwait', p.362.

Initially, Egypt was hesitant about supporting the struggle in Dhufar. The matter was first proposed in a meeting held in 1964 between Abdel Nasser, George Habash, Hani al-Hindi, and Mohsen Ibrahim. Habash recalls this meeting in the following terms:

> Before taking a decision with regards to Dhufar, Abdel Nasser wanted the matter discussed with the Egyptian leadership, meaning General Abdel Hakim Amer, Ali Sabri, and Zakaria Muhyieldin. Abdel Nasser was not very enthusiastic. And he asked that we talk about the matter with his comrades in the leadership.[81]

Meetings that immediately followed were hardly more encouraging:

> Only Zakaria Muhyieldin came to discuss the matter with us, and the absence of the other leaders aroused our suspicions about the official Egyptian position in relation to our goals. When we met with Mr Zakaria Muhyieldin he asked us many questions. He wanted to make sure that we were not using Abdel Nasser as a tool at a time when he was trying to prevent, at any cost, the failure that occurred in the case of the UAR. In short, they told us at the end of our stay that our proposal will be studied, and we left with the feeling that the Egyptian leaders, except for Abdel Nasser, were wondering about the seriousness of our plans in Oman, and certainly with regards to South Yemen as well.[82]

Nevertheless, Egypt became more involved over time, especially through its local representatives in Kuwait. By virtue of its connections to both the DCA and the MAN, Egypt was in a position to influence them towards convergence. The Egyptian government at the time was suspicious of all party divisions and advocated a 'united front' approach to liberation struggles.[83] When the DCA sent an envoy to Cairo to seek assistance in 1964, Egyptian officials invited a representative of the MAN and facilitated a meeting between the two.[84] The Egyptians made it clear that their assistance for any effort in Dhufar was contingent upon the unification of Dhufari political ranks. Concurrent with this pressure, the MAN and the DCA were further pushed towards unity by the Dhufari Soldiers' Organization (DSO). The DSO dispatched three or four representatives from its Qatari branch to negotiate with the two groups in Kuwait.[85] After five days of discussion, a unification meeting was held in Al-Naqura district.

[81] George Habash, *Al-Thawryoona La Yamoutouna Abadan*, Beirut: Al Saqi, 2011, p.64.

[82] Habash, *Al-Thawryoona La Yamoutouna Abadan,* p.64.

[83] Abdel Nabi Al-'Al-Ikri, *Al-Tanthimat al-Yassariya fil Jazeera wal Khaleej al 'Arabi*, Beirut: Dar al-Kunouz al-Adabbya, 2003, p.25.

[84] Fawwaz Trabulsi, *Thufar: Shahada min Zaman al-Thawra*, Beirut: Riad el-Rayyes Books, 2004, p.94.

[85] Interview F.

That event was attended by six representatives from the MAN, four from the DCA and two from the DSO.[86]

On the historic day of 26 December 1964, the delegates unanimously agreed to dissolve their respective groups and form the Dhufar Liberation Front (DLF). Bin Nufl and his associates soon joined them and a committee of five was established to supervise affairs and to prepare for a founding General Conference.[87] This was an event of momentous importance in Dhufari history, signifying a great transformation in the politics of the territory. For the first time, the fight against the Sultans was to be conducted along non-tribalist lines and through an inclusive national body. For the first time, it was to be a struggle for sovereignty and not just for the amelioration of specific localized injustices.

The precise organizational character of the DLF was described in its Charter, which was drafted in Kuwait in the early months of 1965, articulating the following organizational principles: armed struggle; collective leadership; unity of armed struggle in the Arab arena; and opposition to 'tribal, sectarian and racist regimes'. All of these carry the unmistakable imprint of the MAN, and one can reasonably suggest that they were drafted by its cadres. However, several aspects of the Charter reflected compromise with the DCA and the tribalists. Whereas Arab unity was envisioned as the ultimate goal, Dhufari 'freedom and independence' was highlighted as the immediate aim. Likewise, the social and economic aspects of the struggle were vague and underemphasized.[88]

These aspects were left to the DLF's National Council for the Leadership of the Revolution to determine. The National Council was the concrete expression of the principle of the collective leadership. In accordance with the Charter, it was composed of 21 members elected by the DLF cadres in their respective districts. Every DLF member had a right to nominate themselves for election. Decisions within the Council were to be arrived at by consensus, but should that prove untenable, a majority vote of two thirds was required to pass any resolution.[89]

The National Council was invested with 'the right to practice executive power in the Front in all stages and circumstances... [and to] appoint active members of the Front to execute tasks'. Its responsibilities included soliciting international support, consolidating the struggle internally and

---

[86] Al-Mdairis, 'The Arab Nationalist Movement in Kuwait', p.363.

[87] Sources have differed on the exact composition of the committee. See FCO 51/41, 'Dhofar Liberation Front', and FO1016/782, 'Capture of Launch'.

[88] 'The Charter of the Dhofar Liberation Front', in Al-Mdairis, 'The Arab Nationalist Movement in Kuwait', Appendix 5.

[89] 'The Charter of the Dhofar Liberation Front', in Al-Mdairis, 'The Arab Nationalist Movement in Kuwait'.

giving all Dhufaris the 'opportunity to participate in carrying the burden of liberation'. In line with established Nasserist practice at the time, parties were strictly prohibited, and all decisions were to be taken within the national framework of the Council.[90]

As for the implementation of decisions, this was to be done by committees founded to pursue particular objectives and implement general policy. One of these committees was a 'liaison committee', which was established in Kuwait. Its role was to facilitate the supply of money and weapons and to lead the DLF operations abroad. Another committee that was established at this early stage was the military committee.

In strict military fashion, DLF members were bound to the decisions of the National Council and to follow its commands: 'No member in the Front is permitted to refuse any mission he is asked to do, and he has to execute it immediately and then to submit a report including in it his point of view, if he has any, with complete freedom.' This was a direct borrowing from the MAN's famous axiom: 'implement then argue' (*nafeth thuma naqesh*). Members were also required to conduct themselves responsibly and not to abuse their military position in their relations with other citizens. They were moreover expected to pay a regular subscription to the Front, proportional to their income. In case of death or imprisonment, the National Council was responsible for supporting their families.[91]

All of the Dhufari organizations were genuinely agreed on the Arabness of Dhufar and were broadly committed to Nasserism.[92] However, there were important divisions concerning the specific role of Dhufaris within the wider pan-Arab movement. In private, members of the MAN saw their objective as the liberation of the entire Arabian Peninsula from the British and the dynastic rulers. As one leader explained many years later: 'the educated cadres generally belonged to the MAN and they were thinking strategically on the level of liberating the [Arabian] Peninsula, because liberating Dhufar is not enough'.[93] In contrast, other DLF members did not think of their role as lying beyond liberating Dhufar at this stage. They had a sentimental attachment to Nasserism but did not have a clear articulation of comprehensive regional change. Yet, at this stage, the MAN publicly compromised with the DCA and the DSO on the principle of 'Dhufar for the Dhufaris.' As late as 1966, its leading cadre,

---

[90] 'The Charter of the Dhofar Liberation Front', in Al-Mdairis, 'The Arab Nationalist Movement in Kuwait', Appendix 5.

[91] 'The Charter of the Dhofar Liberation Front', in Al-Mdairis, 'The Arab Nationalist Movement in Kuwait'.

[92] Interview F.

[93] Interview F.

Fig. 3. Flag of the Dhufar Liberation Front, found in June 1965 near Thint. Three traditional Arab colours are used respectively from top to bottom: green; white; and red. The text reads 'The Arab Dhufari Republic'.

Mohammad al-Ghassani, asserted in a speech at the Omani Student Confederation in Cairo that 'we believe in Arab unity and struggle for Arab unity but we have a right to an independent state in Dhufar'.[94]

This was a temporary compromise, for there was considerable division over long-term objectives, reflecting the existence of different political rationales within the DLF. The MAN worldview was based on a set of normative values and principles that transcended the Dhufari context. Its cadres rationalized their actions—and measured their effects—in terms of these values. MAN cadres were idealists: their outlook was shaped not by the calculation of individual material needs but in terms of the collective ideal of the just Arab republic. The specific conception of the just republic changed at different junctures but what remained constant were the

---

[94] Abdul Rahman Al-Nuaimi, 'Al-Sibaq 'ala al-Tartibat al-Siyassiya', *Al-Wasat*, 30 October 2008.

emphases on the need for regional transformation and the primacy of principle over immediate local interest.

As for the Dhufarists and the tribalists, they did not share the MAN's republican Arabist idealism. They too had principles, but these were defined in terms of serving the interests of a local community bound by solid social ties and facing a common enemy. Moreover, their conception of the 'community of revolution' differed substantially. The tribalists conceived of tribes acting within a national Dhufari context but the Dhufarists envisioned a Dhufari people operating within the bounds of the broader Arab nation. The republicans belonged to a pan-Arab community of revolution that saw itself—at least since Bandung—as being part of an international struggle against colonialism. For tribalists, the primary location for deliberation was the tribe and for Dhufarists it was the DLF. MAN cadres acted in both spheres but their decisions always took into account, and sometimes originated from, the pan-Arab revolutionary network. They were willing to temporarily coexist with the others but only until the foundations of the struggle became firm.[95] Thus, although they had severed their formal connections to their mother organization upon joining the DLF, they continued to be active within the MAN and attended its Gulf conferences. They also maintained a secret organization within the DLF with an eye to channelling the Front towards serving their broader ideals.[96]

Substantial preparations for the armed struggle were already under way at the time of the unification meeting. The Kuwaiti branch of the MAN decided to use all of its funds at the time, 3,000 Kuwaiti dinars, to purchase weapons for the revolutionaries.[97] Even the MAN headquarters in Beirut was now ready for armed struggle in Dhufar as part of its effort to put greater pressure on the British in South Yemen and to extend the battle of *fard al Jala'a* to the Gulf. In 1964 or early 1965 it issued the following circular for all the Arab Gulf and Peninsula branches:

> …the Movement is studying very carefully the issue of expanding the fight into other fields, to Hadramut, Dhufar, the Gulf and Oman, and this study is in its final stage, aiming to open new battle fields as soon as possible, especially since the apparatus of the Movement in some regions had already been almost finished, during the previous period of preparing for armed struggle.[98]

---

[95] Sai'd Dablan, 'Nushu'u Wa 'Tatawur al-Jabha al-Sha'biyya Li Ta'hrir 'Oman: 1964–1982', diploma thesis, Abdullah Batheeb Institute of Scientific Socialism, Aden, People's Democratic Republic of South Yemen, 1989, p.11.

[96] Interview F.

[97] Barut, *'Harakat al-Qawmiyeen al-'Arab'*, p.396.

[98] Barut, *'Harakat al-Qawmiyeen al-'Arab'*, p.355.

Satisfied with political preparations conducted over the past five years, the MAN now had to find a venue for training and equipping Dhufari fighters. In liaison with the UAR, Iraq was contacted for help. The atmosphere in Baghdad was encouraging, with Abdel Salam 'Aarif in power and a MAN member, Subhi Abdul Hamid, holding the post of Interior Minister. The latter was promptly contacted, and gave his authorization for the training of 140 DLF fighters.[99]

After training the Dhufaris, Iraq facilitated their transportation, providing them with 42 trucks.[100] Some fighters loaded these trucks with supplies and crossed the insalubrious terrain that divided the north of the Arabian Peninsula from its south. Others travelled to Aden, where they were initially stranded by the fighting between the National Liberation Front (NLF) and the British but eventually found their way home via the East Aden Protectorate.[101] Whatever the path, the homecoming was a ragged affair. Spirits were nevertheless high, for essential training had been acquired and more weapons and equipment were expected to arrive. This precious cargo was provided by Egypt via Iraq, and five fighters were left behind, entrusted with first securing and then smuggling it safely to Dhufar.[102] They were accompanied on their mission by six Iraqis: an intelligence officer; two military technicians; a wireless operator and a vehicle mechanic. The eleven of them boarded an Iraqi motor launch and set sail from Basra on 6 May 1965.[103] They did not get beyond Shatt al-Arab, being intercepted by an Iranian navy vessel and taken into custody. This was a double blow for the revolutionaries. In addition to the cadres, Iraqi experts and vital military supplies, the motor launch was carrying pictures of the revolutionaries, training manuals, and internal DLF documents including a list of its leaders.[104] These documents contributed to a heightened state of concern and alert in British circles.[105]

In spite of the setback in Shatt al-Arab, the DLF general conference took place during the first week of June 1965 in a large cave near Wadi Naheez.[106] It was attended by representatives from all the three dissolved

---

[99] Interview F.

[100] FO1016/782, 'Capture of Launch'.

[101] Dablan, 'Nushu'u Wa 'Tatawur al-Jabha al-Sha'biyya Li Ta'hrir 'Oman: 1964–1982', p.11.

[102] FO1016/782, 'Capture of Launch'.

[103] FO1016/782, 'Capture of Launch'.

[104] FO1016/767. Waterfield to British Consulate (Muscat), 1 June 1965.

[105] FO 1016/767. Local Intelligence Committee Aden, 'The Threat to the East Aden Protectorate,', 6 July 1965.

[106] Al-Jabha al-Shabiya Li Tahrir Oman wal Khaleej al-Arabi, *Wathaiq al-Ni'dal al-Wat'ani, 1965-1974*, Beirut: Dar Al-Tali'a, 1974, p.6; Halliday, *Arabia Without Sultans*, p.317; Peterson, *Oman's Insurgencies*, p.193.

Dhufari organizations as well as members of Bin Nufl's group.[107] They officially agreed on the founding of the Front, ratified its charter, and elected a National Council. Most accounts put its membership at 18, while one author states that it was 12.[108] Whatever its exact composition, it was without question a compromise body including former members of the MAN, the DCA, the DSO and the Bin Nufl group.

The MAN's Mohammad al-Ghassani was a highly influential figure within it.[109] A thoughtful and educated man with extensive political experience, he had a reflective and a non-confrontational demeanour, commanding respect in revolutionary circles.[110] The DLF required a man like al-Ghassani in its efforts to bridge tribal divisions: coming from Salalah, he was ideally placed to be a 'consensus figure' amongst the tribes of the *Jabal*.[111] He continued to gain in influence over the next five years, and remained part of the struggle well beyond the demise of the DLF. Throughout its course, the Dhufari Revolutionary War was a collective endeavour that produced very few figureheads—al-Ghassani was amongst those few.

THE ARMED STRUGGLE BEGINS

The fundamental decision of the DLF was the launch of the armed struggle. There was an explicit policy to conduct it along non-tribal lines. To this end, the whole geography of Dhufar had to be re-imagined. The land was historically divided into tribal *diras*. Now, the whole of the territory was conceived as belonging to the citizens, and divisions within it were to be viewed as purely geographical. Moreover, the universality of military reason had to prevail over the particularity of tribal fragments, and the partition of land had to correspond to the organization of theatres of action. Dhufar was accordingly divided into three areas: the Eastern; Western; and Central Areas.[112] Fighters were distributed into corresponding units. Their first fight occurred on 9 June, when an oil company truck was attacked and its driver killed northwest of Thamrit Road.[113] During

---

[107] The British estimate that there were 30,000 inhabitants at the time. See FCO 51/41. 'Dhofar Liberation Front'.

[108] For the compositon of the DLF council see Halliday, *Arabia Without Sultans*, p.317; Riad El-Rayyes, *Thufar: Al-Sira' al-Siyassi Wal Askari Fil Khaleej al-Arabi, 1970-1976*, Beirut: Riad El-Rayyes Books, 2002, p.125.

[109] Al-Amri, *Thufar*, p.80; FCO 51/41, 'Dhofar Liberation Front'.

[110] Interview E.

[111] Interview D(i).

[112] Halliday, *Arabia Without Sultans*, p.319.

[113] See entry for 9 June in DEFE 13/779. 'History of the Dhufar Campaign', Period II.

this action, Said bin-Ghanim al-Kathiri lost his life.[114] The DLF announced him as its first martyr and 9 June as the first day of the revolution. For years to come the date and the man assumed a mythical significance: the former was commemorated in the titles of the revolution's school and its main publication; the latter in the name of a fighting unit.

Following the action, the DLF issued its first public document, the 9 June Declaration of Armed Struggle.[115] The Declaration essentially framed the Dhufari question as a clash between the will of empire and the will of the people, the forces of the Sultan (the domestic agent of British Imperialism) and the DLF (the arm of the Arab liberation movement). The general language of the Declaration was Nasserist and in line with the views of the various organizations that formed the DLF. However, certain parts—particularly a reference to the eventual merger with other revolutionary movements—reflect the MAN's specific outlook. The Declaration was disseminated across the Arab world by MAN publications and various media outlets.[116] As the year progressed, it was spread by Dhufari offices abroad, especially the ones in Kuwait and Cairo.[117]

Optimism and enthusiasm aside, these revolutionary beginnings were marked by difficulties. At first light on 18 June, and with the help of the documents found in the Iraqi launch, a British cordon and search operation was launched in Salalah.[118] Thirty-five members of DLF cells, including leading cadres such as Said Masoud, were arrested and held at RAF Salalah.[119] They were subsequently airlifted to the Sultan's Armed Forces (SAF) headquarters in Bait al-Falaj, where they were subjected to interrogation under the custody of the Sultanate's intelligence officer, Malcolm Dennison.[120] After six months at the army base, they were transferred to Muscat's Jalali prison, a sixteenth-century Portuguese fort. By March 1969, the number of Dhufari prisoners grew to 66, joining another 110 prisoners from Oman proper. These represented the vast majority of the major tribes and classes in Dhufar, including all the large sections of the Qarra and the Kathir, as well as Da'eefs, Khadems, Baharra, and Salalah town families.[121]

---

[114] Halliday, *Arabia Without Sultans*, p.318.

[115] For the text of the declaration, see Al-Jabha al-Shabiya, *Wathaiq' al-Ni'dal al-Wat'ani, 1965–1974*, pp. 9–11. For a translated version, see Gulf Committee, *Documents of the National Struggle in Oman and the Arabian Gulf,* Nottingham: Russell Press, 1974, pp.7–9.

[116] See for example Cairo's, *Al Gumhuriya,* 31 July 1965.

[117] By December 1965, the Cairo office was led by Youssef Alawi and his appointment was announced in the Egyptian media, *Rose El Youssef,* 6 December 1965.

[118] FO 1016/767, Salalah to Headquarters RAF PG, 18 June 1965.

[119] FO 1016/767, Salalah to Headquarters RAF PG, 18 June 1965.

[120] Interview F.

[121] FO 1016/806, List of Dhufari Prisoners in Jalali, 1 March 1969.

Jalali was a terrible place, which even had a depressing effect on British military commanders.[122] It was a dehydrated space, the water ration for prisoners being 'inadequate by any standard'.[123] Water was carried up by three carriers who had 'orders to provide a certain amount of water daily, and no more'. In the extremely hot and humid conditions of Muscat, such a policy amounted to cruelty: 'there is no doubt that shortage of water causes hardships to prisoners, particularly during hot weather'. In addition to thirst, the prisoners also suffered from an inadequate diet. There was evidence of cruel intention on the part of the Prison Warden, Sayyid Shihab: 'the commonest illnesses amongst the prisoners seem to stem from vitamin deficiency... One instance is known of a special diet for a sick prisoner recommended by the doctor being discontinued on orders of Sayid Shihab. The prisoner died.' There were no medical facilities: 'Very sick prisoners can be bedded down under lock and key in the so called "European cell".' Darkness abounded, for there was 'no lighting of any kind in the prisoners' rooms'. Hygiene was not catered for and there were no washing facilities, night buckets, soap or clothing. At all times, the prisoners wore gyves and their ankles were connected by metal bars. As for accommodation, special reinforced concrete cells were built for the Dhufaris in the fort's yard, so as to isolate them from others. Every seven Dhufari prisoners were penned in one small cell.[124] Considerable physical and mental endurance was required to survive such conditions. By 1966, the claustrophobia and physical hardship became overwhelming and the political prisoners staged a hunger strike. Thereafter, more cells were provided and they were now shared by five inmates instead of seven. However, the men continued to be locked in them for 23 hours a day. The fort's yard was the only breathing space, visited for half an hour in the morning and another half hour before sunset.[125]

The health and safety of prisoners could not be ascertained by the outside world. Amnesty International made some queries but these seemed to have offended the sensibilities of the British Consul General, D.C. Carden. The latter went as far as suggesting to his superiors that the Sultan was being extremely merciful to his most rebellious subjects; sparing their lives after they threatened his, imprisoning them when he could have executed them 'as would have happened in most Afro-Asian countries'. In more than one way, the Consul General shared responsibility with the Sultan for the conditions in Jalali. Not only did he defend the Sultan's policy to the British authorities but he also downplayed the

---

[122] MEC-Smiley, Smiley (CSAF) to Waterfield (Military Secretary), 19 June 1960.
[123] MEC-Smiley, 'Jalali Fort', July 1960.
[124] Interview F.
[125] Interview F.

urgency of reform of the prison. In spite of mounting evidence to the contrary, he told the Political Residency in Bahrain and the Arabian Department in London the following:

> ...the conditions in Jalali are, I believe, in various respects good enough. Food is similar to the armys [*sic*]. Water and clothing are adequate. An Indian Doctor visits regularly and if a prisoner is ill can have him moved to an air-conditioned ward in the army hospital...

Projecting some even-handedness to his superiors, the Consul reported that there were some 'valid grounds' for criticism which included the 'leg irons', 'overcrowding', and people staying in prison 'not for a firm sentence but at the Sultan's pleasure...'. Nevertheless, these issues did not change the fact that things were 'good enough,' and no genuine intervention was planned to ameliorate the situation. Unsurprisingly, the Consul could not mask his contempt for Amnesty International:

> ...it would be possible to tell Amnesty International truthfully enough that the Position here is not so bad as they imagine, and that they should probably spend their efforts more usefully by addressing themselves to, say, Prague. But I do not do so...partly because Amnesty International are not likely to be satisfied by any reply but are likely to twist it as best they may to embarrass the Sultan and us.[126]

Instead of answering Amnesty's queries (which were incidentally focused on ascertaining whether specific political prisoners were dead or alive), Carden decided that they should be ignored, as the real agenda behind them was supposedly to 'embarrass' Britain and the Sultan rather than helping prisoners. He therefore proposed that he 'refrain from replying to Amnesty International' and that 'if they should subsequently complain of discourtesy', 'play may be made' of him being outside Muscat.[127] More importantly, he effectively colluded with the Sultan by not pressuring him to reform the incarceration regime prevailing in the Sultanate, something that was well within his powers.

Thus, captured Dhufaris remained literally shackled behind the medieval walls of Jalali for the five long years that lay between the summer of 1965 and the fall of 1970. Following their arrest and the descent of the 1965 monsoon, the Sultan was under the impression that a small tribal rebellion had been effectively suppressed. The Commander of the SAF, Colonel Tony Lewis, even boasted of a 'successful short campaign in Dhofar'.[128] Despite this optimism on the part of the monarch and his British

---

[126] FO 1016/806. 'Amnesty International', minute by D.C. Carden, 21 June 1969.

[127] FO 1016/806. 'Amnesty International'.

[128] John H. McKeown, 'Britain and Oman: The Dhofar War and its Significance', MPhil Thesis, University of Cambridge, 1981, p.26.

officers, the revolutionaries proved to be resilient. At this stage, the DLF fighters barely numbered 200, with only 80 active in the three areas at any one time.[129] One of their daring assaults occurred on 8 November 1965, when twenty to fifty revolutionaries, under the leadership of DLF National Council member Masou'd Ja'boub (Khantour), struck against Mirbat fort.[130] Renowned for his strength and bravery, Khantour used a scaling ladder to climb to the fort's roof. Nevertheless, the commander was shot dead after he managed to throw two hand grenades into the fort court-yard.[131] Thus fell the second casualty in the DLF struggle. Born in 1931 in the Bait Faya region of central Dhufar, he began political work in Qatar in 1962 and participated in the preparations for armed struggle in 1964.[132] A revolutionary unit was named in honour of his memory.

As Khantour's operation illustrated, attacking fixed targets such as forts was difficult and dangerous. Therefore, the revolutionaries more com-monly reverted to planting land mines and initiating hit and run strikes.[133] On 13 March 1966, an action in Wadi Naheez led to the death of the first British casualty in the war, Captain Alan Woodman, along with two sol-diers.[134] Another notable attack was conducted on 24 May 1966. It was led by the celebrated commander Mah'ad al-Bar'ami (al-Shaja'), and marked the first use of rockets by the DLF. The revolutionaries success-fully ambushed an SAF vehicle, killing seven SAF soldiers and a British officer, Major Hamish Emslie. Six soldiers were also injured, but one of them, Emslie's orderly, managed to shoot back, killing commander Mah'ad in the process.[135]

Numerous attacks were also directed at MECOM Oil, damaging sev-eral vehicles and installations and causing the death of the head of the company's Midway Camp.[136] These definitely contributed to its decision to terminate oil prospecting operations on 15 October 1967 and were accordingly of great importance. But the most significant operation was the assassination attempt on the life of the Sultan, conducted by the DLF

[129] FCO 51/41. 'Dhofar Liberation Front'.

[130] Peterson, *Oman's Insurgencies*, p.199; Mohammad al-Amri, *Thufar: al Thawra fil Tarikh al-Omani al Mu'asir*, Beirut: Riad el-Rayyes Books, 2005, p.84.

[131] Peterson, *Oman's Insurgencies*, p.199.

[132] PFLO, *Sijil al Khalideen, 1965–1979*, Al I'lam al Markazi lil Jabha al-Sha'abiya Li Tahrir 'Oman, n.d., p.10.

[133] For a full catalogue of these numerous armed operations consult DEFE 13/779. 'History of the Dhufar Campaign'.

[134] McKeown, 'Britain and Oman', p.29.

[135] Mckeown, 'Britain and Oman', p.31; Peterson 'Oman's Diverse Society: Southern Oman', p.204; PFLO. *Sijil al Khalideen, 1965–1979*, p.14.

[136] He was ambushed on 2 October 1965: DEFE 13/779, 'History of the Dhufar Campaign'.

secret cell in the Dhufar Force.[137] The incident occurred just after 9:40 a.m. on 26 April 1966, when Said bin Taimur was inspecting his troops in the 'Ain Razat Camp outside Salalah. At the call of 'Royal Salute… Present Arms', the Sultan was shot at by Staff Sergeant Said Suhail Qatan and Private Mohammad Taher and, although he managed to escape safely, one of his officers, 2nd Lieutenant Sattar Shah, was killed along with two of his slaves.[138] The Commander of the Dhufar force, Lieutenant Colonel Saki Raja, was also seriously wounded, bayoneted in a grapple with the mutineer Staff Sergeant, who was later shot. In the confusion that followed, a Pakistani Captain, Nur Mohammad, was entrusted by the Sultan with arresting all Dhufari highlanders in the Force. 22 Jabalis were locked up by him while 19 managed to run away, 5 of them being caught later. The rest defected to the revolutionaries and the Dhufar Force was accordingly re-staffed with slaves.[139]

In the wake of this incident, Said bin Taimur went into a long period of isolation, hardly ever seen. Many revolutionaries believed that he was dead and that the British now ruled the Sultanate through a 'phantom Sultan'.[140] Meanwhile, British concern reached new heights, compounded by fears that the UAR would support the DLF further. After all, the assassination attempt was announced in Cairo's *Al Ahram* a week before it happened![141]

Besides these military operations, the DLF was involved in a mass mobilization effort in Dhufar. This process was furthered by the weakening of caste divisions.[142] Like other revolutionary movements in slave-holding societies, the Dhufari one afforded the prospect of abolition for runaway slaves, and it included members of all castes.[143] This attracted oppressed sections of the population to its ranks. By 1966, such was the success of mobilization, that the British reported the existence of a slave ('*Khadim*') component of the DLF.[144] In an operation they mounted across the border in the East Aden Protectorate, they managed to capture Muragha Juma'n al-'Khadim, a prominent leader of the escaped slaves who had been given responsibility for running the DLF supply, military, and educational centre

---

[137] FO371/185364, Carden (Muscat) to Luce (Bahrain), 11 May 1966.

[138] These were Staff Sergeant Sai'd Suhayl Bayt Qatn and Private Salim Bakhit Bayt Kathir: Peterson, *Oman's Insurgencies*, p.202.

[139] FO371/185364, Carden (Muscat) to T.F. Brenchley, 12 May 1966, Annex A.

[140] Halliday, *Arabia Without Sultans*, p.319.

[141] *Al-Ahram*, 19 April 1966.

[142] For the caste hierarchy see Trabulsi, *Thufar*, p.78.

[143] Interview F. Although many slaves had escaped and joined the revolutionaries, complete abolition was implemented following the 1968 Hamrin conference.

[144] IOR/R/20/D/270, 'Joint Force Commander Report on Operation Fate', 11 November 1966. I am grateful to Dr Laleh Khalili for sharing her notes on this file.

in Hauf.[145] The centre operated on Mahra territory. It was created with the help of a Mohammad bin-Humeid, an influential Mahri Sheikh who was disgruntled with the Sultan. At the beginning of the revolution, Mohammad travelled to al-Ghaida and managed to persuade his relatives to allow this centre to open.[146] The British report on its eventual closure declared that 'the loss of this irreplaceable safe area and the capture of a large number of both active rebels and "illegal emigrants" from Dhofar should have a marked effect on both the Front and anyone thinking of joining them'.[147] The operation was even painted as a blow to the UAR:

> After today's grievous blow, Cairo will wish to reinforce and rebuild the DLF, but if it does not know what actually happened or receives a third hand garbled account in about a fortnight's time, confusion will be caused and their efforts will be led astray and their activities will be ineffective...[148]

British officials were aware that Dhufar was but one theatre amongst many in which the regional battle over sovereignty was being fought. The only person who was delusional enough to view the Dhufari situation as a local tribal rebellion was the Sultan himself.[149] He genuinely despised Dhufaris and saw them as uncivilized tribesmen, 'no more than cattle thieves'.[150] In his desperation, he deployed the tactic that he and his predecessors had always used in Dhufar: starving the people. Thus, following the attempt on his life, Sa'id bin Taimur ordered a complete blockade of the Dhufari mountains and imprisoned the inhabitants of Salalah, besieging the town with a barbed wire fence.[151] Anyone trying to enter or leave was shot.

The SAF commander, Colonel Lewis, enthusiastically agreed with these policies. He advocated 'increased military measures such as collective punishments against tribes'. Such punishment would be incurred upon a tribe for 'incidents on its territory or for rebel members from the tribe'. But he also went further, calling for forced dispossession, or what he termed the 'evacuation of free-fire zones'.[152] 'Black areas' such as Wadi

---

[145] IOR/R/20/D/270, 'Joint Force Commander Report on Operation Fate'

[146] 'Dhofar Islocation Rebel Activity.' SIO (Tim Landon) to HH The Sultan, Salalah, 18 March 1970, *RO-5,* p.202.

[147] IOR/R/20/D/270, 'Joint Force Commander Report on Operation Fate'.

[148] IOR/R/20/D/270. 'Transcript of Talk Given by Mr Ellis (RA Mukalla) Over HMS FEARLESS'. 11 November 1966.

[149] Rabi, *The Emergence of States in a Tribal Society,* p.196.

[150] Mckeown, 'Britain and Oman', p.35.

[151] J. Pimlot, 'The British Army: The Dhofar Campaign, 1970–1975', in I. Becket and J. Pimlot (eds.), *Armed Forces and Modern Counterinsurgency*, London: St Martin's Press, 1985, p.28.

[152] Mckeown, 'Britain and Oman', p.33.

Jardum were to be emptied of their inhabitants and the SAF was to shoot any person found in them. Moreover, hostages were to be held wherever the army operated.[153]

Such recommendations were by no means particular to the Dhufari context, belonging to a well-established practice of war defined by Karma Nabulsi as the martial tradition: 'The martialists…claimed war's absoluteness. There was a repudiation of military conflict in anything less than its unadultered form. Any attempts to set limits (whether moral, prudential, or even political) to this natural phenomenon were to be rejected.'[154] In Dhufar, no law was to fetter the imposition of imperial sovereignty. All obstacles had to be removed. The Geneva conventions, already in place for nearly two decades, had no relevance in the minds of the Sultan or the British officers in Dhufar. This is not surprising. Indeed, in the 1949 Geneva conference, 'the British War Office representative…was justifying the maintenance of martial practices in order to defend both the ideology of Empire, and more importantly, the military policies of their colonial armies such as hostage taking and the incineration of rebel villages'.[155] Even after the British failure to legitimate these practices under international law, the Empire continued to act as it did before. It regularly targeted civilians in Kenya, Malaya and elsewhere, although such acts had been comprehensively banned and were now considered to be war crimes.[156]

Besides the Geneva conventions, Britain and its officers in the Sultanate were in contravention of several UN resolutions on the 'Question of Oman'. In December 1965, UN General Assembly Resolution (UNGAR) 2073 expressed deep concern 'at the serious situation arising from colonial policies and foreign intervention by the United Kingdom in that Territory'.[157] The General Assembly considered that 'the colonial presence of the United Kingdom in its various forms prevents the people of the Territory from exercising their rights to self determination and independence'. It called upon the British government to cease 'repressive actions against the people' of Oman, withdraw all troops, release all political prisoners, allow exiles to return, and eliminate 'British domination in any form'.[158]

---

[153] Mckeown, 'Britain and Oman', p.207.

[154] Nabulsi Karma, *Traditions of War: Occupation, Resistance and the Law*, Oxford: Oxford University Press, 2005, p.93.

[155] Nabulsi Karma, *Traditions of War: Occupation, Resistance and the Law*, Oxford: Oxford University Press, 2005 p.106.

[156] For a thorough and chilling account of illegal British acts in Kenya see Caroline Elkins, *Imperial Reckoning: the Untold Story of Britain's Gulag in Kenya*, New York: Owl Books, Henry Holt and Company, 2005.

[157] UNGAR 2073, 'Question of Oman', 17 December 1965.

[158] UNGAR 2073, 'Question of Oman'.

Although it was the outcome of a vigorous diplomatic campaign waged by the Imamate, this resolution applied to the domains of the Sultanate as a whole, and it was based on a UN report that referred to Dhufar in the following terms:

> The people of Dhofar, the Committee was told, were treated by the Sultan as slaves. He was cruel and imposed many arbitrary restrictions on the people... Further, there was no work in Dhofar, no schools, no hospitals, no economic life, no equality and no right to participate in politics... However, the young people of Dhofar had held secret meetings about these matters and although they had no education, some of them had travelled and they all knew their rights.[159]

Yet, rather than altering their policies, Britain and the Sultan intensified them. Accordingly, UNGAR 2238 was passed in 1966. In addition to upholding the resolution of 1965, this new resolution deplored 'the policies of the United Kingdom in installing and supporting any unrepresentative regime in the Territory'.[160] In resolution 2302 of 1967, the General Assembly went further and 'appealed to all member states to render all necessary assistance to the people of the Territory in their struggle to obtain freedom and Independence'.

British representatives at the UN failed in their efforts to challenge those who were making the case for Omani independence. At the Fourth Committee sessions, they had to contend with representatives of the Imamate, as well as Arab republics and Socialist countries. As if that was not enough, they also had to deal with an effective external British speaker, Faris Glubb. Although he was the son of the notorious colonial figure Glubb Pasha, Faris took an anti-imperialist line, holding the position of Secretary of the Committee for the Rights of Oman. Finally, even monarchical Arab states with strong connections to Britain—such as Kuwait and Jordan—took a stance in favour of the various resolutions. These positions were not only expressed within the Fourth Committee, but also in the General Assembly. For instance, in his September 1966 address to the UNGA, the Kuwaiti foreign minister asserted the need to implement UNGA resolution 2073, emphasizing that 'the people of Oman have an inalienable right to self-determination in accordance with their freely expressed wishes'.[161]

---

[159] Ad Hoc Committee on Oman, 1965, p.164. Quoted in Francis Owtram, *A Modern History of Oman: Formation of the State Since 1920*, London: I.B. Tauris, 2004, p.122.

[160] UNGAR 2238, 'Question of Oman', 20 December 1966.

[161] FO 1016/764, 'Extract of a Speech by the Kuwaiti Foreign Minister in the General Assembly', New York, 28 September 1966.

In response to allegations raised against them at the UN, the British consistently asserted that 'The Sultanate of Muscat and Oman is <u>not</u> a British colony' and that there were no 'British forces in the country, apart from some fifty officers and men serving on secondment with the Sultan's armed forces…'. They also insisted that 'there have been no attacks, no bombings, no repressions, no tortures, of any kind whatever' undertaken by the United Kingdom in the 'independent country' that is Oman.[162]

Although united in their disregard of the UN resolutions, the British and the Sultan were divided over the details of how to apply their martialist policies. The former advocated a carrot and stick approach, the latter only offered the stick. Unlike the Sultan, who ordered punishment after defeat, Lewis advised 'leniency' upon submission:

> Rebel movements have only been finally destroyed by leniency. A rebel who has no prospect of surrender terms will fight to the bitter end once he is committed to the movement. If there is some opportunity of pardon, this thought when his morale is low will weaken his resistance and lead him to capitulate. I feel that now is the moment to offer some terms for amnesty to the rebel rank and file.[163]

Such thought belonged to a trend in counter-insurgency theory that was developed in the Malayan and Kenyan contexts: the 'hearts and minds' approach. The logic was to starve and then feed. Accordingly, Dhufaris were to be confronted with a choice between their political will and their physical needs. The first step was to deny both. The second step was to satisfy needs upon their surrender of will. So long as they maintained hope, the logic went, revolutionaries would keep fighting. But should they despair, they would look to addressing their vital needs for survival. Those needs were to be catered for at the moment of submission, beginning with amnesty.

Until his removal in 1970, the Sultan's strategy predominated and no mercy was offered. The instrument of his policy was the SAF. Fighting on Dhufari soil, it did not have a single Dhufari fighter and was entirely led by British senior officers assisted by junior Pakistani ranks. It was staffed by mercenary soldiers, mainly coming from Baluchistan but also from northern Oman. A former SAF commander described his Baluchi men in the following terms:

> These men are pure mercenaries and though they do take an oath of allegiance to the Sultan on joining, having never seen him their loyalty is somewhat

---

[162] FO 1016/764, Lord Caradon to Foreign Office, No.497, 19 December 1966. Emphasis in original.
[163] Quoted in McKeown, 'Britain and Oman', p.38.

superficial. They join the SAF mainly to save money, and when they have saved enough to buy a watch, a wireless, a wife, and a camel—in that order (and the camel being the most important)—they tend to retire.[164]

Racist caricatures aside, the commander captured the fact that the soldiers had no ideals to fight for. In Dhufar, these mercenaries were facing revolutionaries who had left relatively well-paid jobs and better lives abroad to fight for their ideals at home. The low morale of the soldiers could only be counterbalanced by their superior armaments and the backing they received from airpower. Indeed, the use of aircraft began on the same day the revolutionary war was initiated, 9 June 1965. On that day, Provosts flew from RAF Salalah, supporting army operations, dropping bombs and firing guns.[165] As the revolutionary war progressed, airpower became the foremost instrument of imperial sovereignty.

In 1966, however, airpower was so limited that the highlands could only be bombed occasionally. Of far greater consequence at this stage was the policy of siege and starvation, dependent as the Dhufaris were on food imports from the coast. In the past, when Dhufar was isolated and divided, individual tribes eventually acquiesced to the call of hunger. But the DLF was too politicized to yield to this tactic and too integrated in the broader regional fight to surrender. Its members believed that overthrowing the Sultan was possible and, so long as that possibility existed, the sacrifice was worth it. Furthermore, Dhufaris perceived themselves as a people without a choice—collectively punished if they acted, and oppressed if they didn't. Rather than shrinking the DLF ranks, the politics of starvation boosted them.[166] Those who had feared losing their food had lost it by now, and their only salvation was to join the organized political body that was formed by their relatives and friends. After all, these were the ones who had seen and learnt things abroad and some of them had even received formal education.[167] In such an isolated and illiterate society, those that had travelled and been educated were held in esteem.[168] In Dhufar, the former exiles were organized, effectively mobilizing the people for a long revolutionary war.

* * *

[164] MEC-Smiley, 'Report on Tenure', 1960.
[165] Peterson, *Oman's Insurgencies*, p.477.
[166] McKeown, 'Britain and Oman', p.30.
[167] The highest level of attainment was secondary school education. Even as late as 1969, PFLOAG could declare that 'to this day, the ranks of the fighters in Dhufar do not include a single graduate from Arab universities': Al-Jabha al-Shabiya, 'Mula'hathat 'Hawla Ta'hqiq Majalat "Stern"', *Al 'Huriya*, 22 September 1969.
[168] Sa'id Ahmad Al Jina'hi, *Kuntu fi 'Thufar: Mushahadat fi Ard' al-Thawra*, Beirut: Dar Ibn Khaldun, 1974, p.35.

By the close of 1966, Dhufari revolutionary politics had ended its tenth year. As with so many other phenomena in the region, the beginning was with Suez and the connection to the Arab republican tradition. But what began with small groups of migrant youth fearfully assembled in clandestine circles developed into a political and military organization around which most Dhufaris were rallied. For the first eight years, the process of political mobilization happened abroad, but, by 1965, all Dhufari groupings—republican, Dhufarist or tribalist—had made their homecoming and started their fight, joined together in one national front. Open to all Dhufaris regardless of tribe or social position, the DLF assumed four political significations. In its emphasis on 'Dhufar for Dhufaris', it exemplified Dhufari patriotism. In its espousal of Arab unity, it exhibited contemporary forms of Arab nationalism. In demanding the expulsion of the British, it championed anti-colonialism. And finally, in working for the overthrow of monarchy, it practised republicanism. Yet the DLF's military achievements were still modest. The revolutionaries were besieged in the mountains, starved of basic food and military supplies. A British intelligence report summed up the situation:

> They have not [militarily] achieved a great deal, but have created a state of general unrest, provided a rallying point for disaffection, and have shown that given sufficient backing from outside they might well be able to cause very much greater trouble in the future. Their main asset is that they have the goodwill of the Qarra of the mountains. So far there has been no case of Qarra betraying them to the Government Forces.[169]

The revolutionaries had reached an impasse: the people were now rallied and mobilized but equally they were besieged by the Sultan and his British-led troops. The siege had to be broken, but that could only happen from the outside. The only hope was solidarity and support from beyond the borders of Dhufar. In the meantime, the DLF reduced its operations, awaiting the opportunity to resume the struggle for sovereignty.

[169] FCO 51/41, 'Dhofar Liberation Front'.

4

Crises and Constellational Shifts, 1966–1968

The Dhufari revolution, like others across the world, was an act of human will—a quest for negation and affirmation, for the demolition of an established order, and the creation of a new political community. Yet, for all this subjectivism, it was dually shaped and constrained by structural factors, by the determinants of physical and human actuality. The struggle against Anglo-Sultanic rule was both enabled and limited by the surrounding material realities. The fastness of the highlands, the spread of caves, the thickness of wild fig and tamarind forests, and the cloak of the monsoon mist, all afforded perfect cover for the revolutionaries. But the countryside was not sufficiently productive to support a long-term war effort. Water was available but not abundant. Livestock herds were profuse but vulnerable to attack. The soil was fertile in places, barren in others, and mostly uncultivated. Thus, waterholes had to be regularly safeguarded and accessed, livestock protected from army raids, and staple foods imported and safely transported to fields of operation. Popular support in the highlands guaranteed full access to village resources, but the low density of the population and the smallness of settlements rendered the revolutionaries vulnerable. Comprising a substantial percentage of a tiny population, they had no hope of dissolving amongst the villagers 'like fish in water'. In that respect at least, their cover was thin.

Due to the lack of any industrial capacity, weapons, ammunition and clothes had to be procured from abroad. The poverty of Dhufari society meant that these could only be paid for by migrant workers and external aid from friendly states and Arab revolutionary movements. As was shown in the previous chapter, migrant Dhufaris had been funding revolutionary activity since the late 1950s. With the growth of their organizational capacity, cadres regularized fundraising efforts abroad and those working in the Gulf were encouraged to contribute their share. Contributions were viewed as citizenship's due as opposed to philanthropy's offerings. This was in line with a long tradition of exile mobilization that encompassed many other revolutionary structures, including the Algerian FLN and Palestinian PLO. As for foreign support, it was sorely limited in the early years. Much of the modest aid received from Egypt, Iraq, Saudi Arabia, the Imamate and the MAN was drained by Iranian and British patrols at sea and dried up by Sultanate and British raids on overland supply routes and storage depots.

Throughout the course of the revolutionary war, Dhufaris were confronted with three practical challenges: procuring supplies and funds; establishing cross-border bases and supply routes; and maintaining the fighting morale of the population. The first challenge depended on the regional and international context: the willingness of states and movements to aid the revolution. The second was contingent on creating safe enclaves in neighbouring countries, and the third on local revolutionary mobilization and organization. These three challenges were interlinked. International support boosted Dhufari steadfastness and morale, cross-border safe enclaves were essential for maintaining fighting performance, while local perseverance encouraged international support. A fourth, less immediate but absolutely crucial, challenge was to maximize international pressure upon the British so as to increase the diplomatic cost of their presence in Dhufar and Oman and their support for the Sultan.

These challenges were daunting. The military situation in Dhufar had reached stalemate in 1966. The revolutionaries and the army were both weak: the former starved of weapons and supplies and unable to reach the plains; the latter overstretched and incapable of holding territory in the highlands. By the end of 1966, the balance of power had deteriorated from the revolutionary perspective. The Sultan's Armed Forces (SAF) had reached battalion size, with the Northern Frontier, Muscat and Desert Regiments operating on a rolling basis in Dhufar. This expansion allowed the SAF to intensify campaigns in the highlands while simultaneously protecting Midway Road, the sole link between Dhufar and Oman proper. In the meantime, barely any new supplies had reached the DLF from 1966 to late 1967.[1]

This chapter examines the military crisis in which the Dhufari revolutionaries—in their tribalist, Dhufarist and republican varieties—found themselves in late 1966 and 1967. It also outlines four regional developments that shaped their response to that crisis: the June defeat of 1967 and the resulting ideological transformations within the Movement of Arab Nationalists (MAN); the victory of the South Yemeni revolution; the announcement of British withdrawal from the Gulf; and the development of the Chinese connection.

---

[1] J.E. Peterson, *Oman's Insurgencies*, London: Saqi Books, 2007, p.211.

Although these regional developments took shape far away from Dhufar, they had a direct bearing on the revolutionary struggle in that territory. The June 1967 defeat and the transformations within the MAN occasioned a leftward turn in the ideological conception and practice of the struggle, especially amongst the ranks of republican Dhufari cadres. The victory of the South Yemeni revolution consolidated that shift to the left and provided, for the first time, a crucial base of diplomatic and military support. The announcement of British withdrawal heightened the broader regional orientation of the struggle and occasioned further transnational coordination between Gulf revolutionary groups. Finally, the turn to China provided the Dhufari revolutionaries with some modest resources with which to conduct their fight and exposed them to Maoist political and organizational concepts.

CHALLENGES OF 1967

The Sultan's army began 1967 by tightening the siege on the three main mountain ranges in Dhufar—Jabal Qamar in the west, Jabal al Qarra in the centre, and Jabal Samhan in the east. For instance, a 'food denial' operation was undertaken in the vicinity of Taqa that led to the arrest of a Dhow carrying supplies (22 January–9 February).[2] This operation aimed to starve the eastern edges of the Qara mountains, an area that traditionally depended on Taqa for trade and that had close familial links with that coastal town. Further to the east, Sadh, a town with links to Jabal Samhan, was cordoned off and its houses searched on 12 February. Operations were also carried out in the northwest (2–15 February) and the centre, with Wadi Ghasham cordoned and revolutionaries subjected to airstrikes (23 February). In the west, the Muscat Regiment searched the village of Rakhyut and troops were landed by air at 'Gant's Hill' (16 February). In another illustration of popular loyalty to the revolutionaries, these troops were forced to withdraw from the hill after being threatened by the local population.[3]

Such operations were part of a wider and ongoing Anglo-Sultanic campaign, which had two aims: clearing the coastal villages of any revolutionary presence; and making life in the mountains as difficult as possible, mainly through forced-starvation tactics and regular attacks. The former goal took precedence over the latter with the army mainly defending 'base

---

[2] DEFE 13/779, 'History of the Dhufar Campaign', Period II, 27 May 1965 to December 1967.

[3] DEFE 13/779, 'History of the Dhufar Campaign'.

areas'. This was in line with the principle of British counter-insurgency, which stipulated that, in situations where the army lacks the capacity to control all parts of a country, it should prioritize the most populous and economically important areas. After securing those base areas, it would work out of them. The implication was evident: 'this may mean accepting that the insurgent movement gains control over certain remoter areas and that there will be a degree of infiltration across inaccessible borders'.[4] In Dhufar, this translated into the main Central and Eastern coastal villages (with a focus on Salalah) being treated as the base area, heavily fortified and forcibly seperated from their surroundings by the army, while the west and the highlands were viewed as a revolutionary sphere. Yet, although the army did not 'hold' the highlands, it did aim to isolate them and render them uninhabitable, in so far as it was possible.

Most importantly, army operations exemplified the effort to control the physical movement and distribution of the Dhufari population by imposing curfews in the towns and villages and launching strikes on mountain settlements. Their social impact cannot be overemphasized. They suspended established trading patterns, violated the privacy of coastal homes and severed the familial links tying the coast with the highlands. Thus, with the passing of every year, Dhufar's human geography was significantly altered. On the coast, the blockades and curfews, the barbed wire, and the threat of being shot, limited the extent of people's movements and their ability to maintain contact with their families. The trade embargo affected their diet—their ability to import gee butter, livestock and other mountain goods. It further harmed their economic livelihood by disrupting their traditional export activities. Even without the severe restrictions, exports would have been affected by the shortage of goods to sell. Basic necessities, such as sugar and rice, were rationed, brought by the merchants in the coastal towns and villages from Salalah.[5]

The arrival of relatively large military units could have minimally offset some of the economic difficulties on the coast. Yet, although military expenditure increased, its immediate beneficiaries were a very narrow sector of the population, a few individuals handpicked by the Sultan. Goats could only be bought from one merchant. Wood was procured in accordance with strict and detailed procedures imposed by the ruler himself.[6]

---

[4] Robert Thompson, *Defeating Communist Insurgency: Experiences From Malaya and Vietnam*, London: Chato and Windus, 1966, p.57.

[5] KCL-Thwaites, 'Said bin Taimur to Peter Thwaites', 8 January 1970 (Liddell Hart Centre for Military Archives, King's College, London—Thwaites, Brigadier Peter Trevenan, GB 0099 KCLMA Thwaites).

[6] KCL-Thwaites, 'Pat Waterfield to Peter Thwaites', 25 May 1969.

Most of the bulk trade was monopolized by the large Banyan merchant company Khimji Ramdas, and their profits were not channelled into any meaningful local investment. There were no banks in Dhufar through which money could be circulated, and—with the aforementioned withdrawal of the oil company from the region—there were no economic projects save for a few agricultural plantations, often employing slave labourers. Food and clothes were provided to the soldiers within their bases and they purchased little from the local market.

Employment was limited for Dhufaris. The few who worked for the army were monitored personally by the Sultan. Fearful and distrustful of the local population and obsessed with micro-management, he had a marked tendency to check individual profiles of Dhufari employees, and it was not unusual for him to send specific instructions concerning their affairs to senior British commanders. These instructions were often cautionary or punitive, alerting British officers to the base nature of Dhufaris or specifying punishments to be visited upon them. The extraordinarily microscopic level on which the administration was run reflected the pre-bureaucratic nature of the Sultanic state. It also illustrated the Sultan's proclivity for personifying the general. This was matched by his tendency to objectify the particular. Indeed, he did not trust the Dhufari men that worked for him, branding them as 'cattle thieves'. As for the women, he looked down upon them as the 'Jebel Qahbub' (Mountain Whores).[7]

Hardship—caused by the constraints on economic activity, disruption of trade, distortions in the distribution of spending and the circulation of money, as well as limited employment opportunities—was made worse by the Sultan's devaluation of the Muscat rupee in December 1967. The currency was devalued by 14.3 per cent, in line with British pounds sterling, and this caused severe inflation, especially considering the fact that most essential imports were brought from India, which had not devalued its own rupee.[8] This bleak situation existed in spite of the initiation of Omani oil exports on 1 August 1967, with production of crude oil averaging 56,000 barrels daily in 1967 and more than tripling to 240,000 barrels in 1968.[9]

Under the terms of his agreement with Shell's Petroleum Development Oman (PDO), the Sultan was receiving 50 per cent of the profits and 12.5 per cent of the oil production, the equivalent of standard OPEC terms at the time.[10] In 1968, this amounted to an oil income of £25 million,

---

[7] KCL-Thwaites, 'Pat Waterfield to Peter Thwaites'.
[8] FO 1016/790, 'Muscat—Annual Review 1967', 5 January 1968.
[9] 'Crude Oil Production in Middle East and North Africa 1968' in *Middle East Economic Survey*, Vol. XII, No.15, 7 February 1969, p.3.
[10] FO 1016/790, 'Muscat—Annual Review 1967,' 5 January 1968.

a very large sum by Omani standards at the time. Although this influx of income coincided with the termination of the British military subsidy to the Sultanate, it could have still furnished enough to improve the dire economic condition of the population in Dhufar and elsewhere.[11] Nevertheless, ever parsimonious, the Sultan was unwilling to initiate a major spending programme, and this alarmed even his most avid British supporters. The Consul General, who had long admired Said bin Taimur for being a 'tough anglophile', wrote:

> The Sultan has so far failed to take steps to make his rule in Dhofar more acceptable to the people there. Thus, the rebels rather than the S.A.F. enjoy the sympathy and support of the local population.[12]

In spite of this 'sympathy and support', the DLF was experiencing enormous difficulties at this stage.

The military crisis affecting the revolutionaries had profound organizational effects, undermining the position of tribalism and Dhufarism and paving the way for leftist republican ascendancy. The tribalists, as epitomized by Sheikh Mussalam Bin Nufl and his followers, were generally weakened by their inability to draw support from their traditional patron, Saudi Arabia. They had attempted to push the DLF into taking the Saudi side in the Arab Cold War but they were blocked by the other elements. The former members of the Movement of Arab Nationalists (MAN), the Dhufari Soldiers' Association and the Dhufari Charitable Association were all committed to the Egyptian line.[13]

The Saudis had by then reached a general rapprochement with the British and were alarmed at the Dhufari connections to Nasser's Egypt. Moreover, they were concerned by the turn of events in South Yemen, correctly sensing that the struggle in Dhufar could become a natural extension of the revolution in that territory. To top it all, they were likely to have been subjected to the Imamate's negative portrayals of the DLF. Thus, by 1966, they had abandoned their former allies. Dhufarists suffered from similar problems to those besetting the tribalists. Despite their ongoing connection with the Egyptians, they were not procuring adequate aid for the armed struggle. Abroad, they were losing the struggle for positions, especially amongst the growing student elements.

---

[11] The subsidy for 1 April 1966–31 March 1967 was £1,359,095. See DEFE 24/1867 'Agreed Minute—Annex I. Military Expenditure—Part I Army Recurrent Costs', 26 July 1965.

[12] FO 1016/790, 'Muscat—Annual Review 1967', 5 January 1968.

[13] Al-Jabha al-Shabiya, *Al Jabha al Wataniya al 'Arida wa Daruratuha al Tarikhya*, Dirasat 9 Yunyu, n.d., p.22.

Nevertheless, the DLF continued to function and it was responding to the dire situation with attempts to merge with other forces. To that end, a meeting was held between senior DLF and Imamate leaders on 13 July 1966.[14] Although an understanding on the possibility of merger was reached between the two groups, this was never translated into practice and the idea effectively died down. In fact, instead of communion, there developed a saw-toothed animosity, sharpened by divergences in outlook and aims. The Imamate launched an intensive political and media campaign against the DLF, accusing it of having a suspect separatist agenda that contradicted the spirit of pan-Arabism.[15] This campaign seemed to have led to the temporary closure of the DLF office in Cairo. The British Consul in Muscat observed these developments with pleasure:

> Attempts to coordinate the activities of the Dhofar [*sic*] Liberation Force and the Omani rebels appear to be meeting with little success, mainly because the DLF are holding out for an independent Dhofar, whilst the Omanis (or at least the younger generation of them) wish to retain a unitary state. It is reported that this division of aims resulted in a free fight at a meeting of Omani students in Cairo which DLF representatives had been invited to address. So while militarily there has been no let-up, on the political front there is at least a temporary improvement.[16]

A second scheme, which had greater chances of success, was devised by the Egyptians in the same year. In order to undermine British influence, and to pre-emptively counter the Shah, they sponsored the creation of the 'Front for the Liberation of the Eastern Arabian Peninsula'.[17] Under this umbrella, the major revolutionary elements connected to Egypt were assembled: the DLF, the Oman Liberation Front, and the Bahraini National Liberation Front. A founding meeting was convened by Egyptian military intelligence in Sheikh Saqr al-Qasimi's house in Cairo's Duqi district, with the DLF represented by Mohammad al-Ghassani.[18] Following that meeting, a draft National Charter was prepared, articulating the objective of the Front in classic Nasserist terms: 'the economic and political liberation of the region from Anglo-American colonialism, removing its basis and destroying its foundations and the establishment of social justice that would enable the people to benefit from its own material

[14] Falah Al-Mdairis, 'The Arab Nationalist Movement in Kuwait from its Origins to 1970', DPhil, University of Oxford, 1987, p.367.

[15] Abdel Rahman Al-Nuaimi, 'Al Sibaq 'ala al Tartibaat al Siyassia" *Al-Wasat*, 30 October 2008.

[16] FO 1016/765, D.C. Carden (Muscat) to Glen Balfour-Paul (Bahrain), 29 September 1966.

[17] Al-Jabha al-Shabiya, *Al Jabha al-Wataniya al 'Arida wa Daruratuha al Tarikhya*, p.23.

[18] Al-Mdairis, 'The Arab Nationalist Movement in Kuwait', p.367.

resources'.[19] This was to be achieved by coordinated action between the three groups who would be collectively represented by the Front's offices in Cairo while still retaining their autonomy on the ground.[20] The Front project was aborted in the aftermath of the June 1967 defeat (the *naksa*) and subsequent Egyptian withdrawal from the Gulf arena. Thus ended the last ambitious Nasserist project for the region.

THE CRISIS OF THE REPUBLICANS AND THEIR CONSTELLATIONAL SHIFT

The waning of the Egyptian regional role affected the revolution as a whole, including the republican MAN elements. Although profoundly affected by the shock of the 1967 *naksa*, they were the ones that carried the burden of responding to it. They did so by reorienting the entirety of their struggle. To understand their actions, we must go back to their defining characteristics and to emphasize that the fundamental fact that distinguished them from the rest of their Dhufari compatriots was their formal connection to a regional community of revolution underlined by shared political conceptions, organizational methods, codes, rites, and rituals.

On the epistemological level, the communities of revolution belonging to the Nasserist constellation were guided by 'empirical radicalism'.[21] They were radical because they aimed at fundamental change—the destruction of empire and monarchy and the replacement of divided states with Arab republican unity. They were empirical because they grounded their organizational vision in experience as opposed to innate theoretical ideas. This gave them a great deal of organizational fluidity in acting upon the consensus that defined them.

Yet, the 1960s witnessed a shift in the Arab community of revolution from empirical radicalism to radical rationalism, from an experiential epistemology to a theoretical one. Within the MAN, the mother group of republican Dhufaris, the ground was laid for this conceptual revolution over a number of years from the late 1950s to 1967. How did it come

---

[19] 'Al-Nitham al-Dakhili li Jabhat Tahrir Sharqi al-Jazeera Al-'Arabiya al Muh'tal', Appendix 2 in Al-Jabha al-Shabiya, *Al Jabha al Wataniya al 'Arida wa Daruratuha al Tarikhya*, pp.50–3.

[20] 'Mashroo' al-Mithaqq al Watani li Jabhat Tahrir Sharqi al-Jazeera,' Appendix 1 in Al-Jabha al-Shabiya, *Al Jabha al Wataniya al 'Arida wa Daruratuha al Tarikhya*, pp.44–9.

[21] Walid Khalidi, 'Political Trends in the Fertile Crescent,' in Walter Laquere (ed.), *The Middle East in Transition: Studies in Contemporary History*, New York: Praeger, 1958, p.123.

about? Just as success leads to a clustering of communities of revolution into a constellation, crisis leads them to search for alternative constellations with the aid of which they could guide their struggles to victory. The Nasserist constellation was afflicted with a series of crises, beginning with the failure of the United Arab Republic and culminating with the June 1967 defeat. Within the MAN, a battle of interpretation was waged around each crisis, with divergent interpretations carrying profound ideological and practical implications. For instance, those wedded to old nationalist conceptions and al-Hakam Darwazeh's 'two stages of struggle' theory analysed the breakup of the United Arab Republic in terms of immediate and foreign factors (external conspiracy and its internal agents), whereas those demanding change emphasized structural and social factors (the coincidence of *comprador* bourgeois and colonial interests). The former could still adhere to the concept of the unity of the nation in the struggle against empire; the latter asserted that the fight against the national bourgeoisie was a priority in the anti-colonial agenda.

The epistemological transformation within the MAN took place in several spheres, the most conspicuous of which were national conferences. Between 1962 and 1965, long and protracted battles were fought against the old MAN.[22] With their newly acquired radical rationalism, the MAN left (represented by the likes of Mohsen Ibrahim, Nayef Hawatmeh and Mohammad Kishli) emphasized the organic connection between the national and social struggles and attacked the old nationalist separation between the two.

Between 1961 and 1967, the emerging leftist current within the MAN was still acting within the Nasserist paradigm. Yet they sought to create a united organized movement out of it and to infuse it with the theory of scientific socialism. They sought to unite all revolutionary forces in the region under the personal leadership of Nasser. This vision, dubbed as the 'merger with Nasserism', reflected the search for a new pan-Arab vanguard, one that had greater cohesion, unity and ideological consciousness. In the 1965 MAN national conference, the left had managed to impose this agenda. The following months witnessed closer cooperation with the

---

[22] The narrative provided draws on five accounts by MAN participants: George Habash, *Al-Thawryoona La Yamoutuna Abadan*, Beirut: Al Saqi, 2011; Nayef Hawatmah, *Nayef Hawatmah Yatahadath*, Amman: Dar al-Jalil, 1997; Muhsin Ibrahim, *Limatha Munathamat al-Ishtirakyeen al-Lubnanyeen? 'Harakat al Qawmyieen al-Arab min al-Fashya ila al-Nassirya, Tahleel wa Naqd*, Beirut: Dar al Talia'a, 1970; Basil Al-Kubaisi, 'The Arab Nationalists Movement: From Pressure Group to Socialist Party', Unpublished Doctoral Dissertation, The American University, 1971; and Walid Kazziha, *Revolutionary Transformation in the Arab World: Habash and his Comrades from Nationalism to Communism*, London: Croom Helm, 1979.

Egyptian apparatuses in a range of regional theatres, and several MAN branches were even voluntarily dissolved within structures modelled on the UAR's Arab Socialist Union. This experience was shocking for the MAN. In its course, it became increasingly clear that the movement was being treated by Egypt as a tool of its intelligence apparatus as opposed to an arm of coordinated revolutionary action. Although this unsavoury situation was blamed on the conservative 'old guard' rather than Nasser, by the end of 1966 several MAN branches had clashed with the Egyptian security sector and the movement was reasserting its organizational independence.[23]

The failure of the 'merger with Nasserism' policy encouraged the transformation of the MAN. Marxism-Leninism in all its non-Soviet varieties became increasingly popular within the movement. Vietnam, Cuba and China were all sources of inspiration, torch-bearing tricontinental nations that seemed to be charting an independent revolutionary path towards social and national liberation. This not only followed regional precedents (for instance the leftist rebellion at the 1963 Ba'ath party Homs Conference), but also broader global patterns of Marxist rebellion against the Bandung Generation.[24] Still, the shift towards Marxism-Leninism is especially remarkable considering the MAN's historic legacy. The movement's traditional anti-communist stance was notorious, epitomized in such virulently hostile works as al-Hakam Darwazeh's *al-Shiu'ia al-Mahalya* and in such actions as the Kuwaiti branch's establishment of the 'Committee to Combat Communism'.[25] Yet the evangelical anti-communists of the 1950s became the aspiring proletarian vanguard of the 1960s. This reflected the fact that the crises of the decade had heated up the community of revolution. But, above all, it was the fire of the 1967 *naksa* that brought it to boiling point.

The shock of the *naksa* was initially received by the MAN with disbelief bordering on denial.[26] Nevertheless, the following months saw an intense period of *autocritique* and a complete reconsideration of the fundamentals of Arab revolutionary strategy. In July 1967, George Habash convened a meeting of the MAN's national executive committee that resulted in a report entitled 'The Arab Revolution in the face of the Battle of Destiny'. It was argued that June's main stoppage lay in the termination of the war with the military defeat, and the failure to transform it from a

---

[23] Interview A.

[24] David Priestland, *The Red Flag: Communism and the Making of the Modern World*, London: Allen Lane, 2009, p.471.

[25] al-Hakam Darwazeh, *al-Shiu'ia al-Mahalya wa Qadiyat al-Arab al-Qawmya*, Beirut: Dar al Fajr al Jadid, 1961.

[26] See *al-Hurriya*, 19 June 1967.

conventional conflict into a total war of popular national liberation against all colonialist forces in the Arab world. The Vietnamese experience was cited: what was lacking on the Arab level was a long-term mobilization that could lead to the creation of 'many Vietnams' (the phrase was probably borrowed from Che Guevara, who had coined it in February 1967). This was effectively a call for people's war, something that was defined by General Giap in the following terms: 'to educate, mobilise, organise and arm the whole people in order that they might take part in the resistance'.[27] According to Giap, the course of the Vietnamese struggle had proven the results of such a long-term strategy:

> From the military point of view, the Vietnamese people's war of liberation proved that an insufficiently equipped people's army, but an army fighting for a just cause, can, with appropriate strategy and tactics, combine the conditions needed to conquer a modern army of aggressive imperialism.[28]

Inspired by such analyses, the traditional MAN leaders espoused the conclusion that the Arab petty bourgeois ruling elite was unwilling and incapable of initiating a people's war due to its very character, due to an ideology that 'distrusted the masses' and to its structural position and interests, which limited it to conventional warfare. The way out lay in the assumption of leadership by the 'oppressed classes' (workers, peasants and revolutionary intellectuals) and their turn to scientific socialism.[29]

As revolutionary as it sounded, this discourse, as adopted by the traditional MAN leadership, was still inadequate for the leftist current of the movement. Talk of scientific socialism was not enough: a complete shift was required, epitomized in the adoption of Marxist-Leninist organization. The leftists thus continued to agitate against the old MAN figures. The substance of their argument is captured by a famous statement made by Nayef Hawatmeh in the August 1968 Popular Front for the Liberation of Palestine (PFLP) conference:

> If we want to ignite a revolution which will guarantee the liberation of Palestine and consequently the whole Arab world...we have to build our revolutionary party, our Marxist-Leninist party. With the absence of this kind of party, it is impossible to transfer the resistance movement into a real revolution...In Vietnam the revolutionaries are gaining victory because their struggle relies on a theoretical revolutionary base.[30]

---

[27] Vo Nguyen Giap, *The Military Art of People's War: Selected Writings of General Vo Nguyen Giap*, New York; London: Monthly Review Press, 1970, p.92.

[28] Giap, *The Military Art of People's War,* p.95.

[29] Mohammad Jamal Barut, *'Harakat al-Qawmiyeen al-'Arab: al-Nash'a, al-Ta'tawur, al-Mas'air.* Damascus: al-Markaz al-'Arabi lil Dirasat al-Istratijya, 1997, p.424.

[30] Al-Mdairis, 'The Arab Nationalist Movement in Kuwait', p.379.

This voluntarist view portrayed the 1967 defeat as a failure of political will and organization, as opposed to the result of wide-ranging systematic forces, positing that the praxis of theory and organization could resolve any obstacle, no matter how great.

At the Gulf level, Dhufari youth contributed to promoting this line—along with Bahrainis and Omanis, they were amongst its most vigorous proponents. This not only reflected an epistemological reorientation, but also organizational frustration with the old leadership of the MAN, a disaffection that had long preceded the 1967 *naksa*. Organizational power in the Gulf was centred in the hands of the Kuwaiti branch, whose leaders were viewed with suspicion, accused of having 'mild' politics that reflected the branch's 'bourgeois' composition. This grievance was aggravated by regional crises. Two of these had a broad impact. The first was the defeat of the 1965 *intifada* in Bahrain. The failure of the national and regional leaderships to support that uprising effectively reinforced the view that the needs of the Gulf region were being ignored. This compelled Bahraini cadres to declare that they would cease to cooperate with the Movement until it sincerely addressed the concerns of the Gulf branches. They held a meeting in 1965, after which the MAN General Secretariat agreed to pay closer attention to the region.[31] The second crisis occurred when the national leadership of the MAN was accused (quite unfairly it must be said) of failing to stand by the South Yemeni National Liberation Front (NLF) in the face of Egyptian attempts to force it to dissolve into the Front for the Liberation of Occupied South Yemen (FLOSY).[32] The sympathies of most Gulf branches, especially the Dhufaris, undoubtedly lay with the NLF, which was seen to be at the forefront of the struggle in the Arabian Peninsula.

The national and Kuwaiti leaderships were also accused of misdirecting Gulf cadres' energies. Rather than preparing the cadres of that region for the anti-colonial and class fight in their own countries, they were embroiling them in pan-Arab theoretical struggles:

> The Gulf cause is marginal and completely absent from the MAN mind which is busy in daily, and undefined, battles in Greater Syria and Iraq. We find the sons of the Gulf to be party to this conflict, suffering daily and enmeshing themselves in it. So we find that the daily concern of the sons of the Gulf and the focus of their discussions does not go beyond the problematic of MAN-Ba'ath relations, and arguing over which one is better. They are caught up in empty Byzantine discussions, trying to determine which is

---

[31] Al-Mdairis, 'The Arab Nationalist Movement in Kuwait', p.385.
[32] For the MAN leadership's version of this event, see George Habash, *Al-Tharyouna La Yamoutouna Abadan*, Beirut: Al-Saqi, 2011.

better, the slogan of freedom or the slogan of liberation, or analysing the secession and the economic problems of the UAR.[33]

This went beyond the level of vision and extended to practice, with Gulf cadres forced into harmful conflicts within various Arab student unions, especially in Egypt:

> …the sons of the Gulf in the UAR [United Arab Republic] region were dragged into spontaneous and unnecessary battles with the intelligence apparatus in an attempt to control the student unions. But the essence of the problem lies in the following question: what is the goal that is desired from controlling the unions? While working in these unions it became clear to us that the goal was obscure and immaterial, reflecting nothing more than a narrow party vision concerned with satisfying the urge for party control.[34]

Out of these accumulated grievances, the earliest actual step against the pan-Arab and Kuwaiti leaderships was undertaken in late December 1967 with the launch of the first regional conference of MAN branches in the Arabian Peninsula. The conference took place in Beirut under the supervision of National General Secretariat members, Abdel Rahman Kamal and Ahmad Humaidan and in liaison with the leftist current of the movement. It was attended by representatives of the Saudi and Gulf branches as well as Abdallah al-Ashtal, a senior envoy of the NLF, a movement which enjoyed much prestige at that moment, having just won the independence struggle in South Yemen.[35] The Kuwaiti branch was harshly criticized. One delegate accused it of appointing local leaders without consultation with their branches. The Omani delegate, Zaher al-Miyahi, went as far as stating that the 'Kuwaiti leadership with its bourgeois background is responsible for a latent revolutionary area'.[36] At the strategy level, the delegates forcefully pushed for the adoption of armed struggle to liberate the Gulf from the British imperial presence and the Sheikhly regimes. Most of the delegates were in agreement that the first step was to begin armed struggle in northern Oman, especially considering the fact that it was already under way in Dhufar. The Kuwaiti representative, Khaled al-Wasmi, doubted the utility of that strategy in his own country but expressed his understanding for the merits of its application elsewhere.[37]

[33] 'Muhimat al Tantheem fil Kharij', Private Papers of Abdel Rahman al-Nuaimi, n.d., c.1968.

[34] 'Muhimat al Tantheem fil Kharij', Private Papers of Abdel Rahman al-Nuaimi, n.d., c.1968.

[35] Abdel Nabi Al-Ikri, *Al-Tanthimat al-Yassariya fil Jazeera wal Khaleej al 'Arabi*, Beirut: Dar al-Kunouz al-Adabyya, 2003, p.76.

[36] Al-Ikri, *Al-Tanthimat al-Yassariya fil Jazeera wal Khaleej al 'Arabi*, p.77.

[37] Barut, *'Harakat al-Qawmiyeen al-'Arab'*, p.404.

Nevertheless, his stance was seen as embodying a lack of revolutionary orientation.

A new organizational structure was proposed in order to expand the armed struggle and correct the situation prevailing under the Kuwaiti leadership, which had allegedly failed to coordinate work between the various branches, had ignored their individual needs, and had centralized power in its own hands without duly involving local leaders.[38] However, although plans for this new structure were drawn up, they did not lead to any actual results.

More fruitful discussions took place in March 1968 during a meeting of seven MAN members in Kuwait, and the idea of forming a more militant and Gulf-oriented organization was agreed upon.[39] This was translated into reality by the convening in Dubai of an Extraordinary Conference for the Gulf MAN branches on 19–21 July 1968.[40] The conference took place in the context of the failure of the organizational formula that had been agreed on in Beirut in December 1967, the radical decisions of the fourth South Yemeni NLF conference, and the initiation by the MAN left of a series of regional conferences to challenge the national leadership.[41] The leftists—especially the Bahraini, Omani and Dhufari representatives—came with their knives sharpened, resolved to settle their scores with Kuwait. The conference accordingly turned into an ideological battleground. The Kuwaiti representative, Khaled al-Wasmi, protested about the hasty adoption of scientific socialism, stating that 'we do not know exactly what it means'. He questioned the proposed adoption of Leninist organzational principles: 'we can only be committed to Marxism-Leninism as a method of organisation after deep study and research; we cannot commit ourselves to something we do not know'.[42] He further reiterated the inapplicability of armed struggle to the Kuwaiti context. But his pleas went unheard; if anything, they were seen to be driven by 'bourgeois dispositions' and confirmed the necessity of disposing with the Kuwaiti leadership. Accordingly, the Kuwaiti branch's membership was frozen. The only branch to protest this action was Qatar. Overcome with sadness, its representative uttered the bewildered words: 'we want more people, and you are freezing the brothers in Kuwait!'[43]

---

[38] Al-Ikri, *Al-Tanthimat al-Yassariya fil Jazeera wal Khaleej al 'Arabi*, p.78.

[39] MEC. Graham, 'The National Democratic Front for the Liberation of Oman and the Arabian Gulf', SAF Intelligence, 3 March 1971.

[40] Al-Ikri, *Al-Tanthimat al-Yassariya fil Jazeera wal Khaleej al 'Arabi*, p.79.

[41] Barut, '*Harakat al-Qawmiyeen al-'Arab*', p.439.

[42] Al-Mdairis, 'The Arab Nationalist Movement in Kuwait', p.390.

[43] Abdel Rahman Al Nuaimi, 'Al Nuhud al Qawmi wal Watani Ba'da Hazimat Yuniou Wa In'ikasatuh al Hizbiya', *Al Dimuqrati*, Vol.28, 2005.

The Dubai Extraordinary Conference thus declared the Gulf a sphere of action independent of the MAN leadership, and created a formation to replace it in the region. Initially, that formation did not have a name but, two months later, an article in *al-Hurriya* announced it as the Popular Revolutionary Movement (PRM). With this act, the chapter of the MAN was closed and the shift to Marxism-Leninism was completed within the Gulf community of revolution, still shocked by the 1967 defeat but determined to respond to it by means of armed struggle across the Arab world.

ARABIA FELIX VICTORIOUS

As well as being a year of defeat, 1967 witnessed a victory. The NLF had won the fight against British colonialism in South Yemen and formally gained independence on 30 November. This was one of the most important turning points in the Dhufari struggle. The South Yemeni connection to Dhufar was immensely strong. The two regions were tied by geography, history, culture and political organization. Dhufar immediately bordered the easternmost Mahra province of Yemen. Fostered by this propinquity, trade, tribal, and cultural relations flourished for centuries. Moreover, significant sections within the NLF and the DLF shared a common background in the MAN, inhabiting the same moral and political universe and having a nearly identical organizational background and regional objectives.[44] In the pre-independence period, the NLF had always supported the Dhufaris in MAN meetings. It had, moreover, helped in establishing cross-border supply lines. Likewise, the Dhufari MAN cadres stood by the NLF in their conflict with the Egyptians and their sponsored group FLOSY. Thus, revolutionary conviviality began well before the Dhufari armed struggle and continued long after it.

During the celebrations of their country's independence, NLF leaders met DLF representatives. The attendance list reads like a *Who's Who* of the liberation struggle, including President Qahtan al Shabi and three other future Presidents: Salmin; Abdel Fatah Ismail; and Ali al-Bid. As a first act, the NLF communicated its decision to donate arms and equipment used in its revolution to Dhufar. For a few years afterwards, even the uniforms worn by Dhufari fighters were passed on from South Yemen.[45]

The South Yemenis saw the struggle in the Gulf as an extension of their own. Almost every successful revolution passes through an early stage of

---

[44] Interview F.
[45] Interview E(ii).

regional solidarity, and the South Yemeni one was no exception. The notion of spreading a pan-Arab revolution was enshrined early on in the principles of the South Yemeni struggle, which had long advocated liberation 'from Aden to Kuwait'. This commitment was reaffirmed in the post-independence period by both the left and right wings of the NLF. In the Fourth NLF Congress of March 1968, the leftist leader, Abdel Fatah Ismail, emphasized the need to support revolution in the Arabian Peninsula. The same view was expressed in a May 1969 statement by the allegedly 'right wing' President Qahtan al-Sha'abi.[46]

Support for Dhufar made sense not only in terms of this revolutionary logic but also for *raisons d'état*. Viewing the states around them, the Yemeni republicans could only see imperially sponsored monarchies plotting for their defeat. The very survival of the republic seemed to require the spread of its ideals. As Halliday notes, the South Yemenis saw their struggle as a 'model for others in the Arabian Peninsula, and the security of their revolution depended upon the success of kindred revolutions elsewhere'.[47]

This should not be taken to mean that support for the revolutionaries was merely pragmatic or self-interested. Indeed, over the years, South Yemen sacrificed a vast amount of treasure, diplomatic energy and military effort to the Dhufari cause. Abandoning the struggle would have not only relieved that impoverished state from these great expenses and exertions; it could have also aided in its integration into its hostile neighbourhood. Rarely has a state given so much and materially gained so little from its support for a cause. Yet South Yemen continued to support the revolution to the very end. By all accounts, Dhufari leaders were treated as equal comrades, not to be intervened with or told what to do, free in their decision-making and unfettered in their mode of organization.

What explains this policy? One answer that is given in Dhufari circles is that the Yemenis were too traumatized by their experience with the Egyptian apparatuses to ever pull any stunts.[48] A further possible explanation points to the normative foundations of the nascent South Yemen state. The revolutionary principles and actions upon which the state was founded were still fresh, the notion of solidarity still having resonance and popular currency. In such a state, political careers were judged, at least in part, by the length of revolutionary credentials. Indeed, South Yemeni

---

[46] Fred Halliday, *Revolution and Foreign Policy: The Case of South Yemen, 1967–1987*, Cambridge: CUP, 1990, p.140. For a first hand narrative, rejecting the account of Al-Sha'abi as a conservative 'right wing opportunist', see Yevgeny Primakov, *Russia and the Arabs*, New York: Basic Books, 2009, pp.83–4.

[47] Yevgeny Primakov, *Russia and the Arabs*, p.140.

[48] Interview F.

policy cannot be understood without general reference to the distinction between revolutionary and bureaucratic political cultures.[49] The former almost always takes precedence in the early years of a young radical state, although it is often overtaken by the latter with the passage of time. This was the case in the Soviet, Chinese and Cuban cases, as it certainly was with South Yemen. The importance of ideology must also be emphasized. South Yemeni support increased substantially after the leftist takeover of the NLF in the 'corrective move' of June 1969. Even before the 'corrective move', much of the initial Yemeni support for Dhufar came from NLF radical strongholds such as Mukalla in Hadramaut.[50]

Whatever the explanation, Aden was literally turned into a gateway for the revolution. This was part of its general transformation from a cosmopolitan to a revolutionary city, and from an urban space dotted with expatriates and merchants to one filled with established and aspiring revolutionaries. It was a fascinating urban process that was experienced by various Arab cities—Algiers, Cairo, Beirut—at different times, and which is yet to be accounted for in the scholarly literature. Constrained by space, we can only view it from the Dhufari revolutionary perspective. In Aden's vicinity, the Dhufaris were given Camp Jamal. This was located in one of the British RAF's largest former bases, Khormaksar. The camp was fully serviced, and a section of it was transformed into a reception area for the Arab and foreign guests of the revolutionaries.[51] In Aden's port, weapons and supplies were handled. From its airport, Dhufari delegations boarded planes to foreign capitals. Propaganda was printed in its antiquated presses and revolutionary radio programmes were broadcast over its airwaves. Dhufaris were treated in its clinics and accommodated in its old colonial houses. The revolutionaries were introduced to governments in its embassies and to the Yemeni people in the popular demonstrations that filled its streets. In Aden, many a colonial space became a revolutionary one: the

---

[49] For a discussion of how revolutionary culture can be acquired by leaders in the course of a revolution, see Timothy Tackett, *Becoming a Revolutionary: the Deputies of the French National Assembly and the Emergence of a Revolutionary Culture*, Princeton: Princeton University Press, 1996. On Cuban revolutionary political culture, see Richard Fagen, *The Transformation of Political Culture in Cuba,* Stanford: Stanford University Press, 1969. For a common definition of bureaucratic culture, see Max Handman, 'The Bureaucratic Culture Pattern and Political Revolutions', *American Journal of Sociology*, Volume XXXIX, Number 3, November 1933.

[50] For a socio-historic analysis of the radical character of the Hadramaut NLF elements, see Haim Gerber, *Islam, Guerrilla War, and Revolution: A Study in Comparative Social History*, Boulder and London: Lynne Rienner, 1998, p.100.

[51] Abdel Rahman Al-Nuaimi, 'Adan wa Ahlam al Qaramita al Judud', *Al-Wasat*, 13 November 2008.

use of buildings altered and the appearance, background and ends of those utilizing them changed.

In addition to their Aden bureau, which became their main political base, Dhufaris opened an office in Mukalla. Moreover, they had extensive facilities in the Sixth Governorate, including offices in its capital city, al-Ghaitha, and its furthest frontier village, Hawf.[52] They were granted full cooperation from the local leaderships and were afforded tactical, military and economic support. They had complete freedom of movement and were unhindered in their establishment of an intensive network of supply bases and routes. Thus, after nearly two years of isolation and siege, victory in South Yemen gave Dhufaris a sanctuary and a breathing space.[53]

BRITISH 'WITHDRAWAL' AND THE TURN TO CHINA

Aden was not just another *point d'appui* on the British map. It was a pivotal imperial hub, a strategic crossroads. Amongst the plethora of roles it fulfilled, it was 'the base on which Britain's military dominance in the Gulf had hitherto depended'.[54] Thus, when Britain announced in February 1966 that it was withdrawing from Aden within two years, a profound sense of change was felt across the region. The Gulf sheikhs were overtaken by such anxiety on the eve of the Yemeni withdrawal in November 1967 that the Minister of State, Goronwy Roberts, was sent to reassure them of Britain's continued intention to remain in their domains. Two months later, the same minister informed them that Britain was withdrawing from the Gulf by the end of 1971.[55] In actual fact, the sheikhs were bluffed the first time, the decision to withdraw having been reached in July 1967, well before both visits.[56]

After some initial resistance and attempts to dissuade London from its decision, the Gulf rulers and British men on the spot began working hard towards achieving a stabilizing formula under which the small states could be protected. Only a federal arrangement seemed to guarantee adequate security. Amongst the local leaders, Sheikh Zayid of Abu Dhabi took the initiative in pushing this idea. Following joint talks with the Sheikh of

---

[52] Interview D(ii).

[53] FCO 8/366, Hooper (Aden) to McCarthy (FO), 29 February 1968.

[54] Glen Balfour-Paul, *The End of Empire in the Middle East: Britain's Relinquishment of Power in Her Last Three Arab Dependencies*, Cambridge: Cambridge University Press, 1994, p.122.

[55] Balfour-Paul, *The End of Empire in the Middle East*, p.124.

[56] CAB 128/43, 'Conclusions of a Meeting of the Cabinet', 4 January 1968.

Dubai, the two rulers announced that they were forming a federation, to which they invited all other British protectorates, including Bahrain and Qatar.[57]

This initiative was viewed by revolutionaries with alarm: 'at a time when all the powers were busy rearranging their affairs before the year of British withdrawal, we did not see anything in the picture other than a colonialist game for tidying-up the map'.[58] Their response to the initiative was elaborated in a 1969 article published by the Dhufari revolutionaries:

> The latest episode in colonialist policy is the so-called Emirates Federation. This base deformity and impotent colonial excretion will not last...The feudalist Sultanates, Emirates and Imamates will be removed by conscious revolutionary violence. Armed struggle is the only language capable of creating the future of the exploited masses.[59]

According to the revolutionaries, history was repeating itself, the proposed federation being an exact 'replica of the federation of Southern Emirates which had been rejected and brought down by our heroic people in the Yemeni south with the force of arms'. The Dhufari revolutionary leadership vowed to follow the Yemeni example, 'raising its voice high and announcing to international opinion that it is pointing the rifle at the fake federation and sentencing it to death'.[60] But where was the rifle to come from? At this point, the source was none other than China.

To understand the Dhufari turn to China, we must go back a few months before the June defeat, the Yemeni victory, and the announcement of British withdrawal. In February 1967, a delegation led by Mohammad al-Ghassani visited Cairo on an aid-soliciting mission.[61] This delegation, composed of civilian leaders from the DLF liaison committee in Kuwait, arrived roughly at the same time as a military delegation from Dhufar. The two delegations had not been coordinated and tensions were high, reflecting a rising crisis of leadership within the DLF between the more radical figures abroad and the military leadership at home. Objecting to this lack of coordination, the Egyptians refused to give help until there was internal DLF agreement. Thus, no support was given and all hopes were dashed. Other Arab states were also approached through their

---

[57] Rosemarie Zahlan,. *The Making of the Modern Gulf States: Kuwait, Bahrain, Qatar, the United Arab Emirates and Oman*, Reading: Ithaca Press, 1998, p.110.

[58] Abdel Rahman Al-Nuaimi, 'Al-Sibaq Ala al-Tartibat al-Siyassiya', *Al-Wasat*, 30 October 2008.

[59] *Al-Hurriya*, 10 November 1969.

[60] *Al-Hurriya*, 10 November 1969.

[61] FCO 51/41, 'Dhofar Liberation Front'.

embassies but gave nothing other than rejection, consumed by the perilous developments in the region.[62] al-Ghassani described this situation in a letter to his old mentor Ahmad al-Khatib:

> Brother, when I left Kuwait at the beginning of this year, I headed a delegation from the DLF to Cairo. I tell you we asked everyone but met with refusal. All the progressive Arab countries are busy in their own affairs ... these matters kept the real revolutionary outlook away from the eyes of the men in power.[63]

This inevitably led the Dhufari delegation to knock on other doors, contacting various socialist bloc countries through the DLF Cairo office. The only positive response came from the Chinese embassy.[64] The Chinese had long opposed the British presence in the Gulf and denounced Sultan Said.[65] Since 1955, they had developed relations with the Imamate, had offered it military aid and had given it diplomatic support. Moral support was also given and 19 July—designated as Oman Day by a Bandung resolution—was annually marked on the calendar of the Chinese Afro-Asian Solidarity Committee. Aside from having this long history of opposition to the British and the Sultan, the Chinese had other reasons for backing the DLF. In the context of the Sino-Soviet conflict, they sought to enhance their position within the world of national liberation movements. Indeed, according to one account, the Chinese gave their support only after confirming that the DLF had no Soviet connections. Moreover, China was in the midst of the Cultural Revolution, and undergoing the radicalization of foreign policy that accompanied that historical phase. At a time when it was hailing 'world revolution through armed struggle', it was only natural for Beijing to champion a struggle like that of the Dhufaris.[66]

The DLF delegation arrived in China on 23 June 1967, just after the second anniversary of the commencement of armed struggle and two weeks after the June war. It included several senior figures, such as Muhammad al-Ghassani, Salim Musalam (member of DLF Political Committee) and Ahmad Fareh (member of the Military Committee).[67] Hosted by the Chinese People's Institute for Foreign Affairs, they met Defence Ministry officials and were granted light armaments, Marxist literature (mainly

---

[62] Riad El-Rayyes, *Thufar: Al-Sira' al-Siyassi Wal Askari Fil Khaleej al-Arabi, 1970–1976*, Beirut: Riad el-Rayyes Books, 2002, p.130.

[63] 'al-Ghassani Letter to al-Khatib', Cairo, 10 December 1967. Quoted in al-Al-Mdairis, 'The Arab Nationalist Movement in Kuwait', pp.368–9.

[64] Al-Mdairis, 'The Arab Nationalist Movement in Kuwait,' p.368.

[65] Hashim Behbehani, *China's Foreign Policy in the Arab World, 1955–75: Three Case Studies*, London and Boston: Kegan Paul, 1981, p.165.

[66] Behbehani, *China's Foreign Policy in the Arab World, 1955–75*, p.176.

[67] Behbehani, *China's Foreign Policy in the Arab World, 1955–75*, p.176.

copies of the Red Book), and $35,000 to cover shipping costs. The shipment of these items was liaised with Tanzania. The government of Nyerere was close to Beijing at the time (1967, it should not be forgotten, was the year of the Arusha declaration on socialism and self-reliance), and Darussalam even complemented support for the DLF with minor supplies such as tea and sugar.[68]

As modest as it was, members of the DLF received the Chinese aid with jubilation. One cannot underestimate the importance of hope for any armed struggle, especially in the context of a severely unequal balance of power. Support for the revolutionaries in one of their darkest moments boosted their morale and gave them the means, however limited, to persevere. This elevated the already favourable impression of China. al-Ghassani wrote to Ahmad al-Khatib:

> ...regarding our contacts with the socialist bloc countries, we did not receive any reply, except from the PRC, which showed its help in providing some arms...Long discussions took place with the PRC regarding the issue of liberating the Arabian Gulf and at the end it showed its readiness to supply the revolutionary organisations in the Gulf with arms in order to launch armed struggle. I wish that you would contact the PRC and strengthen the relations with it because it is backing the issue of the Gulf especially by arms.[69]

Such evidence from the period illustrates the extent to which the turn to China initially lacked an ideological foundation. There was, of course, respect for the Chinese experience amongst the Dhufari leadership— shared across Arab revolutionary circles—but that should not be confused with Maoist consciousness. That said, the ideological shift that was occurring within the MAN at the time ensured that there was great receptivity to Chinese ideas, a willingness to absorb them that was evident within the more politicized Dhufari circles.

The success of the Chinese revolution and Maoist guerrilla warfare against foreign domination had long animated Arab revolutionaries, and the Chinese rejection of the Soviet policy of 'peaceful coexistence' with the capitalist powers was an additional inspiration for them. Thus, it was unsurprising that Maoism exerted an influence on MAN cadres at a moment when they were searching for a new revolutionary course. This influence increased following the dissolution of the MAN and the

---

[68] For Chinese–Tanzanian relations during this period, see Martin Bailey, 'Tanzania and China', *African Affairs*, Vol 74, No. 294, January, 1975, and George T. Yu, *China's African Policy: Study of Tanzania*, New York: Praeger, 1975.

[69] 'al-Ghassani Letter to al-Khatib', Cairo, 10 December 1967. Quoted in al-Al-Mdairis, 'The Arab Nationalist Movement in Kuwait'.

emergence of its local offshoots, continuing until China changed its international policy and opened relations with Gulf States in 1972. In the late sixties and the early seventies, Maoism was so evident in the discourse of Nayef Hawatmeh, the founder of the Popular Democratic Front for the Liberation of Palestine (PDFLP) that he was satirically dubbed Nayef Zedong. It was so present in the thought of the Popular Front for the Liberation of Palestine (PFLP) that the whole early ideological history of that organization was described as the 'Chinese Phase'.[70] Chinese influences were also evident in all the Gulf branches outside Kuwait, several of which made official internal pronouncements along the following lines:

> ... the Chinese revolution and the national revolutions of third world peoples have initiated a new phase of international struggle... Wielded in them is a strong alliance (workers-intellectuals-revolutionaries-students-soldiers and all sectors of the petty bourgeoisie) in a stubborn confrontation against the imperialist aggression and its local class allies (the comprador bourgeoisie-the military bureaucracy-feudalism).[71]

Closest to Dhufar, similar views had a profound influence on the newly independent South Yemen and were espoused by several of its most prominent leaders. Salmin, Ali Antar, and Ali al-Bidh were especially known for their Chinese sympathies. Their position was paralleled on the Dhufari side by young leaders including Abdel Aziz al-Qadi, Salim al-Ghassani, and Ahmad Abdel Samad.[72] This was to have a major impact on the course of the revolution, as will be illustrated in subsequent chapters...

In conclusion, the Dhufari revolutionaries confronted a military crisis that began in late 1966 and was heightened in the course of 1967. British led counter-insurgency operations and the siege of the highlands led to the deterioration of military and economic conditions. This situation coincided with major regional events that unfolded in 1967 and 1968. These events had a profound effect on the balance of power within the three main currents of the DLF: the tribalist; the Dhufarist; and the republican. The tribalists were weakened by the loss of their patron, Saudi Arabia, in 1966. The Dhufarist position was undermined by the blows to Egypt and its decreasing role in Dhufar and the Gulf. By contrast, the republicans were empowered by new ideological visions and regional and

---

[70] 'al-Ghassani Letter to al-Khatib', Cairo, 10 December 1967. Quoted in al-Al-Mdairis, 'The Arab Nationalist Movement in Kuwait'. p.233.

[71] Al Jabha al Dimuqratiya al Sha'abiya-Al Jazeera al 'Arabiya, 'Al Muntalaq al Istratiji li-Qadaya Hizbina', Unpublished Document, Private Papers of Mohammad Jamal Barut, 1968.

[72] Al Nuaimi, 'Adan wa Ahlam al Qaramita al Judud', *Al-Wasat*, 13 November 2008.

international bases of support. Belonging to a broader regional community of revolution, they were directly tied to the leftward shift that affected that community.

At the pan-Arab level, republicans took the side of the left wing of the MAN against the traditional national leadership of the movement. At the Gulf level, they challenged, along with other regional branches, the authority of the Kuwaiti leadership. Responding to the devastating shock of the Palestinian *naksa*, they subjected their original Nasserist orientation to an *autocritique*, initiating a shift in a more radical direction. The receipt of Chinese support, and exposure to Maoist ideas, contributed to this trend. So did the victory of the South Yemeni revolution, led by the radical NLF. In the wake of that victory, an infrastructure for supporting and supplying the revolution had developed and the total siege that had choked Dhufar since late 1966 was beginning to crumble. Moreover, the South Yemeni struggle against British imperial arrangements offered an example to be emulated. Responding to the announcement of the British withdrawal from the Gulf, as well as to the plan for establishing a United Arab Emirates, the revolutionaries invoked the South Yemeni fight against the British 'Federation of South Arabia' plan, calling for a coordinated Gulf-wide revolutionary response to match the regional imperial scheme. Thus, the political, ideological and military grounds were laid for the transformation of the Dhufar Liberation Front into the Popular Front for the Liberation of Occupied Arab Gulf (PFLOAG).

5

Relocating the Revolutionary Subject: From DLF to PFLOAG

The Dhufar Liberation Front (DLF) was profoundly affected by the unfolding regional developments, the weakening of tribalist and Dhufarist bases of sponsorship, the radicalization of the republicans and the consolidation of leftist external support for them. By late 1967, British intelligence reported that the tribalist leader, Bin Nufl, had 'put out feelers with a view to making his peace with the Sultan, probably because he and his immediate supporters have fallen out with other elements in the DLF which are too leftwing...'[1] Predictably, the Sultan dismissed these approaches, but this did not alter Bin Nufl's alienation from his compatriots. As for the most prominent Dhufarist figure abroad, Yousef Alawi, he continued for a while to be an effective ambassador for the Front. He represented it in the November 1967 New Delhi International Conference in Support of the Arab Peoples and persisted with his pronouncements on Cairo's *Sawt al-Arab*.[2] As late as December 1967, he vigorously connected the Dhufari cause to the international anti-imperialist struggle, announcing that 'there is one matter that cannot change with the lapse of time no matter how much imperialism tries... revolutionaries are revolutionaries wherever they are. Their nature, actions and aims are the same'.[3] Yet, for all this insistence on revolutionary unity, Alawi and his associates had several clashes with the leftists.

The leftist republicans effectively overhauled the DLF. They were empowered by the victory of the Yemeni NLF and their new-found Chinese support. Disappointed with Nasserism and shocked by its setbacks, they were affected by the leftward shift in the Movement of Arab Nationalists (MAN), the rise of its radical rationalism, and the decisions of the Dubai extraordinary conference. Generally, they were inspired by the revolutionary regional atmosphere brought about by the Palestinian

---

[1] FCO 51/41, 'Dhofar Liberation Front', 22 October 1967.
[2] FCO 51/41, 'Dhofar Liberation Front'.
[3] *Sawt al-Arab* (Voice of the Arabs), 12 December 1967.

resistance and they were determined to steer the revolution towards social as well as anti-imperial struggle, and to dispose of all elements opposed to that agenda. Viewing the struggle through a Maoist lens, they saw Dhufar as the base from which all of the region would be liberated through people's war: the countryside from which all of the Gulf city states were to be encircled and liberated. To the DLF rank and file, they brought supplies and weapons and the proclaimed certainty of victory. Their achievements on the ground were already being noted in January 1968: 'In last week Dhofar rebels have shown distinct signs of increased activity indicating both re-supply of arms and improved organisation.'[4] As a result of these achievements, the leftists could count on the support of the fighting base and they were fully determined to utilize it. Thus, radicalized cadres returning from training in China—including Ali Muhsin and Talal Sa'ad—pushed for convening a second DLF conference in September 1968 under the slogan, 'a critical attempt to save the front from inactivity and closure'. One of the factors that encouraged these cadres to hold the conference was the ongoing conflict in South Yemen between President Qahtan al-Sha'abi and Abdel Fatah Ismail. Only six months earlier, the leftist Ismail had been arrested by the 'right wing' of the NLF, and had gone into exile. This convinced the leftist elements in the DLF of the need to take the initiative and to pre-empt any such 'reactionary' moves in their territory.[5] They accordingly convened the second conference of the DLF.

THE HAMRIN CONFERENCE

Preparations for the second conference were undertaken between July and August 1968 and invitations were sent out for all internal and external DLF bodies so as to ensure democratic representation.[6] Approximately 65 delegates assembled in Wadi Hamrin in central Dhufar and deliberated on all the issues from 1 to 20 September 1968.[7] This gathering was joined by a *New China News Agency* reporter and a Communist Party of China official.[8] The presence of the Chinese observers indicated the confidence

---

[4] DEFE 24/1867, Bahrain to Foreign Office, 15 January 1968.
[5] Falah Al-Mdairis, 'The Arab Nationalist Movement in Kuwait from its Origins to 1970', DPhil, University of Oxford, 1987, p. 399.
[6] Mohammad Al-Amri, *Thufar: al Thawra fil Tarikh al-Omani al Mo'uasir*, Beirut: Riad el-Rayyes Books, 2005, p. 95.
[7] Fred Halliday, *Arabia Without Sultans*. London: Saqi, 1999, p. 366.
[8] Hashim Behbehani, *China's Foreign Policy in the Arab World, 1955–75: Three Case Studies*, London and Boston: Kegan Paul, 1981, p.177. Although Bahbahani's claim has

of leftist elements in their ability to steer the conference in a more radical direction.

Leftist elements drafted a fairly lengthy national charter, which was formally adopted at the conference. This time, the revolutionaries firmly relocated the location of their struggle to the realm of universal history, seeing themselves as part of not just an Arab narrative but a global one. Once again, the Chinese imprint is unmistakable. The charter begins by explaining that 'the human struggle which has expanded to include a large part of the world due to the victory of socialist revolution in more than one country has great historical implications on the ability of the international forces of liberation and progress to finally defeat the impe- rialist and reactionary powers'. The 'fighting Arab masses' were part of this struggle undergoing the national democratic phase of liberation.[9]

One of the most ideologically important elements in the charter is its undeclared, but evident, reliance on the Maoist theory of contradictions.[10] A mainstay of the Maoist world view was the need to identify 'principal' contradictions at any given moment. Identifying the contradiction would then be followed by constructing a united front, relying on the peasants and establishing rural base areas, building a people's army, carrying out people's war, and adhering to the policy of self-reliance in the process.[11]

The charter stated that post-oil historical developments had fostered a set of contradictions between the various tribal regimes and tribes (typi- fied by regime and tribal conflicts); and between the tribal regimes created by Britain and the struggling classes oppressed by them (exemplified in popular resistance). In their totality, these coalesced into the 'principal and real contradiction: that between the entirety of the people with all its classes and social contradictions and the colonialist and reactionary authority'.[12] Out of this condition had emerged the previous uprisings in the Gulf. But these were argued to have failed for three reasons: 'the lack of a revolutionary organisation armed with scientific socialist thought and led by a conscious leadership that arises out of the ranks of the masses';

---

been previously dismissed, it is confirmed in British intelligence reports. See FO 1016/790, 'Evidence of Russian and Chinese Support for and Involvement With the Dhufar Libera- tion Front', December 1968. See also FCO 8/366, 'FOH/1072'.

[9] Al-Jabha al-Shabiya, *Wathaiq al Nidal al Watani: 1965–1974*, Beirut: Dar Al-Tali'a, 1974, p. 12.

[10] Mao's theory of contradiction was most famously articulated in his essay 'On Con- tradiction'. printed in Mao Zedong, *On Practice and Contradiction*, London: Verso, 2007.

[11] See Lin Biao, *Long Live the Victory of People's War!*, Peking: Foreign Languages Press, 1965.

[12] 'Al-Mithaq al-Watani Lil Jabha al-Shabiya', September 1968, in Fawaz Trabulsi, *Thu- far: Shahada min Zaman al-Thawra*, Beirut: Riad el-Rayyes Books, 2004, Appendix 3, p.219, original emphasis.

the class character of old leaderships which prevented patriotic *intifadas* from developing into 'an organised armed revolution that leads the masses into final victory'; and 'the isolation of patriotic *intifadas* within their local boundaries and their lack of exposure to neighbouring areas'.[13]

In the light of such an historical vision—underlined by Maoist theory—specific political developments needed to be introduced. Strategic decisions were no longer undertaken on the basis of adjusting to the requirements of immediacy. Instead, they were motivated by a particular reading of history and the distillation of its supposed lessons. By comprehending historical reality, the Dhufari subject could now become its transformative agent, having the necessary rational tools to merge with the flow of events. This grand vision formed the backdrop to the main decisions of the Hamrin conference. Politically, the proposed imperial scheme for the Gulf, the United Arab Emirates plan, was strongly attacked, traditional structures such as the Imamate were berated for their betrayal of the masses, the Palestinian resistance was hailed and—in a gesture of international solidarity—Rhodesia and all other racist regimes were condemned.

At the strategic level, three main decisions were arrived at. The first, commitment to 'organised revolutionary violence', referred to the continuation of the armed struggle. The word 'organised' alluded to the transformation of the struggle from a spontaneous one (the Leninist term for any struggle lacking theory) to one guided by theoretical principles. The second decision, the adoption of a 'revolutionary strategy with comprehensive goals' at the Gulf regional level, 'tying the struggle of Dhufar with the struggle of the masses in the occupied Arab Gulf', entailed expanding the conception of the struggle from one centred on Dhufari independence to one geared to the liberation of the Gulf region as a whole. As mentioned in the previous chapter, this had been the preference of MAN elements from the beginning, but it had been temporarily shelved in order to accommodate Dhufarist and tribalist figures. The third decision, 'unifying the mass popular revolutionary instrument in the occupied Arab Gulf', called for coordination with other revolutionary elements in the Gulf. The implicit reference in that respect was to the Popular Revolutionary Movement (PRM), the regional formation that eventually emerged out of the MAN's Dubai Exceptional Conference of 1968.[14]

These three decisions respectively corresponded to the historical critique of the spontaneity of previous struggles, their isolationism and containment within the units created by colonialism, and their failure to

[13] 'Al-Mithaq al-Watani Lil Jabha al-Shabiya', in Trabulsi, *Thufar*, p.216.
[14] Al-Jabha al-Shabiya, *Wathaiq al Nidal al Watani: 1965–1974*, p.10.

comprehend the historical unity of the Gulf and Southern Arabian regions and their consequent lack of organizational unity. As such, the decisions represented a commitment to rationalize the practices of struggle in accordance with the new theory, and to broaden its boundaries. In order to highlight this commitment, the organization changed its name from the Dhufar Liberation Front to the Popular Front for the Liberation of the Occupied Arab Gulf (PFLOAG). Notably, this new name encompassed Oman but did not refer to it specifically. Dhufaris were still sensitive to Omani domination of their territory, and, although they strived to be part of a broader structure that included Oman, they were not at this stage willing to limit their struggle to uniting with it alone.

Clearly, the movement did not cut its coat according to its cloth, expanding the struggle beyond its material capacities. But at that time of great expectations, horizontal expansion seemed necessary and possible. Indeed, it was complemented with an ideological resolution to 'adopt scientific socialism, which constitutes the historical frame through which the poor masses conduct their struggle to abolish colonialism, imperialism, the bourgeoisie and feudalism; and the scientific method for analysing reality and comprehending the contradictions amongst the ranks of the people'.[15] This effectively entailed deepening the vertical scope of the struggle, ascribing to it the task of social transformation in addition to the political destruction of monarchy and empire. In this respect and others, the resolutions of the Hamrin Conference were nearly identical to those adopted in the conferences that swept MAN branches in 1968,[16] corroborating the contention that the Hamrin conference must be viewed in the context of regional MAN transformations.[17]

Internally, the Hamrin conference represented the culmination of the organizational contradictions within the DLF. The republican current had a tenuous relationship with the Dhufarists and tribalists, who were characterized as unfit to lead a vigorous armed struggle. It was the shift in the balance of power within the DLF—generated by the loss of old sources of support and the gaining of new radical ones—that allowed the republican current to displace the others. Thus, the likes of Alawi and Bin Nufl were effectively marginalized, the former continuing to operate under the old DLF banner.[18]

---

[15] Al-Jabha al-Shabiya, *Wathaiq al Nidal al Watani: 1965–1974,* p.10.
[16] See 'Inbithaq al-Haraka al-Thwariya al-Shabiya',' *al-Hurriya,* 27 January 1969. See also the analysis of the Fourth NLF Congress in Helen Lackner, *P.D.R. Yemen: Outpost of Socialist Development in Arabia,* London: Ithaca Press, 1985, pp.54–9.
[17] Mohammad Barut, *'Harakat al-Qawmiyeen al-'Arab: al-Nash'a,al-Ta'tawur, al-Mas'air',* Damascus: al-Markaz al-'Arabi lil Dirasat al-Istratijya, 1997, p.405.
[18] Interview E(ii).

What relation did this new policy have to the Dhufari rank and file? This book has extensively referred to the tribalist, Dhufarist and republican divisions. However, these divisions existed amongst the vanguard, cadres that held a particular political viewpoint having made a conscious choice to adopt it to the exclusion of others. Almost all were former or current exiles or migrants who had some basic education or organized political involvement and who often came from the coastal towns. In total, these did not number more than a few dozen. Amongst the rank and file, the situation was different. In their circles, exposure to the outside world and to its competing political theories was severely limited: reality could not have been mediated by any concepts other than those orally transmitted.

Experiential factors thus played a fundamental role in shaping the consciousness of most Dhufari fighters. It was the more immediate trials of hunger and oppression, and the promise of progress, that led them to heed their exiled compatriots' call to arms. Likewise their support for one political current or another was, of necessity, very much connected to factors that were not strictly ideological. The most significant were the perceived plausibility of a position, as well as the credibility and rhetorical ability of the person or group presenting it. In practice, these two factors were interconnected. The credibility of leftist figures was boosted by their sustenance of the quotidian needs of the armed struggle and their tribal impartiality—most of them were distant from previous tribal conflicts and disdainful of them. Their ideas were made plausible by reference to other examples—most important of which was nearby South Yemen— and by means of vernacularization, the translation of concepts from the elite language of philosophy to the daily language of the people.

The latter was absolutely necessary. For instance, class struggle, a complex dialectical concept, had to be presented as a matter of common sense with the proletariat and poor peasants standing for the destitute Dhufaris, and the bourgeoisie and imperialism representing their privileged monarchical and British enemies. Consider for example this speech by a Dhufari leader:

> The Sultans and the Shaikhs are selling us to the imperialists. They live in palaces with air-conditioning—these are machines that give cold air even when it is hot...And what falls to our lot is mud, work performed by the sweat of our brow, and humiliation. But we are not slaves, and we have risen in rebellion. Our future is bright, the future when nobody will live at the expense of others and power will belong to the people. Our children will go to school. Doctors will come to our huts. Our oil will help the people to prosper. We shall follow along the road pointed to us by the October revolution in Russia, discovered by the great Lenin.[19]

[19] Quoted in Alexei Vassiliev, *Russian Policy in the Middle East: From Messianism to Pragmatism*, Reading: Ithaca Press, 1993, p.vii.

In simple and concise terms, the speech packed the notions of class struggle, the Manichaeism of colonialism, the *comprador* leader mediating
between imperialism and the toiling people, the technological benefits of
modernity, popular sovereignty and economic development—contrasting
current actualities with the possibilities furnished by 1917.

The fascinating reality in Dhufar was that the concepts being transmitted had in fact undergone double vernacularization. Even the most politicized and educated cadres were not exposed to the Marxist *corpus* in any
serious way. They had received their concepts second hand from deriva-
tive Arabic sources or from Chairman Mao, a master of vernacularization
in his own right.[20] This had two effects: the loss of the original specificity
of concepts; and extreme ideological fluidity. This helps to explain the
constant and rapid ideological changes that were reflected in the Dhufari
struggle, the easy and fluid movement from one theory to another, from
one language of struggle to another. There is nothing specifically Dhufari
about this, and it should not be judged solely as a matter of misreading or
misinterpretation. Indeed, even in the most sanitized, abstract and sophisticated contexts, the travel of theory occasions a process of transformation
and localization.[21]

What mattered at the end of the day were practical applications, especially in relation to the question of organization. The organizational dilemmas of the past were approached in pathological terms and the Hamrin
conference resolved that the Dhufari revolution had previously existed in a
'sick atmosphere'. It was argued that the 'Arab revolution on its march for
liberation' had been accompanied by 'hazy thought'. Leading it, were
'bourgeois class forces...that represented, due to their class and ideological
composition, mercurial middle of the road positions'.[22] These illnesses of
ideological obscurantism and political compromise encompassed the old
DLF leadership, mostly filled with Dhufarist and tribalist elements. The
establishment of a healthy atmosphere required complete change. Thus,
out of the eighteen old leaders of the DLF, only three were re-elected
(Mohammad al-Ghassani, Ahmad Fareh, and Salim Musslam). The new
General Command drew on the ranks of leftist students, Dhufaris active

---

[20] For the role of vernacularization in Mao's thought, see Arif Dirlik, 'Mao Zedong
and "Chinese" Marxism', in Makdisi, Casarino and Karl (eds.), *Marxism Beyond Marxism*,
New York and London: Routledge, 1996, p.123.

[21] For an extensive theoretical discussion of this question see the essays 'Travelling
Theory' and 'Travelling Theory Reconsidered' in Edward Said, *The World, the Text and the
Critic*, Cambridge: Harvard University Press, 1983, and *Reflections on Exile and Other
Essays*, Cambridge: Harvard University Press, 2000.

[22] Al-Jabha al-Shabiya, 'Qararat Mutamar Hamrain', in *Wathaiq al Nidal al Watani:
1965–1974*, p.11.

in the Kuwaiti branch of the PRM as well as local military commanders.[23] These were divided into five committees: executive; political; military; economic; and organizational. Each committee had a chair, and all chairs served on the executive committee. The background of the three cadres holding the most sensitive chairs, outlined in Appendix II, serves to illustrate the extent to which the former MAN elements had consolidated their role in the revolution.

The executive committee was controlled by members belonging to the new intelligentsia that had emerged in the Gulf after the spread of capitalism and education to that region. It was the highest decision-making body within the General Command, and other committees were expected to report to it.[24] Initially, the committees used to meet when necessary. They later began to have weekly meetings but these were never held in a set location and the committees remained mobile. Occasionally, a quorum was not achieved due to military conditions or difficulties of travel. Nevertheless, the principle of 'collective leadership' was generally upheld and the reporting process was committed to within the limitations of the field conditions.[25]

On the military front, the Hamrin conference led to a major overhaul, undoubtedly influenced by Chinese ideas. Mao had famously declared that 'without a people's army, the people have nothing' and PFLOAG sought to create such an army. In accordance with Maoism, the most important feature of a people's army was the role of politics: '[a people's army] does not rely purely on weapons and technique, it relies mainly on politics, on the proletarian revolutionary consciousness and courage of the commanders and fighters, on the support and backing of the masses'. By its nature as a political force, a people's army could maintain a high degree of morale, a will to struggle, and a great deal of cohesion even under the most trying of circumstances.[26]

In the hope of achieving such cohesion, the former Dhufar Liberation Army was renamed the 'Popular Liberation Army' (PLA).[27] This corresponded to the re-characterization of the struggle from one of Dhufari

---

[23] Abdel Nabi Al-Ikri, *Al-Tanthimat al-Yassariya fil Jazeera wal Khaleej al 'Arabi*, Beirut: Dar al-Kunouz al-Adabyya, 2003, p. 98. The exact size of the General Command is difficult to ascertain. This is due to the fact that there was no set number of seats, the numbers and composition shifting in different periods. Accordingly, some sources state that the number was as high as 25, whereas others put it at 21.

[24] Al-Ikri, *Al-Tanthimat al-Yassariya fil Jazeera wal Khaleej al 'Arabi*, p.100.

[25] Interview F.

[26] Lin Biao, *Long Live the Victory of People's War!*, Peking: Foreign Languages Press, 1965.

[27] The old name was used in DLF military communiqués: see 'Jabhat Tahrir Thufar, al Balag'at al Askaria', Private Papers of Abdel Rahman Nua'imi.

liberation to a people's war that was not confined to Dhufar. The PLA represented the professional force of fighters, solely dedicated to armed struggle. Along with cadres of other PFLOAG divisions, all of the fighters received equal pay. Each area was led by a regional company commander and every one of these sat on the military committee of the PFLOAG General Command. Several sources claim that in addition to the three operational areas—eastern, central and western—into which Dhufar had previously been divided by the DLF, PFLOAG added the fourth zone of al-Mamar (the passage) right after the Hamrin conference.[28] This claim is open to doubt. According to a cadre that arrived in Dhufar in mid-1969, there were only three operational areas at the time of his arrival.[29] Similarly, army reports from January 1970 document that PFLOAF forces 'operate in three main groups. West, Central and East', estimating their respective numbers at 600, 200, and 200 fighters.[30] Nevertheless, this new zone was definitely established by mid-1970, having immense strategic value as the main PFLOAG supply line connecting the western mountains with the central ones. Soon after its establishment, it was renamed as 'Ho Chi Minh', to honour the memory of the revered Vietnamese leader and to further connect the struggle to contemporary anti-colonialism.[31]

Between 1968 and 1970, the military structure was developed further. The four regional companies (*Firaq*) were divided into platoons (*Kataib*), and the platoons were divided into sections (*Hatha'er*). A fifth mobile company (*Al Firqa al-Mutaharika*) was later added, so as to aid PLA companies in situations of intense combat.[32] Subsequent additions were the transportation division, which was responsible for arranging supplies, and the communications division, which was responsible for coordinating communications (by 1970, each platoon had a wireless officer using British Racal RA17 sets). Thus, the PLA came to be comprised of the five companies, the transportation and communications divisions as well as the Revolution Camp.[33]

The latter was a training facility formed in late 1968 to raise fighting capability, located between al-Gaitha and Hawf in the sixth governorate of South Yemen. Courses lasted between six and eight months, after which cadres were sent to the PLA. The camp provided political and literacy training as part of its curriculum. This was an implementation of the decision undertaken at Hamrin to develop the PLA towards becoming a 'political fighting

[28] See for example, Al-Amri, *Thufar*, p. 106.
[29] Interview E(ii).
[30] KCL-Thwaites. Box 1, File 2, 'Dhufar Ops', January 1970.
[31] This area is often referred to as 'Ho Chi' to this very day.
[32] Amongst the leaders of that company were Omar Jamida and Sa'id Ali Qatan.
[33] Interview D(ii).

force'.[34] The politicization of the PLA was also undertaken by means of allocating political commissars to the companies and platoons. The trainers in the camp and the commissars were initially drawn from a group of 10 Dhufaris who were sent immediately after the Hamrin conference for a military and political course in China.[35] Their appointment had profound effects on PFLOAG's structure and ideology since they consistently held the most radical views and assumed sensitive positions in the leadership. In the field, they had considerable authority and usually worked closely with the military commanders. In the Revolution Camp, they had full control. By 1970, the Camp was run by five commissars under the direction of Omar bin-Jamida. However, the real holder of influence within it was Abdel Aziz al-Qadi, the young fiery cadre having arrived from Cairo. Through his position in the Camp, al-Qadi had a very broad level of interaction with most PLA cadres. As will be shown later, this was to be the springboard which propelled him to the future leadership of the struggle.

In order to 'create a base upon which the Liberation Army could depend', the Hamrin conference established the Popular Militia, composed of citizens living in each area.[36] This was an attempt to translate the notions of popular line (*khat Jamaheeri*) and people's war ('*harb al Sha'b*) into practice, these notions—with strong Chinese and Vietnamese undercurrents—having acquired great prestige in the post-1967 *naksa* period. As well as carrying on with their normal everyday activities, citizens involved in the militia conducted logistical tasks such as scoping and observation, gathering intelligence and aiding in the transportation and distribution of supplies. Unlike the fighters of the PLA, these citizens were a stationary force that did not move beyond local villages and settlements. They were moreover less well equipped, initially armed with Simonovs and later acquiring some Kalashnikovs. In times of high military alert, they were mobilized to fight with the PLA.[37]

THE BATTLE FOR SOCIETY

As well as these military reforms, radical developments were also introduced at the social level. Amongst these, the assault on tribalism was prioritized. This was in light of the analysis—clearly expressed in the

---

[34] Al-Jabha al-Shabiya, *Shahadat Min al Manatiq al Muharara*, February 1973, p.10.

[35] Behbehani, *China's Foreign Policy in the Arab World, 1955–75*, p. 177, and Trabulsi, *Thufar*, p.121.

[36] Al-Jabha al-Shabiya, *Shahadat Min al Manatiq al Muharara*, p.10.

[37] Interview D(ii).

PFLOAG Charter—that viewed the tribal structure as a divisive presence in society retarding the anti-colonial battle. It was also a response to tribalism's perceived nature as an obstacle to the development of new economic and social relations. Amongst the revolutionary vanguard, the nationalist impulse for the creation of a whole out of fragments—the patching of a society out of tribes—was present and so was the will for socialist modernization. This reflected a global pattern described by Fanon:

> ...the leaders of the rising realise that the various groups must be enlightened; that they must be educated and indoctrinated, and that an army and a central authority must be created. The scattering of the nation, which is the manifestation of a nation in arms, needs to be corrected and to become a thing of the past. Those leaders...rediscover politics...as the only method of intensifying the struggle and of preparing the people to undertake the governing of their country clearly and lucidly...These leaders are led to renounce the movement in so far as it can be termed a peasant revolt, and to transform it into a revolutionary war.[38]

On an immediate and pressing level there was a basic contradiction between two political modes of organization: the popular structure mobilizing all of Dhufari society (PFLOAG); and the tribal structure organizing the people along lines of lineage. This contradiction had practical implications. For the armed struggle to succeed, it had to have a monopoly on violence in the areas it controlled. For the social struggle to be victorious, it required final authority and the ability to implement decisions. In other words, the revolution, in the name of citizenship, had to rise above the tribes.

The tribal structure, as shown in the previous chapter, was bypassed by the creation of Dhufari organizations culminating in the DLF. That represented the emergence of a mode of political action outside the tribe. Nevertheless, although the tribes were effectively incorporated into the struggle, they remained in existence and the contradiction between Front and tribe continued to grow. At least some sheikhs had an uneasy relationship with the revolution. As early as 1966, a number of them had met with the Sultanate's senior intelligence officer. They stated that they were 'tired of the rebels' and that they could pull people out of the conflict if they were offered reasonable terms.[39] Sultan Sa'id bin Taimur rejected the offer, thus undermining the ability of the sheikhs to counter the revolution. With the rise of PFLOAG, the sheikhs' position deteriorated even

---

[38] Franz Fanon, *The Wretched of the Earth*, London: Penguin, 2001, p.108.
[39] FO 1016/765, Carden (Muscat) to Balfour-Paul (Bahrain), 29 September 1966.

further. The reins of economic and military power were held firmly by the revolutionary leadership, separated from the elders by an enormous intellectual and age gap. Furthermore, PFLOAG was openly hostile to the sheikhs' authority. Over the following years of struggle it had managed to seriously undermine it and by the end of the armed struggle in 1976, a British report noted that the revolutionaries 'went some way to break down...tribalism, and many of the jebali sheikhs have disappeared'.[40] Nevertheless, this was not an immediate process. It was a phenomenon that developed over time and that produced its own contradictions.

One of the peculiarities of the Dhufari social structure was the extreme extent to which tribes were fragmented into a multitude of sections and subsections. Thus, compared to their immensely powerful counterparts in northern Oman and in other parts of the Arabian Peninsula, the Dhufari sheikhs had relatively limited influence, commanding only a small number of men within a narrow area. This was an asset for the revolutionaries and a disadvantage for the British and the Sultan who lamented the relative weakness of tribalism, a traditional instrument of British policy in the Gulf: 'what distinguishes Dhofar from Oman and makes the political settlement of the area so difficult is the splintered tribal situation and the absence of influential tribal figures'.[41]

This cause of Anglo-Sultanic weakness was a source of strength for PFLOAG. The Hamrin conference passed a policy of ending all tribal feuds over land and water and banning revenge attacks. It decreed that all vendettas prior to the conference were to be resolved by financial settlements. Should any murders occur following the conference, punishment would be handled by PFLOAG, which would impose the death penalty on anyone convicted. In order to enforce the new rules, the Hamrin conference established *Lijan 'Hal Mashakil al-Sha'ab*, the Committees for the Resolution of the People's Problems. The Western, Central, and Eastern Areas were each accorded a committee comprised of five members appointed by the General Command. The committees were essentially mobile courts 'responsible for judging all non-military violations'.[42] Their creation represented the transference of civil authority from the realm of the tribe to the leadership of the revolution.

In 1969, PFLOAG went further by establishing three agricultural committees. These declared an end to tribal ownership of land and water and the limited agricultural activity that had been practised in the highlands

[40] FCO 8/2707, 'Muscat to FCO', 9 August 1976.
[41] FCO 51/41, 'Balfour-Paul (Bahrain) to Ford (FO Joint Research Department)', 6 December 1967.
[42] Trabulsi, *Thufar*, p. 156.

was now organized by cooperatives. Farming was still undertaken by the tribal subsections and largely consumed within the villages. As for the surplus, it was purchased by PFLOAG, which paid the cooperatives in cash.[43] In order to increase agricultural production, the revolutionaries encouraged sedentism. But this was met with resistance, largely deriving from the traditional tribal disdain for manual labour and preference for herding.[44]

Other holes were poked by PFLOAG's decrees on personal status matters. These pertained in particular to women's issues. The National Charter had addressed the question of women's liberation in the following terms:

> In our country, woman lives a difficult existence. For, she is still imprisoned by the reactionary laws and the worn out customs that do not accord her any human rights. Accordingly, the reintroduction of the rights of woman and her placing on an equal footing with man in rights, duties and social status is a necessity for social justice and the development of human society, so that woman could become a living productive agent in the progressive socialist society.[45]

The Hamrin conference emphasized that 'the extent to which the movement is revolutionary is measured by its view and conception of women'.[46] Precisely because of its audacity, its violation of all previous limits, the liberation of women was the ultimate test of a movement's will to negate the status quo and supersede it with a 'higher' stage of development.

Like others in the colonial world, it was patriotism that brought Dhufari revolutionaries to Marxism-Leninism.[47] However, their acceptance of its precepts and intellectual foundations opened up other arenas of struggle for them, including the fight for women's equality. This derived from the character of Marxist theory as a method of thought that aims 'at a new form of society even when describing its current form … [it] is a "critique" in the sense that all concepts are an indictment of the totality of the existing order'.[48]

In the light of the prevailing Marxist view of women's issues, PFLOAG's publications argued that women underwent double oppression in Gulf

---

[43] Trabulsi, *Thufar,* p.155.

[44] Halliday, *Arabia Without Sultans,* p.382.

[45] 'Al-Mithaq al-Watani Lil Jabha al-Shabiya', in Trabulsi, *Thufar',* p.247.

[46] Munathamat al Mara'a al-Omania, *Musahamat al Mara'a al-Omania fil Haya al Ijtima'ia wal Istiqlal al-Siyasi,* Manshurat Munathamat al Mara'a al-Omania, 1978, p.17.

[47] This was an experience of many anti-colonial Marxists. See for example Ho Chi Minh, 'The Path Which Led me to Leninism'. Ho Chi Minh Internet Archive (marxists.org), 2003.

[48] Herbert Marcuse, *Reason and Revolution, Hegel and the Rise of Social Theory,* Boston: Beacon Press, 1968, p.258.

society. They were dually oppressed as members of the working class and as women.[49] This serves to illuminate the theoretical commitment to women's liberation. Yet, what were women being liberated from? What was their condition in Dhufari society?

In certain respects, Dhufari women had advantages that were not shared in many other parts of the Gulf. In the highlands, they could divorce with relative ease and remarry without stigma:

> If they are incompatible at the beginning, the father [of the bride] returns the bride-price and they go their separate ways. If in later life they decide to divorce, then it is done at no cost. However, if it is she who wants to remarry, then the lover must pay the bride-price to the aggrieved husband. If the divorce is at his insistence, her family will try to dissuade him, but he has the final say. If there are children involved, then the young ones go with the mother and the father pays maintenance. Older children are allowed to choose who to stay with.[50]

Women participated in work and were not socially segregated. They were allowed to smoke (although rarely did so) and could travel without a male companion. As for their dress code, they did not usually cover their faces with the *burgu'*. They wore black *thawbs* 'with a square hole in the top for the head and a hole in each side at the top for the arms,' and loosely covered their heads 'with brightly coloured shawls called *Loosi*'.[51] Although they did not formally take part in tribal meetings—where the men sat on the ground in an open circle, each having a right to speak—they often played an indirect role, congregating 'within earshot' and shouting 'comments from time to time'.[52]

PFLOAG's analysis of this relatively advantaged status of Dhufari women was grounded in an economistic conception of gender relations, clearly influenced by the Englesian view propagated in *The Origin of the Family* and still extremely influential in Marxist analyses of gender relations. In this sort of analysis 'economic causality takes precedence, and patriarchy always develops and changes as a function of relations of production'.[53] In an official PFLOAG article published in 1970, it was noted that four economic characteristics shaped the position of women in the Dhufari highlands: low productivity; absence of the gender segregation in

---

[49] Al-Jabha al-Shabiya, 'Al Mara'a wal Thawra fil Khaleej', *9 Yunyu*, No. 3, August 1970; Gulf Committee, *Women and the Revolution in Oman*, London: Gulf Committee, 1975, pp.27–36.

[50] MEC, Sichel 1/1, 'Sultanate of Oman Demographic Survey, Dhofar 1977'. p.3.

[51] MEC, Sichel 1/1, 'Sultanate of Oman Demographic Survey, Dhofar 1977'. p.1.

[52] MEC, Sichel 1/1, 'Sultanate of Oman Demographic Survey, Dhofar 1977'. p.12.

[53] Joan Scott, 'Gender: A Useful Category of Historical Analysis', *The American Historical Review*, Vol 91, No. 5, December 1986, p.1059.

economic production; the retention of features of a classless society such as common ownership; and women's ability to have economic control within the family.[54] In contrast, whatever oppression existed in the rest of Dhufar and the Gulf was argued to be connected to more developed relations of production, gender oppression paralleling class oppression. 'This conclusion is compatible with and confirms the correctness of the Marxist analysis according to which the oppression of women and the deterioration of their position are a result of the development of the division of labour, and of private property'.[55]

Nevertheless, Dhufar was not completely insulated from its wider environment, and PFLOAG argued that both class and gender oppression in Dhufar derived from the interrelations between Dhufar's 'rural society and the society that surrounds it'.[56] Thus, women were required to serve their parents and families, polygamy was undertaken by the few men that could afford it, and inheritance was unequal. This PFLOAG view blaming Dhufari gender oppression on external influences was not entirely accurate, for there were several patriarchal practices particular to Dhufar: female circumcision was practiced; a half-inch-wide strip of skin was removed from female scalps from front to back in the centre, forming an aesthetic feature that was called *Minzarot*; and caste restrictions and dowry requirements were set on marriage. The latter were intimately connected to the maintenance of a form of social stratification that was arguably more severe than in other parts of the region.

Like most Dhufaris, women lacked the benefit of education but, unlike some of their male counterparts, they did not have the prospect of travelling abroad for work and accessing foreign schooling.[57] Accordingly, whereas roughly 5 per cent of men had basic literacy, not a single woman could read and write.[58] As for the armed struggle, women had so far largely played a supporting role, aiding and feeding the male fighters. On the combat lines, there were hardly any female fighters in the pre-1968 era. The only one whose memory survived the DLF era was the epically named Qamar al-Jazeera (Peninsular Moon), who had reportedly joined the struggle in early 1966 and of whom we know next to nothing.[59]

Whereas PFLOAG took an absolute theoretical position on women's liberation, its practical translation was gradual and partial. This was out of fear of alienating the population. No matter how trenchant, theoretical

---

[54] Al-Jabha al-Shabiya, 'Al Mara'a wal Thawra fil Khaleej'.
[55] Al-Jabha al-Shabiya, 'Al Mara'a wal Thawra fil Khaleej'.
[56] Al-Jabha al-Shabiya, 'Al Mara'a wal Thawra fil Khaleej'.
[57] Halliday, *Arabia Without Sultans*, p.377.
[58] Al-Jabha al-Shabiya, *Shahadat Min al Manatiq al Muharara*, p.33.
[59] Trabulsi, *Thufar*, p.146.

will was incapable of completely transforming age-old social relations within a few years. Thus, revolutionary policies on women's liberation were sometimes faced with resistance. Following the Sultanate victory, many of them were abandoned and reversed with ease. Nevertheless, they are worthy of examination. Shortly after the Hamrin conference, PFLOAG banned polygamy and female circumcision. It further equalized divorce practices and allowed inter-caste marriages. In 1970, it regularized dowries, reducing them to a set token-price.[60] Although there were demands from women revolutionaries for the complete cancellation of the dowry system, this was not undertaken. Equality of inheritance was also introduced but it attracted widespread protest and it was accordingly reversed. At any rate, PFLOAG found great difficulty in its enforcement.[61] At the military level, the doors of the PLA and the militia were opened for women and a special camp was established for them. We have no accurate figures on their participation in the PLA. Some accounts place it at 5 per cent and others estimate that it was up to 30 per cent.[62] In the militia, the percentage was significantly higher. Equally important was the realm of education, where PFLOAG's compulsory education policy was applied to women. By 1973, 350 out of the 1,000 students in its school were girls.[63] The girls lived in separate quarters from the boys but attended classes and military training with them.

As for slavery, it was highlighted by the PFLOAG National Charter as an issue that required immediate revolutionary action:

> ...the imperialists, feudalists and all reactionaries in the occupied Arab Gulf had practiced the slave trade, violating human dignity. This has resulted in confining a large number of our oppressed people under the shadow of enslavement. The revolution, out of its noble principles of freeing the toiling masses of all forms of oppression and exploitation severely condemns this inhuman act, and commits to its complete and radical eradication.[64]

Thus, abolition was declared by the revolution in all the liberated areas. The decision was strongly enforced and slavery was completely eradicated. This was aided by the lack of opposition on the popular level. The percentage of slaves in the highlands was small to begin with (most were owned by the Sultan on the coast) and the decision did not accordingly disrupt economic activity in any profound way. Furthermore, there was general religiously motivated sympathy with the notion of abolition and

---

[60] Halliday, *Arabia Without Sultans*, p. 380.
[61] Interview F.
[62] The first figure is taken from Interview F. The second is derived from Abdel Rahman Al-Nuaimi, 'Tarteeb al Bait al Hizbawi wal Jabhawi', *Al-Dimuqrati*, Vol. 33, 2006.
[63] Al-Jabha al-Shabiya, *Shahadat Min al Manatiq al Muharara*. February 1973, p.33.
[64] 'Al-Mithaq al-Watani Lil Jabha al-Shabiya', in Trabulsi, *Thufar*, p.246.

there was sensitivity to the question due to the presence of former slaves in the leadership and rank and file of the struggle.[65] One of the most prominent was Rajab Jam'an, a former slave of the Sultan who became a member of the PFLOAG General Command.[66]

Viewed from a broader historical perspective, PFLOAG's social policies represented the first arrival of the twin notions of 'society' and 'development' to Dhufar. In certain respects, PFLOAG acquired some basic attributes of an embryonic republican mini-state: establishing a revolutionary leadership that saw itself as representing popular sovereignty; viewing revolutionary territory as an indivisible unit in which a single law prevailed over a conceived social whole; establishing a 'people's army' and acquiring with it an internal monopoly on violence; organizing production and providing basic services.

REVOLUTIONARY PORTRAITS

By declaring itself as a force for the liberation of the Gulf as a whole, the Dhufari struggle came to be seen as belonging to all revolutionaries in the region. This was at least the case for the leftist offshoots of the former MAN (the Ba'ath was still potentially hostile, as was seen in Salah Jadid's rounding up of Dhufaris in Syria in 1969).[67] Leftist regional recognition of this status was confirmed by the featuring of Dhufar on the front page of *al-Hurriya* on 16 December 1968. As the only Gulf armed struggle at the time, it gave support to, and was supported by, surrounding radical forces. In December 1968, two members of the PRM Central Committee, Ahmad Humaidan and Yahya al-Ghassani (Harib), visited Aden. They met with Salim al-Ghassani, chair of the PFLOAG political committee and head of its Aden office. Their talks were centred on expanding the revolution to the Gulf, beginning with Oman proper. Subsequently, PFLOAG provided training for a dozen PRM members (including seven northern Omanis) in the Revolution Camp in Hawf.[68]

Following the Hamrin conference, PFLOAG was in desperate need of cadres who could fulfil political roles requiring a high level of education. Thus, it turned to Gulf students, mostly those belonging to the PRM. The first two to arrive were Laila Fakhro (Huda Salem) and Abdel Muni'm

[65] Interview F.
[66] Interview E(i).
[67] Abdel Rahman Al-Nuaimi, 'Adan wa Ahlam al Qaramita al Judud', *Al-Wasat*, 13 November 2008.
[68] MEC, Graham, 'The National Democratic Front for the Liberation of Oman and the Arabian Gulf'. SAF Intelligence, 3 March 1971.

al-Shirawi (Jihad Salim Ali) from Bahrain. The former was born into one of the richest merchant families in the city of Muharaq. This exceptional woman, 'flaming with beauty and youth', became politically active in her high school days, helping to found the first Bahraini feminist organization. Following graduation, she travelled to Beirut, reading Mathematics at the American University and becoming active in the Gulf student branch of the MAN (which later became the PRM). Having heard from Dhufaris of the revolution's needs, she interrupted her studies and headed for Aden in September 1969.[69] A year or so later, her sister Buthaina followed in her footsteps.

Educated and politically commited, Laila was appointed the women's political commissar in the Revolution Camp. She thereafter played a pioneering role in numerous spheres: education; orphan care; language teaching; women's organizing; revolutionary media; and foreign relations. Like any effective revolutionary cadre, Laila tailored solutions to the needs of her situation. In an armed struggle like that of Dhufar, there were growing numbers of orphans. Many parents were away at the fighting front and there was much concern for children's safety as a result of the regular airstrikes and bombing. Above all, there was an entire population that had never known literacy.[70] In response to these challenges, Laila established the People's School (Madrasat al-Sha'b) on 1 April 1970 in the Yemeni area of Marara, close to the border with Dhufar. Initial enrolment was 60 students, mostly orphaned during the war.[71]

Knowing only her *nom de guerre*, and many having no parent other than her, these children referred to her as 'Mama Huda'. To give them a modern education, Laila handwrote the curriculum for every subject, South Yemeni textbooks being inadequate. She was supported in teaching by four locally educated Dhufari aides and later by the pupils themselves. The latter were taught and lodged in tents and were collectively involved in the daily chores of cooking, wood gathering, and guarding. This was the tiny nucleus of what effectively became a national education project, staffed by revolutionary teachers from across the region and graduating the first generation of literate Dhufaris. Many of these were subsequently sent on scholarships to various Arab and Socialist states, and can now be found in all walks of Omani life. To this very day, they proudly refer to themselves as *Eyal Huda* (Huda's children).[72]

[69] Basima Al-Qassab, 'Laila Fakhro, Mama Huda: An Takuna Mualiman Qadiran ala al-Jura'a'. *Al Waqt* (Bahrain), Issue No. 682, 3 January 2008.
[70] Al-Qassab, 'Laila Fakhro, Mama Huda'.
[71] Al-Jabha al-Shabiya, *Shahadat Min al Manatiq al Muharara*, p.33.
[72] Al-Qassab, 'Laila Fakhro, Mama Huda'.

In the Revolution Camp, Laila was responsible for the political and educational training of young women. She played a central role in translating PFLOAG's theoretical commitment to women's liberation into practice. She launched a campaign against female circumcision and she succeeded in getting PFLOAG to ban it. She also campaigned tirelessly against early marriage, which was widely practised in Dhufar at the time.[73] Along with the other fighters in the women's platoon, she was behind the assault against the dowry, failing to ban it but succeeding in limiting it, as was shown earlier.

Initially, such was the lack of educated cadres that there was hardly any scope for specialization. Multiple roles were often filled simultaneously. For instance, Laila became involved in media work after she was approached by the Bahraini leader, Abdel Rahman al-Nuaimi, with the idea of starting a regular publication for PFLOAG. Liaising with al-Nuaimi and Salim al-Ghassani, she worked tirelessly on that project, editing what came to be the first issue of *9th of June*, the revolution's official magazine. The magazine was typewritten, stencil printed, and distributed in 500 copies during a popular celebration held in Aden on 9 June 1970, the 5th anniversary of the revolution. The first few issues continued to be printed in the same primitive way. They then began to be produced with the 1940s machines of al-Hath printing house in Crater, Aden. Eventually, a professional Bahraini journalist and PRM cadre, Ibrahim al-Bashmi, took over and the magazine was thereafter published in advanced format in Beirut.[74]

Since her youth, Laila had suffered from weak lungs. Her condition substantially worsened after spending two difficult years living in the easternmost areas of Yemen and the Western Area of Dhufar, subsisting on one meagre meal a day and sleeping—like the other cadres—in tents and caves. By 1972, she was affected by a severe lung disease and she left her work in the Revolution Camp and the school to go to Aden.[75] After being hospitalized there, she joined PFLOAG's Political Office and began to work in foreign relations. In 1973, she represented Oman at the International Women's Conference in Moscow. She was also the engine behind the founding of the Omani Women's Organization (OWO). Aside from Omani women's groups in East Africa, this was the first organization of its kind, striving to organize women and represent them at home and abroad

---

[73] Al-Qassab, 'Laila Fakhro, Mama Huda'.
[74] Al-Nuaimi, 'Adan wa Ahlam al Qaramita al Judud'.
[75] Laila eventually died in 2006 as a result of complications arising from the disease she developed during the Dhufari struggle.

as part of a broader revolutionary framework.[76] In the same year of the OWO's founding, 1974, Laila left Aden to work in PFLOAG's office in Baghdad, remaining in exile and living in various countries until Bahrain issued a general amnesty in 2001.[77]

Roughly around the same time as Laila, PFLOAG was joined by Abdel Munim. He came from a relatively prosperous but militantly patriotic family. His father, Mohammad al-Shirawi, was one of the pillars of *Haia't al-Itihad al-Watani*, which had led the Bahraini struggle against the British in 1954–56.[78] True to this family tradition, he joined the MAN Bahrain branch as an eleventh grader in 1963. In August 1964 he was imprisoned, soon after finishing his leaving exams. He was released in 1966 and headed immediately for Cairo, where he enrolled as a medical student and continued his political work in MAN Gulf student circles. There, he was directly recruited into PFLOAG by Ahmad Abdel Samad, who had arrived as the new head of the Cairo office, replacing Yousif Alawi in late 1968 or early 1969. It was arranged for Abdel Muni'm to travel to Aden along with a number of Dhufaris coming from Kuwait and a few Cairo students.[79] Upon its arrival in Aden, the group underwent a two-day crash training course and Abdel Munim was subsequently sent to the Eastern Area, where he was appointed as a political commissar, remaining there for a year. As part of his responsibilities, he conducted literacy classes and gave political advice, as well as delivering political seminars in the evening. His role extended beyond the PLA, interacting with the local militia and population, as well as liaising with clandestine PFLOAG cells on the coast, especially in the town of Taqa.[80]

PFLOAG also began to attract other volunteers. Following a campaign of arrests that had undermined its ranks, the Saudi Arabian Popular Democratic Party began to send cadres to train for guerrilla warfare, in the hope that these would return and wage armed struggle in the Kingdom. Amongst these was comrade Nayef, the first non-Dhufari freedom fighter to die on Dhufari soil.[81] This was the beginning of a trend whereby cadres afflicted by crises in their own countries came to fight in Dhufar. Upon their arrival in Aden, the first person to welcome all of these revolutionaries

---

[76] See Munathamat al-Mara'a al-Omania, *Dawr Munathamat al-Mara'a al-Omania fi Tateer Fa'alyaat al-Mara'a al-Omania*, Manshurat Munathamat al-Mara'a al-Omania, 1978.

[77] Al-Qasab, 'Laila Fakhro Al-Qassab, 'Laila Fakhro, Mama Huda'.

[78] Abdel Rahman Al-Nuaimi, 'Al-Bidayat', *Al-Dimuqrati*, Vol. 26, 2005.

[79] Including Ali al-Ruz, Sai'd Dablan and Nabil Mahad and Rashid Ali from Interior Oman.

[80] Interview E(i).

[81] Al-Nuaimi, 'Adan wa Ahlam al Qaramita al Judud'.

was Salim al-Ghassani (Talal Sa'ad), General Command member, chair of the political committee and head of the Aden office. This short and determined young man had enrolled in Kuwait University after it opened in 1966, studying English literature. While in his second year, he dropped out and returned to Dhufar. An avid reader with a reclusive streak, he was a revolutionary romantic, a type that had emerged with force in the late 1960s Arab world. Once asked by a journalist friend about his love life, Salim answered:

> At the time being, my love is the Kalashnikov and the homeland. I want to see the homeland free. The Kalashnikov is the factor of violence, the path to a free homeland. Later, I will search for a life partner who would not be distant from love. I loved a girl in university but now we're apart. Here I am in the Martyr Khantour Camp and she doesn't know...[82]

Like many of the fighters, Salim had left his personal life behind. From 1968 and for many years onwards, he was dedicated to PFLOAG work; heading its foreign relations, sending and receiving delegations, coordinating with revolutionary groups and countries, writing articles and conducting dozens of media interviews.

Salim's high sense of hope was shared by many a cadre. In spite of vigorous British attempts to collect intelligence, there was great difficulty in doing so, the morale of the fighters and their commitment being an impregnable obstacle. One such fighter was Ahmad Suheil Bait Qatan (Tarish). On 9 November 1969, and in a mine ambush prepared by Spike Powell—a Rhodesian mercenary who later fought and died for his colonial ideals under the Ian Smith regime—he was severely wounded and captured. Refused hospital treatment by the Sultan, the severely injured captive had his leg amputated by a dentist and an army General Practitioner. Following the operation, a British officer tried to interrogate him, reporting the following: 'this man—with most of his face blown away, one arm shattered, one leg off—spat at me. He was very tough and very brave. And even though he was completely at our mercy, we got no information off him.'[83] Such non-cooperation, even under extreme duress, was very common. The British described this as the effect of indoctrination: 'the few prisoners we did take either didn't know much or were too tough and indoctrinated to tell us anything'.[84] 'Indoctrination', in these cases, was nothing other than principled commitment.

---

[82] Al-Jinahi, pp. 75–6.
[83] KCL-Thwaites, Box 2/2, 'Lecture: Dhufar 1960–1970', n.d; see also Box 1/3, 'Peter Thwaites to Said bin Taimur', 31 December 1969.
[84] KCL-Thwaites, Box 2/2, 'Lecture: Dhufar 1960–1970'.

INITIATION INTO THE INTERNATIONAL
COMMUNITY OF REVOLUTION

Following the Hamrin conference, the profile of the Dhufari struggle was raised regionally and internationally. Just as the Dhufaris came to view themselves as part of a universal whole, they came to be internationally seen as a constituent part of a global movement. This had profound implications in the Cold War context. Nearly every political group was approached from a bipolar prism, categorized as an extension of the 'Eastern' or 'Western' blocs. This had various advantages. From 1968 onwards, Dhufar received greater attention from 'progressive countries' and solidarity groups. This raised more prospects for aid and media exposure. On the downside, it aided British efforts to subsume the Dhufari revolutionary war into cold war discourse.[85]

From 1969 onwards, Dhufar was featured on the world revolutionary map (if only as a small corner) and PFLOAG began to receive invitations to international anti-imperialist and communist conferences, unions, student gatherings, women's events and even film festivals. In these affairs, the Dhufari delegates represented and explained their unknown cause and extended requests for concrete solidarity. Initially, little support came. Indeed, in a speech delivered in the 1969 Anti-Imperialist Journalists Congress in Pyongyang, the Dhufari delegate stated: 'after four years of armed struggle and people's war, we are sorry that in the free progressive world only the PDRY and China understand and support our struggle'.[86] This situation was improved over the following years as the struggle continued, accumulating greater exposure, and developing stronger representative mechanisms. For now, however, Beijing was the only weighty capital giving a lift to Dhufar. Its backing progressed, especially after mutual familiarity was developed: the two Chinese observers that were sent to the Hamrin conference came back with favourable impressions of Dhufar; and the Dhufari training mission had returned home with solid allegiance to China.

Nevertheless, the Chinese support at this stage should not be exaggerated. It is all the more important to emphasize this in the light of the fact that in much of the popular literature, especially the memoirs of British servicemen, the fantastical notion of a grand communist plot to overrun the Gulf is often promoted. This was, of course, far from true, requiring

---

[85] FO/1016/790, 'Communist Involvement in Dhofar', D.C. Carden (Muscat), 28 December 1968.
[86] Behebehani, *China's Foreign Policy in the Arab World, 1955–75*, p.161.

much more support than China was willing or able to give. At the elaborate celebrations of the twentieth anniversary of the Chinese revolution, Dhufar did not even make it onto the honour-roll call of national liberation struggles.[87] Little known Dhufar was still a nascent untried member of the revolutionary community, the first extensive report on it appearing in the Chinese press in November 1969. The situation was significantly improved in 1970, when a PFLOAG delegation was invited to Beijing. The delegation, led by Salim al-Ghassani, stayed in China from 28 February to 3 April. After a month of touring, they received high-level attention, meeting Premier Zhou Enlai, Huang Yung-sheng (Chief of the General Staff) and Ji Peng-fei (Vice-Foreign Minister) on 2 April.[88] A few months after the delegation's visit, Dhufar's position was further boosted by the arrival of South Yemeni President Salmin on a state visit (1–13 August 1970). During that visit, South Yemen and China reaffirmed their commitment to the liberation struggle in the Gulf.[89]

One of the effects of the Chinese connection was that Maoism began to circulate more within PFLOAG, especially amongst the circles of political commissars and those exposed to their discourse, emanating from the Revolution Camp. Some of the commissars began to echo Chinese characterizations of the Soviet Union as a 'revisionist' power that had betrayed socialism, mirroring western capitalist imperialism in pursuing a 'social imperialist' policy.[90] In holding this view, they were undoubtedly influenced by the South Yemeni political atmosphere at the time. A leading PFLOAG figure from the period recalls that 'Salmin [the South Yemeni president] was of the opinion that the Soviet Union was a European state that had greedy ambitions. He considered that they were no different than the West, and that China, with its independent character, was right'.[91]

Nevertheless, PFLOAG publications avoided open criticism of the USSR.[92] In fact, great efforts were made to dispel any notion of subservience to China or adherence to its position *vis-à-vis* the USSR. For instance, the PFLOAG politbureau published a response to an article that appeared in the German magazine *Der Stern* following a visit of two of its journalists to Dhufar in 1969.[93] The article had claimed that the 'aim of the revolutionaries

[87] 'Speech by Chou En-Lai', *Peking Review*, vol. 12, no. 40, 3 October 1969, p.18.
[88] Behebehani, *China's Foreign Policy in the Arab World, 1955–75*, p.182.
[89] Behebehani, *China's Foreign Policy in the Arab World, 1955–75*, p.184.
[90] Interview E(i). For the Sino-Soviet rivalry, see Lorenz Luthi, *The Sino-Soviet Split: Cold War in the Communist World*, Princeton: Princeton University Press, 2008.
[91] Interview F.
[92] Behebehani, *China's Foreign Policy in the Arab World, 1955–75*, p. 161.
[93] The article was translated into English: Claude Deffarge and Gordian Troeller, 'Secret War Number Eleven', *Atlas*, vol. 5, no. 18, November 1969.

was to liberate the Gulf with Chinese arms'. PFLOAG answered that claim by stating that 'the national movement in the Gulf, including Dhufar, aims to liberate the region with any weapon, regardless of its source'. Additionally, in response to the claim that it accused the Soviet Union of supporting 'the national bourgeoisie against workers and peasants', PFLOAG responded by noting that 'we appreciate the position of the Soviet Union towards the official Arab liberation movement and we still do not say that the Soviet Union has left us out in the cold and we continue to approach it with hope'. To further clarify its lack of involvement in the ongoing Sino-Soviet conflict, PFLOAG stated: 'all socialist camp countries are our natural allies, just as they are natural allies of all democratic national liberation movements'.[94]

This statement should by no means be read as an appeal to the Soviets. What it did signify was the independence of the movement and its aspiration to avoid any embroilment in the socialist split. The sincerity of this 'non-aligned' position was evidenced by the reception of two representatives from the Soviet Committee for Solidarity with the Countries of Asia and Africa to Dhufar in 1969. One of them was *Pravda*'s Alexei Vassiliev. The other was a military intelligence officer. According to Vassiliev, the two were sent to Dhufar 'to see and understand what kind of organisation this People's Front is, whether it is genuine or merely a fiction, and then to recommend to the Central Committee of the Communist Party of the Soviet Union what to do'.[95] They listened to speeches and observed conditions, satisfied as to the reality of the movement, but were shocked by the 'primitiveness' of the territory (after all, the two were lodged in a hut, with cow hides covering the floor and sacks of grain hanging from the cross beams to protect against the rats). Upon their return to Moscow, a half page report about Dhufar was published in *Pravda*, and some support may have subsequently been sent to the movement.[96] However, there were no grand Soviet gestures at this moment. Dhufari 'primitiveness' could possibly explain this, the Soviets being famously adverse to any revolutionary 'adventurism' and calibrating their support for movements with a strict classification system.[97]

Changes occurred following the Soviet shocks in Sudan and Egypt, with the USSR diversifying its relationships in the Arab world and increas-

[94] al-Jabha al-Shabiya, 'Mulahathat 'Hawla Tahqeeq Majalat Stern', *al-Hurriya*, 22 September 1969.
[95] Vassiliev, *Russian Policy in the Middle East,* p.vii.
[96] *Pravda*, 29 September 1969.
[97] For the impact of classifications upon Soviet policies see Mohammad Haikal, *The Sphinx and the Commissar: The Rise and Fall of Soviet Influence in the Middle East*, London: Harper and Row, 1978.

ing its engagement with liberation movements. In that context, Dhufar began in 1971 to receive more coverage in the Soviet press, and a PFLOAG delegation was invited to Moscow for the first time in early September of that year.[98] Greater aid subsequently began to be received, but it did not by any means match the enormous western support given to the Sultanate. This illustrates the fact that the USSR had no intention of using Dhufar as a base from which to enter the Gulf. In Vassiliev's words:

> ... the Messianic component of Soviet policy in Arabia was far from imply-
> ing practical actions against the local monarchies that had demonstrated a
> high level of stability since the 1960s. Even Soviet support for the Dhufar
> rebels, including the supply of arms, was rendered on anti-British ('anti-
> imperialist') basis and did not imply any interference in Oman's domestic
> affairs.[99]

Indeed, the Soviets always kept an open door to the conservatives in the Gulf, seeking good relations with the newly independent states, including the United Arab Emirates, following British withdrawal in 1971.[100] That said, the minimal support received from the Soviets was much welcomed and it played a role in raising morale. Having initiated itself into the international community of revolution, PFLOAG could now threaten regimes with greater confidence. Conceptually, its revolutionary subjects relocated their struggle from regional to global history, now viewing themselves not just as agents in the realm of pan-Arabism but as partici-pants in the universal march of humanity. So grand was the vision and so small was Dhufar!

[98] Freedman, Robert O, *Soviet Policy Towards the Middle East Since 1970*, New York: Praeger Publishers, 1978, p.67.

[99] Vassiliev, *Russian Policy in the Middle East*, p.333.

[100] Freedman, p. 68. Under severe Western pressure, these relations never really devel-oped. The only Gulf state to have relations with the Soviet Union was Kuwait: Chookiat Panaspornprasit, *US-Kuwaiti Relations, 1961–1962*, London: Routledge, 2005, p.42.

6
Last Stand of the Raj

The historical course of the Dhufari revolutionary movement was not only shaped by the actions of its leaders and cadres, but also by the reactions of the Anglo-Sultanic structure it was fighting against. Likewise, transformations taking place within the Anglo-Sultanic sphere were crucially impacted by the revolution. The Sultanate was as an outpost of the Raj that had, remarkably, survived into the post-colonial era. Revolutionary activity was the primary pressure that was pushing that structure towards the brink, occasioning a conflict of political cultures between colonial conservatives (the Sultan and his British advisers) and colonial developmentalists (the British men on the spot, Shell, and regional neighbours). Due to revolutionary pressure, there was a growing British resolve to strengthen the army substantially, transforming it from an instrument of containment to an aggressive tool in pursuit of state building and the introduction of rentierist developmental strategies. In resisting these policies, the Sultan was on a collision course with his imperial patrons.

THE BRITISH COMMANDER AND THE SAF

An institution like the Sultan's Armed Forces (SAF) cannot be understood without reference to the individuals that staffed it as well as the structures of which it was composed. At the top of the pyramid was the position of Commander of the Sultan's Armed Forces (CSAF). In classic colonial fashion this was always filled by a Briton. It was not until 1985 that an Omani was appointed to it. For the first two years of the Dhufari revolutionary war, the Commander was Colonel Tony Lewis. In April 1967, he was replaced by Brigadier Corran Purdon, an Irishman who belonged to an Ulster military family. Examining the latter figure gives an insight into the bearers of imperial sovereignty.

Purdon's early childhood was spent in the colonial luxury of India.[1] The attitudes, values and practices acquired from his colonial-military upbringing were solidified and reinforced by his secondary socialization. He attended a well-known Irish public school, Campbell College, and spent his holidays in Anglo-Irish military homes. His role models were the young military students that he encountered. In addition to masculinity, he was attracted to the romance of empire and to the notion that British imperialism was a noble endeavour in the service of mankind: 'I was determined to be a soldier, and used to read all the books of that era extolling the manly virtues and the British Empire. Far from exploiting it, as modern day little Englanders would have our youth believe, men and women were proud to devote their lives to serving its peoples abroad.'[2]

This romantic view of empire was undoubtedly shaped by both intellectual and spiritual factors, deriving from Purdon's loyalist education and the set of imperial rituals with which he was surrounded. These included the 24 May celebrations of Empire Day, in which Purdon participated as a piper: 'The Union Flag would be hoisted to the top of [the] flagstaff and three cheers would be given for the King Emperor after the National Anthem.'[3]

True to his imperial romanticism, Purdon spent much of his latter life occupying other countries. He began his post-war career in Palestine. He then served in numerous colonies including Egypt, Hong Kong, Malaya, Cyprus and Borneo. In each of these locales, Purdon was sustained by the Manichaean outlook he had acquired during his childhood and schooling. The world was split between good and evil, pro-British and anti-British forces, his attitude towards colonial subjects vacillating between haughty paternalism towards 'friendly' natives and vehement dislike of 'hostile' ones. For instance, the Hong Kong Chinese were an object of praise, while the Egyptians were despised: 'after Egypt, with its surly hostile locals . . . it was heavenly to be among smiley friendly Chinese.'[4]

The most important imperial experiences that Purdon acquired were of counter-insurgency operations in Malaya and Borneo. This was a background he shared with many of his compatriots fighting in Dhufar. Just as the revolutionaries had sought to learn from the global experiences of anti-colonialists, the British officers reflected on their suppression of revolutions worldwide. The latter, of course, had the experiential advantage of

[1] Corran Purdon, *List the Bugle: Reminiscences of An Irish Soldier*, Antrim, Northern Ireland: Greystone Books, 1993, p.1.
[2] Purdon, *List the Bugle*, p.9.
[3] Purdon, *List the Bugle*, p.9.
[4] Purdon, *List the Bugle*, p.87.

having actually participated in diverse theatres of war. This small group of travelling imperialists, comprising a tiny proportion of humankind, effectively acted as the arm of imperial sovereignty and the implementers of its mission: the political engineering of entire regions of the globe and managing the transformation from the colonial to the post-colonial epochs.

Along with revolutionary thought and organization, the counter-revolutionary experience—personified in the life histories of British officers like Purdon—is a subtle historical thread that connects countries as distant and varied as Oman and Malaya. The histories of these locations may sometimes seem separate in the scholarly literature, but in the trajectory of Purdon and others they appear as one interconnected series of events unfolding, in a similar fashion and in universal sequence, across the breadth and length of the British Empire.

In theory, Purdon's new position as CSAF was under the full control of the Sultan. However, the reality was more complicated. After all, the ultimate loyalty of all CSAFs was to Britain. One of Purdon's predecessors described the situation as follows:

> The CSAF has…the doubtful pleasure of 'wearing two hats' i.e. he is the Sultan's commander and…at the same time he has to carry out certain aspects of HMG's policy. When, as has happened in the past, HMG's policy and the Sultan's do not see 'eye to eye' the CSAF is placed in a very awkward and embarrassing position.[5]

The CSAF was entrusted with four types of forces: the Sultan of Oman's Air Force (SOAF); the Coastal Patrol (CP; later renamed as the Sultan of Oman's Navy); the Oman Gendarmerie (OG); and the Armed Forces (SAF). All of these were stamped with the British seal. The SOAF was founded in March 1959 in a colonial context: the aftermath of the suppression of the al-Jabal al-Akhdar revolt. All of the air force staff, and most of its equipment, were British. Upon Purdon's arrival in 1967, the SOAF depended on four Provosts for offensive purposes. These were so old that they required replacement and, in 1968, an order was made for 12 Strikemasters, light attack aircraft marketed for counter-insurgency use. In March 1969, four of these aircraft were received.[6] The planes were serviced on contract by a British company, Airwork Limited, and flown by eight flight lieutenants on secondment from the RAF.[7]

The CP was a tiny force staffed by northern Omanis and commanded by Jeremy Raybould, a blond man who had impressed the racially minded Purdon with his Aryan features: 'a tall, barrel-chested, power-

---

[5] MEC-Smiley, Box 1 of 2, Smiley to Tinker, 12 November 1960.

[6] 'Sultanate Balance Sheet—First Quarter 1969', D.C. Carden, 14 April 1969, in *RO-4*, p.29.

[7] FCO 8/599, 'Annexe A to ACDS(OPS) 24/3', 14 May 1968.

fully built European. "The original Viking"..."[8] Initially, there was only one motorized dhow in his force, *Nasr al Bahr*. But, in June 1967, this was complemented by a second large dhow, the *Muntasir*. Each of these armed dhows could transport two infantry companies (one battalion between the two), and this made them pivotal to the functioning of operations in Dhufar, which was so far off from the army bases in northern Oman.[9]

While the SOAF monopolized the airspace and the CP patrolled the sea, the Oman Gendarmerie (OG) guarded the borders and frontiers. In the travelling colonial fashion typical of all Sultanate military institutions, this gendarmerie force was founded by Gurkha officers, and its leader retained the Gurkha title of 'Commandant'. All OG officers were British and most of them, if not all, had served in the colonial police services. Upon visiting them in their Sohar headquarters (unsurprisingly named Kashmir Lodge) Purdon was pleasantly struck by their vintage air, reminiscent of the bygone and much lamented Raj:

> They reminded me of those Empire-building, pith-helmeted types in pre-war Barney's Punchbowl Tobacco advertisements pictured strolling through exotic-looking bazaars. They wore dark blue berets with the SAF badge...blue, pre-war British Indian Army-type mazri shirts, web belts, neatly pressed Khaki slacks and sand-coloured suede desert boots.[10]

Like the Gendarmerie, the army itself retained many vestiges of the Raj. English was the language of command and even the rank titles were not 'Arabized'. Moreover, each commissioned rank was followed by the paternalistic designation of 'Sahib'.[11] With Captain, Major and Colonel Sahibs, Oman was a place where the European still retained an exalted position recognized in everyday native speech.

In order to ensure subservience to the British officers and loyalty to the Sultan, the Arab soldiers only belonged to selected loyalist tribes (such as the Hawasinah). This was a telling fact, for the recruitment patterns of armies are an important indicator of the character of a state and the degree to which it commands legitimacy and rests upon a strong base of support. In states functioning through the raw relations of domination, lacking the stability generated by Gramscian hegemony, armies tend to be selective, recruitment exclusively retained for certain groups viewed as 'loyal' and submissive to the ruler. This is especially the case in colonial contexts where collective identity forms the central criterion for recruitment.

[8] Purdon, *List the Bugle,* p.223.   [9] Purdon, *List the Bugle,* p.224.
[10] Purdon, *List the Bugle,* p.225.   [11] Purdon, *List the Bugle,* p.235.

Colonial-style hierarchies were cemented by the fact that commanding officers were British, while the soldiers were Baluch and northern Omani. Neither Arabs nor Baluch were allowed to have formal officer training or to hold any rank above Lieutenant.[12] Officers and soldiers were separate and unequal in all matters, receiving different treatment, lodging, feeding and payment. Even the law applied differently to the British and their colonial subalterns. Every five years, the Sultan and the Political Residency renewed an Exchange of Letters concerning jurisdiction over British personnel. Under this exchange, the Sultan periodically agreed to surrender to the Queen extra-territorial jurisdiction over British troops and seconded officers serving in his domain.[13]

Relations between the officers and soldiers were highly regulated. British officers were given a guide for dealing with their subordinates, steeped in racially premised content: 'These hints are aimed to assist you recognise the essential differences between yourselves, Arabs and Asians and the degree of flexibility required by you to teach the standards and discipline of the British army.'[14] Officers were taught that the 'basic difference' distinguishing them from their native and foreign mercenary underlings was temperament. Arabs and Asians were 'unaccustomed to routine habits', 'talk at length on matters' that seem trivial to Europeans, 'lack the power to concentrate for long periods', can achieve 'surprising' results if encouraged properly, superficially 'form their judgement on externals', require 'contented feeding', 'have a keen sense of humour and the ridiculous', copy their commanding officers, 'are willing and capable of hard work' especially if 'they realise they are doing it to benefit themselves', panic at unusual or new ideas, appreciate being taught games, 'tend to talk round the point of issue', and are 'by nature...excitable.'[15]

Every British officer was given this guide, which illustrates that Orientalism did not just spread in the realm of high culture and literature. Most crucially, it was an essential part of colonial military culture, where the relations of domination acquired an unmediated form. The British officer had to comprehend the nature of his oriental object of discipline, to be certain in his knowledge of this other. But rather than attempt to change it, he had to tame it, bend it to his will.

---

[12] John Graham, *Ponder Anew: Reflections on the Twentieth Century*, Staplehurst, Kent: Spellmount Publishers, 1999, p.315.

[13] FO 93/65/34, R.S. Crawford (PR Bahrain) to Said bin Taimur (Sultan of Muscat and Oman), 31 December 1961.

[14] KCL-Thwaites, Box 2, File 2, 'Guide to Officers and Junior Leaders in Commanding Troops in Oman', 30 June 1965.

[15] KCL-Thwaites, Box 2, File 2, 'Guide to Officers and Junior Leaders in Commanding Troops in Oman', 30 June 1965.

One way through which British will was imposed was by having a mix of Arabs and Baluch. Indeed, this situation produced some serious reflections by CSAF Purdon: 'I consider that our mixture of Arab and Baluch was a good one. I am not sure what the original reason for mixing the Regiments was but I suspect it was "divide and rule" with British officers commanding both Arab and Baluch soldiers.'[16] This assessment of the composition of the army was shared by the PFLOAG revolutionaries, one of whose central aims was to expel British officers. Motivated by the desire of inciting defections—as well as spreading anti-colonial education and propaganda, reducing SAF morale and expressing a class solidarity—they made efforts to reach out to the soldiers. In a leaflet distributed in January 1970 a direct appeal was made to the 'Poor Soldiers in the Mercenary Army':

> O, poor Arab and Baluch soldiers, you are fighting NOT for your own benefit, but for the benefit of the British and for the reactionary Al Busaid who are pushing you into this war which you are NOT able to win, because it is the war of the people... You are fighting against your brothers in faith and nationality. The tragedy... is caused by colonialist rule. You are poor like us... Our war is pointed to the chest of the British and to the reactionaries of Al Busaid and to all traitors but not against you... you are able to save yourselves if you surrender...[17]

Despite such appeals, the revolutionaries had no financial incentives to offer to the mercenaries. For the sake of making a living, many of these had journeyed from Pakistan to the Trucial States, waiting for hours under the burning sun in a desperate attempt to attract the attention of the SAF recruiting officer.[18] Moreover, the backgrounds of the soldiers were so various that it was virtually impossible for them to act in concord. In the estimation of the Sultan's military secretary:

> ...it would be extremely difficult for anyone to subvert the bulk of S.A.F. without the plot being leaked. There... [are] too many different elements in it. The Baluch born in the Sultanate. The Baluch from Pakistan. Other Pakistanis. Indians. Various different Omani tribes. Each of these different elements would inform against the other.[19]

Still, Purdon was not entirely convinced of his soldiers' loyalty to the Sultan, informing the ruler that the 'SAF's Omani soldiers, in particular, did not fight well out of any personal loyalty to him, but because they did

---

[16] Purdon, *List the Bugle,* p.235.
[17] KCL-Thwaites, Box 1, File 2, 'Translation of a Pamphlet Picked Up in Dhofar', MR Salalah to The Sultan, January 1970.
[18] Purdon, *List the Bugle,* p.234.
[19] Carden (CG Muscat) to S. Crawford (PR Bahrain), 23 January 1967 in *RO-2*, p.99.

what their British officers told them to do. The Omanis and SAF were not at all concerned about who ruled Dhofar and the Baluch were mercenaries.'[20] Concerns about loyalty were far surpassed, however, by the dearth of numbers. There were only three battalions of soldiers: the Muscat Regiment; the Northern Frontier Regiment; and the Desert Regiment. Ever since his arrival in 1967, Purdon had been pushing the Sultan towards raising a fourth battalion, a necessity he communicated in their first meeting and insistently repeated afterwards. His requests were as repeatedly rejected.[21]

From a military perspective, the rationale behind raising the fourth battalion was compelling. As mentioned in earlier chapters, the SAF's strategic priorities were to protect Salalah and the rest of the larger coastal towns, as well as Thamrit road (Midway), the only road linking Muscat and Salalah, and the major SAF re-supply route. Protecting Thamrit alone placed a considerable strain on army resources. Recognizing its strategic importance, the revolutionaries had dedicated 100 fighters to conduct operations and plant mines there—roughly one ninth of their forces at the time. The revolutionary ambushes took place particularly at three strategic corners: Baramil corner; Aqabat Hamrir (referred to by the British as ambush corner); and Aqabat al-Hattab (the ramp).[22] On 20 May 1969, the latter corner was even blown up, thus affecting SAF movements.[23] Countering such actions tied down substantial SAF resources: 900 soldiers were sent to guard Thamrit (9 for every revolutionary).[24] With the army overstretched elsewhere, raising an additional battalion was essential for containing, let alone defeating, the revolutionaries. Moreover, substantial armaments were required. In particular, helicopters were crucial for improving operational mobility and effectiveness, facilitating efficient deployment, ensuring fast evacuation of casualties, and offering logistical support. In the absence of airlifting capacity, the maximum amount of time that soldiers could stay away from base was five days. Even with the help of donkeys, soldiers could not carry enough water to sustain them beyond that limit.[25]

Another major obstacle to military operations was the paucity of intelligence. From the very beginning of the revolution, SAF had demanded the establishment of an intelligence network in Dhufar. The Sultan

[20] 'Military Operations in Dhofar'. 5 October 1969, *RO-4*, p.225.
[21] Purdon, *List the Bugle*, p.201.
[22] 'Report of Major R.J.F. Brown (DIO Salalah)', 31 March 1968, *RO-3*, p.179.
[23] 'Annual Review 1969', 30 December 1969, *RO-4*, p.13.
[24] 'Current Situation in Dhofar', D.G. Crawford (Muscat) to M. Weir (Bahrain), 1 November 1969, *RO-4*, p.235.
[25] Purdon, *List the Bugle*, p.201.

disapproved of this. This was not the result of lack of interest in the war. Indeed, if anything, he was completely obsessed with the military situation. He closely followed the daily operations in Dhufar: every evening at 5:30, he received a report via a wireless link set up directly with the operations commander.[26] He maintained an operations map outside his study and had it adjusted fortnightly.[27] Moreover, he was attentive to the smallest details, going so far as ordering that a Polaroid Camera be supplied to the Muscat Regiment so that they could send him pictures of dead and captured revolutionaries for identification.[28] Yet, for all this interest, the Sultan could not help but gloss over the deficiencies in his apparatus.

In the absence of an efficient and well-oiled intelligence machinery, information was mainly gathered by the Dhufar Intelligence Officer (DIO). But even the latter's work was made difficult by the Sultan. The DIO was severely constrained in his ability to pay local collaborators. Additionally, he was required to disclose his sources to the Sultan and these were generally judged to be untrustworthy, if not outright unacceptable. When the first DIO, Major R. Brown, stretched his list of contacts too far, the Sultan dismissed him. He was replaced by Tim Landon, a Sandhurst contemporary of the Sultan's only son, Sayid Qaboos.

The risk to collaborators was great, but the incentives—ideological or material—were evidently small. Even clearance for a collaborator to live in Salalah had to be given directly by the Sultan. This necessitated that each individual case was fully explained to him by the senior officers in Dhufar. For instance, in the case of one collaborator, the exact details of the Salalah neighbourhood in which he wanted to live had to be reviewed by the Sultan, as well as the precise composition of his family. In another case, the commander of the Muscat Regiment had to provide ample justification on a collaborator's behalf: 'He has proved himself and will be valuable for the army but a contented man who has no reason to run away is better than one whose wife [and family]...are on the Jebel and he is always worrying about them.'[29]

Without substantial intelligence, precise information about revolutionary targets could not be obtained, existing cleavages within Dhufari ranks could not be exploited, and new divisions could not be sowed. Even after some vital information was slowly gathered, there was a problem in getting the Sultan to act upon it. This is clearly attested in his failure to

---

[26] KCL-Thwaites. Box 1, 'Said bin Taimur to Peter Thwaites', 22 October 1969.
[27] KCL-Thwaites. Box 1, 'Pat Waterfield to Peter Thwaites', 25 May 1969.
[28] KCL-Thwaites. Box 1, 'Pat Waterfield to Peter Thwaites', 25 May 1969.
[29] KCL-Thwaites, Box 1 File 2, 'Handwritten Notes', n.d., *c.*late 1969/early 1970.

implement the recommendations of an important intelligence report. Tim Landon had drafted it to highlight the fact that 'by encouraging tribalism it is more than likely that the present PFLOAG movement within Dhofar can be isolated and contained within the area of the Jebel Dhofar which is presently occupied by the Qara tribes'.[30]

The premise of the report was the historical conflict between bedouin and settled cattle breeding tribes. The former mostly belonged to the Bait Kathir and the Mahra, while the latter were mostly Qarra. Due to the scarcity of resources, there were ongoing historic conflicts between these various groups. Indeed, as late as 1967, and for two months, the Bait Tabook section of the Qarra were engaged in open hostilities with their Mahra neighbours.[31]

The revolutionaries themselves had striven to transcend such divisions, not least due to the mixing of Dhufaris from different tribes in exile and the subsequent adoption of anti-tribal ideologies. However, as the revolution progressed, it became concentrated in the highlands, which were mainly inhabited by the Qarra. This was due to the fact that the north (which was the geographic realm of the Bait Kathir), and the extremities of the east and west (which were Mahra lands), were more barren areas, in which the revolutionaries could be easily exposed. Landon grasped the significance of this regional concentration, noting that whereas 'the more sophisticated Rebel leaders come from all parts of Dhofar and are supra tribal in their approach to life', the majority of young recruits were young Qarra highlanders.[32] This did not mean that Mahra and Bait Kathir elements were no longer active in the revolution; as Landon readily admitted, many were still committed. However, the heartland of the revolution was in Qarra territory, and the objective was to besiege it and cut it off from the rest of Dhufar.

Whereas tribalism was officially suppressed in the revolutionary areas, it was still operating openly outside the realm of PFLOAG control. Landon thus proposed the targeting of the eastern Mahra and the Bait Kathir. In the case of the former, he suggested that Sheikh Mohammad bin-Humeid be approached. Although the Sheikh had been an active revolutionary supporter in the DLF period (as was shown in Chapter 3), he took a more passive stance during the post-Hamrin era, merely 'giving his blessing to those of his Mahra that work for PFLOAG'. Sheikh Bin-Humeid was also an ideal figure because he was a rare survivor of the revolutionary attack

[30] 'Dhofar Isolation Rebel Activity', SIO (Tim Landon) to HH The Sultan, Salalah, 18 March 1970, *RO-5*, p.201.

[31] 'Dhofar Isolation Rebel Activity', Landon to the Sultan, p.201.

[32] 'Dhofar Isolation Rebel Activity', Landon to the Sultan, p.201.

on tribalism: 'his status...has suffered little among his tribesmen...he remains a Sheikh, free, powerful and no doubt open to persuasion'.[33]

The same could not be said for any Kathiri sheikhs. Splintered to begin with, they were unable to retain their positions in the face of the revolution. However, two of them, Bin-Tufl and Bin-Tamtein, were potential candidates for government work. The former was a prisoner in Jalali, the latter was living in Salalah town. Although they were by no means pro-Sultan, they were no longer revolutionaries. Landon proposed that they be brought over into the Sultanic side. There was clear advantage in recruiting these two Sheikhs: 'with Government help they could soon regain their control over the Bait Kathir and become powerful men again'.[34]

Early on, Landon understood that this approach was cost-effective. All it took was for the sheikhs to be allowed to move between mountain and coast, and be given money and weapons with which they could enhance their position and fight the revolutionaries. The Mahra were to be allocated the eastern coastal town of Sadah to run, whereas the Bait Kathir would be allowed free movement in and out of Salalah. Complemented by some other affordable offerings, tribalism would become an instrument of empire and monarchy:

> Further easily granted concessions could follow; a pair of wells in each tribal area with pump engines, the use of a passport office in Salalah to permit freedom to travel abroad, recruitment of tribesmen into SAF. None of these concessions would cost very much money. They would, however, help to emphasise the advantages of being a Government supporter. They would also re-establish the power of the Sheyukh who are naturally anti-communist and conservative in their outlook and through them the desert areas of Dhoar [sic] can be easily brought under effective Government control at relatively little cost.[35]

Landon hoped that a multiplier effect would occur once his recommendations were put in place. Once relations were cemented with the eastern Mahra, the Sultanate's profile could be raised with the western Mahra, who dwelled on the vital revolutionary supply lines area near the South Yemeni border. A connection with the latter already existed through a collaborator named Busher and it was estimated that a little money would go a long way with them.

By means of encouraging tribalism, the revolutionaries could be encircled from the north (through the desert Kathiris), the east (through the

---

[33] 'Dhofar Isolation Rebel Activity', Landon to the Sultan, p.201.
[34] 'Dhofar Isolation Rebel Activity', Landon to the Sultan, p.201.
[35] 'Dhofar Isolation Rebel Activity', Landon to the Sultan, p.201.

Eastern Mahra), and the west (through the Western Mahra). Their remaining supporters would then be vulnerable to Anglo-Sultanic infiltration and tribalist resurgence:

> Thus encirclement of the Qara tribal areas would be complete, while the PFLOAG would have lost valuable support and credibility. The Qara would be anxious to enjoy similar benefits to their fellow Dhofaris. They would be forced to talk to the Government and accept what the Government was prepared to offer them. The present Chinese backed leaders would lose their credibility and be forced by general opinion to either flee or give themselves up.[36]

As was the usual habit of the Sultan, Landon's report was ignored. However, most of its recommendations were implemented following the 1970 coup. Its importance lay in the fact that it anticipated the character of the so called 'hearts and minds' approach that was later undertaken: the incitement to tribalism and the encouragement of collaboration by means of financial leverage and the manipulation of existing conflicts over land and resources.

For now, however, the counter-revolutionary vision for dividing the Dhufari population was not implemented. As a result, intelligence was still scarce and collaboration rare. With this deficiency in place, Dhufaris had to be fought as a whole. As far as British officers were concerned, every village, hut and assemblage was a potential target, a possible 'enemy' spot.

What was permissible in dealing with this population of 'enemies'? In the absence of any clear regulations and in the presence of Sultanic support for the most severe of policies, this question arose in every situation. The answer was determined by the commanding officers, as can be seen in the two contrasting cases of the Northern Frontier (NFR) and the Muscat Regiments (MR). The NFR was commanded by Lieutenant Colonel Mike Harvey, deploying methods that transgressed even the extremely permissive British army policy of separating 'the neutral sheep from the committed Marxist goats, to support and protect the former and harass and destroy the latter'.[37]

Harvey had a declared aim: 'to keep the Adoo in a constant state of alarm by operations in unexpected areas in continuous momentum'.[38] In accordance with this vision, he attacked everything he could on the Jabal, stretching the limits of the already established practice of collective

---

[36] 'Dhofar Isolation Rebel Activity', Landon to the Sultan, p.201.
[37] Peter Thwaites, *Muscat Command*, London: Leo Cooper, 1995, p.77.
[38] MEC-Hepworth, Box 2/1, 'Operational Charter and Guide for Officers of the Northern Frontier Regiment Proceeding to Dhofar', December 1969.

punishment. During his *roulement* in the latter half of 1968, he issued his 'Emergency Regulations, Dhofar'. These stipulated the closing of the border with South Yemen and the imposition of an curfew after dark across the land. Failing to capture armed men, and finding instead an easy prey in the seasonal Jabali labourers gathering wood to sell in Salalah, he imprisoned them *en masse* and subjected them to interrogation in Um al-Ghawarif, the SAF regional headquarters. Some were kept for days, others for weeks, all 'on suspicion of helping the terrorists'.[39] Harvey was perhaps correct in viewing every Dhufari as a suspect. After all, most Dhufaris were revolutionary fighters or supporters. Nevertheless, his tactic, aimed at intelligence gathering, failed to achieve its aims, hardly bringing any new information. In fact, the disruption and terror caused in this instance and others increased the popular commitment to the revolution. Thus, Harvey's actions—including the imprisonment of the elderly and the dehydration of the populace under the banner of 'water denial'—were described, less than approvingly, by his colleague, Lieutenant Colonel Thwaites:

> He instituted a policy of blowing up or 'capping' wells all over the Jebel which certainly inhibited enemy convoys but also denied water to the locals and possibly innocent Jebalis and their herds. He detained and incarcerated a number of ancient Jebalis in the hope of successful interrogation...[40]

Thwaites belonged to a different breed of men from the aggressive Harvey, and his MR had the reputation, unenviable in a colonial-martialist context, of being 'less hard-hitting than the NFR'. An avid polo-player and a minor playwright, his self-projection was that of a conscientious soldier. His memoirs reveal an element of personal crisis about his presence in Dhufar and a suppressed understanding of his oppressive role there, which occasionally bursts out:

> ...with the beginning of oil revenues in 1967 there was surely something that could be done to relieve the terrible toll of hunger and disease which afflicted the Dhofaris. Was there not a suspicion that we, the British, were lending support to a corrupt regime, whereby the Sultan...and his chosen few, lived in comfort and careless ignorance, while the great mass of the people barely scratched an existence...[41]

Typically, this crisis was resolved by means of cold war categorical abstraction: '[m]any officers, myself included, welcomed Marxist intervention,

---

[39] Thwaites, *Muscat Command*, p.76.
[40] Thwaites, *Muscat Command*, p.76.
[41] Thwaites, *Muscat Command*, p.73.

with its naked policy of terrorism of the innocent as a balm to a troubled conscience'.[42] Thus, anti-communism allowed Thwaites to operate with less guilt than before. Still, moral dilemmas persisted, and these could only be confronted with a measure of Orientalism. This can be seen in Thwaites' account of one of his operations. He vividly recalls how, as his men were invading a village, they were faced with the 'nauseating task' of searching huts that were 'dank and airless with goats and calves mixed up with stale food, sour milk and pathetic, fly-blown children'. He watched them as they forced out the inhabitants packed in the huts, who looked to him 'like clowns getting out of a baby car at the circus'. In response to the wailing and howling of the women, he felt 'like Herod' but he continued watching. His men emptied out the huts of the 'few pathetic belongings' inside them. Thwaites was patient as his men requested permission to burn the houses, having found evidence of the fact that the inhabitants are 'obviously *adoo* [or enemy] women'.

Still clinging to his own self-projection as a moral agent, he thought to himself, 'Must we? Should we? The homes of women and children. This is not total war.' But this thought evaporated as more compelling proof of revolutionary presence was found in the form of two 2-inch mortar bombs. Once the evidence was revealed, the Colonel's Acting Adjutant pressed him to burn all of the huts. By contrast, his First Company Commander, who was sympathetic to the people of the area, looked at him 'expectantly', hoping that he would show mercy. Caught between demands for punishment and pleas for mercy, Thwaites took what he saw as a middle path: he gave the women a chance (ten minutes) to clear their livestock, and burnt one in five of all their houses as opposed to burning them all. Interestingly, he complained about the 'contrived' howling of the women at the sight of their homes burning.[43]

As the cases of Harvey and Thwaites illustrate, under Sultan Said, the British commanders in Oman were exalted to the position of judges, issuing sentences and pardons over Dhufaris. For some, like Harvey, moral reasoning had no place in the field. Whatever they did was justifiable *a priori*, by virtue of the fact that they were fighting communists. For others, like Thwaites, proof of revolutionary activity was required before a decree of collective punishment was issued, and penalties were always measured, if only arbitrarily and in accordance with the whims of the commander. They all burned villages.

[42] Thwaites, *Muscat Command*, p.73.
[43] Thwaites, *Muscat Command,* pp.7–9.

THE TREE LINE BATTLES (1968–70)

In its battle with the People's Liberation Army (PLA), the SAF had numerical superiority, with a total strength of 3,700. However, the army was afflicted by crises of overextension, immobility, and lack of intelligence and collaborators. Purdon had proposed several solutions to this set of problems. He requested a fourth battalion, helicopters, better intelligence, and a 'hearts and minds' approach that would offer political incentives for collaboration. He also wanted direct British support in the form of SAS involvement. With this wish list effectively shelved, he could not sustain an aggressive strategy and the best he could hope for was containment in the face of an ever-growing revolutionary movement.

The single most important factor that shaped strategy—for both the army and the revolutionaries—was a geographic feature that the British dubbed the 'Tree Line'. This was the forested stretch of highland spreading from east to west, Mirbat to Hauf. The long-term revolutionary plan was to establish control over the entire area, to use it as a base from which to attack the plains of Salalah, Taqa, Mirbat, Mughsail, Raysut and Rakhyut as well as Midway Road and, eventually, to take over the plains. The supplies coming from South Yemen provided the main ingredients in this recipe for victory. Thanks to the excellent cover provided by the Tree Line, these could be transported on camels, and the east of Dhufar could remain connected to the west, the mountains could be fed and the revolutionaries armed.

On the whole, the PLA fighters stuck to the tree line on the Jabal. They avoided the open desert where they could be easily targeted by jets and they were also cautious whenever they operated in the plains. They deployed the classic guerrilla tactic of operating in small groups—rarely more than 20 or 30—over a large area. By doing so, they hoped to draw the soldiers into ground of their own choosing, trying to force the army to fragment into 'penny packets' and then defeat it 'in detail'.[44] They also fired mortars, laid British and Soviet mines, and demolished physical structures, including the Sultan's private water supply at Ayn Razat, which was cut by an explosion on 18 July 1968.[45]

During the monsoon of 1969, there was a marked improvement in revolutionary performance. The revolutionaries almost brought down a Strikemaster with automatic fire and the accuracy of their mortar attacks was improving.[46] The thick foliage of the season allowed them to establish

---

[44] KCL-Thwaites, 'Dhofar Ops as of January 1970'.
[45] Peterson, 'Oman's Diverse Society: Southern Oman', p.216.
[46] FO 1016/790, Muscat to Bahrain, 14 July 1969.

positions that were dangerously close to Salalah.[47] Additionally, a significant victory was achieved as a result of the taking of the coastal village of Rakhyut in the western sector, the blowing up of its fort, and the capture of its garrison of '*askars* at the end of August 1969. The village was of no tactical importance to the army but it did have a symbolic value due to its position on the coast. For this reason, the Sultan was furious at its loss and he ordered the SAF to take it back and raze it to the ground.[48] This did not make military sense, running against the main strategic concept of the SAF. This concept—adopted by Mike Harvey in late 1967 and continued ever since—was to establish positions on the Tree Line, going as far west as possible so as to limit revolutionary supply routes. Unable to cover the whole area, the army focused on sensitive parts where the highland routes canalized, effectively forming bottlenecks. Units were stationed in six of these areas. One of these, Haluf, was in central Dhufar. The rest—Adonib, Raydayt, Mughsayl, Janook and Difa'—were in the west.[49] These army outposts were a major source of harassment for the revolutionaries, limiting the transportation of supplies.

Had the SAF launched a land attack on Rakhyut, the whole strategy would have been sabotaged. Troops would have had to be cleared from the 'bottlenecks', thus opening up space for the revolutionaries to rush supplies in. Moreover, the attack on Rakhyut would have undoubtedly entailed very heavy casualties. With 400–600 revolutionaries stationed in the hills around the village, the SAF estimated that it would take at least three companies to attack. The SAF command managed to convince the Sultan against a land assault. It proposed instead the destruction of the village through air strikes. The civilian inhabitants of the village would be dealt with as follows:

> A warning rocket or gun strike would suffice to give warning of bombing run. Alternatively, a few leaflets dropped could explain why we were going to destroy the town 'within five minutes' so that there would be no time to alert the air defence units.[50]

It is difficult to determine how many casualties resulted from the subsequent shelling of Rakhyut. All that can be said with certainty is that the coastal village was turned into a scorched ruin. Nevertheless, the revolutionaries continued to hold it until January 1975.

The Rakhyut victory was followed by a rise in revolutionary fighting audacity. Following the 1969 monsoon, Thamrit road was blown in five

---

[47] KCL-Thwaites, MR Contact Reports 26 & 27, Salalah, 9 August 1969.
[48] KCL-Thwaites, Box 1, Thwaites to Purdon, 7 November 1969.
[49] KCL-Thwaites. Box 2, 'Lecture: Dhofar 1967–1970', n.d., p.6.
[50] KCL-Thwaites, Box 1, Thwaites to Purdon, 7 November 1969.

locations and heavy battles were fought there. By early 1970, the PLA was beginning to take its operations to the plain, something that it had previously been hesitant to do. On 6 January, it led an attack against Taqa fort. After a battle with the SAF, some revolutionaries took shelter in the local mosque and refused to surrender. The mosque was destroyed by the order of the Sultan, increasing popular resentment of his army.[51] On 20 January, the revolutionaries mined the Raysut road. On 26 January, they mortared the RAF airfield in Salalah, and they did so again on 2 and 6 February.[52]

The operations against the RAF were especially significant, delivering a severe jolt to British policy makers. On the military front, the situation was perceived to be so serious that the possibility of further British troops being sent to protect the airfield was even discussed.[53] A second RAF defensive section was thus added, equipped with heavy mortars.[54] Moreover, a Green Archer Mortar Locating Radar was installed in April, and this was successful in detecting revolutionary shells and in facilitating quick counter bombardment.[55] As useful as they were, these steps were recognized as being no more than a bandaid solution to the problem. Under revolutionary pressure, the SAF temporarily gave up the idea of maintaining a strong presence on the western tree line. Troops were now re-concentrated in the central sector of Dhufar. Until more men arrived and more weapons were procured, aggressive action had to be replaced by cautious containment.

THE BRITISH TAKE STOCK

The revolutionaries effectively won the battle over the Tree Line, especially in the West. David Crawford, the new Consul General in Muscat, appreciated the significance of this victory, warning that 'if SAF do not weaken the rebel grip on the Western Areas before May 1970, they may face an even more serious threat in the Central Sector of Dhufar during or at the end of the next monsoon'.[56] So far, the revolutionaries only had Shpagin submachine guns and two or three medium mortars. However, with increasing support from South Yemen, China, and Russia, the arrival

[51] 'Britain's "Secret War" in Oman', in United States Department of Defense, *Military Support to Indirect Security and Stability Surge Operations*, October 2007, p.C-20.
[52] KCL-Thwaites, Box 1, 'Dhofar Ops as of January 1970'.
[53] DEFE 24/1867, 'Muscat and Oman', F. Cooper, 25 February 1970.
[54] 'RAF Salalah: Report by the Air Force Department', 31 March 1970, *RO-5*, p.459.
[55] Chief of the Defense Staff to Secretary of State, 23 November 1970, *RO-5*, p.273.
[56] 'Muscat—Annual Review 1969'.

of Katyusha rockets was a likely possibility that could threaten the RAF airfield and even the Sultan's palace.

These thoughts, previously formulated with hesitation by the old Consul General, found determined expression from the pen of his successor. Nearly every report he sent to the Political Residency was clouded by gloomy assessments of the regime and its prospects of survival. Crawford looked down upon the Sultan, describing him as a 'Babu'.[57] In the colonial lexicon, this term connoted a native clerk employed in the service of the Raj. Moreover, it signified an effeminacy that was counterposed to British masculinity.[58] Unlike the dispatches of his predecessor, which were generally respectful of the Sultan, Crawford's reports transformed the ruler into an object of mockery.[59] They carried a simple message: change had to be pushed for, immediately.

This message was certainly understood by the Political Resident in Bahrain as well as the Arabian Department of the Foreign and Commonwealth Office. In November 1969, the Assessment Staff were asked to prepare a comprehensive appraisal of the situation in Dhufar, so as to 'take stock'.[60] The assessment took a couple of months to prepare but was completed by the end of February. On its basis, a paper was drafted for the Foreign Secretary, outlining the various possible courses of British action and offering conclusions for immediate policy. The paper began with the usual listing of the five major British interests in the Sultanate. The first was to 'prevent the Sultanate from falling under communist, extreme left-wing or Arab nationalist control with the result that stability in the Persian Gulf might be threatened before British withdrawal or Britain's extensive commercial and oil interests might be threatened after withdrawal'. The second was the maintenance of RAF staging facilities on Massirah Island, which were of immense importance to British military activities in the Far East and the Gulf. The third was the maintenance of the flow of oil and Shell's position. The fourth was the furthering of British commercial interests. The fifth was the avoidance of direct British involvement in military operations, at a time when the Sultan was 'able to take the necessary measures himself if he is prepared to do so'.[61]

---

[57] 'Current Situation in Dhufar'. 1 November 1969, *RO-4*, p.235.

[58] See Mrinalini Sinha, *Colonial Masculinity: The 'Manly Englishman' and the 'Effeminate Bengali' in the Late Nineteenth Century*, Manchester: Manchester University Press, 1995.

[59] See for example, 'Dhofar', D.G. Crawford to M.S. Weir, 30 October 1969, *RO-4*, p.226.

[60] McCarthy (Arabian Department) to Stewart Crawford (Bahrain), 6 November 1969, *RO-4*, p.237.

[61] DEFE 24/1867, 'The Sultanate of Muscat and Oman, H.M.G.'s Policy', 25 February 1970.

The revolution was seen to have reached a stage whereby it was seriously jeopardizing these interests, and the assessment paper conclusively showed that 'the situation in Dhofar will progressively deteriorate unless urgent steps are taken'. The way forward lay in the pursuit of development activities in Dhufar as well as the rest of the Sultanate. This was deemed to require 'a major reorganisation of the Sultan's government and administration'. Having already been 'unresponsive to British advice', and exhibiting a 'complex and perhaps unfathomable' character, the Sultan was not expected to pursue such an undertaking without unprecedented pressure.

In this context, five possible courses of action where delineated. The first was to 'immediately increase the British military commitment to deal with the situation in Dhofar'. Whilst this was seen as militarily possible, it was ruled out as dangerous. The commitment would 'be open ended and could continue indefinitely' and it would not necessarily result in an easy victory, not the least because of the difficulty of the terrain. Enormous problems, within Britain and abroad, were envisaged if this option were undertaken, especially with the spectre of Aden still haunting the British imagination:

> ...it would be difficult to justify to parliamentary and public opinion a decision to involve British troops in an open-ended Radfan-type operation in support of a feudal and autocratic Sultan who has the means to help himself but refuses to do so. HMG would also come under considerable criticism from the United Nations and from Arab nationalist regimes.[62]

With this option thrown out of the window, a second possibility was examined, which was to withdraw, or threaten to withdraw, existing British support in the form of seconded officers and the operation of air facilities in Salalah. This was evaluated as equally, if not more, risky. 'These measures, if carried out, would be likely to result in Dhofar falling to the rebels, with unpredictable consequences for Oman and possibly the Persian Gulf States. This would be contrary to British interests.'

The third possibility was to 'attempt to change the regime'. This would entail replacing the Sultan with an alternative figure, such as his son Qabus. The latter was described as 'frustrated and restive' and as sometimes thinking of 'moving against his father'. This option was far from ideal. To begin with, Qabus and other potential candidates were 'unknown quantities with untried capabilities. They might well have difficulty in holding the country.' Furthermore, the change would be difficult to bring

---

[62] DEFE 24/1867, 'The Sultanate of Muscat and Oman, H.M.G.'s Policy', 25 February 1970.

about, and it would put British officers in the SAF in a difficult position, having to act against their employer, the Sultan. Having dismissed this third option, the paper considered a fourth one, which was to maintain the status quo in the hope that the Sultan will see the light. This was also rejected, being declared 'an increasingly forlorn hope', especially considering the need for speedy and firm action to redress the situation.

The report went on to recommend a fifth option: to 'make a major effort at a high level with the Sultan to explain the seriousness of the situation and to jolt him into activity'. It was suggested that such a comprehensive policy review would be the logical step to take before considering other possibilities, all of which were 'dangerous and unsatisfactory'. As part of the review, the seriousness of the situation would be explained to the Sultan, and an indication of what needed to be done would be given to him. Assurances would then be sought, 'perhaps in writing', by which he would promise 'that the essential decisions now be taken'. This would involve a multi-step process that would initially begin with a visit by senior officials, carrying a 'message from HMG to explain the situation to him, to hear his comments and give him time to reflect'. A visit from a senior Minister would then follow, to hear the Sultan's answer and to obtain his firm agreement if possible. Finally, officials would then work on hammering out the precise details.[63] Thus, the conclusion of the long-awaited assessment was for the Sultan to receive a 'grand remonstrance'. The Foreign Secretary, Michael Stewart, adopted this recommendation and decided to review the whole situation with the Sultan within a couple of months, at the beginning of May.[64]

Within the Gulf imperial community, the 'anti-Said' list had grown substantially. Its most notable member was Shell, which held the oil concession in the Sultanate through its subsidiary, Petroleum Development Oman (PDO). Within PDO, the need for asserting imperial sovereignty over the Sultan was emphasized early on. In 1965, a company report asserted that 'someone of high position in the Foreign Office, impervious to the Sultan's charm, should be sent to tell the Sultan what must happen, not what does the Sultan want to happen'. In the same vein, it was emphasized that 'the fiction of the Sultan's independence should be put aside for a while and the Sultan made to understand what is to happen'.[65]

---

[63] DEFE 24/1867, 'The Sultanate of Muscat and Oman, H.M.G.'s Policy', 25 February 1970.

[64] DEFE 24/1855, Michael Stewart to the Secretary of State for Defense, 15 April 1970.

[65] MEC-Peyton, Box 2/2, 'Some Notes on the Political Situation in Muscat and Oman Prepared for the Visit of Mr Barran', May 1965.

The Company's attitude was not caused by any hostility on the part of the Sultan. On the contrary, his era was one in which Shell enjoyed unsurpassed freedom and power. Its officials were the first to admit that they 'enjoyed a privileged position in the country' with 'a minimum of interference from local officialdom', and that, 'as foreigners', they were likely to 'look back on the present as the "good old days" . . .'[66] Nevertheless, the SAF's failed campaign in Dhufar put the immediate interests of the Company under threat. This threat was deemed unnecessary from Shell's perspective, not least because it considered that a quick victory could be achieved if the Sultan was willing to change his ways.[67]

From a long-term perspective, Shell was even more concerned about stabilizing northern Oman, the location of its main operations. As far as it was concerned, the only way forward was to introduce capitalist relations into the country, thus addressing the discontents of established local merchants and securing new loyalties from future beneficiaries. As ever, the question of property was especially pertinent. The lack of a land registry in the Sultanate was bemoaned, described as 'the most important barrier to orderly development'.[68] The restriction of capital mobility was also viewed with alarm, especially due to regulations that prevented people from one part of the country purchasing property in another. This was just one regulation out of many that prevented the emergence of capitalism. Private development projects—such as 'building private houses, shops, or bringing into cultivation land that has been abandoned'—were not officially banned but the fettering web of restrictions made 'such projects impossible for the average Omani to undertake', effectively inhibiting entrepreneurship.[69]

The lack of any redistribution of oil income also concerned the Company. This was especially the case because it was unwilling to undertake such redistribution itself and expected the government to do so. The Company laid all the blame at the Sultan's door, even though its own labour policy discriminated heavily against Omani workers. A three tier hierarchy existed in the Company: at the top of the pyramid were Europeans, who received substantial benefits and services; in the middle were Indians and Pakistanis; at the very bottom were Omanis. PDO of course

---

[66] MEC-Peyton, Box 2/2, 'The Company and the Country, The Environment'. 27 June 1970.

[67] MEC-Peyton, Box 2/2, 'The Company and the Country, The Environment'. 27 June 1970.

[68] MEC-Paxton, 'Problems of Ownership and Development', 22 January 1969.

[69] MEC-Paxton, 'Problems of Ownership and Development', 22 January 1969.

wanted to maximize its profits, and it therefore offered few services to the highly exploitable Omani workers. In contrast, it had to offer some incentives to foreign workers in order to be able to attract them. This did not pass unnoticed by Omanis and their grievances were expressed in various forms. For instance, when a copy of the Company newsletter was passed to one worker

> …he said he did not want another copy; asked why, it appeared he was angry about the title 'News of Our Company'—'It is not our Company', he said 'it belongs to the foreigners for whom the Company builds houses, provides meals, etcetera.'[70]

One of Shell's officials in Oman, William Peyton, had anticipated such problems arising even before the export of oil began. In 1964, he noted that the Company needed to 'provide a bridge' between the Omanis and the 'expats in their midst'. Since services were being offered by the Company to the expats, the government needed to offer services to Omanis. This was necessary so as to ensure that there was no local bitterness against PDO and its foreign employees. Of course, there was no question of the Company itself undertaking these initiatives. However, the Sultan was expected to do so, with some help if necessary.[71]

Three years after oil exports begun, such an integration of services had not occurred, and this was harming the Company's local image as well as its relations with local employees. Increasingly aware of this long-standing problem, and the immediate threat posed by the situation in Dhufar, Shell was anticipating change. At any rate, it was definitely consulted every step of the way. Indeed, on 26 February, at the height of the process of taking stock, the Foreign Secretary ensured he met Shell's representative, David Barran[72] and, in dozens of instances over the following months, the director of its PD(O) division, Francis Hughes, reported to, and advised, British officials on matters of minor and major policy, being recognized as an expert on the Sultan.[73]

The Sultan by now had very few British friends, but his situation was even worse in relation to Arabs. For years, he had purposefully isolated himself from his neighbours. As far as he was concerned, the Saudis were 'hostile', the South Yemenis 'evil', and the Trucial Sheikhs 'inferior'. The only neighbours with whom he had meaningful relations were the Sheikhs of Abu Dhabi. He had met Sheikh Shakhbut in the

---

[70] MEC-Paxton,'Employee Newsletter', 15 August 1968.

[71] MEC-Paxton 'Muscat and Oman, 4-14 April 1964', 4 May 1964.

[72] DEFE 24/1867, 'Muscat and Oman', F. Cooper, 25 February 1970.

[73] For instance see 'John Townsend', D.G. Crawford to M.S. Weir, 16 May 1970, *RO, Vol.5*, p.907.

distant past. More recently, he had held talks with Sheikh Zayid in 1968.[74]

Zayid had long given up on the Sultan and he tried to convince the British to act against him. His anti-Said position was not new.[75] However, Zayid's activism against the Sultan was increased still further by the rising revolutionary tide in Oman and Dhufar. In June 1969, he took his concerns to London. Although he stopped short of calling for the removal of the Sultan, something that he shrewdly avoided in the sensitive atmosphere of Whitehall, he emphasized the need to impose radical changes in the Sultan's policies. The FCO responded by lecturing him on the need to cooperate with his neighbour 'the best way to prevent a revolutionary outbreak was to support the Sultan in his efforts to modernise his state'. Zayid was also reminded that 'HMG believed that the interests of all Rulers were identical'.[76]

The Sheikh was unimpressed by such talk. He expressed his worries about the situation in Dhufar, stating that 'frequent skirmishes were taking place there and the Dhofari dissidents also seem to be falling under communist influence'. He further emphasized that the situation in Oman proper was not as stable as it seemed, noting that the 'Omani dissidents were not a small number of men who could be ignored or suppressed' and that '[d]evelopment plans in Oman would not be enough to stop the situation from deteriorating'. The only solution in his opinion was for negotiations to be held between the 'dissidents' and the Sultan. He believed that most of them were willing to negotiate, stating that he was hosting two Kathiri sheikhs from Dhufar who 'had asked... [him] on behalf of a number of their followers either for Abu Dhabi nationality or for [his] mediation with the Sultan so as to enable them to return to their homes without trouble'.[77] Zayid's intervention on its own was certainly not enough to move the British. Yet his was an important voice in an increasingly loud chorus. His own experience of deposing his brother only four years before had been a spectacular example of the obstacles that could be removed with the replacement of a conservative ruler by one more embracing of modernization and development.

The Sultan was unaware of all of these discussions. Nevertheless, he was familiar with the demands of the British and he seemed to have confidence in his ability to manage them in his signature style. How could his policy

---

[74] *RO-4*, pp.218–19.
[75] Michael Weir, *Michael Scott Weir, 1925–2006, Unfinished Memoires* (unpublished), p.97.
[76] 'Record of Meeting', 27 June 1969, *RO-4*, p.432.
[77] 'Record of Meeting', 27 June 1969, *RO-4*, p.432.

be explained? Several accounts recognize that he was motivated by the desire to minimize spending and maximize his own independent manoeuvring space *vis-à-vis* British officials.[78] One sympathetic observer goes further, suggesting that he was asserting an independent vision of a 'unified tribal state' that was locally sensitive, contrasted with a British one of a modern state along foreign lines.[79] What both explanations miss is the extent to which the Sultan's world view was classically British, exemplifying the values of colonial conservatism coupled with a streak of anti-modernism. This was what made him so resistant to changing his practices. His approach was inspired by precedents from the high age of colonialism. Indeed, the Sultan saw his situation in Dhufar as analogous to that of the Raj in the northwest frontier of India, stating that he 'was impressed by the British who had kept the tribes at bay' in that area.[80]

The Sultan grew up in the shadow of the Raj and he was socialized within its culture, studying in one of its foremost establishments for six years. His *alma mater* was Mayo College of Ajmer. This elite institution undoubtedly maintained the tradition of Macaulay's Minute on Indian Education, with its famous declaration that '[w]e must at present do our best to form a class who may be interpreters between us and the millions whom we govern; a class of persons, Indian in blood and colour, but English in taste, in opinions, in morals, and in intellect'. Said bin Taimur was such a person, sharing in the political culture of the anglicized Maharajas of India as opposed to the Arab Sheikhs of the Gulf protectorates. Unlike the latter, who had an intimate, if hierarchical, relationship to their people typified in the *majlis* style of governance, the Sultan was essentially alienated from Omanis. An informed report noted that:

> He avoids seeing them if possible and when he has to see them he demands a kind of grovelling respect which is totally foreign to Arab rulers—and to Omani Imams in the past—whose courts are traditionally open and remarkably informal. The Sultan's attitude is that only he knows best, that his subjects shall have what he considers good for them, not what they want.[81]

The Sultan was forever haunted by the trauma he suffered from the empty coffers of the early days of his reign. Yet, he was not just hesitant about development on financial grounds: in his conservative colonial world view, development was a dangerous endeavour that could have subversive effects. Equally dangerous was any yielding to popular pressure, his patri-

[78] See, for example, Peterson, 'Oman's Diverse Society: Southern Oman', pp.52–9.
[79] Uzi Rabi, *The Emergence of States in a Tribal Society*, Brighton: Sussex Academic Press, 2006, pp.152–65.
[80] 'Dhofar', D.G. Crawford to M.S. Weir, 30 October 1969, *RO, Vol.4*, p.226.
[81] MEC-Peyton, 'Some Notes on the Political Situation in Muscat', May 1965.

archal authority had to be total and any infringement of it had to be totally punished.

As for the struggle between the Sultan and his British administrators, it should by no means be read as a clash between a local 'tribalist' version of state building and a foreign British one. In fact, what was unfolding in Oman was an internal British debate reflecting the contradiction between two political cultures: colonial modernism and colonial conservatism. The former advocated economic transformation and state building, the latter argued for maintenance of the status quo and minimal gradual change. Until the discovery of oil, the Gulf had been dominated by the conservative vision, embodied in the notion of 'indirect rule', which essentially led to freezing the region in time. However, with the rise of the Gulf's importance and the decline in British power, the vast majority of British officials recognized that a rapid developmentalist programme had to be undertaken so as to allow for the creation of imperially tamed regimes that could survive British withdrawal. The Sultan subscribed to the dwindling conservative vision, advocating an adjusted version of indirect rule with continuing British presence and only gradual interference with the 'traditional' life of the natives.

Said's vision was shared by his advisers, who were viewed by London as low grade, 'extremely conservative' and 'cautious'.[82] The most powerful amongst them was Major Leslie Chauncy. He had dedicated the better part of his youth to the Indian Army and Political Service (1924–1948). He played a 'retarding' role on the development front, preferred 'the old-style Muscat', and was joined in this by his influential wife, who was described by the modernists as a 'forceful memsahib of the old school'.[83] The Raj may have been dead, but it was alive in the minds of this flock. When presented by a British development official with a proposal to establish some primary schools, the Sultan responded with a typically feudal cliché: 'That is why you lost India, because you educated the people.'[84]

Although anti-modernist when it came to anything that could alter Oman's insular condition, the Sultan was willing to introduce modern devices—such as the army and the oil company—to support his rule. However, a strict law of separation applied, whereby these institutions were kept distant from the people:

[82] DEFE 24/1867, 'Muscat and Oman', F. Cooper. 25 February 1970.
[83] FO 1016/790. 'Leading British and American Personalities in the Gulf—1968.'
[84] Quoted in Rabi, *The Emergence of States in a Tribal Society*, p.156.

It appears as if the Sultan has been unable to resolve the conflict between ancient and modern in his own mind. We might draw a line down the centre of a page. On the left side we could list the traditional positions and institutions of Oman... On the right side of the line we can list those positions and institutions alien to Oman... The Sultan seems determined that the subjects in each column should not meet. This attitude makes orderly, peaceful development almost impossible.[85]

Conveniently forgotten in such British reports, with their obsessive fascination with the Sultan's odd psychology and queer choices, were the colonial origins of Sultanic dualism. Indeed, in the days of the Raj, the Empire imposed a separation between the Sultanic institution and local society. The former had to serve imperial interests and was required to run whatever 'modern' structures were needed for that task, while at the same time playing a mediating local administrative function through the less-costly older institutions. Besides the political culture of the Raj, the Sultans of Muscat were bequeathed a structural position whereby they had no power independent of the Empire.

The removal of the social basis of the Sultan's power also meant the absence of any accountability to Omani society, or any desire to develop it. For years there had been no immediate threat pushing the ruler to develop the local military and financial capacity. Nor was there any gripping interest in doing so. Even after the discovery of oil, the Sultan was not dependent on any local power base. His mounting revenues derived from a natural resource as opposed to the economic activities of his subjects. His administration and forces were led, and mostly staffed, by foreigners as opposed to natives.

Moreover, the Sultan had a relatively recent historical precedent to ground him in his inaction. When the al-Jabal al Akhdar revolt threatened him, the Empire had intervened directly and protected his interests. He believed the same could happen in this case. Additionally, he believed in the omnipotence of the imperial power; in the notion that it could defeat internal threats solely by means of sheer force. This belief was clearly not shared by British experts. Nevertheless, his reactionary British advisers and officers ensured that critical foreign voices were suppressed. This was illustrated by the case of J.C. Wilkinson, who was an employee at PDO. In a private conversation with CSAF Tony Lewis in September 1965, Wilkinson criticized some aspects of the state of affairs prevailing at the time, especially in the context of the embarrassing UN Ad Hoc Committee Report[86] that had appeared earlier that year on Oman and the

---

[85] MEC-Peyton, 'The Company and the Country', 27 June 1970.
[86] UN General Assembly, *Question of Oman*, 17 December 1965, A/RES/2073, annex No. 16, document A/5846.

British role within it. Subsequent to this conversation, Lewis pushed to have Wilkinson treated as *persona non grata* on the basis that he had criticized the Sultan. Lewis succeeded, and Wilkinson left, eventually becoming an Oxford don and the most distinguished British scholar of Omani history and society. If anything, this incident reveals the extent to which there was a struggle between developmentalists and anti-developmentalists within British circles, and the degree to which the latter were complicit in the Sultan's policies, not the least by suppressing criticism and independent thought within and without colonial circles.[87]

At any rate, political culture, structural position, prior experience, limited knowledge and sheer belief in the power of the British Empire combined to create a situation whereby the Sultan was playing by the rules of the Victorian game in the post-Suez era. Nevertheless, in his own mind, he was still scoring points. On 31 May 1969, he managed to nip in the bud a plan for RAF withdrawal from Salalah. The withdrawal was planned because the airfield was turning into a risky site, lacking any strategic importance and acting as a drain on resources. The Sultan was determined that the RAF remain so as to ensure that he would not be abandoned if Salalah were seriously threatened. He resisted all the temptations that were offered in exchange for withdrawal, and insisted that an RAF presence in Salalah was a precondition for their use of Massirah Island. The latter was a base of central importance for the maintenance of British supply lines to the Far East and for meeting commitments to CENTO. Consequently, the RAF yielded to the Sultan, who had undoubtedly won the day on this occasion. A few weeks later, on 4 July, he scored another victory by renewing the Agreement for the Secondment of British Personnel to the SAF without making any major policy concessions.[88]

In spite of these achievements, the Sultan had been under enormous pressure to make changes. Having refused so many British demands, he now had to yield to some. Thus, by November 1969, he began to hint at the possibility of purchasing helicopters and raising a fourth battalion. However, these hints did not find a meaningful translation into action until after the arrival of a new military secretary, Colonel Hugh Oldman, on 14 February 1970. Oldman was frustrated by the Sultan's lack of action and he was very forthcoming with him on the need for military development. His demands were also reinforced by the Commander of the British Land Forces Persian Gulf, General Roland Gibbs, and the

---

[87] Draft letter from John Wilkinson to Francis Hughes, 9 October 1965, The letter was in fact never sent. I am grateful to Dr Wilkinson for generously sharing a copy of this document.
[88] 'Oman: Annual Review—1970', *RO-5*.

Sultan finally authorized the purchases of helicopters and the raising of a fourth battalion on 20 March 1970.[89] He also undertook some public works initiatives, in a clear attempt to relieve himself of British pressure. On 20 January, he awarded a contract for the pavement of 260 miles of road in Oman and, on 12 March, he announced a contract for a port in Mutrah.[90]

In accordance with the February assessment, the British were no longer satisfied by such partial responses to their requirements. News of the planned May review was spreading through the ranks of British military and diplomatic officials, and they were keenly anticipating the Sultan's answer.[91] The Sultan was invited to the review on 8 April 1970, receiving a letter from the Foreign Secretary, Michael Stewart, emphasizing the dangerous threat of 'communist elements':

> I am sure Your Highness shares my concern about these dangers and, in this connection, I was glad to learn that Your Highness has recently taken important decisions to strengthen the ability of the Sultanate to guard against them and to assure its future stability. This seems to me the right time to have an exchange of views with Your Highness on likely future developments which might be taken to promote our common objectives.[92]

The review was conducted between the Sultan and the Political Resident (PR), Sir Stewart Crawford on 2–4 May 1970. The PR was accompanied by Anthony Figgis, a member of his staff, as well as the Head of the Arabian Department, Antony Acland. In total, they had nine hours of official discussion with the Sultan and two more hours of dinner conversation. Their talks covered six principal matters: the military situation in Dhufar; civilian measures in support of the military effort in the Dhufari Jabal; development in Salalah plain; the British desire for withdrawal from RAF Salalah; and development in Oman. The Sultan showed some flexibility on most matters. Nevertheless, he was unresponsive when it came to RAF Salalah and the civilian measures on the Jabal. On these matters he was 'polite but unyielding', insisting that development 'would go at the pace he determined for it'. He also made it clear that any British attempt 'to interfere in his internal affairs would be unwelcome'.[93] Regarding the

---

[89] Purdon, *List the Bugle,* p.221.
[90] FCO 8/1669, 'Oman: Annual Review—1970'.
[91] See for example 'Muscat and Oman', Acland to Wright (Tehran), 7 April 1970, *RO, Vol.5,* p.12.
[92] 'The Sultanate of Muscat and Oman, Steering Brief for Review—Annex E'. *RO-5,* pp.399–400.
[93] 'Oman: Annual Review—1970.'

airbase 'he said in terms and with emphasis "if R.A.F. Salalah goes, R.A.F. Masirah goes"...'[94]

As for Jabali development in Dhufar, he argued, that civilian measures could not be undertaken until the military situation improved. In his view

> ...the rebels now operated through the whole length of the jebel, and any civilian effort would require considerable military protection. In any case, civilian activities would present great difficulties, given the nature of the country and the jebali people. With his existing resources, and in present circumstances, it was just not practicable to undertake such activities. SAF's priority task had to be to improve the military situation. Only when this had been achieved, and when greater pacification had returned to the jebel, could effective civilian measures from his own resources be contemplated.[95]

In spite of receiving such a negative reaction from the Sultan, the PR was careful not to press for any hasty action in his summary of the discussion to the Foreign Secretary:

> I should like to have been able to report that we had succeeded in securing substantial progress on all points. In fact, this was unlikely from the start and so events turned out. On the positive side, we obtained confirmation of the Sultan's recent decisions on the expansion of S.A.F., of his firm resolve and that of his military authorities to hold the position in Dhofar militarily until they were ready to move forward against the rebels, of his and their reasonable confidence in being able to do so...We clarified with the Sultan our respective positions over R.A.F. Salalah and over the conduct of British seconded personnel...We were less successful in getting him to commit to the precise measures of civilian development, whether in Dhufar or Oman...[96]

The PR still believed that progress could be made with the Sultan but that this required keeping up 'steady pressure on him over a period'.[97] The Sultan was walking a tightrope with a sympathetic, but increasingly frustrated, Political Resident, his actions soliciting increasing concern from London's highest policy-making circles.

---

[94] 'Discussions with the Sultan of Muscat and Oman at Salalah, 2nd–4th May 1970, Bahrain Despatch of 12th May 1970', *RO-5,* pp.671–98.

[95] DEFE24/1855, 'Enclosures Attached to the Discussions with the Sultan of Muscat and Oman at Salalah: Civilian Measures in the Jebel in Support of the Military Effort', 12 May 1970.

[96] 'Discussions with the Sultan of Muscat and Oman at Salalah, 2nd–4th May 1970', Discussions with the Sultan of Muscat and Oman at Salalah...' pp.687–8.

[97] 'Discussions with the Sultan of Muscat and Oman at Salalah, 2nd–4th May 1970' p.690.

7

The Sultan is Deposed, Long Reign the Sultan!

Britain's Political Resident, Sir Stewart Crawford, was clearly disappointed with the May review: 'When I took an overall view of our discussions with the Sultan at their conclusion, I considered that they had been a useful step in our relations but somewhat disappointing in content, specifically over the speed of civilian development'.[1] Crawford informed the Sultan of his disappointment, and he told him that it might be shared by the Foreign Secretary. Nevertheless, he wanted to see how things would go for a few months, and to review the situation by means of an October 1970 ministerial visit. He believed that the Sultan was willing to pursue some, if not comprehensive, development, that he would at least undertake the projects he had committed to, and that he could be persuaded to do more afterwards. He pinned his hopes on convincing the Sultan to appoint a Chief Secretary. Just as the Military Secretary, Oldman, was able to induce change on the military front, securing major purchases for the army, it was hoped that a Chief Secretary would get the development ball rolling. The Sultan had not rejected that idea in the May review, and that was a good sign.[2] He further showed unexpected enthusiasm about starting a public relations effort to show off developmental achievements in the Sultanate.

All of these signs convinced the PR to give the Sultan a chance, but he was of course aware of the difficulties. Indeed, the beginning of the May Review coincided with the resignation of Robin Young, the Secretary of Development Co-ordination, in protest at the Sultan's refusal to grant him an audience, his ban on him touring the country, and his failure to give him meaningful functions.[3] The Sultan was hiring development bureaucrats, only to prevent them from pursuing their mandates. Even in the few areas where work had begun, fiascos occurred, often the result of cost

---

[1] 'Discussions with the Sultan', 12 May 1970, *RO-5,* p.689.
[2] 'Discussions with the Sultan', 12 May 1970, *RO-5,* p.697.
[3] 'Robin Young's Letter of Resignation'. 8 April 1970, *RO-5,* p.882.

cutting. Khimji Ramdas, the Banyan firm through which the Sultan conducted much of his business, built a water scheme in Sur without carrying out proper surveys and the water in that city became saline as a result.[4] Two hospitals were constructed in Ruwi (just outside Muscat) and Tan'am (in the interior) but they 'had no equipment, personnel or medicines'.[5]

The PR knew of this. He also knew of the frustrations of Whitehead, the main firm advising the Sultan on administrative reform. Throughout 1969 and early 1970, the firm, through its agent John Townsend, had studied ways of modernizing the administration, submitting reports on establishing and running a water board, a reorganized municipality, a department of agriculture and fisheries, roads, a development board secretariat, a health department, and a port authority.[6] They also made further suggestions, including the establishment of a civil offences tribunal with an eye to legal modernization.[7] Most of these suggestions were shelved and in the weeks following the May review, the firm made much noise highlighting that fact. Agitating further against the Sultan, the Consul General wrote to the Residency:

> Whitehead's excellent series of reports…are currently sitting in the Sultan's office sharing space with the efforts of previous experts. It is doubtful if Sayid Said has read the reports since he certainly has not acted upon them. From his point of view, they represent a useful instrument with which to demonstrate to his European visitors his concerns over modern government and development.[8]

Although it was not the fundamental factor in directing the future course of events, the Whitehead affair was one more grievance added to the list. If anything, it signalled the arrival of a new player in the Sultanate community, that of western consultancy firms. Their role in formulating policy only grew over the years and despite its general neglect in the historical literature on the Gulf, this new development merits attention. Indeed, no comprehensive view of the coalescing factors that shaped the construction of the Omani state can ignore the part played by consultancies. For now, however, the technocratic age had to wait.

In spite of their disappointments with him in private, the British were desperate to show off the Sultan's supposed achievements publicly. In late

---

[4] 'Development in the Sultanate', Crawford (Muscat) to Weir, 18 January 1970, p.851.
[5] 'Industrial development in Muscat and Oman', Foreign Office Minute to Mr Blackley, p.894.
[6] 'Meeting, Major Chauncy', Note by Townsend, 18 January 1970, *RO-5*, pp.853–4.
[7] 'Report on Civil Offences Tribunal', Harold Whitehead & Partners, Muscat, April 1970, *RO-5*, pp.896–905.
[8] 'John Townsend', Crawford (Muscat) to Weir. 16 May 1970. *RO-5*, p.907.

May, Muscat's main development official, John Pelly, sent out a press release of completed and planned projects. There were only two ventures that could be seriously talked about: a water pipe scheme for Muscat and Mutrah (which had finally been finished on 27 April 1970, its water carefully priced so as to generate revenue for the Sultan); and the aforementioned two unstaffed and unfurnished hospitals. Confronted with a lack of actual accomplishments, Pelly tried his luck at the art of spin, claiming that £20 million worth of projects had been allocated for the purpose of development. The British Consul General, based on Pelly's own private admissions, noted that this was a 'flattering but not especially accurate figure', which was mostly based on wildly exaggerated estimates for projects that the Sultan might decide to begin in the future. While the press release proudly announced that 'the development of the country has been accelerated', the Consul General made sure he warned his superiors that 'there was not much sign of accelerated development'.[9]

Aware of the dire realities, the British persevered in their spinning. Antony Acland, the head of the Arabian Department, was becoming embroiled in the PR game. Realizing that developmental news 'is going to remain very much on the thin side', he called for intensifying the propaganda effort: 'adverse publicity about the Sultanate is not in British interests since the criticism will inevitably rub off on us. For the time being we must do what we can to reverse this trend by giving what publicity we can to useful developments which are taking place.' In this vein, he indicated that the FCO would feed propaganda to the BBC Arabic service while the Consulate in Muscat should do the same with *Sawt-as-Sahil*, Britain's propaganda venue in the southern Gulf.[10]

Feeding propaganda was important, especially considering the scale of issues the British had to cover-up. British protection of deliberate economic underdevelopment was just the tip of the iceberg, the persistence of slavery having an even greater potential for generating disapproval. As of 1962, the Sultanate was the only place in the world where chattel slavery was still legal, the Sultan owning the largest number of slaves in the country by far. Yet, there was hardly a cry from British journalists—complaints tended to be waged by Communist bloc reporters in solidarity with the Dhufar revolution, contrasting the universal emancipation practiced by the revolutionaries with the slave ownership of the Sultan. Within Britain itself, the only organized effort at challenging slavery in the Sultanate was

---

[9] 'Civil Development in the Sultanate', Donald Crawford (Muscat) to M.S. Weir, 25 May 1970, *RO*, *Vol. 5*, pp.911–13.
[10] 'Publicity for the Sultanate', Acland to D.G. Crawford (Muscat). 4 June 1970. *RO-5*, p.917.

politely conducted behind the scenes by the Anti-Slavery Society, chaired by a Conservative Member of Parliament, Sir Douglas Glover. An anti-communist, he was by no means an enemy of the Sultanate, but he raised the issue of slavery at several private meetings held in the FCO, and in letters sent to the department. Although the society had tried to draw attention to Oman on numerous occasions before, its pleas were usually ignored.[11] However, the recent protests it had been making coincided with the Foreign Secretary's interest in the Sultanate, which had begun following the revolutionary attacks on RAF Salalah.

Lacking any knowledge of the subject, Stewart requested a short note on slavery in the Sultanate. In the note, he was informed that slavery was 'legal in Muscat and Oman. The Sultan himself owns slaves.'[12] British bureaucrats defended this in several ways, including a spectacular deployment of the 'happy slave' argument. It was noted that the British Consul had the right to grant manumission, but the fact 'that very few slaves apply for manumission perhaps indicates that a man is better fed, clothed and cared for as a slave of the Sultan or others than as an unemployed freeman'. This was then supplemented by a genuinely novel analogy: 'in the conditions obtaining in the Sultanate, slavery can be regarded in some respects as the local equivalent of the welfare state'. Of course, all of these expostulations were presented after insisting that Muscat and Oman was 'an independent and sovereign state', a clear effort to imply that Britain (which practically ran most of the Sultanate's affairs at the time) was in no position to interfere in it.[13]

In spite of learning of the situation, the Foreign Secretary (a proud Fabian) made no effort to intervene on this specific issue. To the queries of the Anti-Slavery Society, his underlings responded with redrafts of the above-mentioned minute.[14] Such human rights issues had no bearing whatsoever on British policy. Far more important were the opinions of Shell and the Political Residency. As was shown in the previous chapter, frustration had been brewing in the Company for years and the Political Residency had been subjected to a barrage of anti-Said complaints from the Consul General in Muscat. These were taken very seriously by the

---

[11] This is reflected in the private papers of the Anti-Slavery Society, which detail the extensive correspondences with the British government over Muscat and Oman conducted throughout the 1960s. See Bodleian-RH, ASSP, G958, G959 and G959a.

[12] 'Slavery in the Sultanate of Muscat and Oman'. Note for Secretary of State by J.M. Edes, 4 May 1970, *RO-5*, pp.1002–3.

[13] 'Slavery in the Sultanate of Muscat and Oman'. Note for Secretary of State by J.M. Edes, 4 May 1970, *RO-5*, pp.1002–3.

[14] See for instance, the letter from Evan Luard (FCO) to Douglas Glover (Chairman, Anti-Slavery Society), 27 May 1970, *RO-5*, pp.1000–1.

Deputy Political Resident, Michael Weir, who later described the attitudes of the various players in his unpublished memoirs:

> The Consul-General...came to the conclusion that the Sultan would have to go....Others with longer experience of Oman, including the head of Shell's operations [Francis Hughes]...and the senior British adviser to the government [Colonel Oldman]...came more reluctantly to the same conclusion...Having been closely involved in the two previous British-engineered palace coups in the Gulf I might perhaps have been predisposed to accept the case for a further deposition, but I had been hearing arguments in favour (notably from Shaikh Zaid) for nearly twenty years...The Political Resident...had particular misgivings...[15]

Although they differed in opinion, all these characters shared a belief in the need to keep a close watch on the Sultan. He was on probation but he had at least until October to sort out his topsy-turvy realm. It was not until mid-June that things fundamentally changed. Something tipped the balance: something of such magnitude as to induce a complete change of British policy.

THE REVOLUTIONARY *FOCO* PLOT

Once again, the progress of events was determined by revolutionary initiative. This time however, the location of action was Oman proper as opposed to Dhufar, and the initiator was not PFLOAG, but a sister organization, the National Democratic Front for the Liberation of Oman and the Arab Gulf (NDFLOAG). The origins of NDFLOAG go back to the Dubai Extraordinary Conference held in July 1968 by the Gulf branches of the Movement of Arab Nationalists (MAN). As shown in Chapter 2, the conference led to the abandonment of the MAN and the establishment of a leftist Gulf-wide offshoot organization called the Popular Revolutionary Movement in Oman and the Arab Gulf (PRM).

With the approach of British withdrawal from the Gulf, the PRM vowed to 'carry the task of initiating the armed struggle of the poor masses and the proletariat; to stand in the way of all the powers of counterrevolution; and to undermine imperialist plans'.[16] The most popular theory of revolution during this period was the Guevaran *foco*. This theory, popularized by Regis Debray in his 1967 book *Revolution in the Revolution*, stipulated the establishment of focal points of action out of which armed struggle would spread and expand. The Omani interior was chosen as the initial *foco* for the anticipated revolution, due to its favourable geographic terrain and

---

[15] Weir, *Unfinished Memoires*, p. 97.
[16] Al-Ikri, *Al-Tanthimat al-Yassariya fil Jazeera wal Khaleej al 'Arabi*, p. 83.

conducive political climate. Preparations for the struggle there were not only undertaken by the Omani cadres of the PRM, but by the Gulf-wide network as a whole, which was coordinated by a Political Bureau located in the Deirah district of Dubai and composed of six members.[17]

The PRM cadres in Dubai undertook a campaign to fundraise for the planned action. Contributions were provided by members, including Abdel Rahman al-Nuaimi, who—following the habit of many revolutionaries— dedicated the better part of a handsome salary (he was a senior engineer at the time) towards his political activities. More importantly, the work was sponsored by patriotic Trucial Coast merchants. Without doubt, the most supportive amongst these was Sultan al-Owais, a grand merchant and a poet, who is best remembered today by the al-Owais awards, the Arab world's most prestigious literary and academic honours. Accounting for his historic legacy is an endeavour greater than this space allows. Suffice to note that he played a civic role in the establishment of the United Arab Emirates and that, as leader of the *wi'hdah* (unity) party, he was a major player in a nationalist coup against Sheikh Khaled of Sharjah, a role for which he eventually paid with temporary exile in Pakistan.

Al-Owais was an Arab nationalist who believed in the 'Natural Oman' idea, the unification of the Trucial States with Muscat and Oman.[18] He was joined by other men of trade and commerce who wanted a vehicle for regional modernization and transformation, united in their desire for the removal of Said bin Taimur. Unhappy with the Imamate's stale traditionalism, they turned to the more dynamic Nasserist current represented by the MAN Gulf cadres. Their relationship with the latter went back to the mid-1960s, established with the help of Egypt and the MAN national leadership in Beirut. This relationship was threatened following the leftward shift in the MAN, the newly established PRM having voted to cut off relations with 'bourgeois elements' and to achieve self-sufficiency. However, the desperate need for support occasioned a reconsideration on the part of the PRM Political Bureau. The merchants were thus approached again and they gave substantial financial support.

The donations were collected by Ahmad Saif Bal Hasa (Marwan), PRM central committee member and representative in Dubai. He used much of the funds for the purchase of weapons from Iraq and for their dispatch to their final locations. This was anything but a simple process, its complications revealing outstanding logistical competence. Some of the weapons

---

[17] Abdel Rahman al-Nuaimi, 'Al Nuhud al Qawmi wal Watani Ba'da Hazimat Yuniou', *Al-Dimuqrati*, Vol. 30, 2006; and 'Tarjamat Qararat al-Mutamar al-Tawheedi', *Al-Wasat*, 1 January 2009.

[18] Al-Nuaimi, 'Al-Sibaq Ala al-Tartibat al-Siyassiya', *Al-Wasat*, 30 October 2008.

were sent to Dubai, repacked in oil drums and re-exported to Massanah, a discreet location on Oman's Batinah coast. From Massanah, the shipment was sent to the Omani interior via an inland route. Another consignment was flown to Aden by the South Yemeni Air Force, and this arrangement had to be secured through the good offices of PFLOAG. In Aden, the weapons were repacked into oil drums and shipped to Sur. From that port they were taken by launch to Azaiba and finally taken to the interior. In an early instance of coordination with Palestinian groups, these Iraqi shipments were supplemented by a small amount of pistols given by the Popular Democratic Front for the Liberation of Palestine (PDFLP) via Abdel Rahman Jamal, a Bahraini cadre who did coordination work for the PRM in the Northern Gulf and in Beirut.[19]

Besides the arms, substantial monetary support was sent from Dubai to Oman. To maximize security, monies were smuggled via two routes. Twelve thousand Saidi Riyals were sent to South Yemen and thence into Oman by Nasr Ali (Humaid), a cadre with a launch at Sur. Another twenty-five thousand were taken directly from Dubai by Zaher Ali Matar Al-Miyahi (Ahmad Ali), the Omani revolutionary *par excellence* and a leader of the PRM.[20] Zaher was born in 1941 to a poor family living in the al-Jabal al-Akhdar village of Tanuf. His home suffered British aerial bombardment and was destroyed during the al-Jabal-al-Akhdar revolt (1957–59). In 1957, he, along with his family, sought refuge in the neighbouring town of Birkat al-Mauz. Following the end of the revolt Zaher moved again, this time to Saudi Arabia where he got a menial job in Dhahran airport, working there for two years. In 1961, he joined the Imamate forces and moved to al-Taef for training, but he was quickly disappointed with Imamate inaction, and at some point in the early 1960s he moved to Iraq, where he enrolled in the MAN and became a leading activist in Omani student circles.[21]

Zaher experienced all the successes and failures of his generation of Omanis but his was a more intense experience than most. Painfully feeling the effects of the Palestinian *naksa*, he participated in the 1968 Dubai Conference, helping to draft the MAN's death certificate and sign the PRM's birth announcement. He travelled the region in search of revolutionary connections, visiting the Palestinian camps of the *fedayeen* and giving provocative speeches to Lebanese peasants in Akkar in a heavy

---

[19] MEC, Graham Papers, 'The National Democratic Front for the Liberation of Oman and the Arabian Gulf, A Branch of the People's Revolutionary Movement', Intelligence Department, Sultan's Armed Forces, 3 March 1971.

[20] MEC, Graham Papers, 'The National Democratic Front for the Liberation of Oman and the Arabian Gulf'.

[21] Al-Jabha al-Shabiya, *Sijil al Khalideen, Al Juz' al Awal, 1965–1979*, n.d., *c.*1980, p.171.

Omani accent further obscured by a distinctive stutter. Zaher crisscrossed borders with numerous false passports and an outstanding talent for disguise.[22] Over the years, his seemingly endless assumption of characters became the stuff of in-jokes. Not without a touch of humour, his letters would have such endings as 'Your Comrade, Ahmad Ali (Mana' Said at present),' the earliest *nom de guerre* followed by the most recent.[23]

Zaher was operating in a charged atmosphere. Throughout 1969, the revolutionaries suffered several blows, including the arrest in August of al-Nuaimi, who was effectively directing the PRM politbureau.[24] Nevertheless, the preparations went ahead and the revolutionaries were trickling into Oman, recruiting cautiously. Administrative matters were handled by Juma Ithnayen (Rashid) and the two Ahmads: Ahmad Humaidan (Salim) from Bahrain and Ahmad al-Rubei (Tariq) from Kuwait.[25] These two cadres from the northern Gulf were also responsible for political education. The former was a member of the PRM central committee and, in the words of one intelligence report, he had a 'vast background of political activity'.[26] The latter was one of the main figures behind the leftist split from the MAN in Kuwait and the establishment of the Kuwaiti branch of the PRM in October 1968.

Ahmad al-Rubei had just arrived from Kuwait after an intense set of experiences there. The authorities discovered the PRM branch in Kuwait, and twenty-one suspected members were put on trial before the State Security Court (case number 670/1969), the most sensational case of its kind in Kuwaiti history. Only four of the suspects had managed to escape, amongst whom was Ahmad, who was convicted *in absentia* and given a seven-year sentence.[27] Years later, he would earn a PhD from Harvard, chair Kuwait University's philosophy department, thrice gain election to parliament, and become Kuwait's Minister of Education. For now, this 21-year-old was spreading revolution.[28]

[22] Fawaz Trabulsi, *Wu'oud Adan: Rihlaat Yamaniya*, Beirut: Riad el-Rayyes Books, 2000, pp.131–2; Abdel Rahman al-Nuaimi, 'Tarjamat Qararat al-Mutamar al-Tawheedi', *Al-Wasat*, 1 January 2009.

[23] MEC, Graham, Box 3/6, 'Letter Written by Zaher Ali Matar', 7 October 1972, Annex G, to Report on PFLOAG, 20 July 1973.

[24] Al-Nuaimi, 'Al-Sibaq Ala al-Tartibat al-Siyassiya', *Al-Wasat*, 30 October 2008.

[25] MEC, Graham Papers, 'The National Democratic Front for the Liberation of Oman and the Arabian Gulf'.

[26] MEC, Graham Papers, 'The National Democratic Front for the Liberation of Oman and the Arabian Gulf'.

[27] Falah Al-Mdairis, *Al Tawajuhat al Marxia al Kuwaitia*, Kuwait: Dar Qirtas lil Nashr, 2003, pp. 46–53.

[28] Al Rubei passed away on 5/3/2008. See 'Rah'eel Faris al Kalima', *Al-'Arabi*, issue no.594, May 2008.

The two Ahmads, along with Zaher and Juma'a, were members of the central committee of the PRM's Omani branch. A glimpse at the surnames of other members reveals the degree to which the central committee's composition reflected very diverse tribal and regional backgrounds, with members coming from Bahla, Birkat al Mawz, Sur and other areas. The central committee included two graduates of the Military Academy in Cairo: Bati Khalifa Said and Hafith al-Ghassani. It also included: Ali al-Raisi al-Baluchi; Juma'a al-Nuaimi al-Farsi; Rashid al-Utabi; Ali al-Taywani; and Yahya al-Ghassani. Each of these belonged to one of five committees: administrative; propaganda; finance; political; and military.[29]

The military committee was of particular importance, and it was under the leadership of Yahya al-Ghassani who had served with the Iraqi army as an Engineer Officer for nearly four years, acquiring training in 'all aspects of military engineering including demolitions'.[30] Drawing on this experience, he formed two main fighting groups in the Omani interior, one in Wadi Mahram and another in al-Jabal al-Akhdar. The total strength under his command was 30 men, but this was envisioned as a seed that would grow once successful operations were conducted.

The two main fighting groups were complemented by a third located in the ancient port of Sur and a sabotage unit of 8 men based in Mutrah. Due to its geographic distance, the Sur group was semi-independent, having access to its own locally stored weapons. As for the sabotage unit—which incidentally included Salim Nasr al-Bu Saidi, a member of the extended ruling family—it had access to arms cached in Azaiba and Siddab. With this equipment, it was to pursue several assassination and sabotage targets already identified in a pre-drafted list.

In April 1970, after a year of preparations, the PRM's Omani branch adopted the new name of NDFLOAG. This change was made unilaterally and without due appeal to the central politbureau in Dubai, but it did not represent a split from the PRM. Instead, it signified frustration with organizational problems at the central level, disappointment at the numerous obstacles that had afflicted the work, and aggravation about the politbureau's lack of coordination with other progressive groups.[31] Moreover, it reflected a desire to give the PRM's branch in Oman 'a more regional

---

[29] MEC, Graham Papers, 'The National Democratic Front for the Liberation of Oman and the Arabian Gulf'.

[30] MEC, Graham Papers, 'The National Democratic Front for the Liberation of Oman and the Arabian Gulf'.

[31] 'Taqreer 'An al 'Hiwar Bayna 'Hizb al 'Amal al-'Arabi fi 'Oman wal 'Haraka al-Thawria al-Sha'abiya fi 'Oman wl Khaleej al-'Arabi', May 1971, unpublished private papers of Mohammad Jamal Barut.

and militant title which would appeal to those dedicated to the overthrow of Sai'd bin Taimur.'[32]

NDFLOAG was too much in tune with tricontinental revolutionary theory to wait for objective revolutionary circumstances to develop. Its cadres were imbued with the spirits of Castro and Guevara, captivated by the legend of the *Granma* and the 22 survivors that initiated the Cuban revolution. The ruggedness of al-Jabal al-Akhdar and the interior matched the roughness of the Sierra Maestra; the Omani contempt for Sultan Said was at least equal to Cuban hatred of Batista; and the shabby Sultanic administration was much weaker than the Cuban state. All of these factors suggested that a small revolutionary vanguard could launch a successful armed struggle in Oman, and that it would build up popular support in the process, attracting demoralized soldiers from the SAF. The timing was also right. Revolution had to occur before Britain could strengthen its protectorates, something it was clearly working on as part of its 1971 withdrawal arrangements.

The plan was to begin simultaneous attacks against SAF camps on the early morning of 12 June. The Wadi Mahram group would assault Izki camp, while the al-Jabal al-Akhdar group would hit Nizwa camp. The former would then return to its home base, gather its strength, and then launch an attack on Bid-Bid camp as fast as it could. Once these assaults took effect, they would be followed by a sabotage and assassination campaign carried out by the Mutrah group in their home base, its twin city Muscat, and the oil company complex in Mina al-Fahl. The Sur group would then overthrow government representatives in the Sharqiya province.[33] In the midst of this instability, and as more and more people heard the news, the revolutionary momentum would grow and the Anglo-Sultanic order would be caught between PFLOAG in Dhufar and NDFLOAG in Oman.

At 3:00 a.m. on 12 June 1970, nine members of the Wadi Mahram group attacked the Izki camp, occupied by a company of the Northern Frontier Regiment. The revolutionaries opened fire with rifles, Bren machine guns, and semi-automatics, using walkie-talkies to coordinate their deployment. However, with these light weapons, they did not manage to inflict any serious damage on the camp or any casualties amongst the soldiers. After an exchange of fire, the revolutionaries withdrew, covered by the cloak of darkness. The army immediately sent a follow-up

---

[32] MEC, Graham Papers, 'The National Democratic Front for the Liberation of Oman and the Arabian Gulf'.
[33] MEC, Graham Papers, 'The National Democratic Front for the Liberation of Oman and the Arabian Gulf'.

patrol to chase them with the help of trackers and a beaver airplane and they were located the next day.[34] A fierce fight ensued, resulting in the death of two soldiers and the wounding of one. Three central committee members and two fighters were killed. The rest of the crew were arrested on the spot, or apprehended over the following week, and subjected to interrogation by a specialist intelligence team sent directly from the UK.[35]

From then onwards, it all went downhill for the revolutionaries. The al-Jabal al-Akhdar group did not even carry out their attack on Nizwa camp, only managing to plant a defective sabotage device, which was found on the morning of June 12. Five weeks later, on July 20, the police raided the safe house of the Mutrah sabotage and assassination cell, arresting five of its members and four NDFLOAG central committee members.[36] Although the al-Jabal and Sur groups were largely unharmed, their leaders had now been exposed and were being searched for, their tracking facilitated by the British intelligence network that was spread across the Gulf.

What explains the utter failure of the June 12 insurrection? For years, revolutionary *auto-critiques* attacked the '*foco* mentality' and Debray's Guevaran theory. This trend was supported by the fact that Debray himself had eventually rejected his own formulations, and failed attempts at creating *focos* across Latin America and Africa seemed to confirm the correctness of that rejection. But whereas revolutionary analyses saw defeats such as June 12 from a grand theoretical standpoint, the counter-revolutionaries read them through an empirical prism. The SAF intelligence characterized the issue as one of inadequate training and uneven consciousness amongst revolutionary ranks. The main intelligence report on the June 12 events noted that, with the exception of Yahya al-Ghassani, none of the revolutionaries were properly trained.[37] Although some had been given courses in Iraq, PFLOAG's revolution camp, the Palestinian bases of Fateh in Jordan, and the Egyptian and Syrian military academies, their military record was clearly deficient.

We may add another major reason for the June 12 failure: the choice of targets. The SAF Company stationed in Izki belonged to the NFR, a highly trained and equipped force. Attacking such a force with 9 men was

---

[34] 'Muscat to Bahrain Telegram No. 235', 13 June 1970, *RO-5,* p.356.

[35] 'Security Situation in Oman', 15 June 1970, *RO-5,* p. 357; and MEC, Graham Papers, 'The National Democratic Front for the Liberation of Oman and the Arabian Gulf'.

[36] MEC, Graham Papers, 'The National Democratic Front for the Liberation of Oman and the Arabian Gulf'.

[37] MEC, Graham Papers, 'The National Democratic Front for the Liberation of Oman and the Arabian Gulf'.

clearly a mistake. A more reasonable alternative would have been to organize a series of assaults against the weak structure of *walis* and *'askars* spread across the interior and to engage in popular mobilization in the course of the process. Would the Omani *foco* plot have succeeded in that case? To give an answer would be to indulge in counterfactuality. All that can be said is that the British were not willing to take any future risks. If the PFLOAG revolutionaries provided the long-term causes of the 1970 coup, the NDFLOAG action was the short-term catalyst that determined its precise timing.

PLANNING THE COUP

June 12 had a major impact on the British. In the words of Brigadier John Graham, the new Commander of the SAF (CSAF):

> . . . we became aware of the great number of people both in the coastal towns and in the Interior who had come to support by word or deed the aims and activities of NDFLOAF and the lesser rebel movements. Many were openly dismayed that SAF by its success in the Wadi Mahram had thwarted the overthrow of Said bin Taimur; and we were left in no doubt that other patriots were waiting for further opportunities to strike with greater skill and effectiveness.[38]

The shock was great, not the least because the action was unexpected. As late as 11 June, a conference of all intelligence staff in the Sultanate did not anticipate any immediate threats in northern Oman.[39] After 12 June, all illusions were dissipated. The phrase 'young Omanis' became far more frequently used in British correspondences. This broad social category was deemed a looming threat, a source of British fear that somehow had to be controlled. Thousands of them were abroad, discontented and awaiting change, and dozens were preparing across the Arab world and elsewhere to overthrow the monarchy.

The young people involved with NDFLOAG were by no means restricted to disadvantaged sectors of the population: they included a member of the ruling family; the son of the senior Judge Sheikh Ibrahim al-Abri; two staff members of the British company Cable and Wireless; and three employees of the Ministry of the Interior.[40] In this context, the

---

[38] MEC, Graham Papers, 'The National Democratic Front for the Liberation of Oman and the Arabian Gulf', p.328.

[39] MEC, Graham Papers, 'The National Democratic Front for the Liberation of Oman and the Arabian Gulf', p.324.

[40] 'Telegram No. 241', Muscat to Bahrain, 18 June 1970, *RO-5*, p.361.

Consul General sent the Residency and the Arabian Department a despatch on 14 June, expressing his 'general views' on Britain's relationship with the Sultan, and illustrating the advantages of removing him.[41] In a subsequent despatch, sent on 17 June, he opined that:

> ... if there is a general feeling in the country now, it is that the Sultan's rule cannot go on, since it will lead to a take over [*sic*] after what might prove to be a bitter period of fighting by the young Omanis, encouraged by their Communist supporters. The only alternative, it is generally considered, is for Sayid Tariq and Talib bin Ali working with or without Qaboos to take over the government. Hopefully this will be done with British acquiescence, thus avoiding bloodshed but, if necessary, we would have to be shown painfully the error of our ways for our own good, since it is assumed that we are against the Communists as well.[42]

This was a challenge to the 'wait and see' approach which British Gulf officialdom had previously held on to. The message was that the Sultan would eventually be replaced but the British had a choice: to replace him themselves; or to have him removed by the 'young Omanis', who would then worryingly 'take over' their own country from British hands. The Consul General fired all his guns, and in order to ensure that his superiors understood that this was not just simply a personal predisposition on his part but an objective assessment, he pointed to the SAF Intelligence analysis of the situation: 'This is an interpretation of the current mood in the country I have received from several sources, notably from GII Int. SAF and it is a mood which further incidents of the kind that took place on 12 June would only reinforce.'[43]

The Political Resident, who had hitherto been more cautious in his assessments, was now in support of the Consul General's view that a change of ruler would be favourable to British interests, sending a despatch to that effect on 22 June. The Head of the Arabian Department, Antony Acland, endorsed the conclusions of this despatch, noting that 'all those with long experience of Sultanate and Gulf affairs, including our representatives in the area, are unanimous in concluding that if a change of Sultan occurred, this would be on the whole less disadvantageous to British interests, and to the maintenance of peace and stability in the Sultanate, than a continuation of the present situation'.[44]

---

[41] The CG refers to this despatch in his letter to M.S. Baker-Bates of the Foreign Office's UN (E&S) Department. 21 June 1970. *RO-5*, p.1004.

[42] 'Security Situation in Oman', 17 June 1970, *RO-5*, pp.359–60.

[43] 'Security Situation in Oman', 17 June 1970, *RO-5*, pp.359–60.

[44] DEFE 24/1855, 'The Sultanate of Muscat and Oman: Possibility of a Coup', A.A. Acland to Hayman, 8 July 1970.

The views expressed in these assessments, directly occasioned by the 12 June revolutionary action, were widely shared even at the highest levels of policy. Yet, the initial catalyst for action came from the intelligence officer based in Dhufar, Tim Landon, who was a relatively minor character at the time. The latter had reported on a meeting he had held with Qaboos, noting that the young man was considering launching a coup against his father.[45] It cannot be conclusively determined if Landon had suggested this idea to Qaboos, or whether it was the other way round. However, the circumstantial evidence overwhelmingly suggests that Landon would have most likely made the suggestion. After all, the whole affair was sparked off by someone who was well informed about the atmosphere prevailing in British circles, and who knew that HMG's officials would be receptive to the idea of a coup precisely at that moment in time. Isolated in Salalah, and having no regular British connection other than Landon, Qaboos could not have possibly been privy to the sort of information required for planning such a feat. An element of trust had existed between him and Landon, probably nurtured by their shared background in Sandhurst's 29th intake. Considering the fact that they were part of different colleges and companies, it is highly unlikely that they were close there.[46] Nevertheless, the shared experience gave Landon a unique starting point from which to position himself as Qaboos's middleman, a function that he profited from for the rest of his life. Rising from the relatively humble background of a fourth son of a British officer and a Canadian Hollywood make-up artist, he became one of the largest landowners in Britain at the time of his death in 2007, often referred to as the 'White Sultan of Oman'.[47]

In any case, the Landon message did not have any inherent significance, except in that it precipitated British discussion. For, even if he and Qaboos had wished to carry out a coup, they did not have the means to do so, as they would both have been aware. A coup required SAF approval and implementation, and that meant British authorization. Whilst this was clear to all the players, participants in the British policy discussion at this stage did not initially speak of these matters with such clarity. This was because there was a general reluctance when it came to Said bin Taimur. The Sultan was Britain's oldest and most reliable client in the Gulf, serving it with loyalty and conviction throughout his long

---

[45]   DEFE 24/1855, CBFG to MOD UK, 26 June 1970.
[46]   'Junior Term, September 1960', *The Wish Stream: Journal of the Royal Military Academy Sandhurst,* Vol. XV, No. 1, Spring, 1961, pp.64–7. See also John Beasant and Christopher Ling, *Sultan in Arabia: A Private Life,* Edinburgh and London: Mainstream Publishing, 2004, p.45.
[47]   'Obituary: Brigadier Tim Landon', *The Guardian,* 28 August 2007; 'Obituary: Brigadier Tim Landon', *The Telegraph,* 12 July 2007.

reign. A coup against such a friend could not be spoken of with the same audacity as a coup against an enemy, at least until the initial formalities had been gone through, and the opinions of various officials had been measured. The Landon message therefore offered a convenient pretext for discussion, and a pivot around which the debate could be centred; it gave the opportunity to all participants to lay their thoughts bare.

In spite of his newly found conviction that the Sultan's removal would be a positive end result, the initial response of the Political Resident was as cautious as usual. He notified the FCO of the news, and expressed the view that the SAF's role in this case would be limited to 'maintaining law and order'.[48] No less cautious was the position of his military counterpart, General Ronnie Gibbs, the Commander of British Forces in the Gulf (CBFG). The latter had visited CSAF Graham on 24 June, shortly after receiving word of the potential coup, reporting to the MOD that he 'recognised the difficult problem which could confront CSAF and his commanders in view of the sympathies which particularly the Arab element of the force have for any nationalist movement which promises relief'. Clearly, the popularity of anti-colonial revolutionary action was feared, especially in the ranks of the army:

> It could come to a situation where Tariq the exiled half-brother to the Sultan and/or Talib returns to raise their banner in Oman (perhaps supported by some 6 hundred odd trained Omanis in Iraq) and receives [sic] overwhelming popular support, including the sympathies of the SAF Arab soldiers. Meanwhile it is always possible that gangs similar to the one at Izki will ambush successfully British Officers, and that the arab [sic] soldiers sympathy towards the gang and respect for their daring and success, starts to outweigh loyalty to their British Officers.[49]

This reality in northern Oman was even more worrying considering the fact that the 1971 campaign in Dhofar was 'looking less promising. The strength of the hard-core rebels is now probably 7 hundred and they have a firm grip on the country and the population.' Against this background, General Gibbs recognized that there was a 'mounting case for a change of Sultan and a growing likelihood to unseat him'. He therefore sought the 'views' of the Ministry of Defence (MOD) on the instructions he should give to CSAF Graham as to how 'his battalion in Salalah should react in various possible contingencies', especially those arising if a Qaboos-centred move took place.[50]

---

[48] DEFE 24/1856, 'Chiefs of Staff Meeting, Wednesday 15th July 1970', DMO Brief No 42/70, Ministry of Defence, Army Department, 14 July 1970.
[49] DEFE 24/1855, CBFG to MOD UK, 26 June 1970.
[50] DEFE 24/1855, CBFG to MOD UK, 26 June 1970.

Over the following three weeks, intense discussions and assessments took place in the FCO, the MOD, the Political Residency, and the British establishment in Muscat. In particular, the debate was focused on addressing the following issue:

> …what HMG would do if Sayyid Qabus [*sic*], the heir apparent, were to mount a coup against the Sultan, his father, were to fail and take refuge with the Sultan's Armed Forces (SAF) near Salalah, and if the Sultan were then to instruct the Commander of the SAF (CSAF) (either directly or through the Military Secretary, Colonel Oldman) to hand Qabus over to him.[51]

The opinion of Colonel Oldman, the Sultanate Defence Minister, clearly mattered in this regard. Although he was, at least in theory, appointed by the Sultan and was solely answerable to him, the reality was quite different. Oldman's ultimate loyalty, it quickly became evident, was to the British government rather than the man he was hired to serve and whose interests he was supposed to protect. Not only had Oldman heard of the potential coup and failed to inform the Sultan of it, but he also had no qualms about discussing coup scenarios with British officials. Initially, he was wary of potential outcomes. On 4 July, he reported that he was of the opinion that if Qaboos were to seek refuge with the SAF, the CSAF would have no choice but to return him to the Sultan.[52] Four days later, the Arabian Department asked the Consul General to speak to him again, in the hope that he would have changed his mind. Oldman was still of the same opinion:

> His reaction was immediate. It was that neither he nor SAF could afford not to surrender Qabus in the circumstances envisaged. To do otherwise would remove any prospect of them maintaining a relationship with Sayid Said which would in turn put in question the security of the Sultanate.[53]

It must not be understood from this that Oldman was solidly against (or for) a coup *per se*. What he opposed was a coup without clear instructions from London and direct British involvement. He made it clear that such a coup could unleash a 'chain of events' which would confront him and the SAF 'with decisions extremely difficult to take unless they were assured of HMG's full backing and support'.[54] He insisted that a failed coup would have the probable consequence of unrest and fighting in Salalah, and could 'strain discipline among the lower ranks of the SAF itself'.

---

[51] DEFE 24/1856, 'Muscat and Oman', J.M. Gibbon (Head of DS11) to Defence Secretary of State, 8 July 1970.

[52] DEFE 24/1856, 'Chiefs of Staff Meeting, Wednesday 15th July 1970'.

[53] DEFE 24/1856, Crawford (Muscat) to Acland (FCO), 8 July 1970.

[54] DEFE 24/1856, Crawford (Muscat) to Acland (FCO), 8 July 1970.

Such 'wide disorder' could potentially 'inhibit the immediate return of Qabus to the Sultan', but it would more importantly 'compel the choice of either supporting Sayid Said against the people or of assisting Qabus to restore the situation. The latter would in effect lead to SAF's active participation in deposing the Sultan.'[55]

On 7 July, the Chief of the Joint Intelligence Committee (JIC) Assessments Staff circulated an assessment of the potential coup. The report showed that 'the obstacles in the way of organising a successful coup are formidable'.[56] This was, of course, assuming that the coup would be led by Qaboos, and without British intervention. The following day, a meeting was held at the FCO, chaired by the Under-Secretary of State, Peter Hayman. The meeting was also attended by two high level representatives from the MOD: the Acting Chief of Defence Staff, and the Head of DS11, the MOD department dealing with Defence outside the NATO area.[57]

An FCO Arabian Department note distributed before the 8 July meeting presented Qaboos as a favourable alternative to the Sultan. It was noted that he spoke English, was educated in England, and seemed 'generally very well disposed towards the UK'. Although he did not have any government experience, 'both Oldman, the Sultan's Defence Secretary, and Hughes, the local Shell Manager, think well of Qabus and believe that, with proper support, he could make a good ruler'. It was hoped that 'once he were firmly in the saddle, he would carry out reforms sufficiently quickly to achieve a significant reduction in discontent in the Sultanate, especially in Dhofar but also in Oman'.[58]

The main problem confronting FCO officials was that they did not want Qaboos to be handed to the Sultan if this projected coup, reported by Landon, were to happen and fail. Unwanted consequences that were likely to arise out of such an outcome were negative public opinion in Britain and damage to British standing in the Arab world:

> ... it would be regarded by public opinion in this country, in the Persian Gulf, in the wider Arab world and in the world at large as ... unethical to hand Qabus over for almost certain torture and possible death. Public opinion, particularly in this country would be horrified, and HMG would be widely held responsible for failure to prevent such action by a force commanded by British seconded officers. As a result, there could be

---

[55] DEFE 24/1856, Crawford (Muscat) to Acland (FCO), 8 July 1970.
[56] DEFE 24/1855, 'The Sultanate of Muscat and Oman: Possibility of a Coup'. A.A. Acland to Hayman, 8 July 1970.
[57] DEFE 24/1856, 'Muscat and Oman', J.M. Gibbon (Head of DS11) to Defence Secretary of State, 8 July 1970.
[58] DEFE 24/1856, 'Muscat and Oman', J.M. Gibbon.

considerable damage to HMG's prestige and position, particularly in the Gulf and the wider Arab world...[59]

Equally important was the potential effect on the SAF, its British officers, and the rank and file:

> Many, perhaps all, of the British seconded officers serving with the SAF are believed to be out of sympathy with the Sultan and to favour Qabus. It seems more than likely that they would be distressed and disgusted by an order to hand the latter over, and in consequence a considerable strain would be placed on their loyalty and on the morale and cohesion of the SAF.[60]

Yet, the CSAF was a British seconded officer in the service of the Sultan. How legal was it for him to disobey the orders of the local ruler, to act against his interests, and undermine the security of his hold over the throne? The Treasury Solicitor's opinion was sought to answer this question, and it was swiftly provided, categorically affirming the illegality of the act. Seconded British officers were bound by a confidential agreement made with the Sultan ensuring that they remained as members of the British Armed Forces and were bound by the UK Service Discipline Acts. While this gave the British government the right to give them orders in several contexts, the Treasury Solicitor noted that it did not seem 'consistent with the tenor of the Agreement that such orders should have effect so as to bring about a change in the political situation within the Sultanate so long as the Sultan remains the lawful government of that country...'[61]

Regardless of its illegality, it was decided in the 8 July FCO meeting that Peter Hayman, on behalf of the Arabian Department, was to recommend to Sir Alec Douglas-Home, the Secretary of State for Foreign and Commonwealth Affairs, the approval of a plan to protect Qaboos. This plan was subject to the approval of Lord Carrington, the Secretary of State for Defence, and Prime Minister Edward Heath. It involved instructing the Political Resident that he should, 'subject to his views and in consultation with the Commander British Forces' and without 'arousing the suspicions of either the Sultan or Colonel Oldman', inform Brigadier Graham that he should not hand Qaboos over under any circumstances. If holding Qaboos under SAF protection was to prove too difficult, he was to be handed over to RAF Salalah, where arrangements would be made for flying him out of the country as soon as possible.[62] Indeed, preparations had already been made by the Political Resident for Qaboos's

[59] DEFE 24/1856, 'Muscat and Oman', J.M. Gibbon.
[60] DEFE 24/1856, 'Muscat and Oman', J.M. Gibbon.
[61] DEFE 24/1856, 'Muscat and Oman', J.M. Gibbon.
[62] DEFE 24/1856, 'Muscat and Oman', J.M. Gibbon.

protection at the RAF station. It was carefully decided not to keep a designated airplane on standby there, 'because of the obvious British implication in the event', but to ensure instead that a plane would be available on short notice elsewhere.[63]

Within two days of the meeting, all the necessary approvals were secured and on 10 July the Commander of the British Forces Gulf was instructed to inform CSAF Graham of the plan and the need to implement it, pending further instructions from London. Although Colonel Oldman was not supposed to be informed of this decision, he somehow received word of it. He adjusted his views accordingly and on 12 July he informed the Consul General in Muscat that he has instructed CSAF Graham to prepare two contingency plans, one projecting a successful coup scenario, while the other detailing a response for a failed one. 'Under the latter contingency, SAF would be used to assist Qabus in gaining control of Salalah town and in deposing his father.'[64] This amounted to a proposal to dethrone Sultan Said, put forth by his British Defence Secretary.

Colonel Oldman had effectively been pushed by the FCO into a corner from which only this decision seemed tenable. This was made clear to the British policy makers concerned:

> Colonel Oldman knows that we are ready to fly Qabus out of the country should the coup fail. Colonel Oldman now believes that in view of this, and the time it would take to accomplish, he cannot see how either he or the Sultan's Armed Forces could maintain a viable relationship with the Sultan.[65]

Oldman's effective proposal to dethrone the Sultan was backed by the Political Resident. In the words of his deputy, Michael Scott Weir:

> Stewart Crawford...approved the plan and it duly obtained ministerial endorsement from London. The operation involved the seizure of the Sultan's palace at Salalah by a very small body of troops loyal to Qabus, with the assistance of some British officers...[66]

It must be noted however, that this endorsement did not come without debate. Indeed, there was an initial difference of opinion on the matter between the FCO and the MOD. On 14 July, shortly after the Political Resident's recommendation was sent, a meeting was held at the FCO to discuss the appropriate response to it. FCO officials wholeheartedly embraced the recommendations of Oldman and Crawford. In contrast,

---

[63] DEFE 24/1856, CBFG to Chief of Defence Staff, 8 July 1970.
[64] DEFE 24/1856, 'Chiefs of Staff Meeting, Wednesday 15th July 1970'.
[65] DEFE 24/1856, Acting Chief of Defence Staff to Secretary of State for Defence, 16 July 1970.
[66] Weir, *Unfinished Memoires*, p. 97.

the MOD representatives were reserved about them. Although they were a group of senior officials that included the Director of DOP and the Head of DS11 sections, they stated clearly that they needed 'further guidance' by the highest ranks of government on this matter. The MOD bureaucracy was essentially calling for political clarity:

> Although the end result might be to HMG's advantage, this did not justify the authorisation of seconded officers to take part in planning for the overthrow of the man recognised by HMG as the ruler of the country. A different situation would be created if HMG at any time decided that the Sultan had forfeited HMG's recognition as a ruler.[67]

MOD officials were particularly concerned that the proposed plan, if carried out, would have grave consequences for British seconded officers. Although the Political Resident had emphasized that 'we would of course maintain the public position that we had no foreknowledge', this was not enough. For, maintaining that position would mean that British seconded officers would be 'unable to refute the accusation that they had acted on their own initiative against the person to whom they were supposed to own their loyalty'. This was a matter of grave concern, as 'the standing of British officers, serving with local forces throughout the world, would suffer'. In particular, there was a possibility that Sheikh Zayed of Abu Dhabi 'might seize the opportunity to reduce his reliance on British officers in favour of Pakistanis'.[68]

The divergence of opinion between the FCO and the MOD was resolved at a Chiefs of Staff meeting held on Wednesday, 15 July, which the Commander British Forces Gulf was invited to attend. The FCO sent a high level representative, Sir Edward Peck, UK Permanent Representative to NATO and Chair of the Joint Intelligence Committee. Early on at the meeting, Defence figures expressed their concerns. However, despite their 'misgivings at the possible use of British Officers to assist in deposing a Ruler to whom they are seconded', they agreed to support the FCO's 'approval of Colonel Oldman's contingency planning'.[69] This agreement was initially given 'on the understanding that such a plan would not be implemented without reference to London'. However, shortly after the meeting, even this condition was dropped to take account of the limited time available. Having gone this far, MOD officials saw no problems in accepting an FCO proposal to instruct the Political Resident and the Consul General Muscat that 'if the coup is attempted and it is clear to the

---

[67] DEFE 24/1856, 'Qabus' Imminent Bid for Power in Muscat and Oman', Addendum to DMO Brief No 42/70, 15 July 1970.
[68] DEFE 24/1856, 'Chiefs of Staff Meeting, Wednesday 15th July 1970'.
[69] DEFE 24/1856, Acting Chief of Defence Staff to Secretary of State for Defence.

British officers on the spot that there is no time to refer to London, they will have to use their initiative as they think best, bearing in mind HMG's overall policy'.[70] By 16 July, this decision was officially approved. In the absence of the Secretary of State for Defence, the Minister of State for Defence, Lord Balniel, gave his agreement on behalf of the MOD. Likewise, Joseph Godber, the Minister of State for Foreign and Commonwealth Affairs, agreed on behalf of the FCO.[71]

Several issues are worth reemphasizing with regard to the course of events between the *foco* plot of 12 June and the 16 July British decision to remove Sultan Said. To begin with, serious discussion around removing Sultan Said only began after the 12 June plot. Prior to that point, the idea had been floated around informally in response to the growth of the revolution in Dhufar, and its potentially favourable results were hinted at in some official correspondences. At that stage, however, it was no more than a desire on the part of those frustrated by the Sultan, unlikely to be acted on without major cause. Nevertheless, when that cause emerged, it was no longer difficult to act on. Indeed, frequent, off-the-record expressions of a desire to remove the Sultan, that went back to the mid-1960s, created an extremely favourable atmosphere for welcoming the idea of a coup.

Thus, when the Landon message about the possibility of a coup was sent, it was taken seriously in Whitehall. This was despite the fact that it would have been clearly seen as a bluff by any sober observer of the Sultanate. Upon receiving that message, FCO officials could have responded in two alternative ways. One possible course of action was for them to make it clear that they would never move against a long-term client such as Sultan Said. That would have basically amounted to calling the bluff of Landon and Qaboos, and the pair would have been forced to cease their empty talk of a coup that they could never implement without direct British intervention. Another possible course of action would have been for the British to stand by Sultan Said, informing the ruler of the potential plot against him.

Instead, British officials chose to treat the Landon message and the 'imminent' bid for power that it announced as a serious potentiality, despite receiving a JIC assessment that showed it to be a most improbable event riddled with difficulties. These officials belonged to three main groups: FCO civil servants; MOD bureaucrats and army officers; and British seconded personnel serving the Sultan. None of them suggested protecting the Sultan, for there was consensus on the desirability of his

---

[70] DEFE 24/1856, Acting Chief of Defence Staff to Secretary of State for Defence.
[71] DEFE 24/1856, 'Muscat and Oman', Private Secretary of the Minister of State to PSO/CDS, 16 July 1970.

removal. Instead the discussion revolved around the degree of support that was going to be given to the coup.

FCO officials, in the Gulf and in London, took a maximalist position on this issue. Initially, they pushed for the protection of Qaboos in case he tried to launch a coup and failed. Having convinced a hesitant MOD to accept this in spite of all the illegalities, they put the Sultan's Minister of Defence, Colonel Oldman, in an unenviable position. He knew, as much as the FCO did, that any coup without British involvement was bound to fail, and understood that protecting Qaboos without removing the Sultan would seriously jeopardize the future of Britain's position within the Sultanate. Accordingly, the only choice available to him was to guarantee a successful coup, and that required the involvement of British officers. No sooner had Oldman made this new perspective clear to London than the FCO welcomed it and successfully pressured the MOD into accepting it. This serves to show that there was nothing inevitable about the coup. It could have been derailed if the MOD had stood its ground, or if Oldman had refused to cooperate, or if someone had blown the whistle and informed Said bin Taimur. These were not entirely unlikely possibilities. Nor was the prospect of blockage from Conservative quarters completely improbable. As noted by Sir Michael Weir in his unpublished memoirs:

> Although one must assume that the incoming [Conservative] government was told of the plan, I have always felt that it might have slipped through unquestioned in the confusion of the unexpected victory and the press of other business, and that if some of the diehard rightwingers like Julian Amery and Duncan Sandys, who had a strong fellow-feeling for Said bin Taimur, had learned the details in time they might well have tried to abort it.[72]

Indeed, it is worthy of notice that the discussion around the coup mainly took place within the ranks of the FCO and MOD bureaucracy, with hardly any direct input from elected officials. The latter, including an enthusiastic Douglas-Home, became involved at the final stages, ensuring that power was transferred to Qaboos as smoothly as possible. Although the young Sayid had so far been untried and untested, he held promise for British policy.

QABOOS

Qaboos was born on 18 November 1940 in Salalah. His mother was Mazoun bint Ahmad al-Ma'ashani, daughter of a Dhufari Qarra sheikh, and Sultan Said's third and last wife. He grew up in the environment

---

[72] Weir, *Unfinished Memoires*, p. 98.

of Al-Hisn Palace in Salalah, a constrained space dominated by hierarchy. The two types of figures encountered by Qaboos were servile ones (slaves), or disciplinary characters (his father and British advisers) to whose wishes he had to submit. Completely absent were any brothers, peers, or equals. The effects of this were to continue even after Qaboos took power. As late as 1983, a secret oil company assessment concluded that Qaboos 'has never had any very close Omani friends or followers'.[73]

Qaboos received private tutoring in Salalah, a town that he had never left until he turned eighteen. For many years, the British had attempted to 'persuade the Sultan to see to the boy's education, without success...'[74] In 1958, he was sent to Felsham House, near Bury St Edmunds, to be 'crammed' under a staunchly conservative colonial schoolmaster and clergyman, Philip Romans. In September 1960, he enrolled at Sandhurst. Following the completion of his course there in 1962, he was attached to the British Army of the Rhine for six months as a 2nd Lieutenant at Minden, West Germany. He spent that period with the Cameronians, a Scottish regiment which had played a major role in suppressing the Al-Jabal al-Akhdar revolt.[75]

Following his short placement with the Cameronians, it was arranged for him to leave the British Army on 28 February 1963, flying from Hanover to Gatwick to prepare for a three-month 'world tour'.[76] By order of the Sultan, Major and Mrs Chauncy were to organize the tour and to accompany Qaboos during it. The tour was booked through Thomas Cook and diplomatic facilitation was given by the Foreign Office, which arranged for diplomatic visas and offered the support of British embassies and consulates at all the destinations.[77] It started with a flight from London to Amsterdam on 8 March and finished with the arrival of the cruise ship *Queen Mary*, at Southampton from New York on 3 June, having featured short stops in the Netherlands, Belgium, France, Switzerland, Italy, Greece, Turkey, Iran, Pakistan, India, Burma, Thailand, Singapore, Japan, Canada and the United States.[78] Arab countries were notably, and intentionally, absent from the list.

[73] MEC, Paxton. Box 9, File 2, 'Said Ahmad al Shanfari', January 1983.

[74] FO 371/168725, 'Sayid Qabus', Arabian Department, July 1963.

[75] FO 371/168725, 'World Tour by 2/Lt Qabus bin Said son of HH Sultan of Muscat and Oman', War Office to 1 Cameronians (BAOR), 8 February 1963. FO 371/168725, 'Sayyid Qabus bin Said', Attachment to letter by T.F. Brenchley, 17 July 1963.

[76] FO 371/168725, 1 CAMS to TROOPERS MO4, 22 February 1963.

[77] FO 371/168725, 'Private Visit of The Son of the Sultan of Muscat and Oman', 11 March 1963.

[78] FO 371/168725, 'Private Visit of The Son of the Sultan of Muscat and Oman', 11 March 1963.

During the tour, the red carpet of Shell was rolled out everywhere for Qaboos. This was the first time in his life he received VIP treatment on this scale. This continued following his return to England. Qaboos was given a short course at the Royal Institute of Public Administration, a currently defunct institution that was a major training centre for officials of former British colonies.[79] The Foreign Office then commissioned the Central Office of Information (COI) to take Qaboos on a special tour of England, Wales and Scotland between 10 and 27 July 1963. The tour included visits to British political, cultural and economic establishments. Qaboos was chauffeured to Mansion House, Labour Party Headquarters, Conservative and Unionist Central Office, the Office of Welsh Affairs, Scotland Yard, the BBC, the House of Commons, and the Foreign Office. The young Sayid, who had never before interacted with foreign officials, was introduced to the Minister of State for Foreign Affairs, the Lord Mayor of London, the Lord Privy Seal, Labour and Conservative MPs, the Area Commander of Edinburgh and the head of the BBC's Arabic Service. Hitherto deprived of direct exposure to high culture and luxurious living, he was taken to the theatre to watch a typical English comedy of manners (Noël Coward's *Private Lives*), accompanied to the Glyndebourne Festival Opera to experience Mozart's *Die Zauberflöte*, lodged in luxury hotels, and dined at fine restaurants (including the still fashionable *Le Caprice*).[80]

All in all, Qaboos had as fine and balanced a taste of the United Kingdom as possible in seventeen days. This contrasted sharply with the puritan life he had previously led. Moreover, it offered him an introduction to British political, economic, and cultural life, something that was seen as an important aspect of his training. Above all, this tour was seen by Foreign Office officials as a way to secure Qaboos's future commitment to Britain: 'Sayyid Qabus is expected to succeed his father in due course and with this in mind we are attempting to establish a solid basis of friendship with him'.[81] Thus, under the aegis of the Foreign Office, the summer of 1963 continued to be busy for the 23-year-old Sayid, culminating in a training attachment with the Town Clerk of Ipswich, Suffolk, from 12 to 26 August, arranged for him with the help of the Ministry of Housing and Local Government.[82]

---

[79] K. Jenkins, and W. Plowden, *Governance and Nation Building: The Failure of International Intervention*, Cheltenham: Edward Elgar, 2006, p.18.

[80] FO 371/168725, 'Programme of Arrangements Made by the Central Office of Information on Behalf of the Foreign Office for Sayyid Qabus Bin Said', 10–27 July 1963.

[81] FO 371/168725, 'Sayyid Qabus bin Said', Letter from T.F. Brenchley, 17 July 1963.

[82] FO 371/168725, G.I. Chant (Department of Technical Co-operation) to S.M. Black (FO), 7 August 1963.

It was decided that Qaboos would not receive any formal education. Qaboos's old-fashioned guardian, Mr Romans, had blocked this possibility by stating to the Foreign Office that 'he had come to the conclusion that it would not be useful for Sayyid Qabus to attend a formal course of instruction'. Instead, it was decided by Romans that Qaboos 'should be attached to the Bury St Edmunds Council on a part time basis during the autumn and winter, where he was confident he would obtain valuable experience, by observation rather than by study, of the administration of public accounts's.[83] This was indeed what happened. Thus, after an exciting summer, Qaboos's six-year stay in England had a slow and quiet conclusion. The British commented that 'the Sultan now feels that Qabus has had enough V.I.P. treatment for the present'.[84]

Three things are worth noting concerning Qaboos's experience in England. First, his education was marked by colonialist and conservative influences embodied in the figure of his guardian, a former tutor in colonial India renowned for his reactionary outlook. Secondly, martialism and a love of military ceremony was cultivated during Qaboos's stay, especially during his time at Sandhurst and his service with the Cameronians. Thirdly, Qaboos's education was lacking in academic or analytical rigour. By the age of 23, his Arabic still required 'brushing up' and his written English was 'deficient'. In the only examinations that he ever sat, those at Sandhurst, he achieved 'disappointing' results.[85] He did not 'know very much about economics or politics, and not much about administration beyond what is taught at Sandhurst'.[86]

Nevertheless, Qaboos's education seemed to achieve the effect that his father had desired. Sultan Said explained that his rationale for sending him to Sandhurst was 'to have him brought up as a well disciplined young man without having an overriding sense of his own importance'.[87] Reports from that period indicate that this mission was essentially accomplished, with Qaboos emerging as a 'pleasant, well behaved young man with a good sense of humour'.[88] Although he performed poorly in his exams, he 'obtained glowing reports for his officer qualities, determination and ability to inspire respect of his comrades'. His Commanding

[83] FO 371/168725, Minute by S.M. Black, 11 September 1963.

[84] FO 371/168725, S.M. Black (FO) to J.S.R. Duncan (Muscat), 8 October 1963.

[85] FO 371/168725, 'Sayid Qabus', Arabian Department, July 1963. See also FO 371/168725, S.M. Black (Foreign Office) to J.S.R. Duncan (Muscat), 8 October 1963.

[86] FO 371/168725, G.I. Chant (Department of Technical Co-operation) to R.A. Pilcher (Ministry of Housing and Local Government), 22 July 1963.

[87] MEC-Paxton, Box 9/3, R.A.B. Clough (Doha) to W.D. Peyton (Shell Centre, London), 1 September 1964.

[88] MEC-Paxton, Box 9/3, R.A.B. Clough (Doha) to W.D. Peyton (Shell Centre, London), 1 September 1964.

Officer commented on his 'unfailing courtesy, cheerfulness and strict observance of his religious customs...'[89] The latter point was noted elsewhere. Qaboos did not drink, nor was he interested in women. Even the sight of a belly dancer at a restaurant caused in him visible revulsion.[90] The young Sayid was by no means extraverted; if anything he was excessively withdrawn: 'Qabus is quiet and retiring by nature, and he is therefore not given to expressing himself very freely in conversation'.[91] He was extremely devoted to his father, placing his picture on the dressing table wherever he went.[92]

There was clearly a repressive, and excessively paternalistic, element in Qaboos's upbringing. An informed assessment of his situation at the time was provided by Shell's Bill Peyton:

> It appears as if he has been treated as a child by the likes of Kendall and Chauncy. He was not, for instance, allowed any say in the preparation of his own house at Sallala [*sic*]. Chauncy told me that Qaboos had to come home and 'learn some discipline'. If anything, he is over-disciplined already and there is a danger that what spark of life is left will be snuffed out by further tutoring at Sallala.[93]

Qaboos had little in common with Omanis of his generation, many of whom received religious knowledge, had a patriotic Arabist education, or had received no formal instruction whatsoever. Moreover, Omanis had never seen Qaboos or known anything of him. He was self-conscious about this fact: 'He realises the weakness of his own position and says that he intends, after being made to brush up his Ibadhi theology and Arabic at Salalah...to tour Muscat and Oman'.[94]

Years later, when he did eventually go to Muscat and Oman, Qaboos seemed to have retained his sense of estrangement. His private self was carefully concealed with Omanis, every interaction being a grand public performance. This contrasted with a humble private persona displayed in Qaboos's British years, long preceding the *vanitas vanitatum* that was the mark of his future life on the throne. After a weekend visit from the 24-year-old Qaboos, Peyton reported:

[89] FO 371/168725, 'Sayid Qabus', Arabian Department, July 1963.
[90] MEC-Paxton. Box 9/3, W.D. Peyton (Shell Centre, London) to R.A.B. Clough (Doha), 13 August 1964.
[91] FO 371/168725, G.I. Chant (Department of Technical Co-operation) to R.A. Pilcher (Ministry of Housing and Local Government), 22 July 1963.
[92] MEC-Paxton, Box 9/3, W.D. Peyton (Shell Centre, London) to R.A.B. Clough (Doha), 13th August 1964.
[93] MEC-Paxton, Box 9/3, Peyton to Clough.
[94] MEC-Paxton, Box 9/3, Peyton to Clough.

He is easy and pleasant to have about, makes his own bed, helps with the dishes, romps with the children (who love him dearly) and he did a reasonable job of clipping a couple hundred yards of my roadside hedge.[95]

This sort of domestic attitude was generally reserved for foreigners, with whom Qaboos could feel a reassuring parity or perhaps even a painful colonial inferiority. As for locals, they were the cause of deep insecurities. These were compounded by the fact that he was born to a Dhufari mother. Indeed, he grew up fearing Oman and his inevitable encounter with it: '[Qaboos] says in Oman he is regarded as a foreigner because his mother is Dhufari and because he has never been to Oman. He clearly has no intention ever of settling down in Muscat or Oman and says his family, when he has one, will live in Salalah.'[96] British attempts to convince the Sultan to introduce Qaboos to Oman and to involve him in government failed miserably. They understood the difficulty of their mission early on:

It is greatly to our interest that the Sultan should now bring his son forward so that he becomes known to his people, learns about the country and has some experience of actual government work. Past experience with the Sultan suggests, however, that he will be unwilling to give the boy any real work to do. This will lead to the kind of frustration we have seen in the Sultan's half-brother, Sayyid Tariq, and to a troublesome period when eventually the Sultan abdicates or dies.[97]

These words reflected an appreciation of the Sultan's view of his son. A few months before Qaboos's return to Salalah, the Consul General in Muscat noted that his father 'tended to regard Qabus as a little boy still and that he would require a prolonged period at Salala among his elders and betters'.[98] Further British queries about Qaboos's future role were brushed off by the Sultan. On one occasion, he humorously remarked that his son's time would be spent 'on growing a beard to fit him for his re-entry into Sultanate society'.[99]

The Sultan's plan was for Qaboos to be tutored for a year in Arabic and Ibhadi theology. As early as 1963, he had also indicated his wish to marry him to a girl from the powerful Harithi tribe.[100] For the next seven years, this marriage was talked about but never actually realized. Said bin Taimur clearly made his son's life difficult. After showing him a glimpse of the

---

[95] MEC-Paxton, Box 9/3, Peyton to Clough.
[96] MEC-Paxton, Box 9/3, Peyton to Clough.
[97] FO 371/168725, 'Sayid Qabus', Arabian Department, July 1963.
[98] FO 371/168725, J.S.R. Duncan (Muscat) to S.M. Black (Arabian Department), 6 August 1963.
[99] FO 371/168725, S.M. Black (FO) to J.S.R. Duncan (Muscat), 8 October 1963.
[100] FO 371/168725, S.M. Black (FO) to J.S.R. Duncan (Muscat), 8 October 1963.

outside world, he expected him to remain stagnant in tiny Salalah, repressed, jobless, friendless, and deeply *constrained*. It is important to emphasize this last word, not the least in opposition to the prevalent impression that Qaboos was 'imprisoned' by his father or placed under house arrest. This impression has no basis in the extensive documentation on the period in question. Said strictly controlled his son and kept him under close watch, but he did the same with everyone around him.

What made Qaboos's situation different was that the British were sympathetic to his condition, having a longstanding concern to prepare him for the throne. This concern especially developed following the DLF attempt on the life of Sultan Said in 1966. Carden, the British Consul General at the time, instructed Qaboos on what he needed to do in case something happened to his father. He also asked him to confide in him if he ever wanted to talk about his innermost thoughts. British officials tended to play a paternal protective role with Qaboos, and he certainly felt that. He therefore indicated his frustrations to them over the years, seeking support and indicating his readiness to replace his father. This served him extremely well during the fateful summer of 1970.

CARRYING OUT THE COUP

Shortly after the FCO and the MOD gave their blessing on 16 July for the CSAF and his British seconded officers to ensure the success of the coup, the necessary preparations began. This was not the first time Britain had orchestrated a coup in the Gulf. Only a few years earlier, it had removed Sheikhs Saqr of Sharjah (1965) and Shakhout of Abu Dhabi (1966), the former for being an Arab nationalist, the latter for being anti-developmentalist.[101]

Sunday 19 July was initially suggested as the date for the coup, but the final showdown was postponed to 23 July. This coincided with the anniversary of the Egyptian Free Officers revolution of 1952, the most prominent event in the Arab liberation calendar. Besides its potential symbolic value, the date had an immediate practical use, with most of the Sultan's loyal British advisers, including the notorious Chauncy, being away on summer holiday.[102] From the outset, it was understood that a strict theatrical distribution of roles was to be adhered to. Britain went to great lengths to emphasize that Muscat and Oman was an independent country

---

[101] Rosemarie Zahlan, *The Making of the Modern Gulf States*, Reading: Ithaca Press, 1998, p.117.
[102] Allen and Rigsbee, *Oman Under Qaboos*, p. 29.

and that events within it were free from British orchestration. Ironically, of course, this very need for excessive emphasis reflected the overwhelming reality of the British presence. This reality was clear to the British press, who were advocating greater intervention. *The Economist* of 18 July stated that:

> ...it should be recognised in London that the region's chances of stability are poor so long as the Sultan remains in power. The government can no longer afford to shut its eyes to the dangers of the situation in Muscat. The Sultan and his advisers will have to be persuaded to go before it is too late for an alternative ruler to hold the country together.[103]

It was widely known that Britain controlled events in the Sultanate. Yet appearances had to be kept up for the sake of Qaboos's future legitimacy. British written accounts of the coup—with the significant exception of Sir Michael Weir's unpublished memoirs—continue to present it as his personal initiative to this very day. Curiously, given their reticence in such matters, even a prominent member of the Omani ruling family has provided an alternative assessment. Sayid Badr Bin Hamad bin Hamood Al Bu Said notes that:

> ...there can be no doubt that the planning, timing and execution of the coup reflected the anxieties of the British government, in light of its 1968 decision to withdraw militarily by 1971 from the Arabian Gulf. Thus, the coup, carried out in the name of Oman, at the expense of one Omani Sultan and to the benefit of another, embodied...the involvement of outside powers in the affairs of the Sultanate.[104]

On the ground, this involvement was led by the Commander of the SAF, Brigadier John Graham. For nearly four decades after the coup, Graham continued to insist that he implemented the coup on the basis of his own convictions, following a request from Qaboos, and that the main initiative was undertaken by Qaboos's local supporters. However, in November 2009, he finally admitted to receiving his instructions to overthrow Said bin Taimur from the British authorities in an interview with BBC Radio 4.[105]

In removing Said bin Taimur, Graham was acting as an instrument of British policy. This was a role he loyally fulfilled. On Monday 20 July, he went down to Dhufar for a week in order to manage the coup directly. He was received by Landon, and by Lieutenant-Colonel Teddy Turnill. The latter was an important character in the events that followed, commanding the Desert

---

[103] 'Sir Alec Up the Gulf', in *The Economist*, 18 July 1970, p.15.
[104] Bin Hamood, Badr bin Hamad, 'Political and Economic Development in Oman with Specific Reference to the Reign of Sultan Qaboos', M.Litt, University of Oxford, 1989, p.62.
[105] BBC Radio 4, *Document*, 8:00 p.m., Monday 23 November 2009.

Regiment (DR), the SAF battalion stationed in Dhufar since February 1970. He was already aware of the planned coup and was committed to it. With his participation, the fate of the Sultan was effectively sealed. Unlike most other coups, where there is the hazardous element of a gamble, this one was relatively risk free. The DR was the sole major force in Salalah and, if needed, it could easily neutralize the Sultan's guards and his ineffective Dhufar Force. In order to ensure that such a need would not even arise, a show of strength was to be mounted by the DR supplemented by an SOAF display of airpower.[106] This would send a clear and debilitating signal of British involvement to both the Sultan and his guards.

In terms of his daily routine, Sultan Said was one of the most predictable rulers in the world. His location was fixed: he was always present in the palace of Al-Hisn, hardly ever leaving it since the revolutionary attempt to assassinate him in 1966. His sleeping schedule was also precisely known, organized around the afternoon nap that he usually took. On this basis, the plan was for the DR to surround his palace (where he was bound to be), in the afternoon (when he tended to be asleep), and for the Red Company to force its way through the ranks of his guards (who would be shocked and awed at the sight of the army).

Thursday 23 July was a rainy monsoon day. By the time it had arrived, almost everything was set. Qaboos purportedly sent a letter 'informing' the Commander of the Desert Regiment of 'his decision' to remove his father from power and calling for SAF intervention to 'maintain law and order'. Upon receiving the letter at midday, Turnill (who had been planning the coup for a while) went through the formal motions and asked Graham (who had already issued instructions to carry out the coup) for orders. The latter purportedly commanded him to comply with Qaboos's letter.[107]

So as to maintain discipline, Graham summoned the three most senior non-British officers in the Desert Regiment (DR), representing the segregated units of Omani Arabs, Omani-born Baluch, and Makran-born Baluch. He informed them of Qaboos's 'decision,' and read them 'some of the more stirring sentences' from the letter to Turnill. Graham told the soldiers that he was reacting to the letter on the spot:

> I explained that this [letter] presented Turnill, me and our British colleagues, foreigners in their country, with a conflict of loyalties. But there was I said, no time for me to consult with my superiors in Muscat and London...I stated that I was not going to ask for their advice but that,

[106] John Graham, *Ponder Anew: Reflections on the Twentieth Century*, Staplehurst, Kent: Spellmount Publishers, 1999.
[107] Graham, *Ponder Anew*, p.333.

having told Colonel Turnill to comply with Qaboos' request, I ordered them as good soldiers to go back to their men and to obey all the instructions of their Commanding Officers.[108]

In addition to taking these steps with the Arab and Baluch soldiers of the DR, Graham made sure that he secured Air Force participation, selecting two of the British pilots seconded from the RAF and briefing them 'on the actions they were to take in support of the DR's movements'. He also liaised with the Commander of RAF Salalah, Phil Crawshaw, to ensure that his station's facilities were at his disposal. Having taken these actions, Graham sat by the radio in the SAF's Dhufar headquarters in Umm al-Ghawarif, awaiting the end of the action in the palace, which was scheduled to begin at 13:20 local time.[109] Crawshaw was also following events, closely relaying their progress to the Commander British Forces Gulf.[110] After asking for instructions, he was given the following order: 'important to permit no leakage of information by any means whatever until further orders'.[111]

Teddy Turnill coordinated the action on the ground. After his meeting with Graham, he gathered his British commanders, and informed them of the Qaboos letter. He then 'explicitly ordered' them 'to execute a coup d'état.'[112] Six different groups were included in the action. The DR's Red Company was entrusted with the responsibility of invading the palace and capturing the Sultan. It was to be accompanied by eleven soldiers from the Desert Regiment's all-Arab Recce Platoon, led by Lieutenant Said Salem al-Wuhaybi, the highest ranking Omani in the SAF and the first to be commissioned.[113] This Arab group had no direct operational responsibilities; its men were 'designated as ethnic camouflage' so as to 'disguise what otherwise could be seen as a coup d'état against a friendly monarch executed by an Irishman, an Englishman and a few locals.'[114]

Supporting the palace invaders were Major Dick and his 2 Company, who were given the task of guarding RAF Salalah against any potential attack from the Dhufari revolutionaries. Major Mike and his 3 Company were to form a defensive parameter around al-Hisn, and the SOAF was

---

[108] Graham, *Ponder Anew*, p.333.

[109] Graham, *Ponder Anew*, p.334.

[110] DEFE 71/374, RAF Salalah to HQ BFG, 23 July, 1970.

[111] DEFE 71/374, CBFG to RAF Salalah, 23 July, 1970.

[112] Ray Kane, *Coup d'etat Oman*, Kindle Edition, 2015, Chapter 14, N.pag. Kindle File

[113] In some accounts, Said Salem and his eleven men are described as belonging to the Northern Frontier Regiment (See Peterson, *Oman's Insurgencie*, p.240, fn.1). In fact, as Graham notes, Said Salem had moved from the NFR to the Desert Regiment (DR) in 1967, and his soldiers were also from the Recce Platoon of the Desert Regiment. Graham, *Ponder Anew* , p. 478.

[114] Kane, *Coup d'etat Oman*, Chapter 14, N.pag. Kindle File

instructed to make a display of airpower in which 'two Strikemaster jets would make a low 'frightener' pass' over the palace. Finally, Major Nic was placed with a 25-pounder gun on standby, in case the palace gates needed to be fully destroyed.[115]

The most important role was played by the Red Company, led by its Irish commander Ray Kane. As recounted in Kane's fascinating personal memoirs, Turnill had special instructions for him: 'Teddy took me aside. Use maximum force to accomplish the mission in the shortest time and capture the Sultan alive *if possible*, were his personal orders.' Kane and his company officer Richard Wood were given 60 minutes to round up and brief their '30 odd soldiers, a mix of Omani Arabs and Pakistani Baluchis' and to then storm the palace. Kane 'lied' to his men, telling them that there was 'trouble at al-Husn and the Sultan has requested our help.' He ordered 'a short debussing rehearsal, mainly to stop the soldiers from thinking', and then drove with them and the All-Arab Recce Platoon from Umm al-Ghawarif camp to the palace.[116]

Before the convoy arrived to the palace, and without coordination with the army, one of Qaboos's allies and the son of the governor of Dhufar, Burayk bin Hamud al-Ghafiri, had entered the palace and confronted the Sultan. He was shot by the ruler in his stomach and left wounded. While this could have potentially ruined the coup plan, it had no such effect. The soldiers passed through the defences around the palace without incident. The Hawasina guards of the Sultan, a large segment of the *'askar* entrusted with guarding the exterior of the palace, were bribed so as to ensure the safe passage of the invading convoy,[117] and their commander Hilal bin Sultan al-Hawsini went along with the plot.[118] As for the 500 Baluchi mercenary guard battalion, Major Spike Powell visited their Sheikh and ensured that they stayed out of action.[119]

Ray Kane led the soldiers in single file into the palace. He knocked politely at the palace door. A young staff member half-opened the door and Kane butt-stroked him with his rifle, charging inside with his soldiers. They found 15 palace guards rushing to their rifles in panic. As the guard commander tried to mobilise his men and attempted to load his rifle, he was butt-stroked across his knuckles and chest. Kane then ordered the guards to surrender, and they were disarmed and pushed outside the door. The thirty men of Red Company and the eleven members of the 'Lieutenant Said's all-Arab ethnic camouflage group' were now all inside.

[115] Kane, *Coup d'etat Oman,* Chapter 14, N.pag. Kindle File
[116] Kane, *Coup d'etat Oman*, Chapter 14, N.pag. Kindle File, emphasis added
[117] Kane, *Coup d'etat Oman*, Chapter 14, N.pag. Kindle File
[118] Graham, *Ponder Anew*, p.331.
[119] Kane, *Coup d'etat Oman*, Chapter 14, N.pag. Kindle File

The latter group was then left out of the action, going to ground under the main staircase, and playing no further role in the coup.[120]

As for the Red Company soldiers, they began to look for Sultan Said in the dizzying corridors and rooms of the palace. The Sultan was supposed to be asleep around this time but, in fact, he was spending time with his auditor who had arrived from Muscat that day.[121] The soldiers entered his Majlis, but all they could find was banknotes scattered on the floor. As they began to exit the room, the Sultan began to shoot at them. A round of hide and seek then ensued, interrupted by occasional attacks by the Sultan and his bodyguards. Finally, Kane and his men managed to besiege him in a room that was protected by an armoured glass door. Richard Wood fired heavily into the glass and opened a hole. Around this time, Teddy Turnill ordered Kane to withdraw. In the words of the latter:

> Sheltering behind a building corner, Teddy Turnill shouted an order to me to withdraw, adding that he intended to negotiate with the Sultan. Behind Teddy, Tim Landon, Sultan's Intelligence Officer and Qaboos' best friend, added his voice. Teddy was taking counsel of his fears, or of someone else's. Fuck that, I thought. I assured them it was nearly over, ignored Teddy's order and Landon's protestations and went back to work.[122]

Kane prepared a phosphorous grenade, and he ordered the Sultan to surrender, 'adding that otherwise all inside would be burnt to death'. At this stage, the Sultan was suffering from four bullet wounds. Three of these—in the upper thigh, the abdomen, and the arm—were inflicted by the attackers. The fourth was an accidentally self-inflicted shot in the foot.[123] Since the British did not show any hesitation in wounding him, he probably had no reason to doubt that they could kill him. Accordingly, he agreed to surrender, but only to Colonel Turnill. The Colonel then went into the room, accompanied by Kane and Tim Landon. Now that the fighting was over, Lieutenant Said Salim and his men were also brought into the room, so as to provide an Arab cover to the events.[124] The Sultan was 'clothed in bloodied dishdash and flanked by his loyal, brave, wounded, bodyguards. In his hand and pointing downwards, he held a Mauser C96 'Broom-handle' semi-automatic pistol.'[125] Tim Landon took the pistol and handed it to his orderly. The orderly discharged the pistol

---

[120] Kane, *Coup d'etat Oman*, Chapter 14, N.pag. Kindle File
[121] Peterson, *Oman's Insurgencies*, p.240, fn.2.
[122] Kane, *Coup d'etat Oman*, Chapter 14, N.pag. Kindle File
[123] DEFE 71/374, RAF Salalah to BFG, 23 July, 1970.
[124] Kane, *Coup d'etat Oman*, Chapter 14, N.pag. Kindle File
[125] Kane, *Coup d'etat Oman*, Chapter 14, N.pag. Kindle File

by mistake, and the bullet hit Kane's left calf muscle. The army doctor was brought in to treat the wounds of the Sultan:

> Wounds treated and dignity restored, the Sultan refused to sign an Abdication document presented to him by Teddy Turnill. 'I don't wish to remain a pauper for the rest of my life,' the Sultan lapsed uncharacteristically into peevishness. 'Said, I've had enough of this and I've just had one of my officers shot—sign now,' the exasperated Teddy Turnill insisted. Teddy addressed the Sultan as "Said", while the Sultan reciprocated with "Colonel Turnill". Surrounded by his armed British officers, Sultan Said signed what transpired to be a faulty worded document...[126]

The Sultan was then placed on a stretcher, and clandestinely taken in a covered Land Rover ambulance vehicle to the medical centre at the RAF station, where he was received by Phil Crawshaw. There, he was given some further treatment and was forced to sign another abdication letter in Arabic and English. Shortly thereafter, he was forced to sign a third abdication letter, after it transpired that he had not correctly signed the Arabic draft in the second instance.[127]

Contrary to some published accounts, including those by CSAF John Graham, the Sultan was dignified in his surrender. In the words of Kane:

> Sultan Said bin Taimur acted as an Arab warrior throughout the coup and its immediate aftermath. Before surrender Sultan Said did not, as written in Graham's memoir, say that he had shot himself and wished to surrender to a senior British officer... Nor did the Sultan threaten, with a machine pistol, Teddy Turnill as he and I approached and disarmed the Sultan; nor did he cling to Turnill's shirt begging Turnill not to leave him; nor did he utter, 'the people will kill me'.[128]

The Sultan, in fact, was brave and proud, displaying 'no pain or shock symptoms'. This was

> despite being grenaded and suffering four bullet wounds: a foot wound inflicted by a 7.63 mm pistol bullet travelling at over 1,600 kilometres per hour, and three wounds by 7.62 mm machine gun or rifle bullets travelling at over 3,000 kilometres per hour... Sultan Said's actions and fighting spirit, if performed by a soldier in different circumstances, would have earned the highest gallantry award in any army.[129]

Bravery, however, did not save the Sultan from losing his throne. The day after the coup, he was taken aboard an RAF Casualty Evacuation plane to

[126] Kane, *Coup d'etat Oman*, Chapter 14, N.pag. Kindle File
[127] Graham, *Ponder Anew*, p.336.
[128] Kane, *Coup d'etat Oman*, Chapter 14, N.pag. Kindle File
[129] Kane, *Coup d'etat Oman*, Chapter 14, N.pag. Kindle File

Bahrain, never to see his realm again. Against the Sultan's wishes, the badly injured conspirator Burayk al-Ghafiri was also placed on the same aircraft. This was upon the instance of Qaboos and following authorization from the Commander British Forces Gulf.[130] A schedule was set for the ex-Sultan: initially, he would receive treatment at the RAF hospital in Muharraq; he would then be evacuated to the UK on the night of 24 July aboard RAF Britannia Flight 6394; after arriving at Brize Norton military air base at 08:25 a.m., he was to be received by an Arabian Department official carrying 'a short oral message on behalf of the Secretary of State'. Subsequently, he would be taken by ambulance to the RAF hospital at Wroughton, Wiltshire for further medical treatment.[131]

The Sultan's wounds required more than six weeks of treatment, provided by the British MOD. His physical condition was stable, but there is no doubt as to the profound sense of betrayal that he felt. Aside from four slaves who had accompanied him to the UK, he had no one to count on. Chauncy, who had previously been his most trusted confidant, revealed his true colours and declined his invitation to visit him in hospital.[132] Chauncy feared that calling upon his old master would prejudice his chances of being retained as an adviser by the new Sultan. The new Foreign Secretary, Douglas-Home, was determined not to let this anti-modernist former Raj official anywhere near Qaboos. To that end, he instructed the British Consul to 'discourage any ideas' that the new authorities may have had concerning the retention of Chauncy's services.[133]

Sultan Said was abandoned by those closest to him, including his son and his advisers. Nevertheless, there could be no doubt that the bulk of his frustration was directed at Britain, to which he had always been loyal. When he was visited by an official from the Foreign Office, he told him 'the coup could not have been successful without the help of the British officers serving on secondment with the Sultan's Armed Forces'.[134] In the light of Said's private expressions of anger, some official worries arose about him contesting the British version of events in the media. However, the deposed Sultan never uttered a word against Britain to any journalist, quietly spending the rest of his days in London's Dorchester Hotel until his death of natural causes on 19 October 1972, aged 62.

---

[130] DEFE 71/374, CBFG to RAF Salalah, 24 July, 1970.
[131] 'Coup in the Sultanate of Muscat and Oman', J.M. Edes (Arabian Department) to Hayman, 23 July 1970, *RO-5*, p. 89.
[132] Telegram No. 102, Douglas-Home to S. Crawford, 13 August 1970, *RO-5*, p.78.
[133] Telegram No. 102, Douglas-Home to S. Crawford, 13 August 1970, *RO-5*, p.78.
[134] 'Former Sultan of Muscat and Oman', P.T.E. England (Defence Staff) to Secretary of State, 25 August 1970. *RO-5*, p.80.

Qaboos did not attend his father's funeral, but Brigadier Graham, the man who implemented the plan to depose him, was present, along with eleven other mourners. He wrote in his diaries: 'I was distressed by the hasty and ill-attended burial of this former Ruler, and life-long friend of Britain; a man of great charm and strong personality...I consoled myself with the knowledge that by bringing about his abdication I had enabled him to enjoy two years of peace and freedom from anxiety'.[135]

* * *

Hitherto, the events analysed above have been distorted by an Anglo-Sultanic discourse that was keen, for political purposes, to exaggerate Qaboos's role, presenting him as the planner and implementer of the coup and downplaying British involvement. The picture is further veiled by common mischaracterizations of the motives underscoring the coup, completely excluding the fact that it did not simply result out of the benevolence of Qaboos, but rather due to severe revolutionary pressure. In revising the history, four significant propositions require emphasis. First, the overthrow of Said bin Taimur was not the result of action on the part of Qaboos. The latter lacked the capacity to plan and launch a coup, fearing his father, and having no funds, arms, or mobilizational networks. Secondly, the coup was not simply a result of British implementation but also the outcome of British design. Thirdly, the British were aware at the time of the need to produce a mythological version of events so as to legitimize Qaboos and their efforts were largely successful. Finally, the real author of historical change in this instance was neither Qaboos nor Britain. The coup directly resulted from the revolutionary action of ordinary Omanis, who organized themselves into political groups and took up arms against their ruler and Britain. The revolutionary actions of PFLOAG in Dhufar and NDFLOAG in Oman respectively provided the long-term and short-term causes that lay behind Britain's desire for economic modernization and state building. Having successfully removed the old regime in its quest to confront the revolutionary challenge, Britain was now confronted with the task of constructing the new one.

---

[135] MEC Graham Diaries. 20 October 1972.

8

Constructing the Absolutist State

According to one of its most prominent analysts, absolutism constituted 'the first international State system in the modern world'.[1] The scholarly output on this phenomenon essentially concerns the webs tying the absolutist state to society and the economy.[2] Yet what is often absent is a discussion of a central problem for various non-European countries: the relationship between colonialism and absolutism.[3] The Omani case is a clear manifestation of that problem.

Absolutism is the defining political characteristic of the current regime in Oman. In theory, the Sultan is invested with the *summa potestas* described by Bodin: 'he is absolutely sovereign who recognises nothing, after God, who is greater than himself'.[4] Although subject to divine law, the Sultan is officially the source of civil law and, although originally dependent on Britain, he was given its full support in establishing his own absolute rule. In practice, he has the capacity to dominate the state machinery, having actual control over appointments and decisions. None of his advisers or ministers has a basis for power that is independent of the person of the Sultan. Even the royal family could not be considered to be an intermediate power. Relative to other royals in the region, the Al Said have a small role in the governing process.[5] Thus, 'it is not possible to talk about an "Omani ruling family" as such, but instead of a sole ruler'.[6]

---

[1] Perry Anderson, *Lineages of the Absolutist State*, London: Verso, 1979, p.11.

[2] For the literature on absolutism, see: Michael Kimmel, *Absolutism and Its Discontents: State and Society in Seventeenth-Century France and England*, New Brunswick, NJ: Transaction Books, 1988; John Miller (ed.), *Absolutism in Seventeenth Century Europe*, New York: Palgrave Macmillan, 1990; David Parker (ed.), *Ideology, Absolutism, and the English Revolution: Debates of the British Communist Historians, 1940–1956*, London: Lawrence and Wishart, 2008; Benno Teschke, *The Myth of 1648*, London: Verso, 2003. For a critique of the concept of absolutism, see Roger Mettam, *Power and Faction in Louis XIV's France*, New York: Blackwell Publishers, 1988.

[3] A significant exception is Mahmoud Mamdani's *Citizen and Subject: Contemporary Africa and the Legacy of Late Colonialism*, Princeton: Princeton University Press, 1996.

[4] Jean Bodin and Julian Franklin (eds.), *On Sovereignty: Four Chapters from the Six Books of the Commonwealth*, Cambridge: CUP, 1992, p.4.

[5] Michael Herb, *All in the Family: Absolutism, Revolution and Democracy in the Middle Eastern Monarchies*, Albany NY: SUNY Press, 1999, p.145.

[6] Marc Valeri, *Oman: Politics and Society in the Qaboos State*, London: Hurst and Company, 2009, p.101.

Absolutism is a recent phenomenon in Omani history, beginning with Qaboos. Its establishment required reach: the creation of a state machinery that answers to one individual as it dominates an entire geographic space. The main problem that Britain confronted with Said bin Taimur was his slowness in building such a structure. How was this problem addressed following the removal of the old Sultan? By examining the period between 23 July 1970 (the coup) and 23 December 1971 (the resignation of Prime Minister Tariq bin Taimur), it becomes clear that there was nothing inevitable about Qaboos's absolutism. Indeed, there were several alternatives at the time, including a reformist constitutional vision. Yet, the way in which Britain engineered events and centralized power in Qaboos in the days immediately following the coup ensured the victory of absolutism over reformism.

Anglo-Sultanic historiography shifts attention from this political reality, and focuses instead on the economic development that ensued following the coup, positing 1970 as an *annus mirabilis* for Oman. This account is open to question. On the economic side, serious administrative problems and enormous financial wastage occurred under the Sultan. On the political side, Britain facilitated the domination of Oman by one individual, suppressing more democratic possibilities in the process. Rather than being an exciting time of reform, 1970–1971 was a period of missed economic and political opportunities.

CENTRALIZING POWER IN THE PERSON OF THE SULTAN

Events and policies immediately preceding and following the July 1970 coup are often ascribed to Qaboos. Besides its empirical inaccuracy, this betrays a conceptual deficiency, a failure to highlight the semi-colonial position of Muscat and Oman. Remarkably absent from the literature on Oman is the formal request that the Sultan made to the British following the coup:

> I, Qaboos bin Said, succeeded my father as Sultan of Muscat and Oman on 24th July, 1970. Following the succession, I have received the full support, loyalty and recognition of my family. I now seek H.M.G's recognition of me as Sultan of Muscat and Oman and assure you that the agreements obligations and undertakings entered into between Her Majesty's government and my predecessors will be fully upheld and recognised by me.[7]

---

[7] This was signed on 27 July, four days after the coup: 'Sultan Qaboos bin Said (Sultan of Muscat and Oman) to D.G. Crawford (CG Muscat)', 27 July 1970, *RO-5*, p.27.

This declaration reflected the structural reality by which Muscat and Oman was still under imperial sovereignty—*de facto*, although not *de jure*. In this context, not only was the Sultan seeking recognition, but he was also assuring the colonial power that its interests would not be challenged. This was a small price to pay in return for the services that he was receiving. Indeed, after the British installed him in the place of his father, they made substantial efforts to create a solid foundation upon which his authority could rest.[8]

The morning after the coup, the British Foreign Office emphasized that 'it would clearly be essential for us to give Qabus all the political support, advice, and encouragement we can and above all maintain our assistance to the Sultan's Armed Forces on which the power of any Sultan in Muscat and Oman rests in the last resort'.[9] One of the fascinating aspects of this process is the extent to which the Foreign Secretary, Sir Alec Douglas-Home, was initially involved in even the smallest of details. A flurry of personal exchanges ensued between him and the men on the spot. Six matters required immediate action: giving Qaboos military command; dynastic allegiance; financial control; diplomatic recognition; internal legitimation; and bureaucracy building.

The military was the absolute priority. As was shown in the previous chapter, the British government instructed Colonel Oldman and Brigadier John Graham to shift the army's allegiance from Said to Qaboos. This was the ultimate foundation on which Qaboos's absolutism was built. Without question, the foreign mercenary character of the army was what allowed absolutism to flourish. In this regard, the Omani case was typical. As noted by Victor Kiernan in a classic essay, the role of the 'foreign soldier enlisting for pay' becomes especially pertinent in periods of social reorganization and absolutist state formation.[10] Having no local allegiance other than to his paymaster, the mercenary affords the monarch a foundation for coercion that is independent of his subjects. The problem of military allegiance, faced by all regimes built on direct coercion, was thus readily solved: the British officers were loyal as long as the British government approved of Qaboos, while the Baluchi mercenary soldiers were dependable as long as he paid them.

---

[8] British officials had long reflected on the steps required for putting Qaboos in power should the reign of Said bin Taimur end. See D.C. Carden (CG Muscat) to W. Luce (PR Bahrain), 11 May 1966, *RO-1*. pp.53–4.

[9] Minute by J.M. Edes, 24 July 1970, *RO-5*, pp.22–3.

[10] V.G. Kiernan, 'Foreign Mercenaries and Absolute Monarchy', *Past and Present*, No.11, April 1957. p.66.

As for dynastic allegiance, securing it in 1970 was not a very difficult task considering the weakness of Qaboos's family. The Al Bu Said had not fared well for most of the twentieth century. They 'regarded themselves as privileged and, by the then almost non-existent Omani standards, they were. But many were very poor and some were sometimes hungry.'[11] The familial background of the highest-ranking members was characterized by instability and internal divisions, and some of them continued to live in poverty, even after Sultan Said raised their incomes by 80 per cent in 1966.[12] They also faced other problems, including a 'marked lack of mental stability' amongst their ranks.[13] Divided, poor, disempowered and afflicted with personal calamities, the ruling family was in no position to resist change. If anything, it had an interest in promoting it, even if it came in the name of an unknown figure like Qaboos.

The Sultanate's Military Secretary, Colonel Oldman, played the fundamental role in uniting the family behind Qaboos, right after he received confirmation of the success of the coup from Brigadier Graham.[14] Oldman first sought, and received, recognition from Sayid Shihab bin Faisal, Sultan Said's uncle. He then gathered conveyances from the other royal family members.[15] This happened in spite of the fact that Qaboos had never met any of his relatives. In the meantime, and upon the instructions of Oldman, the first act of the royal family's senior figures was to request official recognition for Qaboos from the British government.[16] Once again, imperial sovereignty was officially appealed to in Muscat and London's acceptance formally sought by the ruling family for the appointment of a new Sultan. Nevertheless, British recognition was deliberately delayed for six days. It was belatedly granted on 29 July so as not to confirm widespread suspicions of colonial involvement in the coup.[17]

At the same time as they worked on securing dynastic legitimation, the British pursued the issue of finances, swiftly arranging for Qaboos to have control over state funds. They had all been deposited in the British Bank of the Middle East[18] but by 25 July, Douglas-Home had applied pressure to make sure that Qaboos could access these funds even before British

---

[11] MEC-Skeet, 4/3, 'Confidential PDO Document on the Ruling Family', 2 November 1975.

[12] FCO 8/568, D.C. Carden (CG Muscat) to S.Crawford (PR Bahrain), 23 January 1967; FCO 8/568, Muscat to Foreign Office.,Tel. No.8, 16 January 1967.

[13] MEC-Skeet, 4/3, Confidential PDO Document on the Ruling Family, n.d.

[14] John Graham, *Ponder Anew: Reflections on the Twentieth Century*, Staplehurst, Kent: Spellmount Publishers, 1999, p.338.

[15] Muscat to Bahrain, Tel. no.294, 24 July 1970, *RO-5.*

[16] Muscat to Bahrain, Tel. no.294, 24 July 1970, *RO-5.*

[17] Muscat to FCO, Tel. No.362, 29 July 1970, *RO-5,* p.36.

[18] Muscat to FCO, Tel. no.299, 24 July 1970, *RO-5,* p.96.

recognition was granted.[19] Equally important at the financial level, was the need to ensure that Qaboos and Shell got off on the right footing. On 24 July, the manager of Shell's subsidiary, Petroleum Development Oman (PDO), informed his superiors that Qaboos was going to send him a message on 25 July 'formally stating that all agreements between PDO and his predecessor will be fully recognised and upheld by him'.[20]

The British also played a delicate game to ensure that Qaboos had the best external outreach possible through their extensive regional channels. Within Muscat, foreign relations were initially dominated by Oldman. As Crawford noted, 'while Oldman retains his position of pre-eminence… his influence on the Sultan in the external relations sphere as in others will be considerable'.[21] Abroad, the British diplomatic network took the initiative. As early as 24 July, the Arabian Department was planning to take action in order 'to get some Arab rulers to come out in… [Qaboos's] support as quickly as possible'.[22] This regional recognition was seen as the first step towards broader incorporation into the international family of nations. In conservative Arab states, British ambassadors were encouraging governments to recognize and support the new Sultan. In 'radical' capitals, they pretended that they did not know much about what was going on in Muscat. For instance, the ambassador in Tripoli was very cautious: 'In their present state of mind, the Libyan government would regard any action on our part to encourage them to express support for Qaboos as proof that Muscat and Oman is not a sovereign and independent state and that Qaboos is a British stooge.'[23]

Back in Muscat and Oman, news of the coup was released on 26 July. A statement signed by Qaboos and addressed to his people promised that he would 'set up as quickly as possible a forceful and modern government whose first aim would be to remove unnecessary restrictions… and to produce as rapidly as possible a happier and more secure future'. It concluded with a grandiose promise of dawn overcoming the night: 'My friends, my brothers: yesterday was dark, but with God's help, tomorrow will dawn bright for Muscat and Oman and all its people.'[24] Thus, contemporary Omani political mythology was born, with Hemera

---

[19] Douglas-Home to Muscat, Tel No. 62, 25 July 1970, *RO-5*, p.97.
[20] Muscat to FCO, Tel. No.84, 24 July 1970, *RO-5*, p.90.
[21] Muscat to FCO, Tel. No.84, 24 July 1970, *RO-5*, p.90.
[22] Handwritten notes, P.T. Hayman to Permanent Undersecretary, 24 July 1970, *RO-5*, p.23.
[23] Hannam (Tripoli) to FCO, 27 July 1970, *RO-5*, p.109.
[24] 'Press Release From the Authorities of the Sultanate', Muscat, Tel. No.312 to Bahrain, 26 July 1970, *RO-5*.

replacing Nyx, her own mother. The propagation of this mythology fulfilled the need for Qaboos to be presented to the Omani people as their lord and saviour.

Inevitably, there was genuine happiness at the overthrow of Sultan Said. Yet negative feelings towards Said were not enough: positive signs of loyalty to his son had to be generated and flaunted. A concerted effort was therefore necessary to manufacture immediate signs of popular support. Considering the extent to which Said's reign was repressive, this was not a particularly difficult task. What was required was to promise change to the desperate population, to lift petty restrictions, and to flaunt these endeavours by means of a vigorous public relations campaign. Indeed, on the day the coup was announced, a media effort was jointly undertaken by Developmental Officer Michael Butler and Sayid Thuwayni, who began to send regular press releases to the Reuters office in Dubai.[25]

Also crucial were organized holidays, celebrations, and spectacles. A few symbolic gestures designed to instil an air of excitement were immediately announced. For instance, 27 July was declared a public holiday. But the thrust of the focus was on Qaboos's visit to Muscat. Sultanate media efforts were complemented by official British propaganda. The Consul General suggested that Britain's main radio outlet in the southern Gulf, *Sawt as Sahil*, announce that 'as a spontaneous gesture, the citizenry of Muscat and Mutrah are at their own expense decorating the streets, making triumphal arches and ensuring in every way that on Thursday Qaboos receives a "royal" welcome'.[26] Besides asserting Sultanic legitimacy, such announcements were designed to heighten the mood of popular jubilation and anticipation. Of course, such means of generating public excitement were hardly exceptional: they were commonly used by numerous regional monarchs from the Shah to King Hussein. Yet, in this case, they carried special signification, representing the birth of a 'New Oman' in which celebrations were encouraged instead of being suppressed. Echoing Sudhir Hazareesingh's work on post-1848 France, it could be said that the Anglo-Sultanic regime 'was not only now more aware of public expectations, but it also understood the strategic necessity of shaping and even anticipating them'.[27]

The leading merchants of Muscat and its twin city Mutrah were at the forefront of the effort to welcome the new Sultan. Many of them sent

[25] 'Text of Press Release Being Issued by the Sultanate Authorities Today', Crawford (Muscat) to FCO, Tel. No.334, 27 July 1970, *RO-5*, pp.114–15.

[26] Muscat to FCO, Tel. No.333, 27 July 1970, *RO-5*, pp.112–13.

[27] Sudhir Hazareesingh, *The Saint-Napoleon: Celebrations of Sovereignty in Nineteenth-Century France*, Cambridge, Massachusetts: Harvard University Press, 2004, p.7.

messages of congratulation on 26 July, the day they learnt of the coup.[28] Undoubtedly, they were keenly awaiting their release from the iron fist of Said bin Taimur's economic restrictions. Some of them had demanded change from the British as early as 1965. Besides expressing joy at the passing of the old regime, merchants were looking towards establishing a solid relationship with the new one. They participated keenly in public displays of loyalty. The richest amongst them continued to spend lavishly on 'Accession Day' celebrations for years to follow.[29]

Joyful reactions were not witnessed in the entirety of the country, as much as they were on display in Muscat and Mutrah. Crawford reported that 'the coup was received with predictable jubilation in Salalah. In Oman, according to preliminary reports, reactions were similar in Fahud, Izki, and Ibri, but more reserved in Nizwa and Sumail'.[30] The Ibadhi heartland was clearly more sceptical about the change in command, traditionally opposed to the institution of the Sultanate, rather than the individual figure of the Sultan *per se*. However, this lukewarm reaction was not only predictable but also negligible in its immediate effects. What mattered most was Muscat, the capital that the new Sultan had never seen. Unsurprisingly then, Qaboos's entry into Muscat on Thursday, 30 July 1970 became an instantly mythologized moment in Omani history.

The very idea of Qaboos going to Muscat as soon as possible was a British one. On 25 July, two days after the coup, Douglas-Home instructed the Consul General: 'Oldman can persuade Qaboos to go to Muscat at once...'[31] The plane that took Qaboos was British: a Gulf Aviation jet chartered by the Foreign Office three days earlier. The Sultan of Oman Air Force (SOAF) fighter formation that accompanied Qaboos on his flight was British manufactured and flown, arranged by the order of Colonel Oldman.[32] The SOAF hangar next to which Qaboos's plane landed was 'superbly prepared and decorated' by two British officers: Lieutenant-Colonel John Moore and Major John Martyn-Fisher.[33] Not to be forgotten, as well, are the 1,100 British-led soldiers that lined the streets between Bait al-Falaj and Muscat, and the journalists who were actively approached and brought to Muscat by the Foreign Office in order to cover the celebrations.

[28] Muscat to FCO, Tel. No.323, 26 July 1970, *RO-5*, p.25.
[29] See, for example, MEC-Paxton, PDO 'Miscellaneous Notes for July–September 1971'.
[30] 'Headquarters British Forces Persian Gulf to Cabinet Office', Tel. No. 271245Z, 27 July 1970, *RO-5*, pp.117–21.
[31] 'Douglas-Home to Muscat', Tel. No.63, 25 July 1970, *RO-5*, p.102.
[32] 'Crawford (Muscat) to FCO', Tel. No.324, 27 July, *RO-5*, p.108.
[33] Graham, *Ponder Anew*. p.339.

In an active British effort to control perceptions of the event, a Department of Information was 'set [up] for the Government at Muscat by the Consulate General to deal with visiting journalists, run the radio-programmes, and to publish a daily information sheet'.[34] In creating this department, the British Consulate relied on help from the army. For a while, the office of Brigadier Graham was publishing the weekly news-sheet in Arabic, Urdu and English. Likewise, Oman Radio began broadcasting from a hut near the SAF headquarters at Bait al Falaj. This effort was managed by two Britons: Captain Peter Walton and Pauline Searle.[35] The latter was a Reuters journalist who had previously worked in Malaya, writing anti-communist scripts and propaganda films for the Film Unit in Kuala Lumpur. Through the facility she helped set up, Qaboos read his first broadcast speech on 9 August 1970.

Qaboos's speech was oriented towards internal legitimation. Perhaps the most important group to whom he appealed were the sheikhs, whose allegiances he effectively promised to purchase:

> We fully appreciate the responsibilities of the sheikhs of the tribes in our country, ensuring their groups' welfare, security, and good behaviour. We intend to facilitate for them to receive salaries in return for undertaking these tasks and responsibilities…[36]

Qaboos was in an advantageous position *vis-à-vis* the sheikhs, holding the full levers of military and financial power. Lacking any other viable alternative, and offered financial and political stability, they flocked to the Sultan. By 28 July, the allegiances of Ahmad bin-Muhammad of the 'Hirth, the al-Khalili brothers of the Ruwaha, Hamid and Mohammad bin-Hilal of the Al-Sa'ad, Salim bin Rashid of the Baluch, as well as the sheikhs of the Duru', the Janaba, and the Sharqya regions were received and officially announced. This trend continued until the end of 1970 with messages complemented by personal visitations in which a sheikh would personally submit on behalf of himself and his tribe, and the Sultan would order services to be extended to the sheikh's region. This act, performed again and again in private, was carefully reproduced through government announcements.[37]

---

[34] MEC-Paxton. PDO Report. 'The Structure of Government'. 2nd Draft, 19 September 1970.

[35] Graham, *Ponder Anew*, p.340.

[36] Sultanat Oman,'*Khutab wa Kalimat 'Hadrat Sa'hib al-Jalalah al-Sultan Qaboos bin Said al Mu'atham: 1970–2005*. Muscat: Wazarat al-I'lam, 2005, p.15.

[37] See, for example, 'Ministry of Information's News Bulletin', 30 December 1970, *RO-5*, p.168.

Every sheikhly visit was the occasion of a Faustian exchange: the alienation of the political in return for the economic. All the announcements sounded the same. It mattered not who the sheikh was or which territory they represented. What counted was the repetition, the constant and persistent re-enactment of the Omani submission to the Sultan. This had become the most important political ritual in the country. Even someone like the sheikh of Bakha, who had previously rejected the authority of the Sultan and styled himself Ruler of Bakha and Dependencies, was now practising this ritual.[38] Moreover, even the sheikhs of areas like Ja'lan, which had always resisted Sultanic authority, now accepted the appointment of a wali.

Yet, the strongest sheikhs were concerned with navigating this novel political terrain, measuring the reach of the new Sultan. In particular, it was essential to test the attitude of Britain, which was still viewed as the paramount power in Oman. It is in this light that we should read a letter sent to the British Consul from one of the most prominent sheikhs at the time, Ahmad al-Harithi:

> I had hoped that the accession of Sultan Qabus would solve the problems confronting Oman, but unfortunately I see the contrary to be the case...I have a suggestion to make subject to the approval of the government of His Highness the Sultan and the government of Great Britain...With your agreement I should like to discuss it with you privately.[39]

In his response to this letter, Crawford took the opportunity to assert Britain's full support for Qaboos, directing Sheikh Ahmad to raise any issues directly with him.[40] Not much later, Sheikh Ahmad was exiled to India and was eventually placed under house arrest when he returned to Oman. Indeed, relations with the sheikhs were not always benevolent and, very early on, signals were sent to those who objected to any aspect of policy. For instance, three 'dissident' Jenaba sheikhs who came to Muscat to protest PDO's labour arrangements in their territory were immediately arrested.[41]

Qaboos's personal authority over the sheikhs was first established through 'whistle stop tours' undertaken in the early weeks of August 1970. All of the Sultan's tours were coordinated by the SAF and Colonel

---

[38] Letter from Hamdan bin Ahmed to J.L. Bullard (PA Dubai), 27 December 1969, *RO-5*, p.173.

[39] Letter addressed to H.M. Consul-General from Sheikh Ahmed bin Mohammed Al Harithi, 18 October 1970, *RO-5*, p.155.

[40] D.G.Crawford (CG Muscat) to Sheikh Ahmad al-Harithi, 2 November 1970, *RO-5*, p.156.

[41] MEC-Paxton, PDO 'Miscellaneous Notes for July–September 1971'.

Oldman, thus risking the potential of revealing 'some undesirable political features'; namely, the British administration of Sultanic affairs.[42] Nevertheless, the merits of the 'meet the people' policy far outweighed the risks. It established the pattern whereby Omanis supplicated their Sultan, and the latter answered their requests in meticulously paternal fashion. The case of Suhar city was typical. When its residents asked for some essential building works and for agricultural equipment, the Sultan granted their request on the spot.[43] The same scenario was replicated elsewhere.

The tours were predictably effective on the coast. For instance, the Sultan's visit to the Batinah was judged a 'resounding success'. More important, the tours had their desired effect in the historically defiant interior. Although it 'had a slow start because the Wali had not arranged things too well', even the Nizwa visit went off without incident: 'once the people heard that Qabus was moving freely round the streets and talking openly to all, large crowds assembled'.[44] This by no means shows that Qaboos was immediately charming. As Brigadier Graham notes, in 'the first year of his reign Qaboos was noticeably hesitant about meeting his people, and when faced with crowds of ordinary folk was patently ill at ease and in his manner reserved and very formal'.[45] However, the Sultan's awkwardness was compensated for by the significance of his presence. Qaboos's visits were meant to illustrate the replacement of neglect with personalized attention. Moreover, just as the Sultan's carrot was revealed in these visits, so was his stick. For instance, a firepower demonstration was held by the Muscat Regiment at the command of Qaboos 'for the enlightenment of the local Sheikhs and many other tribal leaders'.[46]

Just as the sheikhs had to be 'enlightened' by Qaboos's benevolence and power, so did the general population. The Sultan's image was printed on posters, his voice repeatedly echoed over the radio waves, and his words were printed in press releases. This was a great departure from previous Sultanic practice. In the era of Said bin Taimur, the Sultan retained nothing less than an 'aura' in the Benjaminite sense of the term: 'the unique phenomenon of a distance, however close it may be'.[47] Although he was

---

[42] 'Sultanate Scene', Crawford (Muscat) to Weir (Bahrain), 17 August 1970, *RO-5*, p.137.

[43] 'Sultanate Scene'.

[44] 'Sultanate Scene'.

[45] Graham, *Ponder Anew*, p.344.

[46] 'Sultanate Scene'.

[47] Walter Benjamin, 'The Work of Art in the Age of Mechanical Reproduction', in *Illuminations*, New York: Schocken, 1969, p.222.

Fig. 4. Portrait of Sultan Qaboos, Areej (Khor Khuwairi), 17 Sept 1977

obsessed with the mechanical reproduction of all that was around him (in 1961 he had eight cine and still cameras, two of which were continuously operated by his secretary, Hamad bin Hamoud, and a slave), he took a guarded approach to the dissemination of his own image.[48] His aura was shielded by his residence in provincial Salalah, his quintessential hostility to the media, the rarity of his speeches, the paucity of his public appearances and, above all, the inaccessibility of his person.

Counterpoised to this distance was the new semblance of closeness. The coup initiated the age of mechanical reproduction in Oman, and this phenomenon only grew over the years.[49] Yet, even before the mechanical

---

[48] J.F.S. Philips (Muscat) to M.C.G. Man (Bahrain), *RO, 1961*, p.14.
[49] Dawn Chatty, 'Rituals of Royalty and the Elaboration of Ceremony in Oman: View from the Edge', *International Journal of Middle East Studies*, Vol. 41, 2009, p.46.

reproduction of the Sultanic image reached its peak, his shadow was chiselled into Omani consciousness by other methods. For instance, Qaboos's name was imposed upon the calendar through the marking of his birthday. Although he turned 30 on 18 November, celebrations were postponed until 16 December 1970 due to Ramadan. Over the course of a few days, occasions were held across the length and breadth of the land. The principal event was a military spectacle during which the Sultan wore the uniform of a British Army Lieutenant-General and 'took the parade in his honour in a style which showed that he had forgotten none of his Sandhurst training'.[50] The crowd were not only made to see their ruler dressed in colonial wear but they were also subjected to the tunes of the British army, played by the pipe band of the Trucial Oman Scouts. For the first time, they were introduced to the new flag of unified Oman. Even that foremost national symbol was designed by a British officer, Bill Goodfellow, and imported in large quantities from West Germany.[51]

Typically, these sights and sounds of colonial *mimesis* reflected the position of a monarch who, in almost everything he did, constantly copied metropolitan culture. Of course, to use a well known expression in postcolonial theory, Qaboos was 'almost the same, *but not quite*'.[52] Ironically, the British were initially wary about his public displays of anglophilia. Yet, Qaboos insisted and had his way. Right after his first military parade, he held an afternoon tea party for '80 Omani dignitaries and 20 European guests during which he spent most of the time himself serving them with cake and other refreshments'. Other, less typically British, events were also held. In order to heighten the festive atmosphere, 'a group of Arab musicians and singers' gave performances at parties held in honour of the Sultan. They also held concerts for the general public on a stage prepared by the British staff of Radio Oman.[53] The Consul General recognized the exceptional importance of such events:

> ...dancing, singing and music in public was forbidden by the old regime. It is perhaps the transformation from complete prohibition to Sultanic encouragement and participation in public events which will serve to persuade Omanis that the bad old days have really gone... it must be acknowledged that the opportunity to take part in public occasions may be as important to Omanis as the provision of schools, hospitals and roads.[54]

---

[50] 'Sultan's Official Birthday', D.G. Crawford (Muscat) to Michael Weir (Bahrain), 21 December 1970, *RO-5*, p.166.
[51] 'Sultan's Official Birthday'.
[52] Homi Bhaba,. *The Location of Culture*, London: Routledge Classics, 2004, p.123.
[53] 'Sultan's Official Birthday'.
[54] 'Sultan's Official Birthday'.

As much as it depended on the poster and the radio announcement, the cult of the Sultan was furthered by his presence on the parade ground and the concert stage. Receiving a boost of self-confidence at these venues, the Sultan upgraded his own title. In early January 1971, 'His Highness' ordered that he be addressed as 'His Majesty'.[55]

The British understood and appreciated that the main effect of building the Sultan's cult was the consolidation of Qaboos's personal power. Significantly, this in turn meant weakening the position of his uncle Tariq, the only ruling family figure to be reckoned with at the time. In mid-August, less than a month after the coup, the Consul General, Crawford, noted that 'there can be no doubt that the Sultan's "meet the people" policies are building up for him a power base of general acceptance which others, especially Tariq, may in due course find difficult to assail'.[56] By the end of October, the foundations of Qaboos's absolutism became even stronger, the Consul speaking of a 'discernable growth in stature and authority of the Sultan, highlighted by various indications that Tariq is neither as popular, effective or as certain of his ability to cut the Sultan down to size...'.[57] Qaboos was now taking a haughty attitude towards his uncle, boasting that 'the message he received from the interior was that its leaders could only take their orders from him and from no one else'.[58] Had the British not centralized all major decision-making powers in his person during the days following the coup, he would have hardly been able to make such a statement. He certainly would not have felt as secure had his palace not been stacked with figures from the British army, including Tim Landon as his Equerry and Mac Mclean, an ex-Royal Navy officer, as his Secretary. Yet, what was the available alternative to Qaboos's absolutism?

THE CONSTITUTIONAL MONARCHIST ALTERNATIVE

British actions from the coup onwards were directed towards consolidating power in Qaboos's hands. They played the pivotal role in the construction of his absolutist state. Of course, there were alternatives to that system of governance. The most significant one was Tariq bin Taimur's constitutional monarchy project. Tariq was the best educated, most widely

---

[55] Arthur (PR Bahrain) to FCO, Tel. No.12, 8 January 1971, *RO-6*.
[56] Arthur (PR Bahrain) to FCO, Tel. No.12, 8 January 1971, *RO-6*.
[57] 'Sultanate of Oman', Crawford (Muscat) to Weir (Bahrain), 2 November 1970, *RO-6*.
[58] 'Sultanate of Oman', Crawford (Muscat) to Weir (Bahrain), 2 November 1970, *RO-6*.

travelled, and most experienced of the Al Said. He, moreover, had a basis of support within—although by no means command over—communities of Omani exiles, Muscati merchants, local Baluchis and the inhabitants of the Battinah coast.[59] Living in exile during the latter years of Said bin Taimur, he informed the British of his reformist intentions in January 1967.[60] Suffering from a variety of health problems and enjoying life abroad, he wished to return to Oman for only two or three years, during which he would lay the foundations for his vision.[61]

Ignored by Britain, Tariq began to mobilize amongst exiled Omanis. On 15 September 1967, he publicly announced that there would be 'no more despotism', distributing a draft provisional constitution 'in preparation for giving the people the opportunity to choose the system of rule that would accord with the traditions and customs of the country...' Under his plan, the name of the state was to change from the 'Sultanate of Muscat and Oman' to the 'Arab Kingdom of Oman.' This was to emphasize the unitary nature of the state and its Arab identity, and thus facilitate more effective nation building and regional legitimation. In this renamed domain, there was to be a King, a Prime Minister, a Council of Ministers, a Council of State, and a National Assembly. The King was relegated to ceremonial responsibilities, such as representing the state in official functions and receiving diplomatic credentials.[62] He could be impeached by the National Assembly if 'he abused monarchical authorities or endangered the interests of the state'. The same applied to the Prime Minister 'if he gravely abused his authority or endangered the safety and security of the state'.[63]

Tariq's gradualist project offered a fixed transitional period with a semblance of legalism and minimal popular participation, to be followed by the establishment of a more inclusive constitutional monarchic system. With the significant exception of the Dhufaris, who were completely ignored in his initiative, Tariq attempted to please everyone.[64] Although this did not get him very far, he continued to advocate this reformist vision well beyond the 1970 overthrow of his brother, effectively projecting for himself the role of a political, as well as economic, modernizer. By becoming a powerful Prime Minister under a weak monarch, he could

[59] FCO 8/568, Muscat to Foreign Office, Tel. No.8, 16 January 1967.
[60] FCO 8/568, Arabian Department to Bahrain, Tel. No.40, 12 January 1967.
[61] FCO 8/1673, Luce to Acland, 9 July 1971.
[62] FCO 8/568, 'Al Dustoor al Mou'akat lil Mamlaka al 'Arabiyya al 'Omaniya', 11 Jamada al-Thani, 1387.
[63] FCO 8/568, 'Al Dustoor al Mou'akat lil Mamlaka al 'Arabiyya al 'Omaniya', 11 Jamada al-Thani, 1387.
[64] FCO8/568, Carden (Muscat) to Crawford (Bahrain), 22 November 1967.

assume the role of a genuine state builder. Tariq's socialization may have played a role in the development of his vision. Born in 1921, he grew up in Turkey at the height of the republican period. This experience, along with the marginalization he suffered under his brother, possibly explains his interest in constitutionalism. It may also account for his aversion to the word 'Sultan'.

Whatever the extent of its genuineness, Tariq's plan was viewed with deep suspicion. Attacks against him came from both the Imamate and the Dhufari revolutionaries. Initially, the Imamate issued a condemnation of his project as a British imperialist plan. In a strongly worded critique, the Omani Revolutionary Command referred to Tariq as *safah' 'Oman*, 'the butcher of Oman', pointing to his role in suppressing the al-Jabal al-Akhdar revolt. It insisted that it would not be deceived by his initiative: 'The Omani people know Tariq, whom Britain tries to make another of its lackeys, and they know his family and its evil intentions and its cruelty during its long period of black rule, and its connection with imperialism'.[65] Nevertheless, the Imamate eventually adjusted its stance in early 1970, arriving at some form of accommodation, 'born of desperation', with Tariq.[66]

Unlike the Imamate, the Dhufari revolutionaries never really changed their view of Tariq. As had been shown earlier, the republican spirit was by now strongly entrenched amongst Dhufari cadres, and they demanded a complete overthrow of the monarchy, which they saw as organically connected with imperialism. Even after the Qaboos coup, the view of Tariq's status as a British stooge was not adjusted:

> What happened in July 1970 was not unexpected; it was the result of a long-term plan, drawn up by British imperialism to contain, and then liquidate, the prevailing revolutionary trend. In this sense, the overthrow of Said bin Taimur was part of a double plan. First there was the plan for a so-called 'Omani constitutional monarchy'; this had long been advocated by Tariq bin Taimur, Said's brother. The second plan was obviously that of the Union of Arab Emirates. Both were political fronts for British neo-colonialism in the area, in a desperate attempt to advance seemingly patriotic régimes.[67]

In fact, the British opportunistically took a much more conservative line than Tariq. They were concerned with upholding the status quo as

---

[65] FCO8/568, 'A Statement by the Omani Revolutionary Command', 27 October 1967.
[66] MEC-Paxton. 4/4, 'Note: Rebel Activities', 8 February 1970.
[67] Said Seif Talal Saad, 'Interview on the Political Situation in Oman and Dhofar', *New Left Review*, I/66, March–April 1971.

opposed to constitutionalism. To them, the economic and political realms were strictly separated. Thus, they strongly advocated economic modernization and a degree of limited redistribution of oil revenues in Oman but they did not seek political reform. By laying the foundations for the establishment of economic rentierism and providing the military support necessary to uphold Said bin Taimur (and later Qaboos), they inhibited the potential for political development. Quite simply, the path of absolutism was a convenient one for them. Moreover, Qaboos was extremely susceptible to British advice in ways that Tariq, an older man with set ways, was not. Nevertheless, the British understood the need to involve Tariq, and to bring him as close to Qaboos as possible:

> Sayyid Tariq enjoyed a strong position in Oman until his voluntary exile in 1962, and could present a serious challenge to Qaboos if he were unwilling to work with him. Sultan Qaboos is unknown to the people of Oman, and is young and totally without experience in government . . . there seems a reasonable hope that he and Tariq, working as a team, should be able to hold the country together while transforming it to a modern state.[68]

Once again the Sultan had to be told what to do. On 26 July, Oldman was instructed to explain to Qaboos the need to bring back his uncle.[69] Although he was never enthusiastic about this, the Sultan agreed, the 'Foreign Office' insisting on this measure as the 'price to be paid by Qaboos for "fixing" the coup'.[70] Thus, Tariq, who was in Hamburg at the time suffering from a stomach condition, was invited, and duly agreed, to come back as Prime Minister.

At this point, the survival of the Sultanic regime, in the face of the spreading revolution, clearly depended on the creation of a bureaucracy and initiating economic development. This was in turn crucial for the protection of Britain's strategic and oil interests. The British were confronted with a dilemma: how to create a bureaucracy and bring about economic development in a country as bereft of an educated managerial class as Oman? From the prism of comparative decolonization, it can be seen that this question had been asked and answered many times before. However, Oman was unusual in that Britain controlled the country but did not wish to admit that it did so.

---

[68] 'Headquarters British Forces Persian Gulf to Cabinet Office', Tel. No.271245Z, 27 July 1970, *RO-5*, pp.117–21.
[69] 'Muscat to FCO', Tel. No.322, 26 July 1970 *RO-5*, p.107.
[70] MEC-Graham, Graham Diaries, 1 October 1971.

In tackling this dilemma, there were two 'extreme' options: the creation of a British administration or the construction of a bureaucracy principally comprised of exiled Omanis and Arab expatriates. The former was politically unfeasible, although the British deemed it to be superior in efficiency. The latter option was politically preferable, but it came at the risk of slower bureaucratic build-up and threats to the absolutist regime. The British solution to this dilemma was to pursue both courses simultaneously. British involvement was to be intensified at the same time as local involvement was increased. The challenge for Britain was to ensure they tapped into the talents of exiled Omanis while controlling the political inclinations they had acquired abroad for such concepts as democracy and social justice.

Tariq was seen as the principle representative of the exiled Omani professional class and the British had initially reserved the role of constructing state institutions and a bureaucracy for him. Until September 1970, governance was conducted through a temporary Advisory Council headed by Oldman.[71] The keenness to replace this body with a local ministerial hierarchy was understandable. After all, explicit British presence was harmful to Sultanic legitimacy. The dilemma faced at the time was expressed by Sir William Morris, Ambassador to Saudi Arabia:

> I realise that it would be impossible, even if it were desirable, for Qabus and Tariq to move too fast in removing the evidences of British omnipresence in their government; but I think that this makes it all the more desirable that the new born Sultanate Agitprop organisation should be aware of the *need to splash Arab colour over the local scene.*[72]

Colonial reality had to be masked by local discourse and imagery. Splashing 'Arab colour' was especially important on the regional level:

> It probably matters less here than in other Arab countries, but even here it jars when one reads that Oldman has held a press conference for visiting correspondents, and when the official bulletin announces that it is thanks to the generosity of the R.A.F. that the tribal leader of Massirah Island has been able to pay his respects to the Sultan...[73]

Along similar lines, Crawford noted: 'the place of the British in a Sultanate seeking international "respectability" will be a matter which will have to be treated with delicacy by both ourselves and the Omanis'.[74]

---

[71] 'Sultanate Scene', Crawford (Muscat) to Weir (Bahrain), 17 August 1970, *RO-5*, p.137.

[72] Morris (Jedda) to Edes (Arabian Department), 15 August 1970, *RO-5*, p.728. Emphasis added.

[73] Morris (Jedda) to Edes (Arabian Department), 15 August 1970, *RO-5*, p.728.

[74] 'Sultanate of Oman', Crawford (Muscat) to Weir (Bahrain), 2 November 1970, *RO-5*, p.158.

Tariq's arrival as Prime Minister certainly served to improve the situation. He was interested in, if not entirely capable of, launching a genuine Arabization programme. During the second week of August, Tariq held several meetings with Qaboos. The two agreed to appoint four relatively young ministers: Dr Asim al-Jamali as Minister of Health; Saud bin Ali al-Khalili as Minister of Education; Badr bin Saud as Minister of the Interior; and Mohammad Ahmad Al Bu Said as Minister of Justice. Contrary to the popular image of an instant developmental revolution under Qaboos, this ministerial team failed to achieve much during its time in office. In November 1970, Crawford reported that 'in three months, government has done little to improve the well being of the people apart from removing the restrictions of the old regime. The latter was, nevertheless, such a significant advance that it gave both Sultan and Prime Minister a credit balance they have not yet expended.'[75]

Crawford primarily blamed Tariq for governmental failures. His successor, Ambassador Hawley, had a different assessment:

> The Prime Minister... is the most impressive and experienced Omani Minister, although he lives simply and eschews formality...According to one theory he is essentially a talker and not a man of action. I am, however, more inclined to think that he might be an able Prime Minister if his own office was properly staffed and he could rely on a responsive machinery of government.[76]

Staffing deficiencies were indeed a formidable obstacle to ministerial performance and positions vital for bureaucratic functioning were still unfilled. For instance, apart from the Defence Department, government ministries lacked accounting officers and were thus unable to prepare accurate budget estimates.[77]

Corruption was also an issue. As the months passed by, Tariq awarded major contracts without tender to West German companies. Although this was related to Tariq's desire to reduce British economic influence in Oman, it also seemed to contain an element of personal gain. On 2 January 1971, Strabag was awarded a £9.74 million contract for building a road between Muscat and Sohar. Similarly, a £17.2 million contract for the Port Qaboos project in Mattrah was awarded to a consortium led by Hochtief, a company for which Tariq had worked in the past. From the

---

[75] 'Sultanate of Oman', Crawford (Muscat) to Weir (Bahrain), 2 November 1970, *RO-5*, p.158.

[76] 'Impressions of Oman: The First and the Last', Diplomatic Report No. 428/71, 5 August 1971, *RO-6*, p.30.

[77] FCO 8/1673, 'Financial Management of Oman', Hallows (Bank of England) to Sultan Qaboos, 19 March 1971.

latter deal alone, it was suspected that Tariq made £2 million.[78] Tariq by no means set the precedent for the skewed allocation of contracts. Indeed, in the early days before Tariq's arrival, Qaboos's main backer, Colonel Oldman, chaotically assigned projects. But whereas Tariq's German dealings were widely exposed, Oldman's British contracts were treated with discretion, talked about in senior UK circles only. Brigadier Graham, for instance, only learnt of them belatedly, after a meeting with Christopher Kennedy, the Chief Engineer of the Sultanate's Defence Department:

> ...Kennedy announced (we were alone, speaking privately) that Oldman had rushed into signing contracts with Taylor Woodrow et al without getting expert advice, and in consequence was "taken for a ride and has cost the Sultanate over a million pounds in unnecessary expenditure"...the story that his premature signing has caused such loss is news to me. How Tariq will gloat when he hears! I told Kennedy not to speak to anyone on this matter but to keep such thoughts to himself.[79]

Unlike Tariq's German companies, who were generally praised for the quality of their work, Taylor Woodrow was criticized for its 'lax standards and high prices'.[80] Nevertheless, the spotlight was on the Prime Minister. Qaboos himself was speaking at length 'of his doubts about Tariq's financial reliability'.[81] This was, as will be shown later in this chapter, the pot calling the kettle black.

At any rate, Tariq was simply not up to speed on the details of government. He hardly visited his ministries, and did not issue clear instructions for the haphazardly growing bureaucracies. Government coherence suffered from the lack of coordination from his office.[82] How did Omanis view this state of affairs? On 25 May 1971, the Sultanate's Intelligence Officers reported 'disappointment with Tariq and his team'.[83] Qaboos himself was not immune from popular disappointment, the PR noting that the Sultan's 'long absences in Salalah, and the total failure of his ministers to achieve anything, have cost him a good deal of support in the past six months'.[84]

[78] 'Oman: Annual Review for 1971'. *RO-6*, p.8.

[79] Graham Diaries, 9 August 1971.

[80] Graham Diaries, 14 August 1971.

[81] FCO 8/1673, 'Oman: Relations Between the Sultan and Tariq', Luce to Acland, 9 July 1971.

[82] 'Sultanate of Oman', Crawford (Muscat) to Weir (Bahrain), 2 November 1970, *RO-5*, p.158.

[83] Graham Diaries, 25 May 1971.

[84] 'What About Oman? Her Majesty's Political Resident at Bahrain to the Secretary of State for Foreign and Commonwealth Affairs', Diplomatic Report No. 289/71, 26 April 1971, *RO-6*, p.26.

When it came to matters of governance, both Sultan and Prime Minister displayed marked signs of laziness. This caused much anguish in British circles. In his final report as Consul General, Crawford wrote:

> How much time before the Euphoria released by the change of regime evaporates into general discontent and disorder…The Sultan…has not…displayed until now the strength of character or resolution to become a "Shah" or a "King Hussein". He needs to stay in Muscat longer, work harder…perhaps, when he returns in July, he will begin to act more like the benevolent autocrat he wishes to become…[85]

Likewise, Sir Geoffrey Arthur, the new Political Resident Persian Gulf (PR), patronizingly complained to CSAF Graham about the 'dream world in which your young monarch and his Prime Minister function'.[86]

Besides laziness, there was infighting. The conflict between uncle and nephew had two dimensions: it was a struggle for power as well as an ideological clash between conservatism and reformism. Of course, both dimensions were intertwined. Tariq's constitutional monarchy project would have strengthened the Prime Minister's position and weakened the Sultan while the Sultan's quest for absolutism would have raised him above all. Hence, a battle erupted between the two over the issue of constitutionalism. Both of their cases were presented to the British. Tariq spoke 'volubly about his aims to achieve a democratic, constitutional, detribalised, internationalised, Arab and outwardlooking Sultanate'.[87] In contrast, Qaboos 'said that he had spoken to many of the Shaikhs and the Walis in the country, and also to individual members of the government about the question of a constitution. None had wished it at this stage in the Sultanate's development, since it was an irrelevancy'.[88]

Although it sincerely wanted nephew and uncle to work together, Britain gave the Sultan an enormous structural advantage by handing him all the 'sovereign' powers during the first week of the coup and giving him complete backing thereafter. As a result, the Sultan consistently refused to yield to Tariq. He was initially acting on advice given to him by British figures, who had told him 'not to let Tarik touch defence and finance'.[89] But Qaboos was not only being steered by the British in this matter.

---

[85] 'Final Impressions of Oman', Crawford (Muscat) to Arthur (Bahrain), 24 April 1971, *RO-6*, p.13.

[86] 'Final Impressions of Oman', Crawford (Muscat) to Arthur (Bahrain), 11 March 1971, *RO-6*.

[87] 'Sultanate of Oman', Crawford (Muscat) to Weir (Bahrain), 2 November 1970, *RO-5*, p.158.

[88] 'Sultanate of Oman', Crawford (Muscat) to Weir (Bahrain), 2 November 1970, *RO-5*, p.158.

[89] MEC-Skeet 1/1, Malcolm Dennison's handwritten notes to Skeet, n.d., *c*.1991.

Indeed, he was personally disposed towards absolutism. Although he was less interested than the former Sultan in questions of detail, British reports spoke of his resemblance to his father, especially in his love of autocratic decision-making. This trait was not a cause of imperial concern. In the words of the Consul General: 'Several people have said that the new Sultan has many attributes of his father. I think this is so, and they may stand him in good stead.'[90] As his standing and ego grew, the Sultan became more assertive about not only maintaining, but also expanding, his powers. After a meeting with him on 30 October, the Consul General reported the following:

> Sayid Qaboos made clear that his voice would predominate in military, financial and external affairs, and, he stressed, in the award of large commercial contracts. He said, however, that he had no wish to follow his father's example of doing all the work of government himself. "Let them," he said referring to his government, "work out all the details, and if I do not like what they propose or require changes, they can do the work again".[91]

Tariq persisted in opposing this absolutist vision, still demanding an overhaul of financial and defence arrangements. He seemed to be especially concerned with reducing Qaboos's control over the budget, and ending British paramountcy over the armed forces. He spoke audibly about such issues and the ideological basis of his stance on them. At a reception attended by the upper ranks of the Muscat administration, he went as far as declaring himself to be a 'republican' at heart.[92]

Yet, these ideological premises were not the only points of difference he had with Qaboos. Indeed, what made his conflict with his nephew so consequential was the extent to which they fought over administrative affairs. Things were also made worse by the fact that the two rarely met. Qaboos and Tariq both took extremely long holidays at different times. Throughout 1971, they did not overlap 'for a period longer than 10 days together in Muscat...In general they behaved like Box and Cox or the two figures of a Swiss weather clock'.[93] Qaboos's longest absence occurred for an exorbitantly costly tour of Europe that he undertook between 24 April and 10 July 1971. For the duration of that ten-week period, Tariq focused his energies on protesting his exclusion from decision-making,

---

[90] 'Sultanate of Oman', Crawford (Muscat) to Weir (Bahrain), 2 November 1970, *RO-5*, p.160.
[91] 'Sultanate of Oman', Crawford (Muscat) to Weir (Bahrain), 2 November 1970, *RO-5*, p.158.
[92] Graham Diaries, 3 November 1971.
[93] 'Oman: Annual Review for 1971', 3 January 1972, *RO-6*, p.7.

'openly complaining about his lack of power as Prime Minister and criticising the Sultan's own control over defence and finance.' He expressed 'his dissatisfaction by acting the Achilles and refusing to see Colonel Oldman'.[94]

The Qaboos–Tariq rivalry illustrates that there were historical paths open to Oman other than absolutism. Essentially, absolutism was a matter of imperial choice. Britain had the option of backing a constitutional monarchical vision, and insisting on it being upheld. This could have been done either by supporting Tariq and his professed constitutional ideals, or by pressuring Qaboos to alter his own absolutist stance. With full control over the army as well as complete access to Qaboos and immense leverage over him, the latter course of action was available. However, constitutionalism was a non-issue for British officials because Britain's position was best secured by an absolutist Qaboos. Sir Geoffrey Arthur was adamant on this point, advocating a united Anglo-Sultanic front against the advocates of constitutionalism and independence. In a pivotal report to the Foreign Secretary, he emphasized the consolidation of Qaboos's absolutism as the way forward for Britain:

> By temperament the Sultan inclines to autocracy, as his father did. He finds it relatively easy to take decisions, as his father did. He rose to power on the backs of his army and he does not forget this. His army means his British officers and British Defence Secretary, and these are the people he really trusts, together with his British bank manager and some of the senior staff of the oil company.[95]

Arthur insisted that the Sultan and Britain were confronted with the same dilemma. On the one hand, they both desired to maintain British control over all the major decisions. On the other, there was a need for involving Omani former exiles and other Arabs in the administration so as to project as independent image of the country. The British looked down upon the exiles who longed 'for Arab respectability and international recognition'. They were 'people who will talk endlessly about constitutions but who have lost, if they had ever acquired, the habit of hard work'. As usual, the Sultan was in agreement: 'His dilemma is our dilemma, which is perhaps why we find it so easy to discuss affairs with him and why he is so ready to take our advice'.[96]

---

[94] 'Impressions of Oman: The First and the Last', Diplomatic Report No. 428/71, 5 August 1971, *RO-6*.

[95] 'What About Oman? Her Majesty's Political Resident at Bahrain to the Secretary of State for Foreign and Commonwealth Affairs', Diplomatic Report No. 289/71, 26 April 1971, *RO-6*.

[96] 'What About Oman?'

The Sultan was completely disconnected from his local surroundings and was embedded in the British administration in the country. He saw Omanis as incapable and as having motives that did not necessarily serve his interests. In contrast, the British interest completely accorded with his. Nevertheless, he needed to engage with the locals:

> Here he must rely on Sayid Tariq and the other returned exiles and their friends. They hint that the British presence is too obtrusive...He observes that their knowledge is often inadequate and their advice poor. He sees that they, unlike his British friends, do not deliver the goods. He comes to mistrust their motives. They become more inactive and resentful than ever; but they avoid provoking a crisis, for as long as the Sultan keeps his armed forces intact, he is bound to win. Yet their political power grows steadily; and the Sultan is regularly faced with the difficult choice between what is politically expedient and what will lead to efficient government.[97]

Two elements are evident in this analysis. First, the British and the Sultan both subscribed to the 'myth of the lazy native'.[98] As in other colonial contexts, this myth played the function of justifying the British order of domination through positing it as more efficient, and therefore superior, to native alternatives. Secondly, the British were intensely aware of the need to maintain a solid martial basis for the Sultan's absolutist order of domination. They correctly identified the need for monopolizing control over the army, the only institution that could 'rein in the native' in the last resort. With that control assured, domestic politics could be contained within strict parameters.

In this light, the essence of British policy in Oman becomes clear: the political containment of the native to secure imperial interests. However, this was not equivalent to denying reformist Omani figures a say. On the contrary, some freedom of action was given to the Prime Minister and his government staffed by Omani exiles. However, this was done within British-imposed boundaries. The Qaboos–Tariq conflict pertained to the extent of these boundaries, Tariq persistently attempting to push them further. The British allowed for this dynamic to continue, seeing no other alternative 'short of a colonial style administration'.[99] But there was still a determination to maintain Anglo-Sultanic ascendancy. There was simply too much to lose for Britain to pack up and leave immediately:

---

[97] 'What About Oman?'
[98] See Syed Hussein Alatas, *The Myth of the Lazy Native*, London: Frank Cass, 1977, p.2.
[99] 'Sultanate of Oman', Crawford (Muscat) to Weir (Bahrain), 2 November 1970, *RO-5*, p.160.

We cannot afford to let things go too wrong. If we leave things to the Omani government they will go wrong; but if we step in to straighten things out, we shall show up the Sultan as our puppet, widen the division between him and his Government, and leave the latter more resentful than ever of our presence and our influence... [100]

Although Britain had to leave at some point, this could only be done when its local figure of choice, the Sultan, was strong enough to stand on his own. In the meantime, British steering of the internal affairs of the Sultanate was to continue, but on a selective basis and in as discreet a manner as possible. In particular, Britain had to maintain control over security:

We must... be discriminating with our help and in our intervention. The area in which we can least afford to compromise is security... if we see that the security of the State is being put at risk by the lethargy or folly of the Prime Minister or other Ministers, we should not hesitate to warn the Sultan, who will lend a ready ear, and if necessary support the British Defence Secretary, assuming that he is in the right, against an Omani. [101]

Between May and December 1971, this recommendation was put into action. Britain stood firmly behind Oldman and Qaboos, and Tariq's protests against absolutism were ignored.

The British backed Qaboos even though they were aware of his failings. In particular, the Political Resident was appalled by the 'chaotic functioning of the Omani Royal Household and HM's routine'. [102] Apart from burdening the treasury with his *nouveau riche* spending habits, Qaboos was failing to control his slaves. These privileged members of his household were even abusing the country's resources, civilian and military, expecting 'instant conveyance by Landrover or aircraft, sometimes only to visit their family village bearing sacks of bananas but quoting as their authority "His Majesty Wishes..."'. [103]

The Sultan himself was a huge drain on the national budget, not least due to his love of palaces, having a marked interest in royal residences and strong opinions on such matters as the comparison between Schönbrunn and Versailles. [104] This theoretical fascination was translated into a costly obsession. In 1971, at a time when Omani oil revenues were no more than £50 million, and when the state had to dip into its reserves to the tune of £7 million to cover essential gaps in developmental and military

---

[100] 'What About Oman?'
[101] 'What About Oman?'
[102] Graham Diaries, 11 March 1971.
[103] Graham Diaries, 26 May 1971.
[104] Graham Diaries, 28 September 1971.

spending, Qaboos was building three lavish palaces at the same time. With no concern for historical conservation or expense, he demolished the Muscat palace built by his ancestor Said bin Sultan (r.1807–56) and commissioned an Indian firm to build a £3 million building in its place. Equally unsatisfied with his father's old palace in Salalah, he spent £1.5 million on a new royal complex in that town. He also paid £1 million for a palace at Sib.[105] These palaces brought with them additional expenses, the furniture for the one at Sib alone costing £900,000.[106] Up to 20 per cent of the state income from oil for 1971 was therefore spent on palaces. This is not counting the heavy expenditure incurred on the Sultan's travels and other luxury items. Considering that the military was consuming 40 per cent of state revenue, this left a severely diminished amount for other spending.[107]

It was not unusual for individual British figures to criticize Qaboos's expenditure, policy choices, and lifestyle. Brigadier Graham, for example, made sarcastic comments about the Sultan's growing fleet of cars.[108] He also jotted entries in his diary, subtly mocking Qaboos's superstitious approach to military affairs and the close attention he paid to the predictions of 'magicians on the jebel'.[109] Others focused on Qaboos's character, complementing their disapproving statements with homophobic references to his sexual preferences. For instance, Tony Molesworth, the Sultanate's second most senior intelligence officer, stated that 'HM is homosexual and vicious, like his Father, behind the scenes'.[110] Nevertheless, these very same figures served to anchor Qaboos's rule and to further his myth. As much as they were aware of his human failings, they treated and presented him in an exalted manner. In the words of the Sultanate's Intelligence Chief: 'The British put [Qaboos] on the throne and then regarded [him] as the embodiment of all wisdom, bowing down before him'.[111]

British officers and officials created for themselves a heroic myth, insisting on the congruence between their imperial interest and the needs of Oman, the country that they were subjecting to their will. Qaboos and his absolute rule were presented in providential terms, and the British as thanklessly working for the sake of the lazy natives. Thus, in the privacy

---

[105] 'Impressions of Oman: The First and the Last', Diplomatic Report No. 428/71, 5 August 1971, *RO-6*.
[106] Graham Diaries, 5 August 1971.
[107] 'Oman: Annual Review for 1971'.
[108] Graham Diaries, 15 June 1972.
[109] Graham Diaries, 27 September 1971.
[110] Graham Diaries, 21 February 1971.
[111] MEC-Skeet 1/1, Malcolm Dennison's handwritten notes to Skeet, n.d., c.1991.

of his diary, Brigadier Graham writes: 'the British officers go back to their offices most afternoons to catch up with their work; the "brown faces" whose country this is take to their beds each day from lunch to sundown'.[112] This hard work was repaid with ingratitude but that was a worthwhile sacrifice for the sake of Oman's saviour, Qaboos: 'the British are a convenient whipping boy for ignorant and alarmist Omani gossip...But better that we should serve as whipping boys than Qaboos, for in him lies the nation's salvation'.[113]

Undoubtedly, there was the rare Briton who held a vision that opposed the upholding of imperially sponsored absolutism, but such figures were disposed of, accused of madness or insubordination. One example was Company Sergeant Major Knibb, who was the commander of an intelligence team that was sent from Britain to interrogate captured revolutionaries in the autumn of 1970:

> After a few days he refused to conduct interrogations for us. He claimed that his experiences in Aden had led him to sympathise with the Arab 'freedom fighters' to the extent that he no longer wished to be involved in any form of operation against them. He was of course sent back to the UK for medical or disciplinary treatment by his Corps authorities and his place in Bait al Falaj was taken by a commissioned Officer of the Intelligence Corps, Major Sloan, with satisfactory results.[114]

The price of dissent was high: marginalization and disgrace was the cross that the likes of CSM Knibb had to carry.

In order to vindicate their client—to themselves as well as to the rest of the world—British officials separated the economic from the political. They presented Qaboos as a liberal reformer pursuing economic development. The ideal form of governance for the Omanis was determined to be absolute monarchy. This was precisely because it was the form most unrepresentative of aspirations to genuine independence and thus least opposed to British domination. Those who held such aspirations were considered to be inauthentic in their Omaniness, infected with dangerous foreign ideas. As for 'genuine' natives, absolute rule satisfied their desires and suited their needs. Tolerant of the corruption of their masters, they were responsible for their own enslavement. After touring one of the Sultan's palaces, Brigadier Graham wrote: 'Gold plated taps, round blue bath and ultra-plush furniture. We British criticise the expense but his subjects seem to expect it of their Ruler.'[115] Orientalism addressed the contradiction that British

---

[112] Graham Diaries, 14 June 1971.
[113] Graham Diaries, 19 June 1971.
[114] Graham Diaries, 14 January 1971.
[115] Graham Diaries, 2 September 1972.

officials faced. Committed to the Westminster model at home and building absolutism abroad, they needed to blame the native.

Yet, it should not be thought that there was no popular attempt to
challenge the prevailing state of affairs. On Wednesday 1 September
1971, the largest strikes and demonstrations in the history of Oman took
place. These resulted from the workers' mobilization activities carried out
by PFLOAG organizers under the leadership of Zaher al-Miyahi. The
workers' camps in Ruwi were in a state of agitation, and citizens assembled outside Qaboos's palace demanding better wages, the eradication of
corruption, and reform. The government responded with violence. A
demonstrator was shot dead on the pretext of trying to seize a constable's
rifle. Another pulled a gun on a policeman; he was subsequently fired at
but managed to escape. The effort to contain the demonstrations was led
by the Filipino Chief of Police, Felix da Silva, and backed by Brigadier
Graham. The latter helicoptered Oman Gendarmerie forces from their
Sib base and bussed a rifle company from the Desert Regiment camp in
Bid Bid. These forces imprisoned 'troublemakers', and photographers
busily covered 'the disturbances to help identification of others in coming
days'. Policemen were so violent that they felt 'a bit apprehensive about
retaliation'.

A total curfew was imposed in Muscat and Mattrah, and the Sultan
gave typically oppressive orders, instructing the Commander of his Armed
Forces in the following terms: 'If anyone breaks through the curfew posts
to try to reach the workers' camps in Ruwi or at PD(O), you are to shoot
them all!' Road blocks were established across Muscat and Mattrah, and
forces were deployed in workers' camps to 'prevent intimidation of workers'. Sultanate bulletins were broadcast over the airwaves, and loudspeak-
ers were also used. By 4 September, work resumed and the curfew was
'lifted with Police and SAF much in evidence'.[116]

These incidents, requiring severe action on the part of the state, illustrate the fact that the early days of the Qaboos regime were not as jubi-
lantly received as the Anglo-Sultanic histories claim. Popular discontent
was evident, and workers were organized effectively by PFLOAG organis-
ers. The latter established the National Committee of Omani Workers on
15 October 1971.[117] Nevertheless, the severity of the Sultanate response
and the immediate expansion of police and intelligence forces ensured
that future strikes could not break out on such a scale in the future. In the

---

[116] Graham Diaries, 1 September–5 September 1971.
[117] Al Jabha Al-Shabiya, 'Nabtha Saree'a Wa Mukhtasara 'An Masirat al-Thawra
Al-Omaniyya', unpublished, 1985.

meantime, reformist native elements were left to function as the Arab colour splashed over the Muscat scene. This was envisaged as being essential for securing Oman's acceptance into the Arab League and the United Nations.

THE ROAD TO THE UN GENERAL ASSEMBLY AND THE KINGS' CLUB

Joining international bodies was an essential step in facilitating the smooth transfer of Oman from the realm of British protection and into the Westphalian order. In accordance with this long-term interest of theirs, the British were determined to get the Sultanate a seat in the General Assembly, although they were aware of the potential ramifications for their future policy. For Britain, the blessings of UN acceptance were deemed to be mixed. Certainly, this would dispose of an 'international embarrassment that has gone on too long':

> ...but the pressures that may then be placed on Oman from many directions could ultimately erode [the British] special military position in the country, notably at Masirah. Conversely, membership...could provide Oman with the device that article 2(7)...affords to rebut undue inquisitiveness into her internal affairs...[118]

Ironically, the best way of guaranteeing Britain's future interference in Oman was to secure the Sultanate's entry to the UN and its access to the Charter's non-interference clause.

The Road to New York began in Cairo, acceptance to the UN effectively requiring the blessing of the Arab League. To prepare for admission to both bodies, the principles of territoriality and foreign exclusion from domestic governance structures had to be projected. This was in line with the British view that 'it is what a country says rather than what it is or does that gains acceptance in the international community...'.[119] Accordingly, the Sultanate had to present to the outside world a claim over a demarcated territory and an image of native governance. The first step was taken right after the coup with Qaboos's announcement on 6 August 1970 that Muscat, Oman and Dhufar were one territorial unit merged under the official title of the Sultanate of Oman. From that moment onwards, the Sultanate had a clearer territorial claim than ever. The former

---

[118] 'Final Impressions of Oman', Crawford (Muscat) to Arthur (Bahrain), 24 April 1971, *RO-6*, p.13.
[119] 'Final Impressions of Oman'.

title of the 'Sultanate of Muscat and Oman and Dependencies', accurately reflected the fragmentary territorial nature of the Sultanate, and its semi-colonial relation with one of its domains, Dhufar. In contrast, the new title, 'Oman', had a solidly centripetal ring that was typical of a modern nation state. As for native control over governance, this was presented to the world by means of parading Tariq and his Omani ministers.

In order to dissipate the 'widespread belief that Oman was under some sort of British protection', a goodwill mission was sent to Arab capitals. The mission, which was led by the minister of education, Saud al-Khalili, and boasted former opposition figures, set off on 25 January 1971. Notably, it was treated worst at its first destination, Saudi Arabia: 'the question of the Imamate remained a formidable barrier in a country which still gave shelter to the former Imam…'.[120] Although it was well received in other Arab capitals, the mission was informed that the Sultanate had to reach an accommodation with the Imamate as a prerequisite for recognition. The Imamate of Oman had been recognized as a state in exile by most Arab states, and this posed a political and legal obstacle to accepting the Sultanate. Another question that came up was the semi-colonial condition of the regime, some states asking for 'a lessening of British influence as a price for recognition and closer relations'.[121]

Believing that Saudi Arabia held the key to overcoming these difficulties, the British attempted to organize a trip for Qaboos there. In late February 1971, Ambassador Morris in Jeddah informed Saudi Foreign Minister al-Saqqaf that 'Sultan Qabus wants to come here in April but would like a Saudi emissary to send him an invitation'. The Ambassador explained that the British 'wanted the Sultan to stand on his own feet and wished to drop the role of the middle-man' and that they 'thought that such a meeting would be a good step in this process'. Al-Saqqaf 'repeated his assurances that the Saudi Government are well aware that it is in their interest that Sultan Qaboos should succeed, and that they now hold no brief for Ghalib.… Now their interest lay in stability in the Sultanate.' However, al-Saqqaf made it clear that the Sultanate had to settle matters with the Imam: 'unless he was squared, Ghalib might go elsewhere and be used by other trouble-makers. Much the best thing would be for the Sultan to buy him off by offering something in consolation. It would not matter if he were dropped later on.'[122]

The Sultanate did not immediately act on this advice, and the idea of a spring visit to Saudi Arabia by the Sultan did not materialize. Nevertheless,

120 'Oman: Annual Review for 1971'.
121 'Oman: Annual Review for 1971'.
122 Morris (Jeddah) to FCO, Tel. No.124, 22 February 1971, *RO-6*. pp.90–1.

the Sultanate lodged an application to the Arab League on 13 March 1971 and President Sadat of Egypt dispatched Dr Hassan Sabri al-Khuli to Muscat on 2 April. By the end of that visit, an agreement was reached 'in principle' to establish diplomatic relations between the Sultanate and the United Arab Republic.[123] Al-Khuli's visit was an achievement of sorts, considering Egypt's stature and the fact that it had been actively supporting revolutionary forces in Oman for the better part of the 1950s and 1960s. Tariq was encouraged by this development. He hoped that Oman could draw on Egyptian as opposed to Saudi diplomatic support and that this would be enough to secure Sultanate admission to the UN, even if the Arab League was initially bypassed.

Thus, Tariq dispatched a second 'Goodwill Mission' to Arab capitals (notably excluding Riyadh) on 5 June 1971. But the Sultanate's delegation returned with little more than disappointment. Out of those countries visited, only Morocco and Tunisia offered recognition.[124] Others were more cautious, still insisting on a resolution of the Imamate question. Even Egypt seemed to have become less inclined to move without a solution to this matter, the British suspecting it of yielding to counter-pressure from Riyadh.[125] Thus, by the end of June, hopes for joining the UN before the end of the 1971 session had hit rock bottom. That month, the Arab Group in New York decided that the Sultanate would have to be admitted to the Arab League before there could be any progress at the UN. Beneath this cloudy diplomatic sky, the British pressured Qaboos to placate Imam Ghalib.[126] Following his return from Europe in July, the Sultan offered to allow the Imam to return to Oman with the title of Mufti, and to give his brother Talib a ministerial post. Representatives from respected interior families, including Sheikh Hilal al-Khalili, conveyed this message to the Imamate sometime in late July or early August 1971. It was hoped that this would 'render untenable the Saudi attitude of basing opposition to Oman's admission to the Arab League on lack of any accommodation between Sultan and Imam'.[127]

The offer was rejected. Still, in an effort to project a positive reconciliatory image, the Sultanate announced that contact had been made with the Imam and that 'the government had no objection to Shaikhs Ghalib, Talib bin Ali, and Sulaiman bin Himyar returning to Oman as good citizens if

---

[123] 'Oman: Annual Review for 1971'
[124] 'Impressions of Oman: The First and the Last', Diplomatic Report No. 428/71, 5 August 1971, *RO-6.*
[125] 'Oman: Annual Review for 1971'.
[126] FCO 8/1673, Luce to Acland, 9 July 1971.
[127] MEC-Paxton, 'PDO Notes for July–September 1971', August Notes, p.2.

they wished'.[128] The lack of any positive engagement with these overtures aroused Anglo-Sultanic suspicions that 'the Saudis wish to keep the Ghalib issue alive as a cover for their traditional ambitions in Oman as well as in the Trucial states'.[129] This was not necessarily far from the truth. On the one hand, British pressure and the wish to block regional radicalism meant that Saudi Arabia was willing to engage with Muscat and to undermine the Omani opposition. On the other hand, Saudi–Sultanate territorial disputes over Buraimi and other areas were still unresolved. King Faisal may not have wished to play all his cards, and the Imamate was certainly a precious one that he had held on to from the beginning of his reign. Moreover, it is questionable whether the Saudis had full control over the Imam at this stage. Although they had enormous leverage over him, this would not have necessarily been enough to push him into agreeing to the destruction of the ancient institution of the Imamate.

Just when it seemed most unlikely that the Imamate would be wooed and recognition gained before the end of 1971, the Sultanate's quest received a sudden boost. Bahrain unexpectedly gained its independence on 15 August 1971 and Qatar shortly afterwards on 3 September 1971. Both countries were lodging applications to the Arab League, and this symbolically signalled the end of the British era in the Gulf. Thus, there was a moment of enthusiasm for welcoming new Gulf states into the ranks of independent Arab countries. This created an unprecedentedly favourable wind for the Sultanate, and generated broad sympathy for considering its application alongside those of the two small emirates. In this atmosphere, two Sultanate delegations were immediately assembled, one for Cairo, the other for New York. In an effort to dress the Sultanate in a local garb, the Cairo delegation was comprised of traditional interior figures: Sheikhs Saud Al-Khalili; Mohammad al-Harithi; and Sulaiman al-Salimi. It headed for Cairo on 6 September, so as to be present for the 11 September session.[130] Although Qatar and Bahrain were admitted during that session, Saudi Arabia managed to delay the Sultanate's application by a fortnight. Nevertheless, by 29 September, the Sultanate was finally given a seat in Cairo. This news came as a pleasant shock to the Sultan, raising hopes for the Sultanate's application to the UN.[131]

The path to New York was now clear and the Sultanate delegation departed from Muscat on 8 September. Unlike the Cairo delegation,

[128] MEC-Paxton, 'PDO Notes for July–September 1971', August Notes, p.2.
[129] 'Impressions of Oman: The First and the Last'.
[130] MEC-Paxton, 'PDO Notes for July–September 1971'.
[131] MEC-Peyton. 9/3. 'Extract from a note for file—Audience with H.M. Qaboos bin Said on 30th September 1971'.

this one wore a modernist garb. Boasting cosmopolitan local figures, and two non-Omanis, it was headed by Dr Asim al-Jamali and comprised Sayyid Fahd, Ahmad Makki (PA to the Prime Minister), and Omar al Baruni (Adviser to the Sultan). After passing through Beirut to deliberate with the Prime Minister, the delegation arrived in New York on 14 September. As soon as the Sultanate had been admitted to the Arab League, the delegation successfully processed Oman's application through the Security Council, gaining unanimous approval there on 30 September. This was followed by official admission to the UN on 7 October.[132] Thus, Oman's initiation into the international Westphalian order was completed. Tariq provided the local Arab facade that made this possible. However, this ironically rendered him dispensable. Now that the Sultanate had kept up appearances, and was internationally recognized as a result, there was less pressure on Qaboos to engage with his uncle.

By October 1971, the Sultan and the Prime Minister were undergoing one of their 'periodic periods of strain'.[133] At the end of the month, a report by Whitehead Consultants had appeared. The report, recommending the structure of governance in the Sultanate, accepted 'the continuation of the absolute, one-man rule of the Sultan'. Additionally, it made recommendations for furthering Qaboos's hold over strategic sectors, suggesting the appointment of a Petroleum Adviser to the Sultan and to have him in the Ministry of Finance.[134] Although they were aware of Tariq's hostility to these recommendations, the British consultants regardless advocated an absolutist path for Oman. This corresponded to the attitude of Whitehall and the Bahrain Residency. Such attitude did not arise out of a vacuum. Indeed, in projecting their vision for Qaboos, British officials were inspired by the Jordanian and Iranian models.[135] Two decades before, both King Hussein and the Shah had been backed by the British in the face of the popular movements by their subjects. These monarchies were not only models to be emulated but natural allies to be appealed to. Both were eager to help.

The Shah was focused on extending his reach beyond the straits of Hormuz and into the Indian Ocean. He was, furthermore, a cold warrior, concerned with nipping 'communist infiltration' in the bud. Accordingly, Oman, by virtue of its strategic location and its revolution, played a central role in his mind.[136] The British did not have to drag the Shah onto the

[132] 'Oman: Annual Review for 1971'
[133] MEC-Paxton, 4/4, 'Structure of Government', 30 October 1971.
[134] MEC-Paxton, 4/4, 'Structure of Government', 30 October 1971.
[135] See, for instance, 'Final Impressions of Oman', Crawford (Muscat) to Arthur (Bahrain), 24 April 1971. *RO, Vol.6,* p.13.
[136] FCO 8/1677, Arbuthnott (Tehran) to Brian Smith (FCO), 7 August 1971.

scene; he was already imposing himself on it. With hindsight, a veteran British diplomat in Tehran reflected frankly on this matter:

> We certainly didn't say [to the Shah], 'Look, we're strapped. We can't cope with this threat coming from South Yemen. Please, Your Majesty, will you help us? No way. It wasn't that. He thought of it himself. And he pushed himself on them and us... If you talk about the [British] hidden hand in Iran—it didn't exist. If you talk about the hidden hand in Oman—it exists.[137]

Acting on his own accord, the Shah invited Qaboos to the 2500th Imperial Anniversary celebrations at Persepolis. The latter arrived in Iran on Thursday 14 October, 1971.[138] At Persepolis, Qaboos took his first step towards joining the Kings' Club. There, he had his first meeting with King Hussein and was given his first warm welcome by Saudi Prince Nawaf bin Abdelaziz.[139] Most importantly, it was there that he was introduced to the Shah and had his first discussions with him. As was his habit, the Sultan briefed the British ambassador extensively on his experiences. He reported that he was 'gratified' at the way he was treated, and that he was entirely charmed with the Shah, with whom he shared negative opinions on Abu Dhabi, the Palestinians and the Iraqis.[140] However, Persepolis was not just a site for exchanging ideas with other autocrats: it was also a place where concrete offers for help were received. Indeed, the Shah 'expressed a desire for close and cordial relations with Oman and had offered military assistance if the Sultan should need it'. The Sultan thanked the Shah for this offer, but was non-committal about it, awaiting British advice on the matter. By contrast, he accepted a more modest offer of military support from King Hussein of Jordan, beginning with the dispatch of 'three good senior officers' for the special branch.[141] In return for this, Qaboos handed Hussein a 'modest contribution' of $2 million. This elicited disapproval in reformist circles. For one, 'the Prime Minister did not approve of the Sultan's joining the "King's Club" in this way'.[142]

Although he was joyful at these results, the Sultan's initiation into the Club was still incomplete, requiring Saudi blessing. Qaboos had dearly hoped that he would meet Faisal in Persepolis.[143] He desperately wanted a tête-à-tête session where things could be clarified, so 'mystified' was he

---

[137] Harvard University, IOHC, Desmond Harney Interview, 15 October 1985.
[138] FCO 8/1677, Hawley (Muscat) to Arabian Department, 16 October 1971.
[139] FCO 8/1677, Hawley to Acland, 25 October 1971.
[140] FCO 8/1677, Hawley to FCO, 23 October 1971.
[141] FCO 8/1677, Hawley to FCO, 23 October 1971.
[142] 'Oman: Annual Review for 1971'.
[143] FCO 8/1673, Luce to Acland, 9 July 1971.

as to why the Saudis still did not recognize him.[144] For the past four seasons, he had been trying to gain Saudi favour. In the winter of 1971, he had indicated that he wished to pay his respects to Faisal in Riyadh. In the spring, he persisted in this effort but failed. In the summer, he made contact with the Saudi ambassador in London and Sheikh Sa'ad of Kuwait, with an eye to securing their mediation.[145] Now, in the fall, and after Omani admission to the UN, he asked for the intervention of Sheikh Khalifa of Qatar, but to no avail. Finally, his uncle Tariq tried to meet Rashad Pharon in Beirut, but the meeting was cancelled by the Saudis.

The seasons were changing but the Saudis stood still, and this was causing the Sultan to be paranoid, fearing Saudi expansionism. In late October, he told Ambassador Hawley that he would continue to reach out to the Saudis, but that he felt 'that King Faisal could not forget that he was a Wahabi where Oman was concerned'. He also claimed that he had received a report suggesting that the Saudis were massing troops on the border 'possibly with the object of a demonstration, or even an attack, on Abu Dhabi and this might also pose a threat to Buraimi and Omani territory'. Hawley tried to calm the Sultan down, telling him that the British Embassy had not received such information, and that it 'seemed unlikely'.[146]

After subjecting Qaboos to months of perplexity, fear, and insecurity, the Saudis finally yielded to the efforts of intermediaries and agreed to allow him to visit. On 11 December 1971 the young man flew to Riyadh 'with some trepidation'. His fears soon evaporated, however, and he was meticulously well received throughout the course of his three-day visit. King Faisal treated him as an equal and the two got on well. Most importantly, in the Saudi communiqué at the end of the visit, the Sultanate was formally recognized.[147] Qaboos had finally been accepted by all the members of the Kings' Club, welcomed by the royal triad. As for his Imamate opponents, they were effectively abandoned by the Saudis.[148]

Around the same time as the nativist alternative to the Sultanate, the Imamate, was erased from the political map, reformism was dealt its death blow. This was the culmination of a gradual process whereby Tariq was driven to despair. His frustrations grew after Qaboos began to hand immense privileges to new foreign figures. One such figure was the former US Secretary of the Treasury, Robert Anderson. Anderson was brought to

---

[144] FCO 8/1677, Hawley to FCO, 23 October 1971.
[145] FCO 8/1673, Luce to Acland, 9 July 1971.
[146] FCO 8/1677, Hawley to FCO, 23 October 1971.
[147] 'Oman: Annual Review for 1971'.
[148] Graham Diaries, 17 December 1971.

Oman through Qaboos's Equerry, Landon, who had met him in London. In the company of Landon, Anderson flew to Muscat in a private jet. The two were joined by men with suspected CIA connections: a Saudi citizen by the name of Ghassan Shakir and Yahya Omar, a Libyan and a former adviser to King Idris. Shakir and Omar were 'dons' of what later became known as 'the Muscat Mafia'. The Sultanate's intelligence chief, Malcolm Dennison, recalled receiving them at the Bait al Falaj airfield:

> Tim introduced me and told me—not in their presence—the great help they would be to Quboos. They had important contacts in the Middle East, Europe and the USA. Through them doors would be opened thus making it easy for the shy Quboos to meet those who would matter. When I told Tarik this he rubbished it. He said they were nothing and only on the make.[149]

On 6 October, the Sultan gave Anderson a licence to prospect for oil in the south, a concession for other minerals, the authority to obtain legal advice for the Sultanate, and the authorization to appoint Oman's consular representatives in Beirut and Rome. Anderson also secured a general fisheries survey concession for an American company, Mardella. Even Ambassador Hawley described this as being 'of very dubious benefit to Oman'.[150] Tariq understood that this represented nothing less than the organized theft of Oman's resources, and this caused him to resign his Foreign Affairs portfolio on 28 October 1971. Many years later, Dennison remarked: 'I still feel the Mafia robbed Oman and enriched themselves at Oman's expense. I cannot forgive them for this.'[151]

On 14 November, Tariq returned from a ceremony celebrating his son's graduation from RAF Henlow, only to confront further insecurities in his relations with the Sultan.[152] By now, he was completely out of the game, realizing that his reformist battle against Qaboos's absolutism was hopeless. At every step of the way he was opposed by Britain and was therefore incapable of carrying out his vision. Demoralized, and drained by illness and excessive weight, he took another vacation in Europe. He finally submitted his resignation on 23 December. Thus ended the saga of Oman's first and last Prime Minister. From then onwards, the Sultan formally centralized all major ministries in his hands, becoming Prime Minister, Minister of Foreign Affairs, Minister of Finance, and Minister of Defence.

---

[149] MEC-Skeet 1/1, Malcolm Dennison's handwritten notes to Skeet, n.d., *c*.1991.
[150] 'Oman: Annual Review for 1971'
[151] MEC-Skeet 1/1, Malcolm Dennison's handwritten notes to Skeet, n.d., *c*.1991.
[152] FCO 8/1668, FCO Tel. No.394, 19 November 1971.

In hindsight, it could be said that Tariq was bound to fail. He was disposed against absolutism by ideology but he was tied to the absolutist ruler materially. Alienated from the system that the British were building, he was unable to fight genuinely against it. He restricted his effort to 'change from within' and was opposed to the only path that could have generated republican transformation at the time: revolution. Unwilling to up the ante, he submitted to Qaboos, and enjoyed the material fruits of his submission, although he was completely excluded from actual decision-making. Like other Omanis, Tariq was given a choice between the political and the material. Failing in the former path and afflicted by illness and fatigue, he chose the latter.

* * *

In summary, Britain managed the immediate aftermath of the coup of 23 July 1970 by ensuring that Qaboos had military command, familial subordination, financial control, diplomatic outreach, and the means of internal legitimation. While centralizing major powers in the person of the Sultan, it suppressed an alternative vision of reformist constitutional monarchy championed by his uncle and other Omani former exiles. As for economic development, it was severely hampered by the Sultan's control over finances and the chaotic functioning of the nascent government. The ruler channelled more than a fifth of the country's limited oil revenues on palaces, holidays and patronage, and paid little attention to the functioning of his ministries. Inspired by the Shah and King Hussein, and seeking the approval of King Faisal, he was initiated into the regional 'Kings' Club', consolidating his networks abroad so as to further his hold at home. With the removal of the reformist alternative, the only challenge left was that of revolution. The rifles of republicanism were still firing in the south, threatening the very foundations of Sultanic absolutism.

9

Revolutionary Culture

The confrontation between Anglo-Sultanic absolutism and revolutionary forces was not simply a military one: it extended to the very depths of the cultural sphere. The Sultanic conception of culture had its origins in a bifurcated view that saw Dhufari life as the primordial expression of a state of nature, counterpoised with high civilization as embodied in Islamic values and practices. Historically, the desire to challenge local norms was always present but it was tempered by political realities and geographic limits. In the confined areas they controlled on the coastal plain, the rulers could carry out significant cultural interventions, especially ones that trespassed on the lives of the marginalized and the subaltern. For instance, Sultan Taimur bin Faisal (r.1913–1932) banned celebrations of *Diwali*, the Hindu festival, which had long been synchronized with, and incorporated into, the practices of the Muslim poor. According to local tradition, these celebrations had been introduced into Dhufar by a shipwrecked Brahman but the Sultanic authorities saw them as 'alien rites which found a ready acceptance among the lower classes', who had a supposedly imperfect understanding of Islam.[1] Similarly, a Sultanic decree in 1922 banned various practices of African-descended Dhufaris. These included dancing on top of recently dug graves to drive out the evil spirits, as well as gathering in front of the home of a woman about to bear an illegitimate child: 'with shouting and dancing she was exposed before her fellow countrymen; then the woman in question would of her own accord join in the festivities and dance with the others'.[2]

Although the annual expressions of joy and the unorthodox rites of lower caste people were suppressed on the coast, the numerous 'un-Islamic' rituals of the stronger tribes, such as exorcism and magic, were not interfered with. This was in spite of the fact that they were viewed with disdain and disapproval as expressions of loose faith, primordial

---

[1] C.N. Jackson, 'A Note on the Dhufar Province, Southern Arabia', Kuwait, 23 June 1943, *RO1867–1947, Vol. 5*, p.127.
[2] Wendell Philips, *Unknown Oman*, London: Longmans, 1966, p.203.

superstition, and religious ignorance. On the whole, tribesmen were considered to be base and devoid of civilization but, as long as they did not interfere with established power relations, their practices were tolerated. From the late nineteenth century to the early 1960s, the British also highlighted Dhufari savagery, their conceptions underlined by racialism, notions of biological inferiority, and sometimes an objectifying homoerotic gaze. Consider this description of Dhufari highlanders by James (later Jan) Morris, appearing in a book that received widespread applause in 1957:

> ...rough and illiterate though they were, and aboriginal in their bearing, their faces were sometimes of exceptional beauty and refinement. Some of the young men, with their delicate well-moulded features, offered profiles of classic perfection; and they stood around to stare at us with a lovely open-air, natural grace. Do not think, though, that they were exemplars of that noble savage so dear to the eighteenth century. They were handsome enough, but rather wizened, small and stunted; and I am told they could be very mean.[3]

Not only was the Dhufari denied the romanticization accorded to the noble savage but they were not even deemed worthy of a *mission civilisatrice* to alter the supposedly 'primal' state they lived in: no schools were set up for their benefit, be they Christian missionary or Islamic; no musical events were organized, Arabic or European; and no public rituals were celebrated, colonial or Sultanic. The population was subject to the whims and designs of the Sultan, who, in the Arnoldian battle between culture and anarchy, exemplified the former and held the latter in check.

This Anglo-Sultanic attitude was not only reserved for Dhufaris, but for northern Omanis as well, who were presented as 'unruly Arab tribesmen of varying degrees of peaceability; now squabbling with each other, now combining to repel some common enemy; owing diverse loyalties to tribal leaders and misty historical federations; often fierce, rapacious and xenophobic ...'. The only way to contain these 'barbarians' was to keep them locked up behind the Sultanic gates and this required supporting the forces of order and autocracy:

> Was the travelled and urbane Sultan, a paternal autocrat educated in India, the complete and lawful ruler of these difficult people? The British Government, which protected the Sultan's domains for him and largely handled his foreign affairs—in other words which was still the basic power in south-east Arabia—was convinced he was ...[4]

As the local guardian of imperial order, Sultan Said, himself, dwelled freely in the Anglo-Saxon cultural sphere, his references ranging from the plays of

---

[3] Jan Morris, *Sultan in Oman*, London: Arrow Books, 1990, p.35.
[4] Morris, *Sultan in Oman*, p.14.

Shakespeare to Forbes magazine. But he had no intention of carrying out any other policy than one that sought to forcibly ossify local culture and prevent its transformation beyond the limits he set. This did not derive from nativism, for Said looked down upon the native. Rather, it sprang from a defensive colonial attitude that saw native cultural forms in their co-opted state as unthreatening to the established order, unlike oppositional 'foreign' ideas. Here, the 'foreign' becomes associated with sedition, while the local is valorized and equated with loyalty. The privilege of accessing foreignness was solely reserved for the Sultan and his family, and vehemently denied to others.

Only by reference to this can a detailed description of the Sultan's cultural policy be given, explaining not only his behaviour but its ideological and political context. How else can we understand his discouragement of football or his punishment of cyclists in Dhufar? Every sphere of life, including physical activity, had to be orientalized, and its degree of local authenticity judged by the Sultan. By restraining new cultural possibilities, the Sultan could maintain a sense of command and discipline. His order was based on rudimentary methods of social control: they were not carried out by institutions and bureaucracies but rather by an obsessive individual and his ineffectual retinue. Even when it came to handling cultural challenges that could have more serious political repercussions, the Sultan could not effectively cope except through outright bans. This was in contrast to more effective regimes elsewhere in the region.

The case of radio illustrates this well. In the Bandung age, every colonially backed ruler had reason to fear Nasser's *Voice of the Arabs*. But, in places like King Hussein's Jordan, the regime simply made clear its disapproval of those listening to the station so as to spread fear and self-censorship. Sultan Said, however, preferred the more radical option of strictly monitoring the selling of radios and limiting the permits issued for their operation. The end was the same—controlling the dissemination of political ideas—but the method was radically different. Thus, by 1961, there were only 100 radio sets in the whole of Dhufar, roughly one for every 500 people.[5] Unlike the King of Jordan, the Sultan did not establish a permanent radio channel to spread his own vision. For a while, he toyed with the idea, even personally broadcasting a programme by means of an A/C 60-watt transmitter. His first transmission took place on the eve of Eid al-Adha on 25 May 1961, and this developed into a 20-minute-long weekly radio show every Thursday evening. The show typically began with a summary of the news, followed by an instalment on the history of

---

[5] Phillips (CG Muscat) to M.C.G. Man (British Residency, Bahrain), 7 June 1961, *RO–1961*, pp.13–14.

the ruling Al Said dynasty.[6] But the Sultan's new hobby as a presenter, and his attempts to disseminate monarchical loyalty through personally narrating the history of his family, were quickly abandoned.

Besides being a propaganda failure, this was emblematic of the lack of any attempt to create a 'national' culture, or to undertake the first step for such an endeavour: the unification of the language. A substantial number of Dhufaris spoke the Shihri southern Arabic language. Sultan Said took no steps to teach Arabic itself to the mass of the population. His was not a modern national project oriented towards creating a body of subjects that was unified in custom and tongue. At the immediate level, such a project would be costly, incurring relatively hefty, and irreversibly permanent, expenses that the Sultan was not prepared to budget for. In the long term, it was likely to initiate change at a potentially destabilizing level. The Sultan's solution was to rule his subjects in the same way that the British authorities ruled over him: firmly but indirectly. The aim was not to change Dhufaris, but to subjugate them. Accordingly, the practice of cultural imposition was on the whole limited and ineffectual, if not entirely absent. In contrast, acts of cultural suppression were widely applied and felt, and their severity was one of the many factors that animated Dhufari will for political change.

SITUATING REVOLUTIONARY CULTURE

In this context, the quest for cultural transformation did not come from above, but from below, propelled by major socio-economic changes and the experience of Dhufari migrant workers in the Gulf. Subalternity is a status that the marginalized try to break out of, whenever possible, and migrant Dhufaris were no exception. As was seen earlier, they encountered novel conceptions and practices in places like Kuwait and sought to integrate themselves into the broader Arab cultural sphere. At the initial launch of revolutionary activity, their cultural agenda was limited. However, a more expansive vision was inaugurated in the aftermath of the Hamrin conference of 1968, initiating a vigorous form of cultural transformation.

At the outset, it must be emphasized that this endeavour reflected a global pattern shared with other trincontinental contexts. In his *Culture and Imperialism*, Edward Said perspicaciously notes that 'if colonialism

---

[6] Phillips (CG Muscat) to M.C.G. Man (British Residency, Bahrain), 7 June 1961, *RO–1961*, p.14.

was a system, as Sartre was to say in one of his post-war essays, then resistance began to feel systematic too'.[7] Dhufari revolutionary culture was one node in this system, heavily influenced by a cultural style, outlook, discourse, and mode of expression that emanated from left-wing movements operating in other regional centres, especially Palestine and South Yemen. The latter in turn were embedded in a cultural system that included movements ranging from the Cuban to the Vietnamese.

Revolutionary culture was not simply a functionalist instrument. However, this did not mean that it did not play particular political and social functions. One of the most important was to legitimate the revolutionary endeavour by situating it within a broader tradition. The mechanism by which this was done was to constantly assert an organic connection with other revolutions, be they historic or contemporary. Classics of revolutionary literature were often cited, reproduced, and distributed. These ranged from Progress Publishers' official Soviet translation of Lenin's biography to Brecht's 'From a German War Primer'. Classic slogans, such as the Spanish Civil War's 'No pasarán!' (*Lan Yamuru*) were circulated. However, pride of place was given to the Palestinian revolution. References to it are to be found in a wide range of poems, essays, interviews, posters, and drawings, and enormous space was given to Palestinian voices in Dhufari revolutionary publications. This did not only reaffirm Dhufari commitment to Palestine, but it also endowed the Dhufar revolution with a crucial cultural means of legitimation. As noted by Michael Hudson in his seminal study of legitimation politics in the Arab world, there exist core 'All Arab' concerns that have a major impact on the legitimacy of any particular order. The 'legitimacy of given leaders in a given state is determined to an important extent by their fidelity to these core concerns' and 'Palestine is the foremost all-Arab concern, although not the only one'.[8]

If Palestine was important for the legitimation of any regime, it was immeasurably more crucial for revolutionary movements. This form of legitimation was not just externally useful: it held immense internal significance. To appreciate its scale, one must bear in mind that the roots of the Dhufari leadership went back to the Movement of Arab Nationalists, a formation that was primarily established to create an Arab response to the Palestinian *nakba* of 1948. Thus, when a respected Palestinian figure like Sakher Habash wrote poems for Dhufar, he was not only contributing to a process of cultural legitimation outside Dhufari revolutionary circles. Such an act was appreciated at an intimate level, reaffirming the

[7] Edward Said, *Culture and Imperialism*, New York: Vintage, 1993, p.196.
[8] Michael Hudson, *Arab Politics*, New Heaven: Yale University Press, 1977.

revolutionaries' desire to take a step towards liberating Palestine by changing the prevailing reality in the Gulf.[9] Likewise, Palestinian revolutionaries, especially on the left, had a deep affinity for Dhufar and their writings on Gulf revolutionary themes were far from instrumental. One of Sakher's poems entitled 'Palestine is Dhufar' explains the emotion underlying them:

> The earth is filled with storms
> Oh wound that cures a wound
> Oh hurricane that embraces a hurricane
> Who understands the language of revolutionaries
> except for other revolutionaries?
> The faces of hope look alike on the pages of fire
> And Palestine is Dhufar[10]

Such verses of solidarity were unsolicited; they reflected true feelings of camaraderie, motivated by a common experience and a shared moral universe.

Beyond the realm of the poetic, a plethora of Palestinian motifs are to be found. But they do not stand alone. Rather, they lie at the heart of an intersecting web of global words and images that constituted the repertoire of revolutionary culture, and formed the basis for an alternative world view. The two main Dhufari periodicals, the weekly *Sawt al-Thawra* and the monthly *9 Yunyu*, played a major role in constructing this world view, which was principally achieved by constant references to other struggles, especially tricontinental ones. This referential system fundamentally affected such acts as news reporting, which took a special form and flavour in the Dhufari context. Three types of news were deemed fit to print: reports on the revolution; coverage of the regime and its regional and international backers; and items on global revolutionary movements and socialist states. The third named are particularly interesting from the standpoint of revolutionary culture. Such was their frequency and diversity that they kept cadres informed of the latest trends in the tricontinental world.

In Popular Front publications, we find numerous stories of revolutionary beginnings, such as an April 1974 special interview with an Ethiopian 'progressive struggler'—conducted even before the establishment of the Derg—on the growing movement against Emperor Haile Selassie in that

---

[9] Up to this very day, oral historians encounter former Gulf revolutionaries who are literally moved to tears when they think of Palestine and its cause. This has certainly been the experience of this author on several occasions.

[10] Sakher Habash, 'Filasteen Hiya Thufar', Al-Jabha al-Sha'abiya Li Tahreer Oman, *Tisa'a Yunyu*, Year 5, Issue 2, November 1974, p.13.

country. The interview was featured under the title 'Ethiopia: The Revolution of Humanity, Freedom, and Bread'. Despite the mobilizational title, it was characteristically rich in empirical detail, providing in-depth updates and information presented in a descriptive manner.[11] More celebratory, if no less detailed, coverage was given to revolutionary victories. For instance a six-page article on the victory of the people's war in Vietnam was presented under the headline 'Glory to the Fighting People!'. Here, the descriptive material was intensified with declarative statements of opinion, dates and incidents intermingling with normative assertions. A strong sense of identification is present throughout the article, the Vietnamese struggle presented as a matter of pride for every reader, and indeed for the entirety of humanity. Its ultimate victory was portrayed as a profound cause for hope: 'one day in the bright future, our children will be able to play freely, in the same way that Vietnamese children do now'.[12]

Such interviews and reports contributed to a cultural structure of reference that constituted, anchored, and disseminated the revolutionary world view. Every printed item reflected this outlook. Letters congratulating states on their independence were published in full, supporting their leading revolutionary parties. These letters reasserted to Omani readers their belonging to the global community of revolution and informed them of the achievements of other liberation movements. They also elaborated the Popular Front's position with regard to the internal dynamics of each struggle. For instance, readers of the letter sent to President Agostinho Neto on the occasion of Angolan independence were informed that 'the People's Movement for the Liberation of Angola is the sole legitimate representative of the Angolan people', essentially signalling that the Omani revolutionary leadership stood with the Cuban and Soviet-backed MPLA in its conflict with American supported UNITA and FNLA.[13]

Editorials also expressed support for 'sister revolutions'. There was hardly an event that they did not cover, ranging from the first Communist Party of Cuba conference in 1975 (which was attended by the PFLO Secretary General, Abdel Aziz al-Qadi) to the 11th anniversary celebrations of the Zanzibari revolution.[14] Major anniversaries were given huge

[11]'Ethiopia: Thawrat al-Insan wal Hurriya wal Khubz', Al-Jabha al-Sha'abiya Li Tahreer Oman, *Tisa'a Yunyu*, Year 4, April/May 1974, p.31.

[12] Al Jabha al Sha'bya Li Tahrir Oman, 'Al Majd li al-Sha'ab al-Muqatil!', *Tisa'a Yuniyu*, Year 5, Volume 5, June 1975, p.84.

[13] 'Al Lajna al-Tanfithya al-Markazya Tab'ath bi Risalat Tahn'ia ila al-Raees Agostinho Neto', *Sawt al-Thawra*, Year 4, No. 178, 15 November 1975.

[14] 'Cuba Tash'had Hadath 'Atheem', *Sawt al-Thawra*, Year 4, No. 182, 27 December 1975, 'Al-Sha'ab al-Zinjibari Yahtafel bi Eid Intisar Thawratih', *Sawt al-Thawra*, Year 4, No. 136, 4 January 1975.

coverage, an opportunity to provide a historical overview of the particular cause under consideration. October 1917 was annually celebrated with fanfare, and so were the Palestinian, Yemeni, Chinese, Cuban, Algerian, Egyptian, Iraqi, and Vietnamese revolutions. Even obituaries were laden with political meaning and anti-colonial sympathies, promptly published whenever a major international revolutionary figure died. As such, every editorial, anniversary piece, and obituary licensed a discourse of revolutionary affiliation, reflecting incorporation into the anti-colonial cultural system.

REVOLUTIONARY ICONOGRAPHY AND LITERATURE

When we speak of 'cultural transformation' in Dhufar, we must not imagine a sudden and immediate change, or a finalized process with a clearly delineated beginning and end. Nor can we measure such a transformation by the volume of literature, art, or music that was produced, or by the degree to which the revolutionaries created a distinct 'national' culture of their own. In fact, the concern here is to explore rather than measure since canonical assessment exercises narrow down the meaning of culture, both mistaking its nature (by limiting it to the 'higher' tier) and misconstruing the aims of its producers. That they are far from reasonable can be seen even with reference to those world historic revolutions that took place in incomparably larger, immeasurably more populous, and eminently more prosperous lands. A renowned historian of the American Revolution notes that, by the second decade of the nineteenth century 'many thought that Europeans' jibes about America being a cultural wasteland might have been too accurate after all. Where were the great writers, the great painters, the great playwrights?'[15] In the context of the October Revolution, Leon Trotsky went so far as stating:

> Our task in Russia is complicated by the poverty of our entire cultural tradition and by the material destruction wrought by the events of the last decade. After the conquest of power and after almost six years of struggle for its retention and consolidation, our proletariat is forced to turn all its energies towards the creation of the most elementary conditions of material existence and of contact with the ABC of culture—ABC in the true and literal sense of the word. It is not for nothing that we have put to ourselves the task of

---

[15]   Gordon Wood, *Empire of Liberty: A History of the Early Republic, 1789–1815*, Oxford: Oxford University Press, 2009, p.543.

having universal literacy in Russia by the tenth anniversary of the Soviet regime.[16]

In a society that was vastly poorer, far more illiterate, and unquestionably more marginal than revolutionary America or Russia, the initial task of communicating the ABC of literate culture was even harder to achieve. The establishment of the revolutionary school, which was discussed in previous chapters, was a major step forward. Through it, several new art forms were introduced into Dhufar, including political plays encouraged by the school's founder Leila Fakhro (Huda Salem). Theatrical performances, previously unheard of in the tribal highlands, communicated the principles of the revolution to the new generation of Dhufari children, utilized as pedagogical tools directed towards encouraging social change. For instance, one of the plays was organized under the slogan 'there is no social liberation without women's liberation and no women's liberation without social liberation'. Its purpose was to encourage the male pupils to convince their parents to send their girls to school. The plot, enacted with notable improvisation and engaged performance, was simple but immensely radical:

> a little girl was sold into marriage by her father, to an old man, in return for a cow and tomato tins. On the bridal night the daughter refused to be touched by her old husband and ran away to the Lenin School. The mother was...revolutionary but unable to do much.[17]

The school was not the only domain in which Dhufari cultural transformation was initiated. Indeed, there emerged a significant body of revolutionary expression disseminated through a variety of mediums, including the radio, the song, the film, the photograph, the poem, the monthly magazine, and the weekly newspaper. The airwaves were an especially popular and effective venue for disseminating revolutionary culture. Courtesy of Aden Radio, the *Itha'at al-Thawra* ('Revolution Radio') programme was featured as part of the Arab Gulf segment, broadcast every evening between 6 and 8 p.m. On revolutionary anniversaries, *Revolution Radio*'s airtime was doubled, so as to highlight the significance of the occasion.[18] Although there were few radio sets available in Dhufar, it was listened to whenever possible, and even those who lived behind the

---

[16] Leon Trotsky, 'What is Proletarian Culture, and is it Possible', 1923, Trotsky Archive, www.marxists.org (retrieved March, 2012).

[17] Heiny Srour, 'Hindrance and Gender Representation in Documentary Filmmaking', first draft of a presentation at the AUC Symposium of Visual Anthropology in Cairo, 10 April 2010.

[18] Al Jabha al-Sha'abya Li Tahrir Oman wal Khaleej al-Arabi, 'Itha'at al-Thawra', *Tisa'a Yuniyu*, January 1974, p.34.

Sultanic barbed wire surrounding Salalah have vivid memories of it. Recalling his childhood years, a contemporary Dhufari intellectual states:

> The people in Salalah used to congregate around the few radios available to listen to the broadcasts of the revolution from Aden Radio. There was massive enthusiasm for the revolution and it enjoyed a great deal of popularity. Songs used to play a particularly important role in that respect. Due to their impact, the people were willing to reach out to the revolution and to participate in the process of change.[19]

Indeed, although *Revolution Radio* featured news segments celebrating military achievements and criticizing the Sultan and the British, revolutionary songs were its most vital offering, holding significance on at least four levels. First, they had a mobilizational dimension: by celebrating the people, they afforded each citizen a connection with the revolution. Singing them generated collective feeling and emotion and a shared sense of a common task that was grand in its conception, compelling in its motivations, and challenging in its aims.

Secondly, songs furthered the vernacularization of ideas, ensuring their popular spread in a comprehensible and accessible form. Loaded with references to the struggle, they helped disseminate a new vocabulary, featuring terms such as colonialism, liberation and the people. These were of course much more than words: they were concepts, infusing each song with a sense of normative judgement and value-based content. Their repetition, and their particular placement within the moral tale that each revolutionary song told, ensured that they could make a subtle but effective impact on the local political imagination.

Thirdly, songs offered rich material for enacting revolutionary rituals. Of course, the revolutionary song could be, like any piece of art, received with particularity, acquiring a specificity of meaning that was highly personalized. However, reciting it in a collective setting transferred it from the plane of interiority into the realm of ritualized performance, by which a group could re-assert its shared moral conceptions. Dhufari revolutionary songs played that role well beyond the boundaries of Oman, and this can be seen in testimonies of Arab leftist students in America. It was not uncommon for their meetings to end with singing an oath to Tuful, a legendary Dhufari female martyr, swearing by her memory that they will carry out the fight for liberation.[20] This practice

---

[19] Interview M.

[20] This was recounted to the author in a December 2011 conversation with Mr Monadel Hirzallah, a leading Arab-American leftist activist who still remembers the Tuful anthem to this very day.

continued well into the late 1980s, symbolizing and asserting each student's political stance and belonging.

Lastly, and perhaps most importantly, the revolutionary song acted as a verbal site of memory that could be revisited by each individual again and again. Almost every song reminded listeners of the course of the struggle and its major turning points. Sung poems, which had long accompanied traditional performances (such as the folkloric Al-Habout), were now transformed from an instrument for recalling the history of the tribe to a means of narrating the story of the revolution.

Consider one of the most famous of these sung poems, entitled, 'The Hour of Liberation has Struck'. The entirety of the piece was structured around regular repetition of the line: The hour of liberation has struck...Get out colonialism! Your presence will be challenged by our powerful people. Between two *a cappella* renditions of that line performed by a group, a solo voice emerged, asserting a revolutionary principle or telling a story of the conditions that the revolution sought to overthrow. Thus, the Dhufari people were reminded of the 'hunger and backwardness' that they had suffered, and promised complete change by means of armed struggle.

This particular song inspired the title of the most important revolutionary film: *The Hour of Liberation,* directed by the Lebanese feminist filmmaker Heiny Srour. This was not the only film made in support of the revolution. Indeed, the Palestinian artist Sameer Nimer directed the film *The Winds of Change* with support from the Palestine Liberation Organization's Unified Information Office, and the left-wing Egyptian Fua'd al-Tihami directed *Down With Silence* with backing from the Iraqi Cinema and Television Board. Yet Srour's film received the most attention, and it included the most extensive footage from the revolutionary areas.[21]

The way in which that director was drawn into work of solidarity with the revolution is representative of how Dhufar was encountered by a generation of leftist Arab artists. In 1969, Srour was a PhD student at the Sorbonne who was also writing as a film critic in the anti-colonial publication *Africasia*. By chance, she was offered an interview with the PFLOAG representative in Beirut, which she planned to publish in the magazine. Initially, she was uninterested in the representative's description of the revolution, and most of his talk struck no chords with her until she heard him speak of PFLOAG's attitude to women. The official discussed

---

[21] Al Jabha al-Sha'abya Li Tahrir Oman, 'Nasr I'lami Jadid lil Thawra', *Sawt al-Thawra*, No. 129, Saturday 9 November, 1974.

... the 'specificity' of female oppression, the fact that 'women faced a double oppression' in an underdeveloped society, that 'the Front wanted to liberate them because they were the most backward and tyrannised part of society'. His boring, formal voice became warm with gratitude when he described 'women being more revolutionary than men'. Wondering if I was mishearing, I asked him to repeat everything. This he did. Ashamed, I realised that I was suddenly taking abundant notes. For the first time, I was facing an Arab radical man who would volunteer to raise the subject of women's distinct double oppression. And o miracle, who explicitly wanted to stamp it out...[22]

The revolution, and its specific discourse, represented and symbolized various aspirations that were dearly held by diverse sections of the Arab artistic and cultural scene. Some were drawn by its promise of liberation in a strategic part of the region, and the implications that its victory would have at a time when the region was undergoing a post-Nasserist shift to the right. Others were attracted by its economic programmes and its socialist aims. In the case of Srour, she was especially animated by its fight for women and their rights, and this was the aspect she was to focus on the most in her artistic production.

Dropping all her other projects, Srour decided to make the first documentary film shot inside the revolutionary areas, undertaking this task in 1971. One of the main reasons for the rarity of film as a form of revolutionary cultural production was the enormous difficulty that filmmakers confronted in the Dhufari context. Besides the threat of Anglo-Sultanic attacks, there was the challenge of walking enormous distances on rough mountainous tracks, carrying heavy equipment, and subsisting on one meagre meal a day. Srour, along with her left-wing French cameraman and sound engineer, hiked 200 kilometres from the South Yemeni border to the depths of the revolutionary areas in Dhufar, reaching as far as the battle areas along the red line. After shooting some footage, their 16mm synch camera broke down, and they were forced to trudge back the same distance. They then continued shooting after borrowing an 'obsolete, primitive war camera' from the South Yemeni Ministry of Culture, operated by an experienced Yemeni cameraman. In an interview, Heiny described her will to persist against these odds in the following terms:

> Something pushed me to continue, in spite of all the challenges: it was the feeling that this was my revolution. I was living the women's revolution. This did not mean that the female is the only one carrying the revolution, but the

---

[22] Srour, 'Hindrance and Gender Representation in Documentary Filmmaking'.

role that the Omani woman was playing in her people's revolution, and the prized status she held gave me this feeling.[23]

The footage was completed after three months of arduous labour but, even then, it was difficult to produce and PFLOAG lacked the means to finance it. However, as with other cultural outputs of the revolution, solidarity networks played an essential role. At the production stage, the filmmaker was housed and supported in London by the Gulf Committee, which was set up in solidarity with the revolution by well-known leftist intellectuals including Fawaz Traboulsi, Fred Halliday, and Helen Lackner. Financial support for the film also came from UK-based Yemeni workers, who had a long tradition of fundraising for the Dhufar revolution.[24]

Following its release, the *Hour of Liberation* received considerable attention. It was selected for the 1974 Cannes Film Festival and was shown at Venice and the New York Museum of Modern Art. Interestingly, it did not receive the same attention in mainstream art festivals on the other side of the Berlin Wall. Although it was initially selected for International Leipzig Documentary and Short Film Week and for the Moscow International Film Festival, it was withdrawn from both. Nevertheless, it was played at solidarity functions in both the Eastern and Western blocs. Apart from giving the revolution a higher profile and drawing attention to it in new circles, the film performed several other functions. It was widely shown by solidarity committees, used to generate funds and to secure medical donations for the revolutionary hospital.[25] At a visual level, it helped anchor a particular abstraction of the Dhufari fighter. The image of the revolutionary, which in other contexts was typically a young man with long hair and a rough beard, was completely reconceptualized. Here, it was a fatigue-wearing young woman with huge questioning eyes, sporting a short haircut and carrying a Kalashnikov.

This particular conception of the Dhufari fighter was also propagated in other outlets of revolutionary expression. Indeed, it was often to be found on the covers of the monthly magazine *Tisa'a Yunyu*. One of the most striking was the June 1975 cover, celebrating the tenth anniversary of the revolution. The photograph shows a row of armed revolutionary young women. Yet there is an element of gender ambiguity, reinforced by the short haircuts and the unisex fatigues. On the far left, there is a raised Kalashnikov and just next to it is a pair of clapping hands. To the far right, a fighter is waving her hand, the palm shining in the sunlight. At the

[23] Al Jabha al-Sha'abya li Tahrir Oman, 'Min Bayn Jamee' al-Funoun al-Cinema Heya al Aham: Muqabala Ma'a Heiny Srour,' *Tisa'a Yunyu*, Year 5, Volume 5, June 1975, pp.90–1.
[24] Srour, 'Hindrance and Gender Representation in Documentary Filmmaking'.
[25] Srour, 'Hindrance and Gender Representation in Documentary Filmmaking'.

very centre, is a figure of a young woman, her delicate—yet almost boyish—features are fully visible, her face beaming with a broad smile. She seems unthreatening in her appearance, but is clearly vigorous and capable of defending herself, her huge rifle leaning against her shoulder, towering as high as her hairline. Her posture is completely open, absolutely welcoming to all that is around her. Far from bracing herself or shielding her body, her arms are fully raised upwards, as if reaching the sky, with one palm clenching a stick (perhaps even a flag), and the other totally stretched. Her eyes are wide open, fixed on something distant.[26]

This photograph, selected to commemorate the most important anniversary in the history of the revolution, transmitted a specific iconography, telling several stories. A clue to one of these stories is offered by the text at the bottom of the cover: '10 Years of Steadfastness'. The intersection of image and text offers us a narrative centred on revolutionary survival and hope—the smiles of young revolutionary women, their spontaneous moves, their claps, their promising eyes, and above all their joy, could exist in spite of airstrikes, food denial, and grinding counterinsurgency operations. A second story was revolutionary equality: this was not a male revolution; it was a social one that explicitly promoted women's participation and empowerment. But that is not all. In its gender ambiguity, the photograph seems to hold the promise of transcending the traditional binary of femininity and masculinity. There is no suppression of femininity here, but the outward signs that socially distinguish the sexes can hardly be found. A third story that is told is that of individual creativity in an explicitly collectivist context. Here were the women, gathered in one row, yet each was freely engaged in a movement of her own. This was not a military formation in the statist sense of the term: it was a guerrilla unit that was part of a people's army, where institutionalized group discipline was only practised partially and out of martial necessity.

In an influential essay, Linda Nolchin describes how ideological notions of gender-difference determine the content of visual works, embodying themes such as female weakness, passivity, domesticity, or sexual availability. Generally, ideology veils the 'overt power relations obtaining in society at a particular moment in history by making them appear as part of the natural, eternal order of things'. Patriarchal ideology, in particular, presents such qualities as strength and weakness as 'natural corollaries of gender difference'.[27] Yet, as Dhufari revolutionary iconography illustrates, in the same way that ideology can take an explicitly patriarchal character,

---

[26] Al Jabha al Sha'bya Li Tahrir Oman, *Tisa'a Yuniyu*. Year 5, Volume 5, June 1975.
[27] Linda Nochlin, 'Women, Art, and Power', in Susan Feagi and, Patrick Maynard (eds.), *Aesthetics*. Oxford: Oxford University Press, 1997, p.72.

it can also promote a feminist agenda. This, indeed, explains the profusion of the female fighting images in the cultural output of the Popular Front, and the specific nature of this image as an act of complete reversal. Here, the 'natural' order of things is altered. The reproduction of female fighting images naturalizes the position of women as comrades-in-arms, self-determining revolutionary subjects. Passivity is transformed into action and domesticity into public engagement. Weakness turns into strength, and eroticization becomes sexual confidence. In Dhufar, the ease in carrying out these series of reversals partly derived from the lack of an established patriarchal photographic tradition to contend with. Out of this vacuum, the revolution could create its new visual tradition without facing the obstacles found elsewhere.

This task was mainly carried out by solidarity artists. Undoubtedly, the most remarkable, and the one to leave behind the greatest visual record of Dhufari life, was the Iraqi photographer Jasim al-Zubaidi (1940–1991). The story of the revolutionary generation of Arab photographers is yet to be told but it will never be complete without reference to him. As a young photographer, he opened a small photography shop in his hometown of Baqouba. He named it 'Maysaloun', after the 1920 battle during which the Syrian Chief of Staff Yusuf al-Azmah marched with his ragged militia of citizens to a certain death, confronting the invading columns of General Gouraud's French Army of the Levant. In spite of this peripheral beginning, al-Zubaidi was far from being just another provincial photographer. As noted by the Iraqi Photographic Society:

> … his style at that time seemed strange to other photographers around him. He used to capture the faces of poor folk, peasants, and workers, displaying them on his shop walls. His face beamed with joy whenever he saw his wretched customers happy. He desperately wanted to offer something to them, anything to erase even a small particle of their sorrows and worries.[28]

By the early 1960s, al-Zubaidi's talent for documentary photography began to be recognized beyond his small city and he became involved in the Baghdadi journalist scene, eventually invited in 1968 to launch the photography section in the newly established magazine *Alef Ba*. That weekly quickly became the most widely read political and cultural publication in Iraq, and one of the most broadly disseminated in the Arab world until the burning and looting of its printing press, and its resulting closure during the American invasion of 2003.

---

[28] Iraq Photographic Society, 'Al-Fanan al-Raed Jasim al-Zubaidi Rahimahu Allah', <http://www.ispiraq.org/view.23/> (retrieved 15/04/2012).

Although al-Zubaidi belonged to the founding generation of an influential magazine, an enviable status for anyone in his position, he was not satisfied with traditional photojournalism. He was animated by the idea that photography was a revolutionary art, and that it had a role to play in the anti-colonial struggles unfolding across the region. The 1967 war had a major impact on him, drawing him further and further to the cause of Palestine. Eventually, he left *Alef Ba*, spending the reminder of his life in the ranks of the Palestinian revolution, producing prolifically throughout. At various intervals, he visited and photographed aspects of other struggles, such as the Eritrean revolution in 1970. Of course, Dhufar did not go unnoticed by him, and he worked on behalf of the Popular Front on the exhibition and book *Oman: Man and Revolution*.[29] Apart from some images taken by Christian Freund in 1975, most of the photographs in that publication were captured by al-Zubaidi at the difficult moment of revolutionary withdrawal in early 1976. As for the text, it was written by the Iraqi critic Nazik al-Aaraji, who went with al-Zubaidi to Dhufar and who is best known now as a leading proponent of Arabic feminist literature.[30]

Of all the visual records we have of Dhufar, this one comes closest to everyday life. In the photograph, 'Fighters Take a Break in One of the Caves', there is no studied quality.[31] Instead, we find a seamlessly captured moment, illustrating a concrete reality in the day of every Dhufari fighter: the enormous amount of walking done in rough terrain, and the inevitable breaks that are taken. Here, the photographer answers with ease a question that the historian can only tackle with much labour and theoretical mediation: what takes place in those precious fragments of time that lie beyond the theoretical sessions, military engagements, conferences, programme discussions, economic activities, and revolutionary celebrations? In the particular seconds herein portrayed, the fighters sit down and stand in various postures, enjoying a moment of temporary respite. Two notice the photographer and gaze with bemusement at the camera. The rest are silent, some drifting in their thoughts, others smoking. The centrality of the latter activity is captured in another photograph, whose caption reads: 'For the fighter, the joy of smoking is unparalleled by any other, especially after a night of alertness and vigilance'. A kindly looking revolutionary inhales from his traditional *midwakh* pipe in a moment of

[29] Al Jabha al Sha'abiya li Tahrir Oman, *Oman: Al-Insan wal Thawra/Oman: Man and Revolution*. 1976, p.22.

[30] See her influential study, *Sawt al-Untha: Dirasat fil kitaba al-Nisawiya al-Arabiya*, Damascus: Al-Ahali lil Nashr, 1997.

[31] Al Jabha al Sha'abiya li Tahrir Oman, *Oman: Al-Insan wal Thawra*, p.8.

evident contentment, reminding us of the small joys without which the difficult life of a revolutionary could hardly be sustained.[32]

Much of the imagery presented is spontaneously captured, but the collection also includes works that could be classified as belonging to the 'community portrait style', whereby a group is 'photographed in a public setting, with the subjects all looking into the camera and not posed as if engaged in particular activities'.[33] Nevertheless, some of the most striking images are more posed, including an incredibly textured piece introduced by the caption, 'Smiles and confidence are the first things that the Omani revolutionaries welcome you with'. In the background is a group of revolutionaries lying in a cave, but at the heart of this image is a smiling man, wearing what can best be described as a psychedelic 1970s shirt over which a Palestinian *Kuffiyeh* is placed like a shawl.[34] The revolutionary is clearly sporting his own distinctive clothing style. Others around him wear a variety of items, ranging from the traditional Dhufari highland kilt fastened under their waists, to the Panama hats crowning their heads. Besides individuality, the photographer captures the theme of friendliness, implicitly humanizing the revolutionary and providing an almost direct response to the image of the bloodthirsty communist presented by the Anglo-Sultanic authorities.

Friendliness is a recurring theme in the visual trajectory of the revolution. But there are several others that are equally important, all of which could be clustered into two binary categories: revolutionary civility; and counterrevolutionary barbarism. In representing civility, revolutionary photographers took special care to highlight educational and health progress achieved in spite of adversity. In their *oeuvre*, numerous images of humble hospital wards and open-air classrooms are to be found. These are clearly counterpoised with the photographs of demolished buildings, destroyed by airstrikes. The caption accompanying one of the latter images is telling: 'This is the result of the Shah's civilisation'. Clearly, the reference here is to the Iranian Emperor's claim of presiding over a 'great Aryan civilisation', combating what he described as the primitive 'cannibals in Dhufar'.[35] The photograph thus appears as an act of refutation, revealing the 'truth' of the revolutionary written word, and the falsehood of imperial discourse.

---

[32] Al Jabha al Sha'abiya li Tahrir Oman, *Oman: Al-Insan wal Thawra,* p.11.
[33] Michelle Woodward, 'Between Orientalist Clichés and Images of Modernisation: Photographic Practice in the Late Ottoman Era'. *History of Photography*, Winter 2003, Vol. 27, No. 4, p.365.
[34] Al Jabha al Sha'abiya li Tahrir Oman, *Oman: Al-Insan wal Thawra,* p.16.
[35] Al Jabha al Sha'abiya li Tahrir Oman, *Oman: Al-Insan wal Thawra,* p.24.

In parts, revolutionary artworks could be seen as driven by an instrumental energy. Yet on the whole, they emerge as a direct reflection of the world view of the artist, an exposition of their innermost collective thoughts and feelings. This can be seen especially in that crucial medium of Arabic cultural production: the poem. The revolutionary poem is characterized by an exteriority that is perhaps unmatched by any other contemporary poetic form. To begin with, it is always addressed to a collectivity. It is not an intimate conversation with a lover in a drawing room, a self-contained interaction with nature amidst the rolling hills, a battle with fever on a deathbed, or a soliloquy. The poets situate themselves with the fighters at the barricade, amongst the ranks of the citizens assembled in the public square, or (at the highest level) at the centre of humanity at large. They are at the revolutionary moment, when all human relations are fluid and open to reconfiguration, and where the differentiation of time into a present, a past, and a future, brought about by the rise of essentialist individuality, is suspended.[36] In Bakhtinian terms, the *individuum* lives within the collective whole at the revolutionary moment. The emotions that are conveyed are of a public nature, collective feelings that are translated into words and crafted into a verbal structure, living completely 'on the surface'.

Whereas the more interior poetic genres are at their most profound when emotive uniqueness is transmitted, the revolutionary poem is most powerful when it comes closest to capturing, or even contributing to, shaping the general will. It does so by acting as a repository for suppressed popular dreams and aspirations or as a site of tension between actualities and potentialities. Often, it is crafted to act as both, as seen in Qassem Haddad's 'Some Verses from the Sura of the Gulf and Fire'.[37] Haddad is currently recognized as a major poet across the Arab world. However, when he wrote this poem back in 1970, he was a young member of the Bahraini branch of the Popular Revolutionary Movement, just beginning his literary journey. In many ways, the poem belongs to an established twentieth-century Arabic poetic school, one of whose major concerns was the problem of tradition. The principal figure exemplifying this school is Badr Shaker al-Sayyab, crucially influenced by the work of T.S. Elliot. Yet, far from seeking to 'maintain that all historical periods are equally corrupt' or that the 'past was superior to the present' (two beliefs that, according to

---

[36] See Bakhtin's discussion of the Folkloric bases of the Rabelaisian chronotope. Mikhail Mikhailovich Bakhtin. 'Forms of Time and Chronotope in the Novel', in *The Dialogic Imagination.* Austin: University of Texas Press, 2008. pp.206–7.

[37] Qassem Haddad, 'Ma Tayasarah Min Surat al-Khaleej wal Dima'a,' Bahrain, November 1970, in PFLOAG, *Tisa'a Yunyu.* No. 10, March 1971, pp.21–2.

some readings, could be seen simultaneously in the essentially conservative Elliot), Haddad aims to anchor those episodes from the past that hold revolutionary potential, utilizing them to re-select a tradition from which a new beginning could emerge.[38]

Accordingly, his poem is centred on two figures: Rahmah bin Jaber al-Jalhami and a Dhufari revolutionary named Tuful. The former was born in the mid-eighteenth century to the *Utoub* tribe. During his lifetime, two branches of the *Utoub*, the Al-Khalifa and the Al-Sabah, established control over Bahrain and Kuwait respectively. Sidelined by their ruling arrangements, he waged war on both, raiding their ships and disturbing their trade for decades. He died in an epic naval battle in 1827 during which he was encircled and massively outnumbered. Choosing the path of self-annihilation over surrender, this 70-year-old man killed himself and his entire crew by means of a massive cannon explosion that involved the sacrifice of his own young son. In the words of a British report from the time:

> Thus ended Rahmah bin Jaubir, for so many years the scourge and terror of this part of the world, and whose death was felt as a blessing in every part of the Gulf. Equally ferocious and determined in all situations, the closing scene of his existence displayed the same stern and indomitable spirit which had characterised him all his life.[39]

Rahma was traditionally presented by the British and the ruling Gulf families as the ultimate bloodthirsty pirate. Yet, Haddad transforms him into a revolutionary warrior, a symbol of defiance in the face of the despotic ruling families. Thus, he is recalled from the depths of the past to reawaken the spirit of resistance in the sons and daughters of the Gulf:

> And if a bird comes flying,
> rising from the drowsiness of history,
> he shall sleep over our slumber
> and then perhaps...
> Let the ships, the Gulf vessels, raid us
> Let his sword... The sword of Rahmah
> (It is not like it has been said oh stupid folk and
> smart ones. For, the pirates of the sea do
> not know the meaning of sacrifice)
> But they have lied, and we drank sewer
> water...
> Tasted the pain of separation.

---

[38] For this reading of Elliot, see, for example, Terry Eagleton, *After Theory*, London: Penguin, 2004, p.179.

[39] India Office, *Bombay Selections XXIV*, p.528. Quoted in J.B. Kelly, *Britain and the Persian Gulf, 1795–1880*, Oxford: Clarendon Press, 1968, p.213.

The return of Rahmah al-Jalhami signals the awakening of the revolutionary tradition, and brings about the potential for re-writing history and confronting the real pirates, the ruling Princes and Sultans:

> Let the sword of that Jalhami knight come to us;
> Let us bend our history, giving it a sip from the blood
> of truth, becoming for once, men and audacity;
> opening the gates of the sky with our feet; bringing mercy upon ourselves,
> So that we no longer splash our children with the
> blood of tears and await the coming of
> the Pirate-Princes (every minute they arrive)
> while we sleep over hunger
> and nakedness…

Carrying the sword of Rahmah allows for the initiation of a new humanity, boasting its own insurgent traditions, transgressing against all that was held to be sacred:

> Our proverbs we shall re-write; and
> our traditions redraft.
> There shall be for us, oh land of childhood,
> our own Quran.
> We choose verses from the Sura of Death
> so that they may recite.
> And from the Sura of Blood and Prostitutes…
> We shall also select from the Sura of Revolutionaries
> For our Children, so that we recite, but in a new voice
> that resembles that of victims who rejuvenate themselves
> with birth, crossing the bridges of martyrdom.

In this pugnacious reconceptualization of the sacred, Qassem refers to the chapters and verses of revolution in language that has been jealously reserved for the holy Islamic scripture. While it could be superficially read as a simple contravention of religion, the message here is the abandonment of fatalism, the displacement of the notion that the laws of the earth are determined in heaven. The new people belong to a humanity that creates its own history, reconceptualizes its life anew in accordance with the revelation that is revolution. The reciter of the new revelation is called Tuful, a common Dhufari female name, and a well-known fighter in the Popular Liberation Army.[40] The significance of having a woman as the public reciter of the Quran is not to be overlooked here, for such a role is

---

[40] Note that the poem was written before the death of the first female casualty of the Popular Liberation Army, Tuful Mutaye', on 19 Feburary 1971. However, it was published by the front right after her death. See PFLOAG: 'Awal Shaheedah min Jaysh al-Tahreer al-Sha'bi: Tuful Mutaye", *Tisa'a Yunyu*. No. 10, March 1971. p.21.

traditionally reserved for men. But Tuful overturns the tables, and she speaks of 'revolutionaries made of sparks' fighting in the 'land of fog' (an old name to which Dhufar was sometimes referred). She preaches a new belief, rooted in the aesthetics of heroism, directed against monarchs who were cloaked in the garb of the old traditions, dwelling in a base paradise of male lust, but destined to a hell burning with the fire of revolution:

> A child in the spring of danger called Dhufar
> Listen... Fire begins to eat the robe of all Sultans,
> all those Kings that sell the breast of my homeland
> in the slave girl markets

Tuful recites to the children of the Gulf and informs them of a prophesy, promising them a new life in a liberated Arabia without princes and kings. Her message overcomes the fear of death, that most debilitating force:

> Listen to what Tuful tells us
> And if she tells then believe her
> For what Tuful says is the say
> Open the books of the night and erase; step upon them.
> Let us be, for once, like that Jalhami Knight
> that does not lose anything if he dies...
> I mean that when he battles death he has nothing to
> squander other than suffering.

In the literary tradition of yesteryear, women were often presented as the conveyors of falsehood and empty chatter. In contrast, they emerge here as the credible narrators, purveyors of the truth that was kept hidden from the people by their rulers, a truth in which the new traditions will be rooted. That truth becomes the thread tying past, present, and future, its promise flowering in the act of citizens joining together in arms, liberating the whole Gulf from its distant south:

> When the knights come, when they roam
> we shall be together.
> The knights are made of paper and imagination,
> and it is the Jalhami that breaks the genie's bottle held
> by the British advisor.
> Dhufar
> Dhufar
> Dhufar
> It comes to us with the Eid
> Across the South... the Gulf
> We will be together, together, and together
> (From now on, whenever two of us meet,
> there shall be the homeland)

The new republic emerges by the very act of its own citizens congregating, aware of their revolutionary past, fearlessly fighting for their future, resurrecting Rahma al-Jalhami in their actions. Here, it matters not whether the portrayal of Rahma is accurate or not. To the historian, his actions undoubtedly have little to do with the revolutionary aspirations of the 1960s and 70s. Yet, in the words of T.S.Elliot: 'the difference between art and the event is always absolute... The ode of Keats contains a number of feelings, which have nothing particular to do with the nightingale, but which the nightingale, partly, perhaps, because of its attractive name, and partly because of its reputation, served to bring together.'[41] What matters for the revolutionary poet is the construction of the legend and, through it, the expression and propagation of popular insurgent feeling.

The Dhufari audience for this type of poem was limited. Considering the low literacy level, the complicated constructions of free verse could only be savoured by the revolutionary intelligentsia. As much as they expressed a general sensibility, these were poems to be read and reflected upon, and more memorable and simpler rhyming verses could be better disseminated. In vocabulary and content, these were closer to the art of punchy rhyming polemic rather than poetic expression:

> Revolution and long people's war
> Original leftist principles we uphold
> Every invading horde
> Its presence we abort...
> Collaborators you have changed
> The older thrown and the new tamed
> Pampered Qaboos you have plumed
> Enthroning the boy you groomed
> England moved ahead
> Political intrigues she led
> Collaborators she bred
> Hopes of gain filled her head...[42]

Often coming from cadres in the Popular Liberation Army, such verses were important for sustaining morale and spreading the political assessments of the Popular Front at any given moment. Far from being the highest form of revolutionary composition, they were nevertheless an important part of everyday cultural expression. Similar verbal forms were also used for military purposes. For instance, the old song 'Nana' was

---

[41] T.S. Elliot, 'Tradition and the Individual Talent', in *The Sacred Wood: Essays on Poetry and Criticism*, London: Faber and Faber, 1997, p.42.
[42] 'Thawra wa Harb Tawila', Al-Jabha al-Sha'abiya Li Tahreer Oman, *Tisa'a Yunyu*, December 1971, p.17.

sung by shepherds in the local Shihri dialect, its lyrics adjusted to inform revolutionaries of the movements of Anglo-Sultanic troops.[43]

Although such popular cultural forms were not always expressed in Arabic, the Popular Front went to great pains to launch a programme of Arabization, solidly anchoring Dhufar in the broader regional cultural sphere. This was not an imposed process, for knowledge of Southern Arabic dialects was not seen as conflicting with expression in Arabic. Indeed, although Arabic was not the native tongue of the majority of highlanders (Kathiris being an exception), those belonging to the Qarra and other non-Arabic-speaking tribes saw themselves as Arabs and they were keen to gain literacy in the Arabic language, their native dialects having no written tradition. The intelligentsia had already learnt Arabic during their years of exile and migration in the Gulf and all revolutionary publications were accordingly published in that language. Yet, much work was done at the mass level as well, especially within the school and the literacy classes given to members of the Popular Liberation Army and the Militia. This process of Arabization had the most profound long-term cultural impact on Dhufar. Such was the scope of its eventual spread that Arabic is now universally spoken across the territory. Although it was initiated by the revolutionaries, it was taken to its logical conclusion by the Qaboos regime, which was also keen to Arabize but for completely different ends.

The main difference between the revolutionary and regime approach to Arabization pertained to the question of 'national culture'. In asserting a new culture, the revolutionaries followed the pattern described by Fanon:

> Today Arab doctors and Arab poets speak to each other across the frontiers, and strive to create a new Arab culture and a new Arab civilisation. It is in the name of Arabism that these men join together, and they try to think together…The living culture is not national but Arab. The problem is not as yet to secure a national culture, not as yet to lay hold of a movement differentiated by nations, but to assume an African or Arabic culture when confronted by the all-embracing condemnation pronounced by the dominating power.[44]

The aim of the revolutionaries was amalgamation into the broader Arabic cultural sphere rather than a delineation and emphasis on a narrowly defined 'national' culture that was particularly 'Omani'. In contrast, the regime was actively using Arabic language education for the purpose of

[43] Interview D(i).
[44] Frantz Fanon, *The Wretched of the Earth*, London: Penguin Classics, 2001 [1963], p.172.

'Omanization', appropriating Dhufar into the Sultanic realm. Its quest was to emphasize the distinctiveness of Oman in relation to the countries surrounding it—imposing its national dress, emphasizing its particular seafaring tradition, the legacy of its Indian Ocean empire, its forts, daggers, and literature (all of which had little to do with Dhufar). The essence of this policy was to invent cultural sameness within the boundaries of the nation state and to assert difference beyond them.

AUTHORITY AND RELIGION IN ROYALIST CULTURE

The essence of Sultanic cultural policy after the 1970 coup was to create a basis for the development of pro-monarchist and loyalist sentiments, countering revolutionary culture in the process. While the Said bin Taimur regime had failed to undertake this task, initiating no major initiatives worthy of consideration, the Qaboos era began with an expedited programme of radio broadcasts, publishing, image production, and televised activity. As was shown in the previous chapter, Radio Oman launched its operations from the military base of Bait al-Falaj one week after the 1970 coup. Its programmes were carefully managed by British anti-communist propagandist Pauline Searle, drawing on her previous experience in Malaya. In December 1970, a subsidiary station was established in Salalah, offering a five-hour programme in the Dhufar region. By 1975, broadcast strength grew from 1 kilowatt to 100 kilowatts and the programme duration was expanded to 14 hours. This was supplemented by the creation of a television station, which commenced its operations in Muscat in November 1974, and extended its presence to Salalah one year later.[45] Sultanate newspapers also began to be published. The first to appear was the weekly (and later daily) *Al-Watan*, whose inaugural issue was printed in Beirut on 28 January 1971. The second was *Oman*, launched on the 'national day' anniversary on 28 November 1972 through the efforts of Jordanian anti-Nasserist and anti-communist journalist Amin Abu al-Sha'ar. He was seconded to the Sultanate as a media adviser, having served in numerous propaganda, censorship, and official media roles in Amman. These culminated in his 1971 establishment of the *Al-Ra'i* official newspaper in the context of Black September, and his heading of Jordanian Radio, which essentially functioned as an intelligence arm during that stark period of martial law.

[45] Abdulmonam Al-Hasani,. 'Teaching Journalism in the Arab World: Recent Obstacles and Future Plans in Oman', Paper presented at the IAMCR conference, Cairo, July 2006.

With the help of such figures as Searle and Abu al-Sha'ar, the new media platforms were used to propagate a royalist culture centred on veneration and celebration of the trinity of God, the homeland, and the monarch. Although coming last in this order, the monarch was actually the most important in it, state managed religion and a royalist form of patriotism both being deployed for his benefit. Notably absent was a fourth term: the people. They were conceived as subjects whose role was to submit and obey the Sultan and, by doing so, serve God and the homeland. This conception formed the basic foundation for the reformulation of the 'authority relationship' in Oman, fashioning it in terms suitable for the new system of absolutism that was being imposed. Regardless of where it is to be found, the authority relationship

> ...assumes two essential elements in the mental attitude of he who is subject to authority: a certain measure of freedom (voluntariness: recognition and affirmation of the bearer of authority which is not based purely on coercion) and conversely, submission, the tying of will (indeed of thought and reason) to the authoritative will of an Other.[46]

The will, thought, and reason of Omanis was being bound tighter and tighter under the impact of the enormous expansion of the army, the police, and the intelligence structure of the *mukhabarat*, all of which were directed internally for the purpose of controlling and monitoring the populace. But this was not enough: without the spread of royalist culture, the voluntary recognition and affirmation of the Sultan's authority could not be effectively achieved.

Royalist culture was centred on the constant narration and representation in various mediums of one major story: the 'the launch of the age of renaissance, development, and construction under the leadership of his Majesty the Sultan the builder of Modern Oman'.[47] In shorter form, this was referred to as *al-Nahda al-Mubaraka*, 'the blessed renaissance,' a name that carried clear religious connotations. Of course, it was not possible to present the hero, the Sultan, as a holy figure, nor could he be accorded the status of God's representative on earth. That would have gone against Islamic practice, especially in its Ibhadi form. Yet, the idea was to position the Sultan as the protector of religion against the forces that seek to destroy it. In that sense, he was the 'Hand of God' on earth, destroying the Almighty's enemies. This can be seen clearly in various examples of royalist iconography, including the poster 'The Hand of God Destroys Communism'. Here, we see a closed fist with the Sultanic crest tattooed

---

[46] Herbert Marcuse, *A Study on Authority*, London: Verso, 2008 [1936], p.7.
[47] See for example, coverage of the second national day celebrations in *Al-Watan*, No. 76, 18 November 1972.

on it, smashing the communist star. Similar messages were transmitted elsewhere. For instance, one of the posters hung inside the classrooms of the military school read: 'Brother soldier, do not become an apostate…Communism is atheism'.[48]

As the 'Hand of God', the Sultan shielded the faith from the relentless assaults of communists. Posters and paintings portrayed him as an almost transcendental figure, soaring in his dignified posture above his godless enemies. Religious motifs were constantly utilized to remind Omanis that his was the reign of justice on earth. Indeed, the Sultan constantly re-enacted the story of the second caliph, Omar ibn al-Khattab, traditionally associated with justice. Like Omar, he inspected the affairs of his subjects, making sure that all was well in his realm by means of 'surprise visits' and encounters with the 'ordinary man'. These clearly contrived visits were presented as being spontaneous. Their hero was celebrated for his even-handedness and courage in opposing all those who denied his subjects their rights. This was emphasized in such headlines as 'His Majesty the Sultan Orders that Workers Should be Fairly Treated'.[49]

Fig. 5. SAF recruiting poster featuring the slogans: 'The aims of communism include: apostasy, atheism, domination and slavery' and 'Communism is the enemy of religions and homelands'. Sib Camp, 7 April 1975

[48] Assem Al-Sheedi, 'Rih'la Fi Thakirat Jarida', *Jaridat Oman*, Tuesday, 13 March 2012.
[49] *Al-Watan*, No.1, 28 January 1971.

In order to entrench the idea that adversaries of the Sultan were enemies of God, the Sultanate, under the direction of its British and Jordanian propaganda advisers, solicited the production of several articles, pamphlets, and books. The most ambitious in scope was *The Dhufar Revolution: A Struggle Between Communism and Islam*, written by an anti-communist author, Fouad Karam. As the title suggests, the book describes revolutionary evil in all its aspects, while illustrating that it is bound to be defeated by Islam. The Sultan here is not only represented as the protector of religion, he is also highlighted as the saviour of the Omani homeland, the wider Arab nation, and the Palestinian cause from a wicked threat that threatens to destroy them from within. The Dhufar revolution was described as a perfidious plot 'aiming at the Soviet capture of Gulf oil' as well as 'separating Dhufar from Oman for the purpose of establishing another "Israel" in the Gulf region that implements the plans of International Communism and serves its interests so that it could become, with Aden, a staging post for controlling the states of the region'.[50] In an earlier book, Karam noted that all Arab communists were colluding with a 'global Jewish conspiracy', which had been outlined in the *Protocols of the Elders of Zion*: 'Karl Marx is the son of Zionism, and Communism is the daughter of Zionism, and they are twins working for the same goal, which is the erasure of the Muslim and Christian religions'. In fact, 'due to the efforts of Arab progressives, Israel—after taking over Jerusalem—has been able to jump ahead towards its final goal of...building Solomon's temple'.[51]

Thus, political fear is deployed as a mobilizational tool in the service of the throne. As noted by one scholar: 'for political fear to arouse us, the object of fear must belong to the realm of politics and yet somehow, in the minds of the fearful, stand apart from it'.[52] The revolutionaries were subject to a process of mystification, reduced to a political phenomenon that can only be understood by reference to supra-material realities. They were at once placed at the centre of politics, but expunged from the realm of the rationally analysable. The message was simple: in the absence of the Sultanic order, an iniquitous alliance of international communists will take over the world with the help of progressive Arabs, destroying Oman and ultimately demolishing the al-Aqsa mosque and building the Temple of Solomon. By establishing a fear of such conspiracies as the 'ground for public life', the Sultanic regime effectively attempted to bury the 'grievances

---

[50] Fouad Karam, *Thawrat Dhufar, Sira'a Bayna al-Shuyu'ya wal Islam*, Beirut: Haqa'iq 'An al-Marxiya Series, 1973, p.51.

[51] Fouad Karam, *Wa Da'at al Jawlan*, Beirut, 1970, pp.60–1.

[52] Corey Robin, *Fear: The History of a Political Idea*, Oxford and New York: Oxford University Press, 2004, p.4.

and controversies that underlie it'.[53] More importantly, it restored the political precepts of the *status quo* with vigour. Generally speaking, 'political dangers like war or insurrection . . . require a society to define or affirm its beliefs, to mobilise against the threat on behalf of its political values'.[54] In the Sultanic realm, the political values that the regime was keen to ensconce were obedience and submission to the Sultan.

Affirming such values, in the context of a revolution that radically challenged Sultanic authority, required the deployment of various arguments and positions along the lines described above. These reflected a strand of anti-rationalism whose earliest manifestations are to be found in the European counter-revolutionary tradition of the Comte de Maistre, the Vicomte de Bonald, and Friedrich Schlegel. Emerging in response to the French revolution, this tradition was underlined by the attempt to affix respect for the *status quo* as 'the psychological basis for the social order of domination'. Here, the 'principle which upholds state and society is not the truth as arrived at through human insight, but faith: prejudice, superstition, religion and tradition are celebrated as the essential social virtues of man'.[55] That said, the form of faith offered by Sultanic literature differs from that seen in traditional Omani political commentaries. Up to the early twentieth century, these writings exhibited forms of enchantment rather than anti-rationalism. In such works as al-Salimi's *Tuhfat al-A'yan*, little understood and incomprehensible political intrigues were occasionally explained with reference to magic. But that was a neutral tool that could be used for good or evil, and it was moreover a stable and known category that could be understood 'rationally' within the parameters and confines of the prevailing local world view. The purpose in such classical texts was not to instil unhinged fear of a lascivious 'enemy' and faith in the protection of the earthly ruler, but rather to reveal the wisdom of God as he orders the unfolding of history. More importantly, all the concepts offered were rooted in a stable epistemological and ontological framework, reflecting a system of belief rather than fleeting arguments offered at whim.

At this juncture, however, it must be emphasized that the jumbled and evanescent nature of Sultanic discourse did not mean the lack of an ordering principle. Although it drew on an incoherent reserve of words and images— borrowed from religion, tradition, anti-Semitism, Cold War propaganda, and counter-revolutionary thought—royalist discourse essentially revolved around one stable centre: the Sultan. Any argument serving the Sultan was likely to be used. The substance of the arguments did not matter, and belief

[53] Karam, *Thawrat Dhufar, Sira'a Bayna al-Shuyu'ya wal Islam*. p.3.
[54] Karam, *Thawrat Dhufar, Sira'a Bayna al-Shuyu'ya wal Islam*. p.5.
[55] Marcuse, *A Study on Authority* p.71.

in them was not necessary. British propagandists did not believe in Islam, yet they appealed to it in their works. Jordanian royalist journalists were not subjects of the Sultan, yet they glorified him in their editorials. They were opposed to Palestinians, but hailed the Sultan as the protector of the dispossessed. By engaging in royalist cultural production, they were simply fulfilling a task they were hired for: creating a counter-revolutionary tradition.

This evident lack of sincerity kindled a great deal of bitterness in revolutionary cultural circles. These included men and women from across the Arab world who strongly believed in the principles they preached, and were indeed risking their lives for them. They derided what they saw as a mercenary culture that instrumentalized religion, tradition, and fear in the service of monarchy and empire. In one of his poems, Sakher uses classical Islamic references to question royalist discourse, which he characterizes as the 'religion of oil', preached by Sultanic media outlets:

> The age of oil spreads its religion with the sword
> Its tribute is loyalty
> The middleman purchases the map of the sky
> and buys the martyrs…
> For Oil has bought life and wants the hereafter
> to come to him bowing

Sakher effectively appropriates and subverts religious language to revolutionary ends. By doing so, he engages in a long tradition established by writers across the tricontinental world.[56] In this poem, he retells the story of the Ridda wars that threatened Islam right after the death of the Prophet Mohammad: Arabia is lost to the forces of the 'imposters', and the Muslims are left with the three towns of the Hijaz. Most of their soldiers are far away, led by Osama bin Zaid in an arduous fight against the Byzantines. The Caliph Abu Bakr al-Sideeq remains composed despite this perilous state of affairs, relying on the greatest General in Islamic history, Khalid ibn al-Waleed (widely known by the sobriquet 'God's Raised Sword'). These Islamic figures—the 'true believers'—stand for the revolutionaries, confronting Musaylama (the ultimate 'imposter') who instrumentalizes religion for earthly gain:

> Prayer is lost in the Prince's palace
> Apostacy till when?

---

[56] Revolutionary writers engaging in this tradition not only subverted religious themes but extended their endeavours to numerous other genres (including detective fiction!). See, for instance William Nichols, *Transatlantic Mysteries: Crime, Culture, and Capital in the 'Noir Novels' of Paco Ignacio Taibo II and Manuel Vásquez Montalbán*, Plymouth: Bucknell University Press, 2011.

Let the sword take its course Oh son of al-Waleed
Have you come to accept heresy in an age when oil produces
airplanes?
By God, the Caliph did not allow it back when the
Treasury was made of date fruit...
Perplexed am I by the flying swarms of the Day of Judgment
Dhufar has changed its colours son of al-Waleed
Bring me the raised one! (It was tried by the Caliph...and in
September it was a sharp cutter).
In the meantime, the army of Osama departs beyond the
boundaries of the spirit, lost in the desert, panting in its
search for the colour of the religion of Oil.
The Sideeq lies imprisoned and two
Musaylamas are playing with the Book
Qaboos embracing the truth...[57]

A revolutionary editorial critiquing Sultanic educational policy in the Sultan's Armed Forces conveyed the same message in plainer prose:

> The teachers attempt to convince the Omani youth that the revolution and its slogans reflect apostasy and atheism, as well as hostility to God, the homeland, and the people. They present the treachery, theft, and exploitation practiced by Qaboos and his colonial masters as a wise and correct policy that aims at the progress of the Omani people, and the preservation of its religion and beliefs. Brainwashing is not only practiced with regards to local issues, but it is extended to cover fateful Arab national issues. Thus, America becomes the friend of the Arabs and Israel is here to stay; the Palestinian revolution is nothing more than a form of terrorism that is practiced by forces that are controlled by international communism![58]

As clear as this was to the revolutionaries, it was not necessarily evident to Omanis living outside revolutionary areas. In the Gulf region, monarchy was the norm rather than the exception, and its cultural and ideological dominance was pervasive. The world view that the Sultanate was promoting had much in common with the discourses and practices emanating from nearly every regional capital, backed in full force with enormous funding from Saudi Arabia. Its themes corresponded to a global royalist tradition that had a long lineage, projecting 'images of fortitude, legitimacy,

---

[57] Sakher Habash, 'Al Janoub wal Thawra...Oman.' Al Jabha al Sha'bya Li Tahrir Oman. 'Al Majd lil Sha'ab al-Muqatil!' *Tisa'a Yuniyu*, Year 5, Volume 5, June 1975, p.92–3.

[58] Al Jabha al Sha'bya Li Tahrir Oman, 'Ay Jaysh Thalika al-Lathi Yasa'a Qaboos wal Biritanyoon Li Takweeneh Fi Biladina?', *Sawt al Thawra*, Year 4, No. 182, Saturday 27 December 1975.

and paternal care'.[59] These images were not just confined to the sphere of propaganda. Indeed, royalist themes were expressed through the revival of traditional Arabic cultural genres such as the poetry of *madeeh'* (praise). Characteristically, one of these orally transmitted poems, attributed to the late Dhufari oral poet Malgout (widely known as Bin-Turoom), celebrates the connected themes of Sultanic benevolence and popular submission. The poet refers to the Sultan with the word *Habbab*, a title by which slaves address their Master:

> You remain a Habbab that is merciful
> to his slaves...
> A Habbab who is rightly guided, and doesn't
> wish anyone trouble
> Before you we saw rulers of misery and suffering
> But you are a Habbab who brought motors for
> the people...

The grassroots appeal of such language must not be underestimated, especially at a time when Sultanic absolutism seemed unstoppably powerful— citizens witnessed its most spectacular expansion over their lives, enjoying the financial patronage that came with it.

Yet, every word was certain to make the inheritors of Rousseau and Marx, Mao and Che, Nasser and Habash, cringe. They contested the very conception and use of culture, engaging in a perennial battle whose global unfolding was summarized by Manuel Vázquez Montalbán in one of his last speeches. On the one hand, there was the revolutionary conception that 'questioned the established order' and intended to transform it. This will for transformation was expressed in such aforementioned acts as photographically reconfiguring female iconography or poetically re-reading regional history through the lens of anti-monarchical resistance. On the other hand, there was the royalist practice of integrating culture 'into a body of established truths, defined by power, thus turning access to culture into a means for people to come to terms with the established order'.[60] This practice took the form of integrating religious and historic tradition as a means of glorifying the monarch and asserting both his authority and benevolence. This clash between revolutionary and royalist visions continued unabated, well after the end of the major military confrontations described in the following chapter.

---

[59] For such images and their anti-revolutionary usage in another context, see Marilyn Morris, *The British Monarchy and the French Revolution*, New Heaven: Yale University Press, 1998, p.134.

[60] Manuel Vázquez-Montalbán, 'Revolutionary Culture'? *Le Monde Diplomatique.* January, 2004.

10

From Citizenship to Subjecthood, Episodes from 1971–76

The Dhufar revolution was confronted by the tide of absolutism and the new cultural, political, and economic realities it carried to the surface. Spreading from Oman proper, absolutist centralization initially enveloped the Dhufari plains and gradually rose to cover the highlands. The success of this phenomenon depended on three factors: civic disintegration; regional monarchical consolidation; and geographic division. These mechanisms allowed for the destruction of the last Omani space for autonomous civic mobilization. They ensured the transformation undergone in the status of the highlanders from citizens, fighting voluntarily, recognizing no higher human authority and receiving no patronage, to subjects whose loyalty was secured by a combination of threat and material cooptation.

CIVIC INTEGRATION AND DISINTEGRATION

One of the earliest and most important effects of revolutionary mobilization was the creation of a supra-tribal civic space in which all sectors of Dhufari society could participate. The revolutionary notions of equality and fraternity were central to that endeavour. Fighters were equal regardless of their tribal position, and were tied by voluntary (as opposed to predetermined) solidarities and bonds. Throughout the struggle, the revolutionary leadership confronted the mammoth task of preserving this autonomous space and strengthening these bonds. How were they to unify a historically fragmented society? How were they to transform tribal subjects into citizens? The answer lay in radical destruction and construction. The object of destruction was the tribe, and the goal of construction was the modern polity. Both tasks were to be undertaken by the party: an organized body of men and women who upheld a universal Marxist-Leninist ideology.

Marxism-Leninism is an ideology of centralized organization premised on iron-clad discipline in the quest for revolutionary transformation. Making its Dhufari appearance in the post-1968 period, its practical introduction to a pre-existing struggle was bound to be ridden with complexity, especially when the theory itself was only vernacularly and partially comprehended. PFLOAG came to be treated by leftist leaders less as a Front, and more as a party. The principal aim was to create a formidably organized force, bound by ties rendered unbreakable by ideology. This was expressed in the Maoist slogan *al-Fikr Yaqud al-Bunduqiyya*, 'thought leads the rifle'. This slogan was promoted as the mark that distinguished the Dhufari revolution from kindred struggles, especially the Palestinian one, which was deemed to romanticize the rifle at the expense of ideology. But who was to provide thought in illiterate Dhufar? None other than the Political Commissars, the main agents of centralization within PFLOAG. Every PLA unit had three ranks of Commissar. 1st Commissars were given immense powers: they even had the authority—unquestioned until the 1971 Raykhut Conference—to 'outweigh a tactical military decision'.[1]

The Commissars' authority was reinforced with displays of knowledge. Almost every one of them—including those with limited reading competence—was armed with an Arabic translation of the Red Book.[2] Other texts they relied on included PFLOAG's *'Sifaat al-Munadil al-Jayyid*, based on Liu Shao-Chi's *How to be a Good Communist*.[3] Moreover, they were occasionally distinguished with such symbols as hexagonal red stars and Mao badges. Such books and symbols were not only signs of affiliation but also of representation. Commissars were the bodies that represented the central authority of the revolution in the various areas: the links that intellectually and visually tied geographically spread revolutionary hubs. It could be said that their counterparts within the local conservative tradition were the *walis*, who embodied the Sultan's authority in distant regions, and the Islamic preachers, who carried religious authority to the smallest of villages. The Commissars oversaw the reproduction of centralizing practices in every Dhufari gathering. The literacy class, the evening political discussion, and the *autocritique* circle did not simply fulfil strictly delineated individual functions; they also acted as common political rituals in which hundreds of people were simultaneously joined, united in time although divided by space.

---

[1] MEC-Graham, 'Captured Enemy Documents—3rd National Conference of Rakhyut'. 15 December 1971.
[2] Interview E(i).
[3] Abdel Nabi Al-Ikri, *Al-Tanthimat al-Yassariya fil Jazeera wal Khaleej al 'Arabi*, Beirut: Dar al-Kunouz al-Adabbya, 2003, p.101.

One of the main obstacles that confronted the proponents of ideological centralism was that their message was deemed incompatible with religion. This was especially the case in the more sedentary parts of Dhufar where faith was strongly rooted, namely the Eastern Area. Addressing this issue divided opinion within PFLOAG, as illustrated by a series of incidents that took place between the autumns of 1969 and 1970. The chain of events was initiated by operatives connected to the disgruntled old-DLF figure Youssef Alawi, attempting to undermine the leftist leadership. They began to distribute gifts (especially watches) to gain leverage, simultaneously initiating a campaign to shift the allegiance of the population. Their slogan was simple but effective: to defend religion against communist infiltration.

During an evening political education session, the local militia in the town of Taqa reported this development to Abdel Munim al-Shirawi, 3rd Political Commissar. He in turn gave word to Saud al-'Ansi, the leading Military Commander in the Eastern Sector. The two decided that the only solution lay in public displays of religiosity and to focus on the anti-colonial as opposed to communist precepts of PFLOAG. They began touring villages, leading the prayers wherever they went. Although this produced positive results at the local level, it solicited a harsh response from leaders such as Abdel Aziz al-Qadi. As the trainer of Commissars in the revolution camp, the latter was building a considerable base of support. Concerned at any sign of 'reactionary thought', he threatened to try al-Shirawi and al-'Ansi for betraying secular revolutionary principles.[4] Central control was thus imposed, ending an initiative attuned to local conditions as opposed to ideology.

The quest for centralization also affected the distribution of commanders within the Popular Liberation Army (PLA). Another example from the East illustrates this point. In 1970, up to thirty military leaders in that sector were moved elsewhere, exchanged with others chosen by the General Command.[5] Although this may have made sense in centralizing military terms, it upset a delicate tribal balance within the region and caused some discontent. As successful as anti-tribal policies were within the PFLOAG organizational structure, tribalism still held an undeniable social significance: the leadership and fighting units were supra-tribal, but non-combatants continued to live in tribal congregations. Although tribalism's political expression declined with the revolutionary assault against the Sheikhs, it remained the foremost unit of

---

[4] Interview E(i).
[5] Mohammad Al-Amri, *Thufar: al Thawra fil Tarikh al-Omani al Mo'uasir*, Beirut: Riad el-Rayyes Books, 2005, p.170.

social and economic organization, its primordial links continuing to harbour a latent political potential.

The same could be said for the social norms that were being centrally challenged through such initiatives as the ongoing programme for women's empowerment. This programme was reinforced by the growth of female political education. In 1971, British Intelligence noted that it 'appears that political indoctrination of civilians has been more successful amongst the women than the men. This may well be because the women are attracted by the idea of promised emancipation through the doctrine of communism.'[6] Women's radicalization threatened established gender norms, and so did their arming and incorporation in the PLA. Whereas divisions were mostly unmixed, mixing began to be practised in the Mobile Unit. This did not mean, however, that mixing was imposed without due consideration of local conditions. Indeed, during the 1971 Rakhyut Conference, mixing within the *halaqas*, the political discussion circles, was seriously considered, but the decision on it was cautious. It was agreed that the Front would examine the potential for 'the mixing of men and women within halaqas and ascertain whether or not this is acceptable as there are differences between areas and it is up to the custom of the individual area'.[7]

The most ambitious decisions on gender were undertaken in areas with a radical core of female cadres. For instance, by 1971, women in Wadi Naheez 'made it known that they consider themselves to be equal to the men in every way'. Unsurprisingly, proponents of patriarchy read such moves through a sexualized lens. Thus a collaborator reporting the decision claimed that the women '[declared] that they are "available" for any male fighter at any time'.[8] Ironically, the collaborator's vision conceived the revolutionary world dually as a sphere of emasculation (by means of the violation of honour) and of fantasy (by virtue of female 'availability'). Such a conception reflected the world view of the perceiver as opposed to the reality of the perceived.

The contradictions arising out of centralization policies were most acutely felt in the Eastern Area. There, the coup and a general amnesty announced by Qaboos on 1 September 1970 introduced a political opening that allowed for division. On 12 September, a mutiny erupted, expressed in terms that emphasized the need for the reaffirmation of religion, restoration of public morality, and the assertion of control over the female body. Political Commissars were characterized as 'atheists'

---

[6] MEC-Graham, 'Captured Enemy Documents'.
[7] MEC-Graham, 'Captured Enemy Documents'.
[8] MEC-Graham, 'Captured Enemy Documents'.

conspiring to 'demolish religion and Islamic traditions'; members of the General Command were accused of 'deviance'; and women in the revolution camps were described as 'whores'.[9] This was the discourse in which local discontent was expressed: it was universal in that it appealed to the supra-tribal world of religion and conservatism. However, this was only one layer, covering deeper contradictions between centralizing thought and practice and established local structures. Although both the central and the mutinous leaderships claimed otherwise, speaking in the language of universals, these contradictions pertained to the realm of the tribal particular.

Indeed, the mutiny occurred in areas dominated by the Ma'shani, a powerful Qarra tribe to which Qaboos's mother, Mazun, belonged. The ascent of their son to the throne, and the amnesty he granted, boded well for the Ma'shanis' future. Accordingly, the majority of the mutiny's leaders belonged to that tribe. It should be emphasized that this does not mean that all Ma'shanis participated: some continuing to be loyal to the Front. Nevertheless, major figures from the tribe were central to the unfolding events. One of them was Mohammad bin-Salim, paramount Sheikh, PFLOAG General Command member, and the father of Sultan Said's first wife. Another was Salim bin-Mubarak, Deputy Commander of the PLA in the Eastern Area.[10] To these figures, leaving the revolution outright did not make sense. From the standpoint of their own interest calculation, that would have led to undesirable results, separating the Ma'shanis from Dhufari society. From an emotional perspective, it would have amounted to abandoning a rich heritage of struggle to which the tribesmen had given more than five years of their lives and to which they had sacrificed some of their finest fighters. Moreover, it was highly unlikely that consensus could have been achieved within the tribe against the revolution. Realistically, the best course lay in steering the revolution into accepting Qaboos. This was impossible as long as PFLOAG was committed to Marxism and Republicanism: challenging this commitment was essential.

The priority was to arrest and expel armed elements from areas other than the Eastern Sector so as to allow for greater tribal manoeuvring space. As long as political decisions were made by anti-tribal Commissars and the military situation was controlled by supra-tribal commanders, the Ma'shanis were tied to the central control of the General Command. Expelling these figures would allow for the restoration of tribal autonomy.

---

[9] Al-Jabha al-Shabiya, 'Hawla Harakat al-Thani 'Ashar min September', 12 January 1971, *Wathaiq al Nidal al Watani: 1965–1974*, Beirut: Dar Al-Tali'a, 1974, p.91.

[10] Al-Amri, *Thufar.* p.170.

Thus forty PFLOAG General Command, PLA and militia members were arrested on 12 September.[11] That same day, negotiations were held in Jabal 'Aram between representatives of PFLOAG's military committee and the leaders of the mutiny, resulting in the release of the detainees. Subsequently, a warning was sent by the mutinous leaders to all non-local PFLOAG members present in the Eastern Sector, leading to the departure of almost eighty cadres from the area. Having achieved their objective, the mutinous leaders then held another set of negotiations in Darbat, with a General Command delegation led by Mohammad al-Ghassani. An agreement was reached by which the new status quo was upheld until the National Charter had been re-examined and a Committee elected to investigate divisive issues and figures.[12]

At this point, the General Command was left with two options: to cede control in the East, allow the Ma'shanis freedom of manoeuvre in relation to the regime, and reconfigure the ideological and organizational structure of the revolution; or to restore centralized control. Unsurprisingly, the latter course was chosen, so as to preserve discipline and military efficiency, and suppress tribalism. However, the unusual severity and cruelty with which this was done had a disastrous impact on the present and future of the revolution. Units were sent to the Eastern Sector from other parts of Dhufar, and the mutiny was totally crushed by 30 September. Under the influence of an ultra-leftist purging mentality, more than thirty cadres were executed.[13] These were mostly Ma'shanis, but their ranks also included some mutineers from other Qarra sections.[14]

Such internal violence was unprecedented. For the first time, lethal punishment had been administered within the revolution on a large scale, tearing the fabric of the Dhufari body politic and destroying the bonds of camaraderie. The families of the executed were traumatized and some of their relatives who were enrolled in PFLOAG began to harbour new vengeful attitudes towards the leadership. Tribalism, which had gone into a temporary slumber under the effects of collective mobilization, was reawakened. There were now cadres who raised their rifles with the Front but turned their hearts towards revenge.[15] More significantly, a new character, fear, had made its presence felt. It fed on the callousness in handling revolutionary lives, the ease with which they were terminated. As the space for expressing alternative views progressively narrowed, suspicious

---

[11] Al-Jabha al-Shabiya, 'Hawla Harakat al-Thani 'Ashar min September'.
[12] Al-Amri, *Thufar*, pp.173–4.
[13] Interview E(i).
[14] Al-Amri, *Thufar*, p.175.
[15] This was a sentiment consistently expressed by defectors from the Eastern Area. See, for example, Graham Diaries, 30 September 1971.

actions or opinions were liable to be described as counter-revolutionary. Although this did secure an immediate improvement in revolutionary discipline, it ultimately served the Anglo-Sultanic authorities.

Revolutionary mobilization aims at anti-colonial unity, while colonial counterinsurgency tends towards indigenous division. However, there are multiple paths to unification and division. In the post-1970 context, heavy-handed centralization was the revolutionary path of choice, while tribalism was the bedrock of Anglo-Sultanic policy. This echoes the situation in other former British domains. For instance, in several African colonies, there existed two opposing paths famously referred to by Mahmoud Mamdani as a colonial-tribalist 'decentralised despotism' and a nationalist 'centralised despotism' pursuing forced modernization.[16] The difference in the Omani case is that tribalism was no longer the instrument of a decentralised despotism (as it was in the Said bin-Taimur era) but the agent of a highly centralized absolutist system.

Following the coup, the absolutist administration took a series of measures to divide the people of Dhufar. These echoed the Landon Plan of March 1970, described in detail in Chapter 5. There were two dimensions to Anglo-Sultanic strategy: incorporating Dhufari elements that were discarded by the revolutionaries; and encouraging splits within the revolution itself. The focus was to be on the tribes inhabiting the eastern and western peripheries of the Jabal, the desert sections of the Al-Kathir and the Mahra. The desert Kathiri structure required effective reconstruction, its leadership having collapsed as a result of the revolutionary assault on tribalism. Accordingly, one of its Sheikhs, Mussalam bin-Tufl (not to be confused with Bin Nufl, who also defected to the Sultanate), was released from Jalali prison and, on 13 August 1970, he was sent by the Sultan on a mission to visit Habarut with an SAF Platoon. There, he informed exiled Kathiri Sheikhs that they were allowed to go back to their lands and enter Salalah, that a shop was going to be opened for them in Thamrit, and that their followers would be offered opportunities in development projects and PDO operations.[17]

On 21 August, a larger meeting was held between PDO representatives and Kathiri sheikhs, and the latter gave a positive response. Subsequently, Kathiris began to be hired by PDO in their tribal lands at Mushqin and Arba.[18] This by no means led to ending Company–tribal tensions. Indeed, Kathiri workers launched a strike against PDO soon after they were hired. Nevertheless,

---

[16] Mahmoud Mamdani, *Citizen and Subject: Contemporary Africa and the Legacy of Late Colonialism*, Princeton: Princeton University Press, 1996, p.8.

[17] MEC-Paxton, 'August Notes', 1970.

[18] MEC-Paxton, 'Monthly Report', February 1970.

what mattered was that the Bedouin sections of the tribe were being effectively incorporated into Anglo-Sultanic patronage networks. One of the personalities who helped solidify this was Dhufar Development Officer and main liaison with the Kathiris, Robin Butler. Simple developmental projects were pursued under his direction. The first of these was the drilling of a water-hole in Barsa on 10 October 1970, an event attended by Butler and loyalist Kathiri Sheikhs.[19] Undoubtedly, this was meant to increase the local leverage of the Sheikhs as well as the government.

Kathiri urban branches were even more positively inclined towards Qaboos. Like others amongst the 7,500 inhabitants of Salalah, they were exhausted by years of war, and welcomed improvements in their material condition regardless of its political source. This contrasted substantially with attitudes in the Jabal. In September 1970, a PDO report noted:

> There is little or no sign of the mountain tribes responding to the Sultan's amnesty; the grip of the hard core rebels is still very strong…Tribesmen and others from the Salalah plain, however, have reacted favourably to the amnesty and the relaxing of restrictions on movement into and out of Salalah. Some of them have come forward as volunteers to join the Sultan's Army. The best of these are now under training in Oman.[20]

Several figures from important Kathiri families in Salalah were quickly incorporated into high positions. For instance, Said al-Shanfari was increasingly trusted as a 'go-between and a fixer' for the Sultan in Salalah and was eventually appointed as Petroleum Minister in 1974. Al-Shanfari, who had previously worked in Saudi Aramco and learnt some English there, benefited from contracts awarded after the coup, amassing a large fortune. His feelings for Qaboos were 'somewhere between reverence and hero-worship', and the Sultan who had 'never had any very close Omani friends or followers' developed a 'high regard' for him.[21] Another Salalah Kathiri, Abdel Aziz al-Rawas, was appointed Dhufar Information Officer and later became Information Minister. The absorption of such figures helped consolidate the Sultan's patronage networks within Salalah.

Of course, not all Salalah Kathiris joined the Sultanate. Indeed, urban members of the tribe continued to hold high rank within PFLOAG. Moreover, Jabali Kathiris were still largely committed to the revolution and were represented on the General Command. This was generally the case with all the tribes on the Jabal, until the suppression of the September 12 mutiny. Following that incident, things began to change, with Anglo-Sultanic forces receiving their first batch of defectors. The revolutionaries

---

[19] MEC-Paxton, 'August Notes', 1970.
[20] MEC-Paxton, 'PDO Monthly Report', September 1970.
[21] MEC-Paxton, 9/6, 'PDO Assessments', 1983.

gave them the dishonourable title *mutasakiteen* (the fallen ones); the British named them Surrendered Enemy Personnel (SEP). Descending from the revolutionary highlands to the Sultanic plains, they were lavishly paid, clothed, armed, fed and organized into counter-revolutionary units—*Al-Firaq al-Wataniyya*, 'the National Brigades'—under the control of the British SAS.

The *firaq* cannot be simply brushed off as traitors and collaborators. What was once a clear fight for economic subsistence and anti-colonialism under Said, became far murkier under Qaboos. The foundations for a rentierist economy, whereby the ruler spent some of the oil rent on economic development, were laid right after the coup. Dhufaris who accepted Qaboos's absolute rule were promised immediate financial benefits, something that had been denied to them under his father and that could not be given to them by the impoverished revolution. As for the anti-colonial dimension, it was complicated by the new language and symbolism of the regime. Years later, revolutionary *autocritiques* analysed the success of this phenomenon in terms of the failure to instil adequate anti-colonial consciousness:

> Some fighters felt that their fiery arrow had hit the heart of their main enemy Said bin-Taimur, unaware of the fact that their real enemy was the British presence in Oman and that Said bin-Taimur was nothing more than one of Britain's stooges, replaced by the appointment of Qaboos as the new ruler over Oman.[22]

Undoubtedly, this voluntarist analysis helps to explain why some cadres left the struggle, while others continued to fight for many years. After all, it cannot be denied that the political character of the struggle was sharpened. However, the structural dimension must also be emphasized, the material lure of submission having been so great. Considering that giving up was more profitable and far less risky, it is quite remarkable that most Dhufari rifles were still shooting for PFLOAG. The distinct objective factors that enabled revolution—economic oppression and state weakness—were being overturned. But its subjective vehicle—anti-colonial republican mobilization—was becoming stronger. Accordingly, it took nearly six years for the Anglo-Sultanic order to get Dhufaris to fight on its side in Dhufar. It took another five years for the revolutionaries to leave Dhufar, and twenty-four years for the Front to draw its last breath.

This is not to belittle the scale of the internal split in the post-mutiny atmosphere. There was only one defection in September 1970 but, by

[22] Al-Jabha Al-Shabiya, *Aqlamat al-Harb fi Oman wa Maseer al-Firaq al-Qabalya fi Thufar*, n.d., *c.*1975, p.12.

March 1971, there had been over one hundred.[23] These defectors could not be mobilized solely in the name of the Sultan. There needed to be a broader ideological cover under which they would fight and a universal ideal for which they would sacrifice. The British found religion to be convenient in this respect, recasting the nature of the struggle from one between an imperial power and a local anti-colonial movement to one between Islam and international communism.[24] The 'religious approach' against communist parties had long been pursued by the British, and was used in Iraq as early as 1949.[25] Drawing on this tradition, Anglo-Sultanic forces presented the *firaq* as conducting a jihad against foreign-backed infidels, giving them the names of Muslim conquerors and anti-colonial heroes.

This was counterpoised with PFLOAG practice. Following its radicalization, The Front had adopted names that emphasized the internationalism of struggle, and belonged to the community of global revolutions against colonialism and capitalism. This emphasis upon the universal modern march of progress under the red flag was countered with Islamocentrism. Accordingly, Anglo-Sultanic forces renamed the Red Line, the 'Green Line' and the first *firqa* was christened Firqat Salah al-Din. Subsequent ones were called after Abu Bakr, Omar and Tariq bin Ziyad. Added to these were Arab nationalist names such as Firqat al-'Uruba. Even Gamal Abdel Nasser, Britain's foremost historic enemy in the region, had a *firqa* named after him, supervised and trained by the SAS. The *firaq*, in the words of Colonel Oldman, were 'supported, organised and controlled by SAF through the SAS', and this made it all the more crucial that they have a native ideological base from which to discredit the revolutionaries.[26]

The initial pattern of defection was collective. Firqat Salah al-Din was initially founded by Ma'shanis under the firm leadership of Salim bin-Mubarak and 28 of his followers.[27] It subsequently absorbed defectors from another major eastern Qarra tribe, al-'Amri, as well as some from the Central tribe, Bait Qatan. 'Amri defectors joined, under the command of former PFLOAG military leader Ahmad al-'Amri (Qartoob), after the SAF and the *firqa* successfully captured the eastern town of Sadh on

---

[23] John Graham, *Ponder Anew: Reflections on the Twentieth Century*, Staplehurst, Kent: Spellmount Publishers, 1999, p.346.

[24] For an extensive theoretical treatment of processes of 'recasting', see Frank Furedi, *Colonial Wars and the Politics of Third World Nationalism*, London: I.B. Tauris, 1994.

[25] Hanna Batatu, *The Old Social Classes and the Revolutionary Movements of Iraq*, London: Saqi, 2004, p.694.

[26] FCO 8/1667, 'The Dhofar Rebellion—An Evaluation by the Defence Secretary of the Sultanate of Oman, Colonel HRD Oldman', 13 September 1971.

[27] MEC-Graham, 'Operation Storm Fortnightly Report', 5 May 1971.

23 February 1971.[28] Qartoob was followed by 35 men and this helped bolster the *firqa*'s prestige. However, problems began to arise following the death of Salim bin-Mubarak in March, following a heart attack.

The situation exploded on 22 April 1971 when the *firqa* members were reported as 'being difficult about their future employment'. Their SAS commander flew over to Mirbat and heard their grievances. He reported that 'in the main the problem was a tribal one with the original SEPs, who are Maasheni and the Qartoob group who are Al Umr [*sic*] declining to serve together'. The following day, the *firqa* was paraded and the British commander issued an order for the men who still insisted on their position to hand in their weapons and be discharged. The majority of the *firqa*, 60 out of 88 men, did so.[29] Although they were rebuked for their action, they managed to achieve their objective: the British were now convinced that the *firqas* should be tribally organized.[30]

By the beginning of May 1971, the SAS arrived at six general conclusions concerning the *firaq*. In their estimation, these forces were 'essential' for victory. However, they were 'selfish and self-interested; unstable and grasping' and were expected to pose a long-term 'political problem for the Sultan and his government'. In the light of inter-tribal clashes, they had to be reorganized on a 'one tribe, one firqa' basis, their 'strength limited to about 70 men'. To attain 'discipline and pride' they needed to be uniformly dressed and armed. Furthermore, 'close personal relations' had to be maintained between them and their SAS leaders. Above all, they had to be kept 'busy' and watched 'with suspicion'.[31]

The Ma'shanis were now enrolled in Firqat Khalid bin al-Walid; the Al-Kathir in Firqat Al-Nasr; the Qatn and the Central Area tribes in Firqat Salah al-Din; the Al-Amr in the Amri *firqa*; the Sudh tribes in Firqat Gamal Abdel Nasser; the Western Area tribes in Firqat Tariq bin Ziyad; and so on. This had decisive effects on the local social structure, contributing substantially to the re-tribalization of Dhufar. It also allowed for the reintroduction of a tribal elite class. Within tribes, individual *firqa* commanders gained in strength. Between tribes, the old powerful houses such as the Ma'shani, Qatn, and the Amri regained ascendance *vis-à-vis* such disadvantaged social groups as the Khuddam, Daifs and Shi'hris. The latter groups had assumed leading positions in the revolution but they were re-marginalized within the newly emerging mode of social organization.

[28] J.E. Peterson, *Oman's Insurgencies: The Sultanate's Struggle For Supremacy*, London: Saqi Books, 2007, p.257.
[29] MEC-Graham, 'Firqa Salahadin-Discipline', 27 April 1971.
[30] 'MEC-Graham, 'Operation Storm Fortnightly Report', 5 May 1971.
[31] Graham Diaries, 5 May 1971.

British officers clearly did not trust their *firaq* subalterns, not least due to their resistance to the established order of discipline and punishment. This continued to be the case throughout most of the war. A turning point, however, was a meeting designed to chastise the *firaq* leaders at the highest level possible. On 27 December 1973, the Sultan addressed a threatening speech to these leaders, voicing his 'displeasure of their apparent lack of initiative, lack of information on enemy movements, discipline and unwillingness to come to grips with the enemy'. He then 'promised rewards to those who were loyal and penalties to those whom he considered two faced or idle', and gave leaders a commission for good service. Prior to the meeting, 'the Firqat leaders were disarmed and entered in an uncooperative mood'. However, after listening to threats of 'dire consequences should they be found wanting or disloyal', they were 'obviously shaken' and at the end of the Sultan's talk they sat 'bolt upright in their chairs like chastened children. They all pledged their loyalty.'[32]

In spite of the fact that their performance varied over the course of the early 1970s, the value of these former revolutionaries was understood at the highest levels from the very beginning. Colonel Oldman emphasized that 'it was on the Firqats who knew the country and who had a better motivation than many of the Northern Omanis serving with the SAF that defeat or victory would probably ultimately depend'.[33] In the same vein, he noted that 'only [through] success by the Firqat...can a true counter-revolution against communism be created'.[34] The *firaq* fulfilled several essential functions: they provided indispensable intelligence on revolutionary movements, locations, supply-lines and strategies; they acted as 'flying fingers' for the SOAF, guiding pilots as to the settlements they should strike; they contributed to the poisoning of revolutionary water sources; and they engaged the revolutionaries in major battles. Above all, they acted as an engine of revolutionary division, fighting over the allegiance of their own tribal members. On the Jabal, a 'with us' or 'against us' approach began to be taken by both *firaq* members and revolutionaries.

One of the litmus tests for the allegiance of tribal settlements was the provision of supplies. Those that provided food to the revolutionaries were attacked by the *firaq* and the government. The same fate befell those who were hesitant in joining the *firaq*. This was a consistent pattern encouraged by Qaboos. For instance, on 10 June 1972, he ordered that the Amri tribe be bombed for being 'too dilatory' in joining the

---

[32] FCO 8/2022, 'Oman Intelligence Report No. 56', 16–29 December 1973.
[33] FCO 8/1667, 'Record of Meeting Held at British Residency Bahrain' 7 August 1971.
[34] FCO 8/1667. 'The Dhofar Rebellion—An Evaluation by Defence Secretary'.

government.[35] Likewise, the revolutionaries attacked those who joined the government or refused to sell them food. Essentially, they treated this question from the standpoint of a national wartime measure: any citizen who denied support and implicitly or explicitly engaged with the Anglo-Sultanic authorities could be charged with treason, which amounted to a death sentence. As evidenced by their extreme rarity in the pre-September 12 mutiny period, such disciplinary measures sanctioned by severe martial laws were oriented towards ensuring unity. However, they often produced an opposite effect, particularly in the socially torn Eastern Area.[36]

The *firaq* were especially detrimental to revolutionary morale because their very creation personalized the war. For British officers, Dhufaris belonged to a featureless mass that was attacked impersonally. The identity of fallen locals did not matter to the British, and the name of the killer did not concern the revolutionaries. In contrast, the *firaq* were not just fighting a multitude, they were targeting individuals who had a vivid presence in their lives. Previously, death simply signified enemy loss or heroic martyrdom. Now, the object of death lost its namelessness. It assumed a bodily shape and a voice; it acquired relatives, friends, memories and a chain of social signification.

By 1974, there were 1,000 *firaq* members and, by the end of the war in 1976, there were nearly 3,000. The most important effect of these paramilitary units was the transformation of the people of Dhufar from citizens, who fought voluntarily for a political structure that they created, to controllable subjects who fought for material reward under the command of a British officer, Lieutenant Colonel Colin McLean, and in the service of an absolute monarch.

Just as he had no interest in sharing power in the Omani north, the monarch wanted to be absolute in Dhufar. However, whereas the British were keen proponents and practitioners of absolutism in the north, they desired a more accommodating approach in Dhufar, so as to co-opt the revolutionaries. The hawkishness of the Sultan and his love of power prevented a settlement because, although the British controlled the application of government policy and shaped its course, they were uninterested in challenging the Sultan when it came to its general outlines. Like his father, Qaboos ruled Dhufar as a personal domain: 'The Sultan continues to consider Dhofar as a special area under his own partial control. This is not popular with either the Prime Minister or the Government.' The situation did not appeal to Dhufaris either: 'The concept of Dhofar as an

---

[35] Graham Diaries, 10 June 1972.
[36] MEC-Graham, Intelligence Summary 452, 4 December 1971.

Omani province complete with old-style Wali and Qadhi is of no interest to the Communists. It is also doubtful whether the soft-core and non-communists are attracted by anything less than some form of self-determination within the Oman.' Nevertheless, the Sultan was not prepared to allow anything beyond Dhufari attendance in 'some form of Municipal Council attached to the Province Administration'.[37]

Whereas the British understood that there was a serious possibility of defeat in Dhufar, the Sultan did not. It was accordingly 'impossible to persuade him to move to a more liberal attitude'. It was also difficult to convince him to pursue a peaceful solution, since he was just as committed to the total eradication of the revolutionaries as they were determined to destroy the monarchy. Indeed, martialist influences, centred on the glorification of war and chiselled into Qaboos during his Sandhurst days, were regularly in evidence. For instance, one of Brigadier Graham's entries read: 'The Sultan seems impatient for military action; also distinctly blood-thirsty. He has told me not to have any compunction about hurting civilians in enemy held areas.'[38] The thoughts of the Sultan were sometimes expressed in more violent forms, punctuated by an exaggerated sense of his power. In a 1974 discussion with Prime Minister Wilson, he noted that while 'it would not be impossible to exterminate everyone living in the difficult mountain areas concerned,' he 'had no desire to do this' and 'wished instead to persuade people to see reason.'[39]

Aware of the hawkishness of the Sultan, Oldman lamented that 'no thought or action has yet been taken to attempt a deal with the rebels'. He hoped that an indirect channel could be used to contact 'non-communist leader [Mohammad Ahmad] Ghassani', and suggested that the British government should pressure Qaboos to do so.[40] The latter was typically resistant to this. Qaboos's stance was mirrored on the revolutionary side by Abdel Aziz al-Qadi (Abu Adnan). Al-Qadi led a current of belief that refused any form of settlement, influenced by the history of the South Yemeni NLF in their road to independence. Challenging him was a school of thought represented by Ali Mohsen, member of the General Command and a seasoned revolutionary who had been active from the very beginning of mobilization in Kuwait in the 1950s. In 1971, al-Qadi managed to place Mohsen under arrest, and the latter's life was spared at the last minute due to South Yemeni intervention. Thereafter, Mohsen left for Aden and headed from there to Kuwait, where he spent

---

[37] FCO 8/1667, 'The Dhofar Rebellion—An Evaluation by the Defence Secretary.

[38] Graham Diaries, 12 February 1971.

[39] FCO 8/2244, 'Record of a Conversation between the Sultan of Oman and the Prime Minister', 1 November 1974.

[40] FCO 8/1667, 'The Dhofar Rebellion—An Evaluation by the Defence Secretary'.

the rest of his life.[41] The political importance of this event was enormous, signifying the decay of the principle of collective leadership that had long guided the revolution. Even the highest-ranking revolutionaries were now open to accusations of opportunism and revisionism.

Al-Qadi's radicalism can only be understood with reference to his previous experiences. Although his family originally came from Sur, he was born and raised in Dhufar, where his father was a judge under Said bin-Taimur. His insistence on civic politics and his trenchant hostility to tribalism were undoubtedly influenced by his upbringing in a relatively educated household, tribeless in a tribal environment. During the early 1960s al-Qadi lived in Kuwait, where he was an active member in the MAN, leaving it to go to Cairo in 1963.[42] During the following four years, he emerged as a prominent member of the Yemeni Students' Federation in Cairo, in which many Dhufari students were involved. He was also a leading participant in the political battles over the Omani Student Federation, effectively challenging its president and the future ruler of Sharjah, Sheikh Sultan al-Qasimi.[43] Following the Hamrin conference in 1968, he came back to Dhufar and became a member of the Economic Committee, commencing his work as a Commissar in the Revolution Camp. During this period, al-Qadi was heavily inspired by the Chinese and Vietnamese revolutionary experiences. Moreover, he had a Stalinist outlook, clearly evidenced in a pamphlet he wrote on classes in Dhufari society. This was complemented by Stalinist practices including the emphasis on 'correct analysis', and the suppression of other viewpoints.

Nevertheless, al-Qadi was immensely popular. Besides a level of education that was high by Dhufari standards, several factors gained him respect. One of his former comrades and ideological opponents, Abdel Rahman al-Nuaimi, notes:

> The Comrade was held in high esteem amongst the party members and the front leaders, due to his incorruptibility, humility, material austerity, and energetic follow-up with issues in Dhufar. The majority of cadres used to support him without any notable contestation.[44]

These traits catapulted him up the leadership ladder, with a push from his friend and fellow ideologue Abdel Fatah Ismail, PDRY's Chairman of the

---

[41] Interview D(iii).

[42] Ahmad Ubaidli, 'Ikhtilafat 'Hawl Jabhat Tahrir Thufar Wa Rabitat al-Talaba', *Al-Waqt*, 28 March 2010.

[43] See Sultan Al-Qasimi, *Sard al-That*, Beirut: Al-Mu'asasa Al-Arabiya lil Dirasat wal Nashr, 2009.

[44] Abdel Rahman Al-Nuaimi,. 'Tarteeb al Bait al Hizbi wal Jabhawi', *Al Dimuqrati*, Vol.33, May 2006.

Presidium of the Supreme People's Council.[45] By early 1971, al-Qadi had become the strongest figure in the revolution, surpassing Mohammad al-Ghassani. Other radical figures such as Ahmad Abdel Samad and Salim al-Ghassani also grew in stature and influence.

SPREADING THE FIGHT

With both sides uninterested in a settlement, radically clinging to their absolutist and republican visions, they had no choice but to escalate the conflict. The revolutionaries took the fight to the Omani north, the Sultanate heartland. The Sultanate took to the liberated areas in the Dhufari highlands. To understand the new revolutionary strategy, the Rakhyut and Ahlaish conferences of 1971 need to be examined. With the revolutionary ranks unified behind their 'no settlement' approach, PFLOAG began planning a national conference, the third since the 1965 and 1968 conferences of Wadhi Nahiz and Hamrin. The conference was convened in the village of Rakhyut in June 1971, attended by 75 delegates.

The notes of Ahmad Abdel-Samad, 1st Commissar of Ho Chi Minh unit and General Command member, were captured shortly after the conference, and these offer a detailed insight into its proceedings. After a minute of silence in honour of the martyrs, the General Command submitted a general report, the first since its election three years earlier. This was followed by an official military report, which contained strong criticism of the campaign:

> Positive and negative points were brought out, each area was taken separately and the revolutionary standard of each unit was discussed. The negative points were: a. Lack of discussion or debrief after any contact; b. Lack of ammunition conservation during contacts and, in particular when firing at aircraft; c. Adequate reconnaissance not carried out; d. Lack of appreciation of enemy forces; e. Lack of coordination between units; f. Criticism of the Military Committee; g. Lack of technical experience; h. Negative use of defence; i. The need for better deployment; j. Lack of material supplies...[46]

This criticism reflected a growing military reflectivity resulting from the return of cadres from training courses in China and the USSR. These cadres, along with former servicemen with the Trucial Oman Scouts, began to address some of the weaknesses even before the conference. Indeed, by mid-1971, performance had already progressed substantially:

---

[45] Interview F.
[46] MEC-Graham,. 'Captured Enemy Documents'.

Contacts...immediately pre- and post-monsoon showed a considerable improvement in enemy military skills and it was at this stage that some of the Front members who had received military training abroad returned to the jebel.[47]

The foremost symbolic testament to this improvement was the shooting down of a Strikemaster fighter jet in September 1971.[48] In spite of this, the situation became critical, especially in the Eastern Sector, where defection and the creation of *firaq* constituted a major threat. In order to counter the depletion of PLA ranks in that sector, it was decided to move units from the west.[49] By the end of the summer, fighters were effectively concentrated in the East, as can be seen in Appendix III.

Other military decisions took a longer time to implement. For instance, on the technical side, a decision was taken to improve such areas as weapons maintenance, and to build a workshop to that end. The lack of expertise in this field was affecting performance adversely and the situation was only improved after the arrival of a cadre from Bahrain, comrade Nouh, who began to operate in 1972.[50] Similarly, steps to further self-sufficiency were only seriously undertaken after the arrival of the Bahraini leader, Abdel Nabi al-'Ikri, an agricultural engineering graduate from the American University of Beirut, who initiated an experimental farm in Dhufar, training more than 150 farmers, distributing new crop seeds, and overseeing planting efforts.[51]

The Rakhyut Conference officially opened PFLOAG ranks to more Arab and international volunteers. Most importantly, it authorized the newly elected General Command to unite PFLOAG with other revolutionary groups in the Gulf, especially NDFLOAG. This was undertaken at the Unification Conference, which took place in December 1971 in the Ahlaish area. The unification of NDFLOAG and PFLOAG had long been on the agenda of both fronts. The Popular Revolutionary Movement (PRM), the mother group of NDFLOAG, had resolved to achieve this in its third conference, as part of a general effort to regulate its various branches.[52] This reflected a general consensus that intensifying operations in Oman proper would be the only way to relieve the pressure on the Dhufar front and achieve wider liberationist objectives. The idea was to

[47] MEC-Graham, 'Captured Enemy Documents'.
[48] MEC-Graham, 'Thirty Months: A Brief History of the SAF, April 1970–September 1972,' p.18.
[49] MEC-Graham, 'Captured Enemy Documents'.
[50] Interview G.
[51] Interview D(i).
[52] Abdel Rahman Al-Nuaimi, 'Tarjamat Qararat al-Mutamar al-Tawheedi', *Al-Wasat*, 1 January 2009.

merge the fronts and retain the PRM as the vanguard party that would lead them and that would include Marxist-oriented cadres from both groups. NDFLOAG was to become part of the only active, and the longest standing, armed struggle against the Sultanate, while PFLOAG was keen to benefit from NDFLOAG's ability to open another front in Oman proper. Besides its organizational significance, this merger allowed for a new conception of Oman as a united territory including Dhufar, a conception driven by the revolutionaries themselves, pushed from below. Ironically, this contrasted with the attitudes of Dhufaris fighting on the government side, who were still demanding some form of autonomy in spite of the Sultan's insistence on the indivisibility of their territory from Oman.

A thorough account of the Ahlaish proceedings is available based on a report given by one of its attendees, Said al-Mughtisi, after his arrest in December 1972, as well as reflections written by some Bahraini participants many years later. The National Front was represented by eight delegates. The Popular Front was represented by 13 delegates. PFLOAG dominated the agenda due to its relative strength in relation to NDFLOAG, which had been enormously weakened after the failed *foco* attempt of 1970. Nevertheless, there were major points of contention. The discussions were 'mainly an intellectual battle' between al-Qadi and al-Nuaimi, 'and occasionally' between Zahir al-Miyahi on the one hand and Ahmad Abdel Samad and Salim al-Ghassani on the other.

NDFLOAG was reproached for 'its mistake [the June 1970 plot] which had led to arrests being made and crippled its movement, and for its inability to continue the struggle'. In its turn, PFLOAG was criticized for not including the name Oman in its title, al-Miyahi insisting that 'Oman stretched from Dhofar to Abu Dhabi and had to be mentioned; Oman was one thing, the Arab Gulf another'. PFLOAG leaders responded by insisting that including the name Oman was succumbing to imperialist plans to divide the Gulf region. This dilemma was resolved by selecting a name that had already been proposed in the preparatory meetings: the Popular Front for the Liberation of Oman and the Arab Gulf (also PFLOAG), a slight modification to the older name, the Popular Front for the Liberation of the Occupied Arab Gulf. The new title affirmed both Omani specificity and the broader Gulf context. Moreover, it retained the word 'front', as the PFLOAG charter insisted that the phase it was confronting was that of National Democratic Liberation, requiring a broad popular alliance of classes: 'the people in its entirety must rise against imperialism and its reactionary allies: the Emirs, Sultans, feudalists and compradors. All classes—excepting the feudalists, compradors and all traitors—have a common interest in resisting these enemies, and must unite against them in one broad front.'[53] However, revolutionary theory diverged from praxis. PFLOAG was less of a front and more of an alliance of two groups, led by a single vanguard Marxist-Leninist party, the PRM. Even anti-imperialist organizations, such as the Arab Action Party, were excluded from it.[54]

Organizationally, it was agreed to divide PFLOAG's map of operations into five regions (*aqaleem*): the Southern Region (Dhufar); Northern Oman (including the UAE); Qatar; Bahrain; and Kuwait. The main focus of action was on opening a second front in Northern Oman. Accordingly, soon after the conference, Zahran al-Saremi, Mohammad Talib Al Bu Said and Saud al-Marzouqi travelled from Aden to Beirut with Qatari passports, and later headed to Dubai separately. They were joined in Dubai by Hilal Mufaragh, Batti Khalifah al-Hinai, and Zaher al-Miyahi. This core group of organizers entered Oman by different routes in February 1972, immediately beginning to recruit and instil enthusiasm for revolutionary action. Zaher was the foremost figure in this regard, playing 'a most important part both as an energetic organiser, a persuasive recruiter, and a procurer of arms'.[55]

For military purposes, Northern Oman was divided into the Central and Eastern Areas. The Central Area was organized in turn into four districts: Rostaq to Sib; Muscat to Sib; Fanjah and Sumail; and Izki to Bahlah, including Nizwa and al-Jabal al-Akhdar. The Eastern Area included three districts: Sur; Ja'lan; and Masirah. Executive, Military and Financial Committees were established in each area. In accordance with the old practices of the now dissolved Movement of Arab Nationalists (MAN), each district had cells and circles of supporters. Supporters were admitted as cell members only after they underwent six months of political education. In addition to the district cells, a special cell was established in the SAF organized by Lieutenant Hamid Majid al-Mukhaini and Lieutenant Khalfan Salim al-Wahaibi. The two officers recruited five other soldiers into the group. The latter were not informed of PFLOAG, but they were organizing against the government and the British-Baluch-Pakistani presence in the army.[56]

Noms de guerre were allocated to cadres, and recognition codes were used for dealings with contact men. For instance, cadres approaching Awadh al-Jabri, the PFLOAG contact man working in al-Rahma hospital

---

[53] Al-Jabha Al-Shabiya, 'Barnamej Al-Amal al-Watani Al-Dimuqrati' December, 1971, *Wathaiq al Nidal al Watani: 1965–1974*, Beirut: Dar Al-Tali'a, 1974.
[54] Interview F.
[55] MEC-Graham, 'PFLOAG Activities in Northern Oman', 20 July 1973.
[56] MEC-Graham, 'PFLOAG Activities in Northern Oman', 20 July 1973.

in Muscat, were required to ask, 'Has Bashir al-Aaraj had a heart operation?' Written communications were conducted by post or delivered by
hand. Postal letters were sent to a Muscat PO Box owned by al-Jabri or to
an address in Dubai. Codes were used in them as well. For instance 'to be
sick' referred to being arrested, and the word 'father' signified Zaher al-
Miyahi. PFLOAG pamphlets and publications were delivered by launch
via the South Yemeni embassy in Kuwait. Besides this help, South Yemen
also provided financial aid. The rest of the budget was covered by donations from revolutionary organizations and supporters abroad as well as
local fundraising. On the local level, members paid 10 per cent of their
salaries. The money was mainly used for incidental expenses and to pay
for the families of those who died during the June 1970 action.[57]

Between June and October 1972 meetings were held at cell, district
and area command levels and a Fundamental Conference of the Central Area was held on 2–3 June 1972. Out of these meetings, a programme of work was agreed upon in three stages: mobilization of the
masses; organization of the masses; and preparation for armed struggle.
By October 1972, the third stage was being pursued, training conducted and arms distributed in Sur, Rustaq and Sib. A few cadres had
prior training. Seven of them had reportedly received training in PFLP
camps in Jordan in 1970, under the auspices of their former organization, NDFLOAG. Other cadres had been trained in Iraq and some had
served in the Abu Dhabi Defence Force. Some may have also received
training in Fateh camps in Syria and Lebanon. More trained fighters
could have been brought in from abroad but logistical problems prevented this. For instance, there was an offer from Fateh to send Palestinian cadres to undertake military operations against the Jordanian
officers who were present in the Sultanate. Zaher al-Miyahi declined
this offer. Although he valued the importance of such an operation,
and emphasized that it was a PFLOAG priority, he noted that it would
be very difficult to 'bring in the comrades' and to arrange their 'entry,
concealment, and transport'.[58]

As for arms, a shipment of Chinese weapons was sent from al-Gheida in
PDRY to Sur in Oman aboard Al-Mansoor, a launch owned by PFLOAG.
The standard of the weapons was not entirely satisfactory, which drew
exaggerated complaints from Zaher, directed at the central committee in
Dhufar. For instance, whereas there was a large amount of slab explosives,
there were not enough detonators to explode them. Nevertheless, the

---

[57] MEC-Graham, 'PFLOAG Activities in Northern Oman', 20 July 1973.
[58] MEC-Graham, 'Letter Written by Zaher Ali Matar al Miyahi Dated 7 October
1972'.

weapons were just enough to start, and it was hoped that more would be gained from attacks against the SAF.[59]

Action was planned to begin on 1 January 1973 with the assassination of intelligence personnel identified by the SAF cell. Following this, groups would withdraw into fighting areas to which the SAF would be lured and ambushed. This plan was agreed with the lessons of the June 1970 action in mind: rather than attacking well-guarded SAF units, they were to be dragged into ambush ground of revolutionary choice. The location that the revolutionaries had best prepared for this was Wadi al-Jawabir, which was stocked with arms, rations, and medical supplies. It will never be known whether this new tactic could have succeeded. Certainly, the revolutionaries had a chance. This time, they were larger in size, far better led and organized and relatively well armed. For months, they were undetected, in spite of the fact that in 1972, 'the entire resources of the Northern Oman intelligence effort was [*sic*] directed to the search for indications of PFLOAG activity and cell formation'.[60] Although the objective conditions were significantly less conducive to revolutionary action than in June 1970, organization was far better in January 1973. Clearly, lessons had been learnt and experience gained. For months, the intelligence forces were misled into monitoring two launches, at a time when the revolutionaries had already smuggled their arms in a vessel completely unsuspected. This was the work of Zaher al-Miyahi. By now, he had revealed himself to have mastered his craft—able to operate cells, conduct conferences, and train cadres in a highly monitored area without a single leak.

Nevertheless, Zaher's vision was denied actual application. It took only one contretemps, a revolutionary defection, to turn the tables completely. In the summer of 1972, PFLOAG's General Command sent its information officer in Aden, Awadh Badr al-Shanfari, to Cairo. The plan was for him to surrender to Sultanate authorities, gain their trust, and then operate in Salalah. Awadh handed himself to the Sultanate Ambassador in Cairo, arriving in Muscat in September 1972. There, he decided to genuinely defect: 'Privately, and only to the present Director of Intelligence . . . [he] confessed that he had been sent by PFLOAG . . . to re-activate the cells in Salalah, this he did not want to do and he threw himself on the mercy of His Majesty Sultan Qaboos'. During his debrief, Awadh mentioned that a member of the ruling family, Mohammad Talib Al Bu Said, was operating as a PFLOAG organizer. Another defector, a young man who was brought to the capital for debriefing, spotted Mohammad Talib in Mutrah. He was duly arrested, after having his identity confirmed

[59] MEC-Graham, 'PFLOAG Activities in Northern Oman', 20 July 1973.
[60] MEC-Graham, 'PFLOAG Activities in Northern Oman', 20 July 1973.

by Awadh al-Shanfari. Initially, Mohammad resisted interrogation and did not confess to anything. He was then sent to Salalah for further interrogation, suspected of being involved in activities in Dhufar. There, he lost his nerve and 'stated that he was concerned with PFLOAG preparations in Northern Oman which were at a fairly advanced stage'. He was immediately returned back to Bait al-Falaj and revealed details about the organization and its members. Two days later, on 23 December 1972, the authorities launched Operation Jason, arresting 60 people. In the second phase of the operation, 22 more arrests were made. Eight female revolutionaries were arrested in the third and final phase, bringing the total to 90 arrests. A special interrogation centre was then set up in Sur during the first week of January 1973. Based on the interrogations, it was decided to prosecute 69 of the arrested for 'belonging to a Communist Organisation'. Eleven were eventually executed. Significantly, several revolutionaries managed to evade this fate, warned by Lieutenant Hamid Majid of the arrest of Mohammad Talib. Among them were three important leaders: Zaher al-Miyahi, Saud al-Marzuqi, and Abdullah al-Shammar.[61]

The revolutionaries were youthful, their average age being 28.5 years. By Omani standards, more than half were highly qualified and leading members of the community, while the rest represented the working and peasant classes (See Appendix III). Drawing on the work of James Scott, we may note that this remarkably broad composition reflects the fact that whereas the 'public transcript' in the Sultanate revolved around loyalism, there was a vigorously oppositional 'hidden transcript'.[62] Had PFLOAG been successful in bringing this hidden transcript to light, the potential for mass-mobilization would have been substantial. Indeed, the Sultanate intelligence noted that this 'was no haphazard affair planned and mounted by a small number of young men and women who were dissatisfied with the progress of their country...'. On the contrary, this was a relatively disciplined effort conducted by cadres of an organization 'dedicated to the overthrow of all traditional forms of Government in the whole of the Arabian Gulf'. Although PFLOAG failed this time, the Sultanate intelligence anticipated a comeback: 'Those who escaped arrest, Zaher Ali in particular... are certain to be planning their next assault'. These were now 'infinitely more experienced in revolutionary techniques. They will therefore be most careful in the selection training and indoctrination of their

---

[61] MEC-Graham, 'PFLOAG Activities in Northern Oman', 20 July 1973.
[62] For a detailed discussion of the 'hidden transcript' concept see J.C. Scott, *Domination and the Arts of Resistance: Hidden Transcripts*. New Haven and London: Yale University Press, 1990.

members, the organising of their new cells, the caching of their weapons and supplies, the picking of their targets, and, above all the choice of time to strike.'[63] Against these potential threats, British intelligence officers remained vigilant.

The revolutionary focus on opening a second front in the Omani north was mirrored by the Anglo-Sultanic attempt to achieve a permanent foot-hold in the liberated areas. By the end of the 1971 monsoon, Anglo-Sultanic forces had developed their capacity substantially in eight principal ways: 300 former revolutionaries and returned exiles were now organized into five *firaq*; SAS elite forces had arrived; the raising of the fourth SAF battalion (the Jebel Regiment) was completed; an Armoured Car Squadron had been acquired; the command and logistical structures were improved; the Dhufar Gendarmerie and the 'Askar forces were enlarged with 450 additional Baluchi soldiers recruited for the defence of Salalah plain; static defences on the plain were boosted; and the SOAF was substantially expanded.[64]

With these reinforcements, paid for by a defence budget that drained 40 per cent of the Sultanate income, the SAF endeavoured to impose Sultanic sovereignty on the Eastern coast. To that end, the SAF and the SAS captured the coastal village of Sadh, consolidated the defence of Taqa and Mirbat towns, and took over Aroot in the far West so as to block supplies to the East. Moreover, the SAS established Civil Action Teams to provide the bare minimum of development required to gain local allegiance to the person of the Sultan. This, however, was not enough. In September 1971, Colonel Oldman assessed the situation as follows:

> SAF have put the Salalah and coastal plain to the east further out of reach of physical capture by the rebels, but has not been able to remove the threat of long range harassing fire to the vulnerable points on the plain. No part of the enemy environment [the Jabal] has been seized and cleared, and the physical liquidation of the Communist hard core has not been solved. The stalemate has been maintained with the edge in favour of SAF. This edge would rapidly disappear with rebel reinforcement in men, weapons and efficiency. The most feared reinforcement would be the arrival of the 120 millimetre rocket launcher capable of hitting the VPs [vital positions] on the plain from within the jebel environment.[65]

The challenge was to establish positions in the highlands, and this began with the launch of Operation Jaguar. The location of that operation was initially planned to be the Central Area, where the supply routes could be

---

[63] MEC-Graham, 'PFLOAG Activities in Northern Oman', 20 July 1973.
[64] FCO 8/1667, 'The Dhofar Rebellion—An Evaluation by the Defence Secretary'.
[65] FCO 8/1667, 'The Dhofar Rebellion—An Evaluation by the Defence Secretary'.

cut. However, the location was changed to the Eastern Area. This was motivated by a variety of factors:

> It was there that the anti-Marxist rising had taken place during the previous autumn [*sic*]; the greatest number of SEP's to date had come from that area; and it was the homeland of the strongest tribal firqas formed so far. Further, the local people had a particular bond with the Sultan through his Mother. The terrain also offered some important advantages: relatively little dense scrub, good fields of fire, observation over considerable distances and an abundance of sites for the speedy development of airstrips for SOAF's Skyvan and Caribou aircraft. Indeed the countryside was to remind one of Salisbury Plain at the end of a long dry summer.[66]

Under SAS command, Jaguar began on 2 October 1971 with the moving of 1,000 troops to the Jabal. By 11 October, 100 square kilometres of the Jabal had been 'cleared'. There were three options available to the revolutionaries in response: concentrating their forces further and attacking the new Anglo-Sultanic positions; splitting their forces into smaller units and initiating a series of small engagements; or temporarily withdrawing and waiting for the Anglo-Sultanic forces to move further west. From a tactical perspective, the latter two options were the correct ones, since the revolutionaries were facing an army with heavier weapons, greater numbers, and air cover. However, the revolutionaries chose to concentrate their forces in the East. This move illustrated one major weakness in the revolution: the lack of a highly trained strategic planning corps. Whatever its failures, the revolutionary concentration made it extremely difficult for Anglo-Sultanic forces to take over the area. Nevertheless, after fierce fighting, the Sultanate managed to achieve dominance, if not complete control over the Eastern Area. Achieving full control was dependent on receiving further aid from regional monarchic forces.

REGIONALIZING THE WAR

In the aftermath of the withdrawal from the Gulf, the presence of British troops in Oman was perceived as a necessary inconvenience. In the words of FCO Under-Secretary Anthony Parsons:

> It horrifies me...that we have quite so many British officers in the Sultan's forces. However, the problem is that they never get a breather in which they could set about Arabising without seriously damaging the efficiency of the

---

[66] MEC-Graham, 'Thirty Months: A Brief History of the SAF, April 1970–September 1972', p.22.

Forces as a whole. They are dealing with pretty jungly people whose loyalty is in inverse proportion to their level of education: hence potential officers are perhaps the least reliable people... To Arabise in the middle of the war would probably be fatal... The one thing we are keeping a very close eye on—an obsession of mine—is that we should not be sucked in any deeper: i.e. that we should not allow ourselves to be drawn into a mini-Vietnam.[67]

Yet, much greater intervention was required to win the war. The Sultanate did not have the soldiers or the weapons necessary to defeat the revolutionaries. This was in spite of the enormously rapid growth of its forces. In 1971, there were 5,096 soldiers led by 201 officers. By early 1975, there were 10,356 soldiers in the army, 216 in the Air Force, and 314 in the navy. Still, this was not enough to defeat the estimated 800 PLA members backed by a militia of 1,000. This was not just a question of numbers; it was also one of money. Enormous funds were diverted to defence and this was straining the economy. Moreover, defence spending never seemed to be enough. Although the oil revenues for 1972 only amounted to RO 51 million, the defence budget was RO 30 million.[68] This unhealthy diversion of funds crucial for development was unsustainable, rendering the unpopular war in Dhufar even more detestable. Enormous financial wastage ensured that even when Sultanate funds multiplied after the October 1973 oil boom, there was still not enough money to cover both development and defence. This is not to mention the private expenses of the Sultan, his advisers, and the 'Muscat Mafia'. The oil revenue for 1974 rose to RO 340 million, while the budget only showed an income of RO 240 million. As the British embassy noted, 'the balance must have gone on the Sultan's personal expenditure, certain schemes which are controlled by the Palace, investment overseas, and commissions'.[69] By 1975, corruption and reckless spending nearly brought the Sultanate to its knees.[70]

The only solution to these military and financial problems lay in approaching other dynastic states in the region. Thus, Anglo-Sultanic pleas were sent to Abu Dhabi, Jordan, Iran and Saudi Arabia. The struggle between revolution and absolutism was taking a more pronounced regional character, Dhufar offering the first serious test of the ability of these states in combating republicanism and enshrining monarchical sovereignty.

Abu Dhabi provided generously. In August 1971, it gave 1,000 Sura rockets, temporarily unavailable from the UK, as well as substantial

---

[67] FCO 8/2006, Anthony Parsons to Le Quesne, 12 February 1973.
[68] FCO 8/2006, 'Oman: Annual Review 1972', 7 January 1973.
[69] FCO 8/2454, 'Oman: Annual Review for 1974', 7 January 1975.
[70] FCO 8/2454, 'Then and Now', Diplomatic Report No. 159/75, 12 February 1975.

financial subsidies.[71] In 1972, it sent £3 million in civil aid. Further funds were transferred in 1973, including £1.7 million for a road connecting Taqa with Salalah.[72] The Sultan was unimpressed with this help, deciding that he was entitled to far greater aid from his wealthy neighbour.[73] By 1974, Abu Dhabi had increased its support, giving RO 10 million (US$28.95 million) for an air defence scheme, and providing a garrison for Sohar to free Sultanate troops for fighting in Dhufar.[74] In 1976, it gave Oman RO 15 million, with more funds promised for 1977. Still, the Sultan remained demonstrably cool to Sheikh Zayid. In spite of the fact that he was invited to make a state visit to Abu Dhabi in 1973, he failed to reciprocate the invitation until November 1976.[75]

Relations with Saudi Arabia were hardly warmer. King Faisal did not put his weight fully behind the Sultan. He had recognized Qaboos in December 1971, sent a military delegation to Oman in 1972, and promised aid, but his support was rather limited. The Saudis shared intelligence on the PDRY, sent some equipment, and provided diplomatic backing, but they did not give large-scale aid until 1975. This was a result of their suspicion of the British, whom they knew to control the Sultanate. The Saudi Minister of Defence, Prince Sultan, held the view that the British had to let go of their stranglehold over Oman. Similar views were held by Saudi Ambassador Salih al-Suqair.[76] The Saudis sought to fill the British gap with their own influence and to force the Sultan to yield to their line in return for support. This factor was augmented by territorial ambition. In March 1974, King Faisal stated that 'he wanted the question of the Omani/Saudi boundary out of the way for good and all'.[77] By the end of the year no progress had been achieved, and the Saudis were still indicating interest in the Buraimi villages.[78] This continued to be the case until Faisal's assassination. Thereafter, on 18–20 May 1975, the Saudis negotiated with the Omani Foreign Minister, Qais al-Zawawi, an agreement for $200 million in loans and grants, effectively saving the Omani economy from collapse. A significant percentage of this aid was allocated to a 'triangular operation' whereby British experts were given Saudi money to undertake a large-scale development programme oriented towards pacifying Dhufar. At one point, it was suggested that the transfer of funds

[71] Graham Diaries, 22 August 1971.
[72] FCO 8/2022, 'Intelligence Report no.54', 16 November–1 December 1973.
[73] FCO 8/2006, 'Oman: Annual Review 1972', 7 January 1973.
[74] FCO 8/2454, 'Oman: Annual Review for 1974', 7 January 1975.
[75] FCO 8/2944, 'Oman: Annual Review 1976', 1 January 1977.
[76] FCO 8/2010, 'Oman/Saudi Arabia/UK', 6 October 1973.
[77] FCO 8/2223, 'Oman/Saudi Border', 18 April 1974.
[78] FCO 8/2223, 'Buraimi', 16 December 1974.

would be conditional on opening a Saudi corridor through Omani territory to the Indian Ocean. The Sultanate adamantly resisted that condition and the money was eventually given unconditionally.[79]

Things ran smoother with King Hussein of Jordan. In the post-Black
September context, he was an isolated actor in search of a role. Conveniently,
the Gulf region was opening its doors to him, its rulers seeking 'safe' Arab
security expertize to gradually fill in the gaps left by the British withdrawal. Supporting them would not only secure him much-needed financial backing, but also a strengthened position in relation to the Americans
and the British, from whom he could request more arms and backing in
return for his services. For its part, Britain encouraged Gulf rulers to
approach Hussein, deeming him the ruler most compatible with its
regional policy in the Gulf. This was politically expedient and economically convenient. As one official noted: 'we are on something of a financial
hook in Jordan and it is very much in our interest that Jordan should
obtain financial aid...'.[80]

In December 1971, Qaboos wrote to Hussein, complaining of the
revolutionary threat he faced, and asking for support. In response, the
King promptly offered twelve 25-pounder guns, which were delivered a
few months later. On 8 March, he was formally informed that Britain
'welcomed Oman's looking to Jordan for assistance'. Subsequently, the
King gave Amer Khammash, his former Defence Minister and a retired
Lieutenant General, the responsibility for coordinating support to Oman.
After a thorough debrief in London, Khammash arrived in Muscat on
15 April 1972 and toured all operational areas. He met Colonel Oldman
and discussed with him the form of help required. Oldman asked for
non-combatant assistance from Jordan in the form of an engineering unit,
telling Khammash that 'he did not think he could administer a Jordanian
combat unit without more helicopters and fixed wing tactical support'.[81]
Upon his return to Amman, Khammash reported to King Hussein. The
King then contacted his financial and military patrons, the Americans,
enquiring as to whether they 'would object to his sending American
equipment to Oman and also if he could have replacement equipment in
Jordan'. The Americans gave him their blessing, on the condition that he
cooperated with King Faisal and the Shah. The latter was informed of this
new development during Nixon's visit to Tehran. Joseph Sisco, who had
accompanied the President, raised the matter with Foreign Minister

---

[79] FCO 8/2687, 'Oman: Annual Review 1975', 1 January 1976.
[80] FCO 8/1858, 'Jordanian Assistance to SAF', Gore-Booth (NED) to McGregor
(Arabian Department), 27 January 1972.
[81] FCO 8/1858, Defence Attaché (Muscat) to MOD, 3 May 1972.

Khalatbari, telling him that 'when King Hussein was in Washington he had expressed interest (to President Nixon and Officials) in Jordan becoming active in the Persian Gulf. The Americans had welcomed this kind of initiative and had expressed the hope that the Jordanians would consult closely with Iran and Saudi Arabia as their thinking developed'.[82]

At this stage, there was a need for Anglo-American discussion over policy. In particular, there needed to be a mechanism for dealing with the pro-western states in the region: Jordan; Saudi Arabia; and Iran. The Americans had suggested forming a committee in Amman, including the American and British ambassadors, to oversee support for Oman. The British managed to convince them of a less formal arrangement, whereby matters would be more loosely discussed, with Colonel Oldman in Muscat taking the lead role, and Iran, Jordan and Saudi Arabia liaising directly with him. To finalize matters and reach a synchronization of policy at the Gulf level, Anthony Parsons and PRH Wright were sent to Washington on 26 June 1972.[83]

Significantly, Parsons was told in a meeting with Sisco that the US was not interested in becoming directly involved in Oman.[84] Busy with other theatres of operation, they were willing to let Britain manage the details of policy in its former Gulf domains. When it came to the question of Dhufar, their knowledge was limited. This continued to be the case until the summer of 1973. The appointment of a new Under-Secretary of Defense, Bill Clements, aroused some interest in the unfolding events. Clements was a close friend of Nixon and an associate of ARAMCO. He had long been involved in Gulf affairs, and wanted an examination of the situation prior to giving evidence to a Defense Congressional Committee hearing. He dispatched Colonel George Maloney to Oman to assess the progress of the campaign. Maloney had been involved in counter-insurgency operations in Vietnam and was therefore deemed suitable to this task. He first passed by the Ministry of Defence in London in August, and then went to Dhufar. After an extensive visit, he reported his findings to the Sultan, the British, and the Americans. In spite of some criticisms, he was on the whole satisfied with the British performance and recommended that the US keep its distance.[85] The American role therefore remained indirect. Washington was happy to let London ride this tiger. Moreover, rather than instigating action on the part of its Iranian and Jordanian clients in the region, the US simply authorized their actions and supported them.

---

[82] FCO 8/1858, Murray (Tehran) to FCO, Tel. No.601, 22 June 1972.
[83] FCO 8/1858, Ramsrotham (Tehran) to FCO, 16 May 1972.
[84] FCO 8/2010, 'US Interest in the Arabian Peninsula', 18 October 1973.
[85] FCO 8/2010, 'US Interest in the Arabian Peninsula', 18 October 1973.

Having secured American backing in 1972, Jordan began to be more involved in Oman. On the personal level, Qaboos and Hussein developed close relations. They exchanged several visits and there was even talk during 1972—never amounting to action—of marrying the King's daughter, Aliya, to the Sultan.[86] At the military level, intelligence officers and military trainers continued to be loaned to the Sultanate, Omani air force and army personnel received training in Jordan, and the Sixth Squadron of the Jordanian Royal Engineers was sent to Oman in 1974. In December of that year, the Sultanate requested a Special Forces battalion to guard the Salalah–Midway road, having failed to convince Sheikh Zayid to send troops for that purpose.[87] King Hussein responded favourably to that request, dispatching the 91st Parachutist Battalion of the Special Forces in March 1975. The following month, Jordan gave Oman 31 old Hawker Hunter planes. These were inadequate for such a major front as the Arab–Israeli one, but were immensely useful for a state like the Sultanate, which was fighting revolutionaries who did not have an air force. Initially, Jordan had sought to sell the planes to Rhodesia but UK pressure prevented this from happening.[88] An alternative possibility for the planes, a purchase from Iraq, was frustrated by the Shah. Eventually, it was decided to offer them as a 'gift' to Oman, on the tacit understanding that compensation would be given to Jordan in return.

From the very beginning, Hussein was uneasy about the progress of the war. Since early March 1975, he had been complaining to the British and the Americans about Omani financial wastage. The King could not understand why the Omani defence budget of £180 million, 'was necessary for an army of only divisional size, i.e. twice as much as he spends on an army six times as large'.[89] More significantly, he was under the impression—inaccurate it must be emphasized—that the war was being unnecessarily prolonged by British contract officers. As far as he was concerned, they were too slow in promoting Omani officers. This reminded him of the critical situation prevailing in Jordan prior to the Arabization of the army in 1956.[90]

Hussein's critical views were reinforced during a visit to his troops on 20 April 1975.[91] The Jordanian Commander, Tahseen Shurdum, had

[86] FCO 8/2006, 'Oman: Annual Review 1972', 7 January 1973.
[87] FCO 8/2219, Muscat to FCO, Tel. No.435, 14 December 1974.
[88] FCO 8/2480, Private Secretary to 10 Downing Street, 'King Hussein', draft letter, 9 May 1975. For the full details and documentation of Jordanian sales to South Africa and Rhodesia, see FCO 36/1702.
[89] FCO 8/2480, 'Steering Brief', 9 May 1975.
[90] FCO/2459, Balfour-Paul to Weir, 4 March 1975.
[91] FCO/2459, 'King Hussein's Current Preoccupations', Balfour-Paul (Amman) to Urwick (NENAD), 25 April 1975.

given him a long list of complaints. These reflected the location of the 91st Battalion, mistrust and coordination failures, as well as tactical disagreements. Geographically, the Battalion was stationed on the Midway Road, an area that had already been rendered quiet. Having not seen much action, the troops were under the impression that the revolutionary presence was weak and that the British were prolonging the war to serve their own agenda. On the level of coordination, there had been a few incidents. The most serious occurred when the battery at Salalah mistakenly fired into the Jordanian area. As for the tactical differences, they revealed themselves when the Jordanian forces baptized their operations by burning a village house, an action that was not in line with SAF's new strategy of winning 'hearts and minds' in the areas under their control (though of course not in revolutionary-held areas). The 91st Battalion failed to comply with the SAF policy, relations between them and the highlanders becoming negative to the extent that they became embroiled in a tribal blood feud with the Bait Qatan tribe.[92]

The Jordanians' heavy-handed approach was unsurprising, considering the fact that their most recent experience was Black September, during which they had participated in inflicting thousands of Palestinian civilian casualties in a matter of weeks. Nevertheless, Shurdum's complaints were viewed as 'malicious' by CSAF Perkins, and he wrote a letter to the Jordanian Chief of Staff, Zaid bin-Shakir, to defend himself:

> I know that Tahseen feels we should be more ruthless with those of the local population who may not be particularly cooperative, but he is judging the problem against the background of guerrilla activities elsewhere. The Jebalis here were not well treated under the previous regime, hence their suspicion. We need to win them to our side...and I am sure you would agree that we shall not do that by burning them out. I am conscious that...91 Battalion are in an area with but little immediate warlike activity...I have been tempted...to use the 91 Battalion for some other more aggressive task...but I would then be open to the charge of using allied troops for the toughest tasks.[93]

The uneasy relations between the SAF and the 91st Battalion upset the Jordanians. So did the severe criticism that they received from a number of quarters. The dispatch of their forces elicited from the revolutionaries a communiqué:

> To our brothers in the Jordanian Arab Armed Forces...By the memory of the fragrant blood that has been spilled in Dhufar to defend Qaboos instead

---

[92] Interview F.
[93] FCO 8/2480, Letter from Major General K Perkins to Lieutenant General Sharif Zaid bin Shaker, 26 April 1975.

of being spilled in the land of beloved Palestine, we call upon you to end this crime, and to announce your opinion honestly and to refuse to serve in Oman...We swear that our hearts get torn when we hear of the death of any of you; and he who dies fighting his brothers does not die a martyr. However, for us there is no choice but to fight for our freedom, and to sacrifice for our land, honour, and national independence...[94]

Statements from the Jordanian opposition expressed similar sentiments. An official joint declaration was issued by the Federation of Jordanian Trade Unions, the General Union of Jordanian Students, the Bathists, the Communists and various other groups. The Jordanian people, it stated, condemned sending soldiers to Dhufar

> ...just as it had previously condemned preventing our army from fighting in the October war...The real role for our sons and brothers in our Arab Jordanian Army is not fighting their brothers in Oman, but combating the enemies of the Arab nation and supporting the Arab revolution, not undermining it.[95]

An intensive media campaign was also initiated by the Palestinian resistance, in solidarity with the 'revolutionary heroes' in Oman and against the monarchical regime.[96] This had an immediate impact on Hussein, who had informed the American Ambassador in Amman that 'one of the things that particularly disturbed him had been rumours of heavy casualties among Jordanian troops in Oman, which had been exploited against him by the Palestinians'.[97] A widely quoted article released by the Palestinian News Agency (WAFA) reported that 35 bodies had arrived in Jordan in April 1975 and that this had caused demonstrations in the city of Salt. The report added that an increasing number of officers were declaring their refusal to serve in Oman, leading to the arrest of 30 officers in May, including three Colonels.[98] This report may have been inaccurate in portraying officers as 'refusing to serve', considering that all the Special Forces deployed to Oman were volunteers, attracted by the significantly higher rates of pay there. Nevertheless, the report was not without substance. Indeed, in a conversation with the Shah, King Hussein 'talked about the effect in Jordan of the casualties sustained by the Jordanian forces,

---

[94] Al Jabha al-Shabiya, .''Ila Kul Jamaheerina al-'Arabiya fil Urdun.', June 1975, Private Papers of Abdel Rahman al-Nuaimi.

[95] 'Ghalayan Sha'abi Fil Urdun', *Al-Hadaf,* 28/3/1975.

[96] See, for example, 'Ma'ziq al-Nitham al-Urduni fi Oman', *Filasteen al-Thawra,* 18/5/1975; 'Mazoufat Insihab al-Quwat al-Urduniya', *al-Hurriya,* 18/8/1975.

[97] FCO 8/2459, Amman to FCO, Tel. No.044, 21 March 1975.

[98] Palestinian News Agency (WAFA), 'Itiqalat wa Tasreehat Wasi'a Fil Jaysh al-Urduni'. 9/5/1975.

particularly the fact that the rebels had decapitated the dead and that it had therefore been impossible to show the bodies to the relatives on their return to Jordan'.[99]

Internal and Palestinian factors coincided with Syrian protests at King Hussein's relocation of his troops from the main theatre of confrontation with Israel. In the context of exceptionally close Jordanian–Syrian relations during this period, this final source of pressure proved decisive. Hussein's decision to remove the troops was taken after a visit to Dhufar on 14–16 July, and announced on 19 July.[100] The official explanation was that the 'troops were sent to Oman for six months, and that period has now finished'.[101] Although the Sultan requested that 'if the Jordanian battalion could not stay at least one company should remain', the King felt unable to oblige.[102] Hussein made this decision after being assured that the Iranians would supply more troops. As far as he was concerned, the Jordanians had played their role, giving Arab cover to an essentially Anglo-Iranian campaign. Having achieved this political goal, they now had to secure their home front. Prime Minister Zaid al-Rifai noted that 'participation in this remote and little understood war had been highly unpopular with the Jordanian public...The order for withdrawal had been enthusiastically welcomed here.'[103]

Having failed to convince King Hussein to change his mind, the Sultan asked the FCO to intervene. However, his request was sent out belatedly, six weeks after the King had announced his decision, rendering British efforts futile.[104] The 91st Battalion was withdrawn in September 1975, without prejudice to the presence of the Jordanian Engineering Squadron, Training Officers, and pilots. Muscat eventually came to terms with Amman's decision. The CSAF noted that although 'the Jordanian troops were good, it had been difficult to employ them effectively'.[105]

Unlike Jordan, Iran had no qualms about providing unconditional support. The Iranian role has often been discussed with reference to the Nixon doctrine. Such an analysis is partial, however, explaining Iran's practices solely in terms of its position as a sub-imperial power in the service of American policy. A more comprehensive analysis would have to take account of Iran fitting the pattern of 'middle power' politics, pursuing

[99] FCO 8/2459, Parsons (Tehran) to FCO, 8 September 1975.
[100] FCO 8/2459, 'Jordanian Troops in Oman', Tel. No.201, Amman to FCO, 21 July 1975.
[101] 'Abu Zaid: Kul al-Quwat al-Urduniya Satus'hab', *Al-Siyassa*, 2/8/1975.
[102] FCO/2459, FCO to Muscat, Tel. No.284. 24 July 1975.
[103] FCO 8/2459, Amman to FCO, 31 August 1975.
[104] FCO/2459, FCO to Amman, Tel. No.322, 28 August 1975.
[105] FCO 8/2459, 'Jordanian Forces in Oman', Muscat to FCO, 31 August 1975.

a proactive as opposed to a reactive stance. The 'drive towards regional supremacy', a classic practice of emerging middle powers, was a central feature of Iranian policy in the 1970s and it is in this context that its intervention in Oman can best be understood.[106] Although Iranian policy fit perfectly with American imperialism and its Nixon doctrine, it had motivations independent of it.

Iranian involvement initially took the form of gifting military supplies to the Sultanate. On 15 August 1972, Operation Caviar was launched, providing the SAF with sixty C130 sorties loaded with arms, including three Augusta-Bell 206 Helicopters.[107] Three other helicopters with their crews were also provided. The Shah had offered to send combat troops as early as 1971, but the Sultanate was hesitant about accepting them so soon after the Iranian occupation of the three UAE islands. In August 1972, the Shah once again suggested sending a Special Forces unit. London advised Colonel Oldman of the political difficulties that could arise from this but the FCO decided not to block acceptance of the offer. This was in spite of protestations from Sheikh Zayid, who had warned both Tehran and London of the grave political implications. The British logic was that they had long been urging neighbouring states to assist the Sultan, and that military needs trumped diplomatic difficulties:

> Foreign military assistance may make the campaign in Dhofar a less tidy business to run, but it is in our interests, and the Sultan's, that Oman should receive such help as she can from her friends.[108]

By October 1972, the offer of a 150-strong Special Forces unit had been accepted, but the utmost level of secrecy was kept, as there was a need for non-Arab countries to 'be circumspect in their involvement for the good of Oman as well as their own position in the Arab world'.[109] Moreover, there was a conscious effort to dissociate Britain from the endeavour. A guidance telegram was issued to various British Heads of Mission on how to manage this issue. Douglas-Home stated that British missions should maintain the line that 'it is for the Sultan to decide how best to defend his country'.[110]

In late 1973, a larger Imperial Iranian Battle Group of 1,500 men was sent to Dhufar. Their mission was to open the strategic 'red line', the road

---

[106] A. Ehteshami and R. Hinnebusch, *Syria and Iran: Middle Powers in a Penetrated Regional System*, London: Routledge, 1997, p.28.
[107] Graham Diaries, 3–15 August 1972.
[108] FCO 8/1859, 'Iranian Special Forces in Oman', 10 October 1972.
[109] FCO 8/2006, Defence Attaché Muscat, 'Annual Report for 1972', 14 January 1973.
[110] FCO 8/1859, Douglas-Home to Henderson (Doha), 27 October 1972.

linking Midway base (Thamrit) with Salalah. On 20 December 1973, they attacked from both north and south, supported by enormous fire power. After heavy fighting, they managed to control the road, which had been effectively held by the revolutionaries since 1969. Having succeeded in their mission after heavy fighting, they remained to protect the road until October 1974:

> The Iranians protected themselves with vigour and without subtlety. Night after night...thousands of rounds were blazed off into the blue. They seldom, if ever, hit anyone, but the enemy, and indeed everyone else, were forced to keep their distance.[111]

Besides this role, the Iranians agreed in 1974 to provide air defences in Dhufar against potential attacks from South Yemen and an enormous 4,000-metre runway was built in Midway (Thamrit) to house their F5s and Phantoms.[112]

The presence of Iranian troops caused enormous tensions with several Arab states, and generated a South Yemeni diplomatic offensive against the Sultanate. With the 1974 Arab summit in Rabat approaching, the Sultanate needed to take a defensive line. On 10 October 1974, this led Deputy Foreign Minister Qais al-Zawawi to make a statement to the heads of diplomatic missions and the press in Muscat, announcing Iranian withdrawal.[113]

Zawawi's statement caused a diplomatic crisis with Tehran. For, although Iran was withdrawing its battle group, the Sultanate had requested from it a much larger Imperial Task Force to conduct operations in the Western Area. On 23 October, the Shah personally protested the statement to the British Ambassador in Tehran, who summarized the conversation as follows:

> [the Shah said that he] had no intention of staying where he was not wanted...The Sultan should make clear to him, the Shah, that he still wanted Iranian troops in Oman. He had not done so. He had sent a slightly equivocal message...He thought that Qabus's Tactics would be to leave matters vague until after the Arab summit so that he could assure his Arab brothers in Rabat that the Iranians were withdrawing. This would be typically Arab. But the Shah would not send the Brigade for which the Sultan and General

[111] John Akehurst, *We Won a War: The Campaign in Oman, 1965–1975*, Wiltshire: Michael Russell, 1982, p.22.

[112] FCO 8/2454, 'Then and Now', Diplomatic Report No. 159/75, 12 February 1975. The Iranian role has been explored in much greater detail in a book based on the archives in Tehran; see Mohammad Jafar Jamangar, *Bahran Zufar va Regime Pahlavi*, Tehran: Mouassasat, 2004.

[113] FCO 8/2219, 'Text of Statement', 15 October 1974.

Creasy had asked for to carry out the new operation until Qabus made it plain that Iranian troops were still required.

Parsons concluded by noting that the 'Shah was at his most school masterly and Qabus will have to state his position unequivocally in order to get things back on an even keel'.[114] Over the following weeks, Qaboos and the British tirelessly worked to placate the Iranian monarch. Having made his point and initiated this 'storm in a teacup', the Shah had an obvious interest in commencing operations, and in mid-November, he informed the British that he would send a large taskforce as a 'birthday present' to Qaboos, the Sultan's birthday falling on 18 November.[115] Accordingly, by December 1974, 95 C130 sorties had been sent, accompanying 2,900 Iranian troops.

As a result of Iranian intervention, revolutionary parties on both sides of the Gulf commenced cooperation. In an internal circular issued in January 1974, PFLOAG announced to its cadres that it stood

> ...with the Iranian national democratic liberation movement in one trench against Iranian reaction and American imperialism. The latter wants to entrench nationalist hatred between the Iranian and Arab peoples, so that it can undermine them both, at a time when the Arab and Iranian reactionaries stand together...[116]

Close relations were established with the Tudeh party, Mujahedin-e Khalq, and Feda'i Khalq. The last named sent a few cadres to fight in Dhufar.[117] Additionally, at least two of the teachers in the Revolution School belonged to that group.[118]

Beside these Iranian parties, the Shah's intervention brought two important states to the revolutionary side: Libya and Iraq. Initially, Libya was sympathetic to Qaboos, who had visited that country in December 1972 and appealed to Qaddafi's anti-communist position, seeking any support available against PFLOAG. Qaddafi promised to help, sending to Muscat a military delegation of four officers led by Lieutenant Colonel Hamid Bilqasim on 10 January 1973.[119]

However, upon learning of Iranian intervention, Qaddafi completely changed his position. Two PFLOAG figures, Said al-Ghassani

---

[114] FCO 8/2219, 'Parsons to FCO', 24 October 1974.
[115] FCO 8/2219, Tehran Tel. No.466, 15 November 1974.
[116] Al-Jabha al-Shabiya,. 'Ta'mim Dhakili' No.13, 23 January 1974. (unpublished).
[117] Al-Ikri, *Al-Tanthimat al-Yassariya fil Jazeera wal Khaleej al 'Arabi*, p.126.
[118] Interview H.
[119] Riyad El-Rayyes, 'Hikayat al-Sultan wal 'Aqeed wal Malik', *Al-Nahar*, 7 March 1975.

and Mohammad Salih, were already in contact with Libya, and as a result of their efforts, Qaddafi sent an investigatory delegation headed by Mohammad al-Qashat. The delegation walked 100 kilometres from the South Yemeni border to the Western sector, where they spent three days. They met with PFLOAG leader Mohammad al-Ghassani, inspected the terrain, and witnessed prayers in the Liberated Areas, something that debunked the notion of revolutionaries being infidel atheists. Following their visit, a PFLOAG representative office was opened in Tripoli by Said al-Ghassani, and the revolutionaries began to receive support from Libya, which continued well into the mid-1980s.[120]

Besides relatively large financial donations, Libya provided medium and light weapons. It also gave diplomatic backing. On 28 February 1975, Qaddafi published a letter to Qaboos, beginning with a reminder of the positive disposition that the Libyan leader initially had towards him: 'you know how optimistic we were after you overthrew your father under the pretext that he was a reactionary and a collaborator, and that we intended to help you on the basis that you were a revolutionary young man'. Qaddafi followed this opening by emphasizing the Libyan position:

> We were hoping that we could reach an internal Arab solution...but we were shocked to find that you ignored your Arab brothers and sought help from foreign states, and you took the issue away from us and placed it in the hands of the King of the Persians. We were baffled as to how you could allow yourself to violate the dignity of your people and the honour of your nation to commit an act so stupid as to allow foreign regular armies to occupy Muscat first and then Dhufar second so that they could finally take over the southern part of the Arabian Peninsula as a whole.

Accordingly, Qaboos was asked to alter his policies, or otherwise face the threat of war:

> We call upon you for the last time to order the immediate withdrawal of foreign troops. Should they refuse your request then you should inform us so that we could fight them along your side. If you do not do this, then we warn you of a war in which you would be on the side of the invading foreigners, while we stand on the opposing column with our Arab people there. I have told you about this many times in the past without announcing or publicising it, so that I could protect you from scandal. However, you have scandalised yourself with your own hands and the presence of thousands of Iranian soldiers gives you no scope for saving face...We are now warning you and taking pity on you at the same time. Our warning comes because

---

[120] Interview F.

you have committed a grave sin, and our pity is there because you face the fate of a leper mule.[121]

Like Libya, Iraq had originally attempted to establish relations with the Sultanate. In 1972, it sent an ambassador to Muscat, but he was informed that he was unwelcome.[122] Still, Iraqi policy remained cautious. This was evidenced by the stance of its delegation during a conference in Moscow on 25–31 October 1973. A PFLOAG internal circular noted that:

> The position of the Iraqi delegation was good, as it expressed its willingness to support and present our cause. However, the delegation clearly stated that Iraq was unwilling to mention Iran by name and to expose its role. It justified this by noting that the Arab nation was confronting a fateful battle and that Iraq itself had sacrificed many things in order to neutralise Iran.[123]

Iraqi support became much more significant in 1974, largely due to the desire to counter Iranian intervention. Higher-level contacts were established with Palestinian help. PFLOAG enlisted the good offices of Naji Alloush, a prominent leader and intellectual who had split from Fateh and had strong connections in Baghdad. Alloush was happy to oblige and the road was paved for an official PFLOAG visit to Baghdad in 1974. The delegation had a highly successful meeting with Vice-President Saddam Hussein, who had by now secured his position as 'the dominant figure' in Iraq.[124] Although his support for the revolutionaries was clearly connected to his conflict with Iran, he nevertheless expressed himself in the language of solidarity:

> Saddam held our requests in his hand and said: 'our people in Iraq cannot be full while our people in Dhufar are hungry'. He then asked: 'where are you going?' They answered: 'to Libya and Algeria'. So he said: 'By the time you get back to Aden, you will find the weapons there'. And so it was.[125]

Besides sending these weapons, Iraq began to finance the revolutionaries, reportedly sending them 100,000–120,000 Iraqi dinars every year.[126] Iraq continued to support the revolutionaries until 1982. That year the Front's Baghdad office was closed due to its refusal to support the war with Iran, which it saw as part and parcel of the American policy of 'creating regional wars and unnecessary conflicts that occupy and drain the parties opposed

---

[121] Wakalat al-Anba'a al-Libya, 28 February 1975.
[122] FCO 8/2006, 'Oman: Annual Review 1972', 7 January 1973.
[123] 'Ta'mim Dakhili Nisf-Shahri li A'daa al-Jabha al-Sha'biyya', n.d., *c.* November 1973 (unpublished).
[124] Charles Tripp, *A History of Iraq*, Second Edition, Cambridge: CUP, 2000, p.215.
[125] Interview F.
[126] Al-Amri, *Thufar*, p.216.

to Israel, and cause the sort of unrest that is conducive to American military plans for the region'.[127]

Following the Iranian intervention, the Arabic press vastly increased its coverage of Oman. This greater popular interest coincided with discussions at the official Arab level. During the Arab League Council meeting on 25–28 March 1974, the question of Iranian intervention was deliberated, and the North Yemeni delegate, Abdullah al-Asnaj, suggested forming an official Investigative Committee to examine the situation. This led to the passing of Resolution 61, which laid the official basis for the creation of a commission comprised of seven members.

The members of the Commission were: Secretary General Mahmoud Riad; Egypt; Tunisia; Libya; Algeria; Syria; and Kuwait. The Commission held its first meeting in the headquarters of the Arab League on 21 April 1974. South Yemen and PFLOAG insisted that it must visit the liberated areas. While Libya pushed for this, Sultanate allies within the Commission (the Secretary General, Egypt and Tunisia) ensured that a visit never took place. Finally, the Commission held its last meeting on 19 May 1975. Its delegates issued the following recommendations: Arab collective action to pressure foreign troops to leave Oman; the dispatch of an Arab observer force to the area; the need for an Arab framework to specify the parties to the conflict; the commencement of negotiations with the parties specified under the supervision of the Arab League.[128] There were no specific steps attached to these recommendations. In a special internal circular, the revolutionaries mocked this outcome with reference to the Arab proverb: 'After a hard labour, the mountain gave birth to a mouse'.[129]

FROM PFLOAG TO PFLO

Even before the Commission commenced its work, the Front was suspicious of it. In an internal circular to its members, it described the context of mediation efforts as the post-October 1973 war 'reactionary spread'. Accordingly, the Front emphasized that

> All comrades must arm themselves with greater awareness of the following issues: Mediation is a liquidationist project. It was initiated by North Yemen and received the blessing of the reactionary regimes (it is quite possible that

---

[127] Al-Jabha Al-Shabiya, *Al Barnamij al-Siyassi*, Aden: Da'irat al-I'lam wal Di'aya wal Tahreed, 1982, p.29.

[128] Jam'iat al-Duwal al-Arabiya, Al-Amana al-'Ama, 'Taqrir Lajnat Janub Oman', 15 August 1975.

[129] 'Ta'mim Dakhili Haam ila Kafat A'daa al-Jabha', August 1975 (unpublished).

Saudi Arabia is behind it). This liquidationist project has two elements: a) It aims to peacefully terminate the revolution. b) In case we do not adopt a new tactic it aims to tighten the Arab siege on the revolution, and to characterise it as the cause of all problems, an obstacle in the face of Arab solutions, and outside of the Arab Front!

Nevertheless, there was a need for engaging Arab diplomacy and the Front indicated to its cadres its intention to revise its entire strategy:

> Our strategy 'from Dhufar to Kuwait' requires reconsideration in our coming conference, so that we can arrive at political decisions that are suitable for the new circumstances prevailing in the Arab Gulf following the artificial independence of its states. These decisions must also reflect the graveness of the situation and Iranian intervention in the 'Sultanate of Oman', and make use of all the contradictions in the Gulf region to isolate the regime from its other reactionary allies. This would allow us to win the great round in Muscat. For, victory in Muscat will constitute a great leap for the progressive Arab revolution as a whole and will propel our position in the entirety of the Arab Gulf region.[130]

The last point was the most important. Ever since they joined the Movement of Arab Nationalists in the fifties, revolutionary cadres saw their task as liberating the entirety of the Arab Gulf. The shift towards a more limited notion of a struggle over Oman had huge implications. This new vision must again be viewed in its wider regional context. The idea of stagism—focusing on the possible rather than the desirable—was making its presence felt in the various revolutionary theatres. For instance, one of PFLOAG's sister groups, the Popular Democratic Front for the Liberation of Palesine (PDFLP), was pushing for its implementation in Palestine during this time.

More locally, PFLOAG's non-Omani Gulf cadres—Bahrainis, Kuwaitis and Emiratis—were pushing for change.[131] They first suggested the idea of localizing the strategy of struggle in an internal PRM circular issued in 1972. This circular, coming from the vanguard party leading PFLOAG, caused confusion within the rank and file, which had long been mobilized under the slogan of regional unity. Nevertheless, the full-scale Iranian offensives of 1973 and 1974 convinced the leadership of the need for change. First, the regional revolutionary horizon was narrowed by the arrival of the new player. Secondly, a local strategy was likely to aid in encouraging regional states to delegitimize and isolate Qaboos in the light of his dealings with the Shah.

---

[130] Al-Jabha Al-Shabiya, 'Ta'mim Dakhili Hawla al-Wasata Ma'a al-Khawana fi Muscat', n.d., *c.* April 1974 (unpublished).
[131] Al-Ikri, *Al-Tanthimat al-Yassariya fil Jazeera wal Khaleej al 'Arabi*, p.121.

As a result, the leadership began to prepare its cadres for a shift in strategy to be undertaken in the Second National Conference for PFLOAG. An internal circular was distributed before the conference that gave a succinct analytical overview of the general regional situation, concluding that the PFLOAG local branches 'have reached a degree of maturity and ability to conduct tasks on the local level, and they are therefore able now to confront the political reality within each political entity'.[132] Within the conference, delegates were agreed on the need for a revised organizational formula, but the discussions focused on the relations between the new organizations within each country. Abdel Aziz al-Qadi, the Secretary General of the Dhufar branch of the PRM, wanted to keep the PRM as the vanguard leadership of all the newly independent organizations. Abdel Rahman al-Nuaimi, Abdel Nabi al-'Ikri, and Zaher al-Miyahi objected to this.[133]

On 5 July, the decisions of the Second Conference were announced: organizational independence within each political entity; the operation of the Omani cadres in PFLOAG to be in one united group; emphasis on maintaining regional cooperation between the various newly created local groups.[134] Thus, the Popular Front for the Liberation of Oman and the Arab Gulf ceased to exist. This marked the historic demise of the last Gulf-wide political organization. In its place, there came to be two main organizations: the Popular Front in Bahrain and the Popular Front for the Liberation of Oman (PFLO). PFLO's creation led to the anchoring of the 'Omanization' of the struggle, a process which had begun with the Ahlaish conference of 1971, but had now developed fully. Although it had a majority Dhufari composition, PFLO's cadres referred to themselves as Omanis. Oman as a whole was treated as one national entity. Although its borders did not correspond to the Sultanate borders, since PFLO considered the UAE territories to be part of Oman, this remained a significant development. Whereas the Sultan imposed Omani 'unity from above', the revolutionaries organized for 'unity from below'. Interestingly, at this stage, some of the Dhufaris working for the Sultan continued to harbour a separatist agenda, while the revolutionaries officially boasted a unitarian platform that saw Dhufar as an integral part of Oman. Ironically, however, the increased focus on Oman corresponded with a reduced capacity for operating in the north. The last major

---

[132] Al-Jabha Al-Shabiya, 'Hawl al-Khat al-Siyasi wa Istratijiyyatina al-Nidaliyya', July 1974 (unpublished).

[133] Al-Ikri, *Al-Tanthimat al-Yassariya fil Jazeera wal Khaleej al 'Arabi*, p.122.

[134] Al-Jabha Al-Shabiya, 'Ta'mim Hawl al-Mu'tamar al-Thani Lil-Jabha al-Sha'biyya', n.d. (unpublished).

revolutionary operation conducted there took place in the Hazm area on 29 October 1974. Zaher al-Miyahi, Saud al-Marzugi and two other revolutionaries were intercepted at a road block as they were driving a Sharjah registered Land Rover filled with weapons and explosives. After a firefight, Zaher was killed and Saud was injured and arrested along with his other comrades. They were later executed by the Sultanate authorities.[135] Thus ended the saga of the most ardent revolutionary figures of Northern Oman.

In spite of this painful blow, the PFLO continued. Besides narrowing its vision from a regional to a national one, it also adopted a more flexible political line that attempted to address some of the local criticism that had been voiced against it. This was a continuation of the 'moderating policies' undertaken since 1972. On 15 August 1972, Popular Councils were established in each area, to increase local participation in decision-making. Each council included 7–11 members, representing the citizens, the popular militia, and the PLA. The majority of seats were reserved for the citizens, and elections were held in the various districts to fill them.[136] This reflected a process of ideological appraisal that entailed shifting the emphasis from the social struggle to the national one, so as to create the 'broad national front' required for the national liberation phase of struggle. To this end, concessions were given to non-communist cadres. For instance, in November 1972, revolutionary units were renamed after Omani fighters: Ho Chi Minh (West), the Central, and Lenin (East) units respectively became Shaheed Said Giah, Ali Masoud, and Said Addhahab units.[137]

PFLO's new internal regulations explicitly stated that 'any member who mocks religions, attacks the traditions of the people that are not harmful to the revolution, or flirts with women will be subject to serious disciplinary measures...'.[138] Such a regulation came out of the need to counter government and *firaq* characterizations of the revolution as attempting to eradicate religion, undermine tradition, and violate female honour. Likewise, a tighter policy on executions was undertaken, emphasizing that treason sentences required 'thorough, detailed, and

[135] Al Jabha Al-Shabiya, 'Nabtha Saree'a Wa Mukhtasara 'An Masirat al-Thawra Al-Omaniyya', 1985 (unpublished); 'Oman: Annual Review 1974'.
[136] 'Al-Laiha al-Dhakiliya Lil Majalis al-Sha'abiya,' in Al-Jabha al-Shabiya Li Tahrir Oman wal Khaleej al-Arabi, *Wathaiq al-Ni'dal al-Wat'ani, 1965–1974*. Beirut: Dar Al-Tali'a, 1974, pp.94–7.
[137] FCO 8/2245, 'The Popular Front for the Liberation of Oman and the Arabian Gulf', IRD Report, July 1973.
[138] Al-Jabha Al-Shabiya, 'Al-Nitham al-Dhakili lil-Jabha al-Sha'biyya Li-Tahrir Oman', Article 49, 1974, private papers of Abdel Rahman al-Nuaimi.

extensive' investigation, higher leadership approval, and could be subject to reversal.[139]

Maoist views were generally on the retreat. In large part, this related to the shift in Beijing's position towards the struggle. In July 1972, a six-person senior PFLOAG delegation had visited China. It was led by the Chairman of the Central Committee, Ahmad Abdel Samad, and included executive committee members Abdullah Hafith and Amer Habkook. After twelve days of 'extremely deep' discussions, the delegation came to the conclusion that there was a fundamental shift in relations between China and revolutionary forces in the region.[140] At the time, China was becoming painfully aware of the fact that its own oil reserves could not satisfy its needs. Developing relations with the Gulf power brokers, including Iran, became essential. In June 1973, the Chinese Foreign Minister visited Tehran and announced that his country supported Iranian regional policy.

Chinese abandonment did not mean that the revolutionaries were left alone. Indeed, by 1973, they had managed to develop several regional and international connections. Links with the Palestinian Revolution were exceptionally close. Initially, the Front was closest to the Popular Democratic Front for the Liberation of Palestine (PDFLP). In the aftermath of the Rogers Initiative, and on the eve of Black September, Mohammad al-Ghassani held talks on PFLOAG and PDFLP cooperation, issuing a joint communiqué in August 1970.[141] Close relations were also established with the Popular Front for the Liberation of Palestine (PFLP). The PDFLP and the PFLP seconded several cadres to Dhufar, including several teachers and a physician, Dr Nazmi Khorshid (Marwan), who operated al-Shaheed Habkook hospital, established in November 1969.[142]

Relations also developed with Fateh, with the help of Abbas Zaki, Palestinian Ambassador and Dean of the Diplomatic Corps in Aden. In late 1971, Fateh officially invited PFLOAG to Beirut. In 1972 Fateh sent weapons, although they were light and old, and PFLOAG donated them to the Eritrean struggle.[143] More than its material value, Omani—Palestinian

---

[139] Al-Jabha Al-Shabiya, 'Al-Nitham al-Dhakili lil-Jabha al-Sha'biyya Li-Tahrir Oman', Article 55, 1974, private papers of Abdel Rahman al-Nuaimi.

[140] Interview F.

[141] 'Bayan Mushtarak', Aden, 19 August 1970 in Al-Jabha al-Shabiya Li Tahrir Oman wal Khaleej al-Arabi. *Wathaiq al-Ni'dal al-Wat'ani, 1965–1974*. Beirut: Dar Al-Tali'a, 1974, pp.98–104.

[142] Al-Jabha Al-Shabiya, 'Nabdha Saree'a Wa Mukhtasara 'An Masirat al-Thawra al-Omaniyya', 1985 (unpublished). Nazmi Khorshid, who was trained at Damascus University, was a founding cadre of the DFLP. See Qais Abdel Karim and Fahed Suleiman, *Al-Jabha al-Dimuqratya, al-Nasha'a wal Masar*, Beirut and Damascus: Dar al-Taqadum al-Arabi and al-Dar al-Wataniya al-Jadida, 2000, p.8.

[143] Interview F.

cooperation was significant for its symbolic weight. As was suggested in the previous chapter, Palestinian support carried prestige, and allowed the revolutionaries to claim the moral high ground over Qaboos in Arab popular circles. The legacy of this can still be found in such cultural locations as Muthafar al-Nuwab's 'Oh My Killer', one of the most famous poems in modern Arab literature. Nuwab, who had visited Dhufar, linked the Sultanate acts there with Black September, Qaboos with Hussein. Like Nuwab and other Arab intellectuals of his generation, PFLOAG saw its revolution as being inherently tied to the Palestinian one. In fact, it conceived of itself as opening a second front against imperialism, the sponsor of Zionism.

Although less significant for the Omanis than Palestine, Vietnam was another grand struggle with which PFLOAG was linked. Dhufar was often dubbed 'Britain's Vietnam', and the revolutionaries regularly referred to Vietnam in their communiqués and internal discussions. At the invitation of PFLOAG, the National Liberation Front for South Vietnam sent a delegation to the Liberated Areas, led by Executive Committee member Pho Dung-Jiang. The delegation toured the territory between 16 and 26 September 1972, and issued a joint communiqué with PFLOAG.[144] This Far Eastern connection was more than matched by Cuba. After a visit from a Cuban delegation, a much-needed medical team of six doctors was dispatched, allowing for the establishment of the Martyr Fatima Ghanana Hospital (named after a renowned female fighter) and the Omani Red Crescent on 26 July 1974.[145] The Cuban doctors operated just outside Dhufar on the PDRY border, and continued to provide essential treatment even after the end of the armed struggle.

The Palestinians, Vietnamese and Cubans raised morale and provided valuable assistance in a variety of fields, but the revolutionaries' main military backer after 1973 was the Soviet Union. Having been abandoned by China, PFLOAG began to approach the superpower more vigorously through the Embassy in Aden and the Afro-Asian Solidarity Committee in Moscow. The Soviets, concerned with the increasing Iranian role, provided training to a few dozen fighters and a wide range of light weapons, including Katyushas. They also granted a request for SAM 7 rockets to counter the huge number of Iranian helicopters and fighter jets that were operating in Dhufar. These weapons had an instantaneous effect, shooting

---

[144] Al-Jabha Al-Shabiya, 'Al-Bayan al-Mushtarak lil-Muhadathat bayna Wafd Jabhat al-Tahrir al-Watani li-Janub Vietnam wal-Jabha al-Sha'biyya', Dhufar, 26 September 1972, in *Wathaiq al-Ni'dal al-Wat'ani, 1965–974*, Beirut: Dar Al-Tali'a, 1974, pp.104–6.
[145] PFLO, 'Nabdha Saree'a Wa Mukhtasara 'An Masirat al-Thawra al-Omaniyya', 1985 (unpublished).

down a Strikemaster on 19 August 1975.[146] On the solidarity level, the Soviet Committees for Solidarity with the Revolution in Oman were formed on 26 October 1975, with branches in Moscow, Leningrad, Kiev, Astrakhan, Tashkent and Kharkov.[147]

GEOGRAPHICAL DIVISION

The PFLO's new line from 1974, and the increasing aid it was receiving, were not enough to counter the territorial expansion of absolutist control. Accordingly, the Dhufari highlands were transformed into a geographically divided space. This was just as crucial to the course of events as social division. On 19 July 1972, a major revolutionary attempt at countering this trend was launched. The plan was to take over the Fort of Mirbat through a full-scale offensive. The presence of British SAS troops in that position delayed the revolutionary offensive. By a twist of fate, the foggy monsoon skies cleared, allowing the SOAF to bomb the revolutionaries, inflicting severe casualties. As a result, 29 fighters were killed and 11 were captured, and the dead bodies were paraded in Salalah market, dealing a heavy blow to revolutionary morale.[148] Likewise, as was shown earlier, the 1972 revolutionary attempt at opening a second front in Northern Oman failed due to last minute intelligence. Both of these incidents were a significant victory for absolutism. However, the British were aware that these revolutionary reversals were not enough. In the words of PR Wright, head of the FCO's Middle East Department: 'The Sultan has had two considerable strokes of luck: the fortunate outcome of the Mirbat battle and the success of Operation Jason. But both were "damn close-run things," and I think... [it is] right to guard against over-optimism.'[149]

The regionalization of the war was the fundamental factor that impacted on revolutionary morale. The arrival of the Imperial Iranian Battle Group in December 1973 allowed for overwhelming the revolutionaries in the Central Area, who had been effectively blocking the Midway road since 1969. By October 1974, the road was completely controlled, and a huge step towards turning the central highlands into a divided geographical space had succeeded. The deployment of Jordanian Special Forces along

---

[146] FCO 8/2687, 'Oman: Annual Review 1975', 1 January 1976.
[147] 'Wathaiq al-Mu'tamar al-Ta'sisi Li-Lijan Munasarat al-Thawra fi-Oman Li-Omoum al-Ittihad al-Sovieti', Moscow, 26 October 1975 (unpublished).
[148] FCO 8/2006, 'Oman: Annual Review 1972', 7 January 1973.
[149] FCO 8/2006, PR Wright (FCO) to DF Hawley (Muscat), 23 January 1973.

the road on 27 February 1975 ensured that it remained pacified, and freed Anglo-Sultanic forces for operations in the Western Area, the remaining stronghold of the revolution. Even more significant in the Central Area was the role of the Jordanian Engineers Squadron. On 13 May 1974, it began building the 53-kilometre Hornbeam line, running from Mughsayl on the coast to the edges of the desert, completing it in August that year.[150] This line effectively developed an earlier installation, the Leopard line, a series of picquets guarded by patrols. These were now connected by a high fence of thick wire surrounded by anti-personnel mines, preventing revolutionary movements from the Western Area to the Centre and the East.[151]

Finally, the arrival of the 2,900-strong Imperial Iranian Task Force, and its backing by massive airpower in late 1974, allowed for the initiation of yet another stage of geographic division. The goal now was to divide the Western Area. The Force began its operations on 2 December 1974, aiming to clear a line from Iraq in the north to Rakhyut in the south and to establish another line of barbed wire, mines and patrols along that stretch. The Iranians suffered immense casualties in the process. 33 of their soldiers, including their commanding officer, were killed, and an equal number was injured. Anglo-Sultanic forces also suffered heavy blows, including the death of a battalion commander, Major Bradell-Smith, and the injury of another battalion commander, Mike Lobb. Nevertheless, the operation continued, its success guaranteed by numerical superiority, heavy firepower, and complete air dominance. It took the combined Anglo-Sultanic and Iranian force an entire month to take over Rakhyut, which had been the symbolic revolutionary capital since 1969 and which finally fell on 6 January 1975.[152]

At this stage the whole of Dhufar was ablaze, with three helicopters shot down in March and April and minor contacts occurring across the land, including a heavy battle with the revolutionary 9 June Brigade in the Central Area. Most of the heavy fighting took place in the west, however. The installation of the Damavand line in February coincided with Anglo-Sultanic focus on the most important revolutionary supply hub, the Shershiti cave complex. Attacks on this area were consistently repulsed, facing stiff resistance. However, the newly divided landscape made the revolutionary task much harder. The Iranians blocked access from the Western to the Central Area, while the Jordanians blocked access from Central to the Eastern Area. In the meantime, the western strongholds were

[150] FCO 8/2454, 'Oman: Annual Review for 1974', 7 January 1975.
[151] Akehurst, *We Won a War*, p.20.
[152] FCO 8/2687, 'Oman: Annual Review 1975', 1 January 1976.

increasingly besieged. The 600 or so remaining PLA men were facing a combined international force of 10,000 men (referred to since 1973 as the Dhufar Brigade). Whereas the revolutionaries were effectively imprisoned, the Dhufar Brigade could move at will with its helicopters and planes. The arrival of SAM 7s in August helped, but rockets were unavailable in great numbers. In total, 23 were fired in Dhufar, 3 of them hitting their target.[153] The real turning point came in mid-October, when the SAF occupied the coastline below Sarfait, thus blocking all revolutionary supply lines from South Yemen. By the end of the month, the main revolutionary local supply depot at the Shershetti Cave complex fell after a longstanding siege and a large-scale attack reinforced with the ex-Jordanian Hawker Hunters. Finally, on 1 December, the coastal village of Dhalkut fell, the last PFLO permanent position in Dhufar.[154]

The battles of 1975 proved to be the most intense of the war. Besieged fighters caught in a desperate situation sang the swan song of the revolution. All of them could have surrendered and received immense monetary gain and comfort, but they fought to the last breath. In the words of Major General John Akehurst, the Commander of the Dhufar Force, the fighters' 'bravery and skill against overwhelming odds earned our admiration and respect'.[155] His sentiment was shared by nearly all of the British officers who led the fight against the revolutionaries.

* * *

The final victory of absolutist monarchy in Dhufar was achieved by three means: civic disintegration, regional monarchical consolidation, and geographical division. These processes allowed the Anglo-Sultanic forces to take the battle to the revolutionary domains in the highlands. The revolutionaries responded by uniting their forces and attempting to open a front in Oman proper, thus exporting the battle to the territories dominated by the Sultanate. Abandoned by fortune on at least two pivotal occasions in 1972, their strategy did not succeed. Nevertheless, they remained a formidable force that still had a chance at a counter-offensive. Moreover, they were politically responsive, adjusting their discourse and slogans. It was the involvement of new regional forces that tipped the balance. By 1975, the combined impact of Iranian, Jordanian and Anglo-Sultanic forces—backed by generous funding from Saudi Arabia and Abu Dhabi—overwhelmed the revolutionaries. Thus the indigenous inhabitants were defeated on their own land by a foreign force seeking to determine who governed them. The land and the people were now divided, and the sovereignty of the absolute ruler prevailed.

---

[153] Akehurst, *We Won a War*, p.143.
[154] FCO 8/2687, 'Oman: Annual Review 1975', 1 January 1976.
[155] Akehurst, *We Won a War*, p.109.

These coalescing factors allowed Qaboos to announce victory against 'international communism' on 11 December 1975:

> Victory is the fruit of the sacrifice of our sons the soldiers and the National Firqas and all the friends who contributed and helped. It is a sacrifice in which they gave lives and offered them in a holy manner to save their homeland and sacrifice for their Islam, and save peace and security from the corruption of communism that calls for terror and decadence on earth.[156]

This contrasted with the statements of revolutionary leaders: 'the decision to end or not to end the revolution always remains in the hands of the people and not in the hands of invaders, ruling traitors and collaborators'.[157]

The PFLO formally withdrew its forces to South Yemen in January 1976.[158] Nevertheless, almost 120 revolutionaries remained in Dhufar, and PFLO shelling operations continued within the territory until 30 April 1976.[159] For years to come, hundreds of revolutionaries continued to live abroad. South Yemen, in particular, supported them faithfully and unconditionally. However, as the prospects of success were progressively diminishing, cadres began gradually to return to Oman and surrender. In spite of this process, PFLO continued to function, raising a new slogan: In the Path of Self-Reconstruction and Continuing the Revolutionary War. The idea was to rebuild the intellectual, political and military basis of struggle and to continue it.

Why did PFLO opposition to the absolutist regime continue? This question is pertinent, considering that economic development was rapidly commencing in Oman, and the Sultanate was generously rewarding surrender. Part of the answer may be found in a speech by Al-Qadi, a member of the PFLO Central Executive Committee:

> Fundamentally, our struggle is not just about economic development. We are principally strugglers for freedom and independence, fighting for the liberty of our Omani people...What is the point of all of these reforms if the people does not have a say in anything, even in the choice of its own rulers?...We do not reject schools, hospitals, wells, and mills. But we want that under a republican Oman, independent, democratic, progressive and

---

[156] Saltanat Oman, *Khutab wa Kalimat Hadrat Sahib al-Jalala Qaboos bin Said al-Mu'atham: 1970–2005*, Muscat: Wuzarat al-I'lam, 2005, pp.73–4.

[157] 'Kalimat al-Rafiq Abdel Aziz Abdel Rahman al-Qadi', 9 June 1977 in Al-Jabha Al-Shabiya, *Wathaiq al-Ihikra al-Thanya 'Ashara lil-Thawra al-Omaniyya*, Aden: Al-Lajna al-I'lamiya al-Markaziyya, 1977.

[158] Al Jabha Al-Shabiya, 'Nabtha Saree'a Wa Mukhtasara 'An Masirat al-Thawra Al-Omaniyya', 1985 (unpublished).

[159] Akehurst, *We Won a War*, p.176.

non-aligned…We are not children who would stop if Qaboos builds us a few hospitals, schools, a port and a television station. When a child cries, he is given a mint and goes quiet. But we are not children. We are genuine strugglers.[160]

Cross border operations therefore persisted, and a few cells remained within Dhufar until 1979. According to revolutionary records, the last operation occurred in the Eastern Area on 9 May 1979.[161] As for political organizing and civic mobilization, it continued in exile for many years, was frozen after the fall of the Soviet Union, and silently ended after the 1994 Yemeni civil war. That, however, is a different story.

---

[160] 'Kalimat al-Rafiq Abdel Aziz Abdel Rahman al-Qadi', 9 June 1977 in Al-Jabha Al-Shabiya, *Wathaiq al-Ihikra al-Thanya 'Ashara lil-Thawra al-Omaniyya*, Aden: Al-Lajna al-I'lamiya al-Markaziyya, 1977.

[161] Al Jabha Al-Shabiya, 'Nabtha Saree'a Wa Mukhtasara 'An Masirat al-Thawra Al-Omaniyya', 1985 (unpublished).

Conclusion

In his opening speech at the 1955 Afro-Asian Solidarity Conference, Nasser declared: 'I do not know of any other age in which the peoples of the world have agreed on one goal as they have done now: to unite in working towards achieving a truly international system. Shall we transform this dream into a genuine reality?'[1] That dream, and the effort to achieve it, was the essence of the 'Bandung spirit'. Through its trajectory and its framework, this book has sought to explore the nature of this spirit, and of its opponents. But rather than viewing it from the perspective of an established and sizeable centre, this spirit has been examined from a periphery of a periphery: Dhufar in the south of Oman. From this vantage point, the book has aimed to set out a narrative that is particular to the Omani and Arab context, while engaging with the broader analytical themes that pertain to the process of imperial sovereignty and its contestation.

In presenting this narrative, this book has pursued three aims: historical retrieval; revision; and contextualization. The purpose of retrieving the history of the revolutionaries in Dhufar was to shed light—as faithfully as possible—on their world. The approach was neither to judge nor romanticize, but to understand, appreciate, and analyse. History is regularly unkind to the defeated, the marginal, and the oppositional. This is even more the case when writing history becomes the suppression of an inconvenient past in the service of the present, or even the celebration of imperial deeds. In contrast to the practice of describing the revolutionaries from without, this book has attempted to offer a more persuasive account from within. It reads against the colonial archives and utilizes revolutionary documents, publications and interviews, in order to provide a sense of a rich and lost world of backgrounds, personalities, networks, ideologies, and practices.

A second aim was to revise the history of Oman. This was done by two means. First, state-centrism was challenged. Rather than reading Omani

---

[1] Gamal Abdel Nasser, 'Opening Speech at the Bandung Conference', 19 April 1955.

history as a self-contained story of the rulers and their economic, bureau-cratic, and military trajectories, this work has offered a narrative of con-testation, resistance, and struggle on the part of immensely vibrant popular movements. In their scope and persistence, these movements were unparalleled within their Gulf regional context, playing an essential and neglected role in shaping the economic, social and political history of Oman. Furthermore, this work offers a history concerned with political alternatives as well as realities. It presents absolutism as only one of several paths that Oman could have taken. It also explained its construction as an imperial project, thus re-emphasizing an under-emphasized link between colonialism and absolutism. Colonialism does not always lead to absolut-ism. But in some contexts, including the Omani one, absolutism could not arise without colonialism. Had it not been for direct British interven-tion, the Sultanate would not have been able to survive revolutionary movements, let alone achieve comprehensive political dominance.

Finally, this book has aimed at contextualization. Events that unfolded in Oman during the years 1965–1976 were embedded in the broader cur-rents of Arab and international history. The story of the struggle between imperial and popular sovereignties is fundamental to Arab and broader tricontinental histories during the period in question. In the case of Oman, the Sultanate was dependent on global networks of imperial and monarchical solidarity, while the revolution was strongly tied to transna-tional revolutionary networks and communities of revolution in the Arab world and beyond. Indeed, Dhufar offers a microcosm from which to illustrate the centrality of South–South connections in Arab political and intellectual history during the period concerned. It was precisely in these connections that the 'Bandung spirit' was alive, and it was through them that it spread, even to the most peripheral and impoverished corners of the world.

* * *

It remains to be said that this work was originally completed as a doctoral thesis on 9 June 2010, the 45th anniversary of the launch of the Dhufar revolution in Oman. Written some months before the 2011 Tunisian revolution and new era it heralded, it reflected the stark mood of the his-torical moment, underlined by the melancholic search for a revolutionary tradition that was nearly forgotten. Nevertheless, recent events have revealed the latent revolutionary forces in the region and the enduring relevance of the themes discussed here.

Revolutions, by their very nature, are forward-looking, emphasizing utter novelty and complete disjuncture with the past. This has certainly been the axiom upon which the revolutionary conceptual tradition was built, constructed in its modern form at least since 1789. So powerful was this act of separation that De Tocqueville could write that no nation 'has devoted more effort than the French in 1789 to distinguish, as it were, the two periods of their destiny, to create a gulf between what they had been up to that point, and what they sought to be from then on'.[2] In the Arab world today, as the revolutions and uprisings unfold, similar sharp distinctions are being drawn between what was, what is, and what is yet to come. Yet, if this work has shown anything, it is that the unfulfilled hopes of the past continue to persist. Indeed, the challenges that the Dhufar revolution confronted, external control and internal political and economic development, remain alive in the present. And just as was the case in the past, effective responses to these challenges can only be mounted in the context of a sweeping regional spirit that can raise localized discontent out of its isolation, opening the possibility of change in people's minds. In the past, this spirit was exemplified in Nasserism and the Bandung dream. Today, it is reflected in the demands of democratic movements. Whether these movements are to succeed or succumb to co-optation or counter-revolution is a matter yet to be determined.

In spite of the attempts of the Sultanic regime to isolate Oman from the vicissitudes of pan-Arab politics, the country has been far from immune to regional changes. On 19 February 2011, significant demonstrations began to take place, some of them violently suppressed. The regime responded a week later by using two of the major political tools that it had previously developed in the context of the Dhufar revolution. The first was diverting popular discontent, transferring the blame for political ills from the person of the Sultan to his ministers. The second was the absorption of political demands by means of economic spending. Cabinet changes and new social provisions were announced, including a major increase in student allowances, the 'establishment of an independent commission for the protection of consumers' and 'studying the possibility of forming co-operatives', and the enhancement of civil servants' retirement plans. By utilizing these means, the Sultanic regime has temporarily contained democratic movements. Yet—as has been shown again and again throughout the Arab world and elsewhere—as long as absolutism persists, the potential for future revolutionary action remains.

[2] Alexis De Tocqueville, *The Ancien Regime and the French Revolution*, London: Penguin, 2008, p.7.

Estimated Population of Dhufar according to the Sichel Censuses of 1977 and 1979

Area	Population	Percentage of Total Population
Al-Najd	4,578	6.7%
Coast	3,092	4.5%
West	2,217	3.3%
Jabal	16,470	24.5%
Marbat	3,000	4.5%
Salalah	35,000	52%
Total	67,200*	

* MEC-Sichel 1/1, 'Sultanate of Oman Demographic Survey: Dhofar 1977', p.36.

PFLOAG Executive, Political and Military Committee Chairs (September 1968–1971)

Name	Committee	Background
Mohammad Ahmad al-Ghassani	Executive	From a renowned Salalah merchant family. Worked in the 1950s in the Kuwaiti Petroleum Company. Founded Dhufari branch of the MAN. Elected to the DLF leadership in 1965. Although highly politicized with a strong Nasserist background, he was also an accommodating and ideologically flexible figure.
Salim Ahmad al-Ghassani (Talal Sa'ad)	Political	Mohammad al-Ghassani's brother. Studied in Kuwait under the sponsorship of the MAN's Arab Gulf Cultural Association. Attended Kuwait University as part of its first cohort, but dropped out in 1967 and returned to Dhufar to join the struggle. Associated with the Maoist line within PFLOAG.
Ali Mohsen	Military	From the Aa'l Hafeeth of the Aa'l Abu Bakr bin Salim, an Ashraf family. Joined the MAN in Kuwait. Split from the MAN in 1962 and helped found the Socialist Advance Party (SAP), but returned to the MAN after the SAP's dissolution in 1964. Studied in Kuwait under the sponsorship of the Arab Gulf Cultural Association. Was military commander of the Eastern Sector from 1968 to 1971. Known as a consensus figure.

SAF Intelligence Estimates of PLA Deployment in Dhufar (September 1971)*

Eastern Sector (Lenin Unit)		
Firqa	**Size**	**Location**
Al-Shaheed Madrum	70	West of Wadi Darbat
Al-Shuhadaa	70	East of Wadi Darbat
Firqat al-'Amal	25	n/a
Mobile Unit	70	Roving Commission
Total	235	
Central Sector		
Guevara	60	North
Tarish	100	South
Total	160	
Ho Chi Minh Sector (Al Mamar)		
Al-'Ula	50	n/a
Al-Shaheed Mohammad Mussalam	50	n/a
Al-Firqa Al-Thalitha	50	n/a
Total	150	
Western Sector		
Al-Shaheed Saif	50	n/a
Al-Shaheed Ahmad Aradha	50	n/a
Stalin	50	n/a
Total	150	
Grand Total	**695**	

* MEC-Graham, 'Intelligence Summary 448', 15 September 1971. This table does not include units stationed in PDRY, nor does it include estimates of the militia, which had a larger membership than the PLA.

SAF Intelligence Analysis of 69 of the Participants in the 1972/73 *Foco* Plot*

Employment	No.	Average	Education
White Collar Workers	13	23.7	Oman 2 Abroad 8 No Record 2
Teachers	14	24	Oman 3 Abroad 10 No Record 1
Self-employed	7	30.5	Oman 1 Abroad 1 No Record 5
Labourers/Agriculture	13	28	Oman 2 Abroad 1 No Record 5
Drivers	6	27	Oman 0 Abroad 1 No Record 5
Sheikhs	3	38	Oman 1 Abroad 0 No Record 2
Military	7	29	Oman 0 Abroad 3 No Record 4
Seamen	2	33.5	No Record
Wali	1	50	No Record
Student	1	19	Oman
Unemployed	2	30.5	Oman 1 No Record 1

* MEC-Graham, 'PFLOAG Activities in Northern Oman', 20 July 1973.

Major Qarra and Kathiri Tribes in Dhufar*

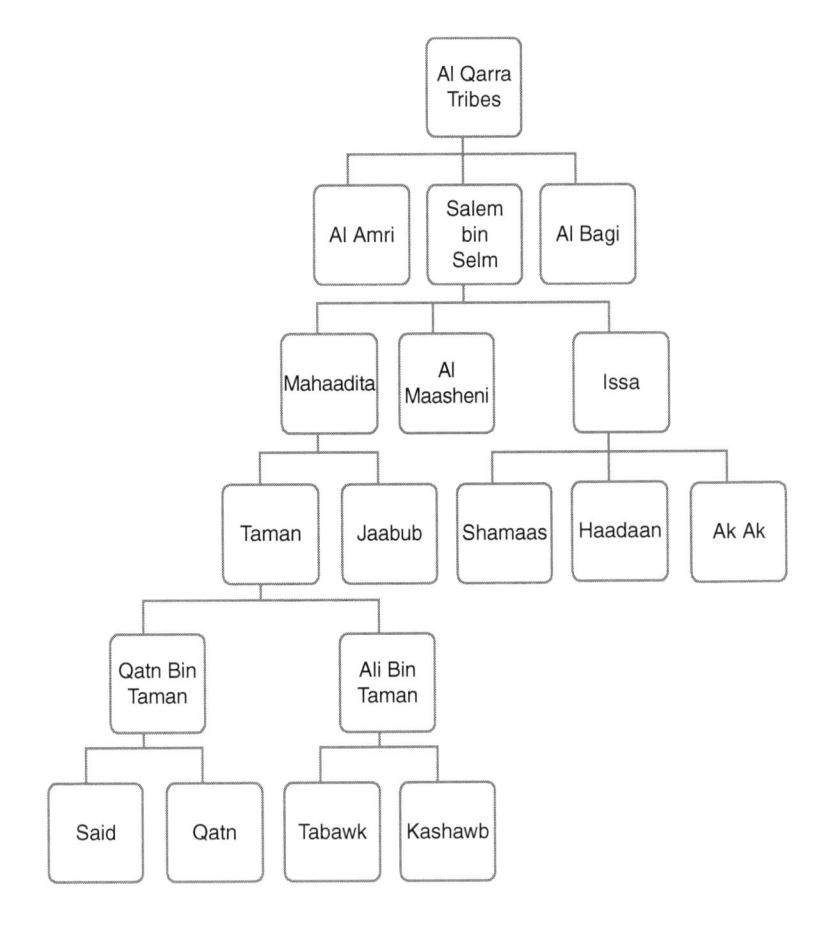

* MEC-Sichel 1/1, 'Sultanate of Oman Demographic Survey: Dhofar 1977', p.18.

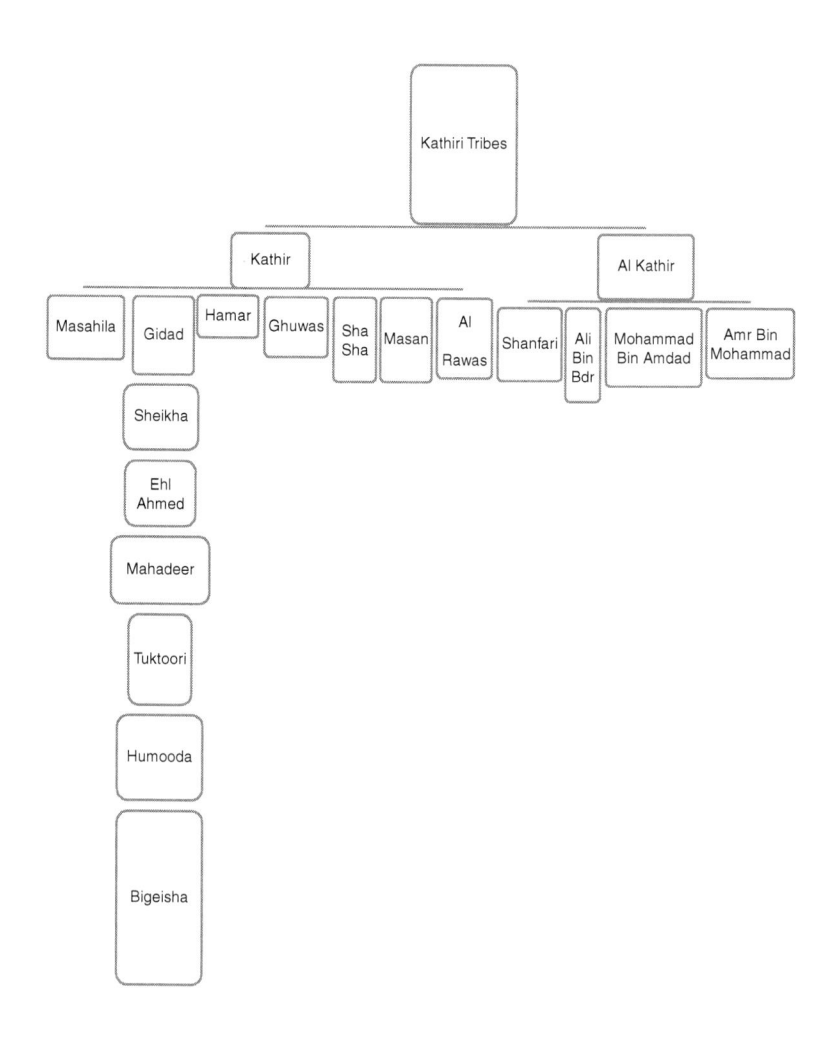

Bibliography

I PRIMARY SOURCES

(i) Archival Sources
The National Archives, United Kingdom

Records of the Cabinet (CAB).
Records of the Foreign and Commonwealth Office (FCO).
Records of the Foreign Office (FO).
Records of the Ministry of Defence (DEFE).
Records of the Treasury (T).
Records of the War Office (WO).

Oman Collections, Middle East Centre Archive, St Antony's College, Oxford

Ashley, Edward, GB 165–0399.
Graham, John David Carew, GB 165–0327.
Hawley, Sir Donald Frederick, GB 165–0338.
Hepworth, Charles, GB 165–0410.
Paxton, Jeremy F.E., GB 165–0331.
Peyton, William Durham, GB 165–0330.
Searle, Pauline, GB 165–0328.
Skeet, Ian, GB 165–0329.
Smiley, David, GB 165–0336.

Bodleian Library of Commonwealth and African Studies at Rhodes House, Oxford

Papers of the Anti-Slavery Society, MSS. Brit. Emp. s.16–24.

Liddell Hart Centre for Military Archives, King's College, London

Thwaites, Brigadier Peter Trevenan, GB 0099 KCLMA Thwaites.

Private Archives

Al-Nuaimi, Abdel Rahman, Private Document Archive, Manamah, Bahrain.
Barut, Muhammad Jamal, Private Document Archive, Aleppo, Syria.

(ii) Interviews
a) Mohsen Ibrahim (Member of the National Leadership of Movement of Arab Nationalists and founder of its Left Wing Current): Beirut, Lebanon, 16 December 2005.
b) Fawaz Trabulsi (A Leading Lebanese Leftist and Solidarity figure with the Revolution in Dhufar): Beirut, Lebanon, 16 December 2005.
c) Hisham al-Shihabi (Head of the Popular Front's clandestine organization in Bahrain in the early 1970s), Oxford, United Kingdom. 2 June 2006.

d) Abdel Nabi al-Ikri (one of the Founders of the PRM; PFLOAG Foreign Relations Representative; Delegate to the 1971 and 1974 Conferences). Interviewed on the following dates: i) Manamah, Bahrain, 4 August 2006; ii) Manamah, Bahrain, 27 August 2007; and iii) Oxford, United Kingdom, 27 July 2008.

e) Abdul Mun'im al-Shirawi (PFLOAG Political Commissar and first Arab solidarity fighter in Dhufar). Interviewed on the following dates: i) Manamah, Bahrain, 5 August 2006; and ii) Manamah, Bahrain, 24 August 2007.

f) A high-ranking Dhufari Leader who requested anonymity: MAN cadre; DLF founder; and a prominent political figure in the PFLOAG and PFLO periods. Interviewed on 10, 11, 12, 13 and 14 September 2006.

g) Comrade Nouh (Bahraini volunteer; operator of PFLOAG's repairs workshop): Manamah, Bahrain, 25 August 2007.

h) Teacher at the Revolution School who requested anonymity: Manamah, Bahrain, 31 August 2007.

i) Buthaina Fakhro (Bahraini volunteer; co-founder of the Omani Women's Association; PFLOAG delegate to several international conferences; longest serving teacher at the Revolution School): Manamah, Bahrain, 27 August 2007.

j) Sideeq al-Majid (Bahraini teacher at the Revolution School): Manamah, Bahrain, 27 August 2007.

k) Abdallah al-Nibari (Former Member of Kuwaiti Parliament; Prominent MAN leader; and active in solidarity and fundraising for the revolution): Oxford, United Kingdom, 8 August 2009.

l) Helen Lackner (Founding Member of the Gulf Committee in Solidarity with the Revolution): Oxford, United Kingdom, 1 August 2008.

m) Two Dhufari Intellectuals who grew up at the time of the revolution and requested anonymity: Cambridge, United Kingdom, 22 March 2009.

Oral History Programmes

British Diplomatic Oral History Programme, Archives Centre, Churchill College, Cambridge.

Iranian Oral History Project, Centre for Middle East Studies, Harvard University.

(iii) **Other Primary Sources**
Published British and Sultanate Documentary Sources

Burdett, A, *Records of Oman 1966–1971*, 6 Volumes, Cambridge Archive Editions, 2003.

Saltanat Oman, '*Khutab wa Kalimat 'Hadrat Sa'hib al-Jalalah al-Sultan Qaboos bin Said al Mu'atham: 1970–2005,* Muscat: Wazarat al-I'lam, 2005.

Published Revolutionary Documentary Sources

Al-Hindi, Hani and Al-Nas'rawi, 'Abdul Ilah (eds.), '*Harakat al 'Qawmiyeen al 'Arab: Nashatuha wa Ta'twuruha 'Abra Wathai'qiha, 1951–1968*, Volume 1, Parts 2 and 4. Beirut: Mu'asasat al-Ab'hath al-'Arabiyya, 2002 and 2004.

Al-Jabha Al-Shabiya Li Tahrir Oman, *Wathaiq al-Thikra al-Thanya'Ashara lil-Thawra al-Omaniyya*, Aden: Al-Lajna al-I'lamiya al-Markaziyya, 1977.

Al-Jabha al-Shabiya Li Tahrir Oman, *Sijil al Khalideen, Al Juz' al Awal, 1965–1979*, n.d., *c*.1980.

Al-Jabha al-Shabiya Li Tahrir Oman wal Khaleej al-Arabi, *Wathaiq al-Ni'dal al-Wat'ani, 1965–1974*, Beirut: Dar Al-Tali'a, 1974. Translated as *Documents of the National Struggle in Oman and the Arabian Gulf*, London: The Gulf Committee, 1974.

Official Revolutionary Publications and Studies

Gulf Committee, *Arms Build up in the Indian Ocean and the Gulf*, 1974.

—— *Women and the Revolution in Oman*, London: Gulf Committee, 1975.

Al-Jabha Al-Shabiya Li Tahrir Oman, *Aqlamat al-Harb fi Oman wa Maseer al-Firaq al-Qabalya fi Thufar*, n.d.

——*Al Ghazou al-Irani li Oman fi 'Aamih al-Thani*, Aden: Al-Lajna al-I'lamiya, 1975.

——*Al-Jabha al-Wataniya al-Arida wa Daruratuha al-Tarikhia*, Dirasat 9 Yunyu, n.d.

—— *Oman: Al-Insan wal Thawra/Oman: Man and Revolution*, 1976.

—— *Al- Qabila: Min Ayna Wa Ila Ayn?* Dirasat 9 Yunyu. 1981.

——*Al-Barnamij al-Siyassi*, Dirasat 9 Yunyu, Aden: Da'irat al-I'lam wal Di'aya wal Tahreed, 1982.

Al Jabha al-Shabiya Li Tahrir Oman wal Khaleej al Arabi al-Muhtal, *Qatar wal Ist'imar al-Jadid wal Inqilabat*, Dirasat 9 Yunyu, Beirut: Dar Al-Tali'a, 1972.

——*Al-Tanaqudat Fi-Itihad al-Shuyukh*, Dirasat 9 Yunyu Beirut: Dar Al-Tali'a, 1973.

——*Al-Wad' al-Tabaqi fi Oman (Al Saltana)*, Dirasat 9 Yunyu Beirut: Dar Al-Tali'a, 1973. Translated as *Oman: A Class Analysis*, London: Gulf Committee, 1974.

—— *Shahadat Min al Manatiq al Muharara*, February 1973.

——*Al-Thawra al-Omania, 1957–1959*, Dirasat 9 Yunyu Beirut: Dar Al-Tali'a, 1974.

Al-Jina'hi, Sa'id Ahmad, *Kuntu fi 'Thufar: Mushahadat fi Ard' al-Thawra*, Beirut: Confedraliat 'Talabat 'Oman wal 'Khaleej Al 'Arabi fi Lubnan and Dar Ibn Khaldun, 1974.

Munathamat al-Mara'a al-Omania, *Al-Mara' al-Omania wa Musawatuha fil Qanun wal Waqi'*: Dirasa Muqadama ila al-Mutamar Al-Alami lil Mara' al-Munaqid fi Berlin fil fatra min 20–24 October 1975.

——*Dawr Munathamat al-Mara'a al-Omania fi Tateer Fa'alyaat al-Mara'a al-Omania*, Manshurat Munathamat al-Mara'a al-Omania, 1978.

——*Musahamat al Mara'a al-Omania fil Haya al-Ijtima'ia wal Istiqlal al-Siyasi*, Manshurat Munathamat al Mara'a al-Omania, 1978.

Munathamat al-Shabab al-Omani, *Barnamij al-'Amal wal Nitham al-Dakhili: AL-Mutamar al-Awal al-Muaqid Min 25 ila 28/12/1977*, 1977.

Omani Red Crescent, *Health Work and the Revolution in Oman*, 1981.

Revolutionary Periodicals

9 Yunyu (Aden and Beirut).
Al-Khat al-Ahmar (Aden).
Gulf Solidarity (London).
Sawt al-Thawra (Aden).

Newspapers and Magazines

Al-Ahram.
Al-Arabi (Kuwait).
Al-Dimuqrati (Bahrain).
The Economist.
Filasteen al-Thawra (Beirut and Cyprus).
The Financial Times.
Al-Hadaf (Beirut).
Al- Hurriya (Beirut).
Al-Jumhuriya (Cairo).
Al-Kifah al-Arabi (Beirut).
Al-Nahar
The *New York Times.*
Oman.
Peking Review.
Rose el-Youssef (Cairo).
Al-Safir (Beirut).
Al-Sharara (South Yemen).
Al-Siyassa (Kuwait).
Al-Tali'a (Kuwait).
Al-Waqt (Bahrain).
Al-Wasat (Bahrain).
Al-Watan (Oman).

Arab Memoirs and Reflections

Darwish, *Munadil Min Oman, Mohammad Amin Abdullah,* Nicosia: Dilmun, 1990.
Al-Deeb, Fathi, *Abdel Nasser wa Tahrir al-Mashriq al 'Arabi: Shahadat Fathi al-Deeb,* Cairo: Markaz al-Dirasat al Istratijya wal Siyassiya bil Ahram, 2000.
Habash, George, *Al-Thawryoona La Yamoutouna Abadan,* Beirut: Al Saqi, 2011.
Hawatmah, Nayef, *Nayef Hawatmah Yatahadath,* Amman: Dar al-Jalil, 1997.
Al-Khatib, Ahmad. *Al-Kuwait: Min al-Imara ila al-Dawla, Thikrayat al- 'Amal al Wa'tani wal 'Qawmi,* second edition ('Kuwait: From the Emirate to the State, Memories of the Patriotic and Nationalist Work'), Casablanca and Beirut: al-Markaz al-Tha'qafi al- 'Arabi, 2007.
Al-Nuaimi, Abdel Rahman, 'Al Nuhud al Qawmi wal Watani Ba'da Hazimat Yuniou', *Al-Dimuqrati,* Vol.30, 2006.
—— 'Tarteeb al Bait al Hizbi wal Jabhawi', *Al Dimuqrati,* Vol. 33, May 2006.
—— 'Adan wa Ahlam al Qaramita al Judud', *Al-Wasat.* 13 November 2008.

Al-Nuaimi, Abdel Rahman, 'Al Sibaq 'ala al-Tartibat al-Siyassiya', *Al-Wasat*. 30 October 2008.

—— 'Tarjamat Qararat al-Mutamar al-Tawheedi', *Al-Wasat*, 1 January 2009.

Srour, Heiny, 'Hindrance and Gender Representation in Documentary Filmmaking'. First draft of a presentation at the AUC Symposium of Visual Anthropology in Cairo, 10 April 2010.

Trabulsi, Fawaz, *'Surat al-Fata bil Ahmar, Ayam Fil Silm Wal 'Harb*, Beirut: Riad el-Rayyes Books, 1994.

—— *Wu'oud Adan: Rihlaat Yamaniya*, Beirut: Riad el-Rayyes Books, 2000.

Ubaidli, Ahmad, 'Ali Hussein: "Allama al-Talaba Al-Riyadiyat wa Sina'at al-Cream Caramel" Kalima Fi Ta'been Khalaf Zein al-Din, Niyabatan "an Azdiqa'a al-Faqid"' (unpublished), n.d.

British Memoirs and Reflections

Akehurst, John, *We Won a War: The Campaign in Oman, 1965–1975*, Wiltshire: Michael Russell, 1982.

Arkless, David C, *The Secret War: Dhofar, 1971/1972*, London: W. Kimber, 1988.

De La Billiere, *Looking For Trouble: SAS to Gulf Command—The Autobiography*, New Edition. London: Harper Collins, 1995.

Fiennes, Ranulph, *Where Soldiers Fear to Tread*, New Edition, Mandarin, 1995.

Gardiner, Ian, *In the Service of the Sultan: A First Hand Account of the Dhofar Insurgency*, Barnsley: Pen and Sword, 2006.

Graham, John, *Ponder Anew: Reflections on the Twentieth Century*, Staplehurst, Kent: Spellmount Publishers, 1999.

Gwynne-James, David, *Letters from Oman: A Snapshot of Feudal Times as Oil Signals Change*, Victoria, British Columbia: Trafford Publishing, 2008.

Henderson, Edward, *This Strange Eventful History: Memoires of Earlier Days in the UAE and Oma,* London: Quartet Books, 1988.

Innes, Neil, *Minister in Oman: A Personal Narrative*, Cambridge: Oleander Press, 1987.

Jeapes, Tony, *SAS Secret War: Operation Storm in the Middle East*, London: Greenhill Books, 2005.

Kennedy, Michael Paul, *Soldier 'I': SAS*, London: Bloomsbury Publishing, 1990.

Perkins, Kenneth J, *A Fortunate Soldier*, Oxford: Brassey's Defence Publishers, 1988.

Sibley, Paul, *A Monk in the SAS*, Traford Publishing, 2006.

Thwaites, Peter, *Muscat Command*, Barnsley: Leo Cooper, 1995.

Weir, Michael, *Michael Scott Weir, 1925–2006, Unfinished Memoires* (unpublished).

II SECONDARY LITERATURE

Unpublished Theses

Alabdulkarim, Adel, 'Political Economy and Political Development in the Arabian Peninsula: the Case of the Sultanate of Oman', PhD dissertation, University of Southern California, 1997.

Bin Hamood, Badr bin Hamad, 'Political and Economic Development in Oman with Specific Reference to the Reign of Sultan Qaboos', MLitt thesis, University of Oxford, 1989.

Al-Hinai, Abdulmalik A, 'State Formation in Oman, 1861–1970', PhD thesis, London School of Economics and Political Science, 2000.

Cooper, Tristan, 'The Popular Front for the Liberation of Oman and the Arab Gulf: The Role of External Forces in its Political Development (1963–1975)', MPhil thesis, University of Oxford, 2000.

Dablan, Sai'd, 'Nushu'u Wa 'Tatawur al-Jabha al-Sha'biyya Li Ta'hrir 'Oman: 1964–1982', Diploma thesis, Abdullah Batheeb Institute of Scientific Socialism, Aden, People's Democratic Republic of South Yemen, 1989.

Hildebrant, Anke, 'Ecohydrology of a Seasonal Cloud Forest in Dhofar', PhD thesis in Hydrology, Massachusetts Institute of Technology, 2005.

Al-Kubaisi, Basil, 'The Arab Nationalist Movement: From Pressure Group to Socialist Party', PhD dissertation, The American University, 1971.

McKeown, John H, 'Britain and Oman: The Dhofar War and its Significance', MPhil thesis, University of Cambridge, 1981.

Al-Mdairis, Falah, 'The Arab Nationalist Movement in Kuwait from its Origins to 1970', DPhil thesis, University of Oxford, 1987.

Muqaibel, Salim bin-Aqeel, 'Thawrat Thufar, 1965–1975', Higher Diploma thesis, Institute of Arab Research and Studies, Arab League, Cairo, 2001.

Thiab, Lazim Lafta, 'Al-Mu'arada al-Siyassiya Fi-Saltanat Oman, 1955–1975', Masters thesis, Basra University, 1984.

Published Books, Chapters, and Articles

Abdel Karim, Qais and Suleiman, Fahed, *Al-Jabha al-Dimuqratya, al-Nasha'a wal Masar,* Beirut and Damascus: Dar al-Taqadum al-Arabi and al-Dar al-Wataniya al-Jadida, 2000.

Abdullah, Muhammad Mursi, *Imarat al-Sahil wa Oman wal Dawla al-Saudia al-Ula,* Al Juz' al-Awwal, Cairo: Al-Maktab al-Misri al-Hadeeth, 1978.

Alatas, Syed Hussein, *The Myth of the Lazy Native,* London: Frank Cass, 1977.

Allen, Calvin. 'The State of Masqat in the Gulf and East Africa, 1785–1829', *International Journal of Middle East Studies.* Vol. 14, 1982.

—— *Oman: The Modernisation of the Sultanate,* Boulder, Colorado: Westview Press, 1987.

Allen, Calvin and Rigsbee, W. Lynn II, *Oman Under Qaboos: From Coup to Constitution, 1970–1996,* London: Frank Cass, 2002.

Al-Amri, Mohammad Sa'id Duraibi, *Thufar: al Thawra fil Tarikh al-Omani al Mo'uasir,* Beirut: Riad el-Rayyes Books, 2005.

Anderson, Perry, *Lineages of the Absolutist State,* London: Verso, 1979.

Aristotle, *The Politics.* Carnes Lord Translation, Chicago: University of Chicago Press, 1985.

Bailey, Martin, 'Tanzania and China', *African Affairs,* Vol.74, No. 294, January1975.

Bakhtin, Mikhail Mikhailovich, *The Dialogic Imagination,* Austin: University of Texas Press, 2008.

Balfour-Paul, Glen, *The End of Empire in the Middle East: Britain's Relinquishment of Power in Her Last Three Arab Dependencies*, Cambridge: Cambridge University Press, 1994.

Barut, Moh'ammad Jamal, *'Harakat al-Qawmiyeen al-'Arab: al-Nash'a, al-Ta'tawur, al-Mas'air*, Damascus: al-Markaz al-'Arabi lil Dirasat al-Istratijya, 1997.

Batatu, Hanna, *The Old Social Classes and the Revolutionary Movements of Iraq*, London: Saqi, 2004.

Beasant, John and Ling, Christopher, *Sultan in Arabia: A Private Life*, Edinburgh and London: Mainstream Publishing, 2004.

Behbehani, Hashim, *China's Foreign Policy in the Arab World, 1955–75: Three Case Studies*, London and Boston: Kegan Paul, 1981.

Benton, Lauren, 'Empires of Exception: History, Law, and the Problem of Imperial Sovereignty', *Quaderni di Relazioni Internazionali*, Vol.54, 2007.

Bhaba, Homi, *The Location of Culture*, London: Routledge Classics, 2004.

Bhacker, M Reda, *Trade and Empire in Muscat and Zanzibar: Roots of British Domination*, London: Routledge and Kegan Paul, 1994.

Bierschenk, T, 'Oil Interests and the Formation of Centralised Government in Oman, 1920–1970" in *Orient*, Vol. 30, 1989.

Bin Huwaidin, Mohammed, *China's Relations with Arabia and the Gulf, 1949–1999*, London: Routlege Curzon, 2002.

Bodin, Jean and Franklin, Julian (eds.), *On Sovereignty: Four Chapters from the Six Books of the Commonwealth*, Cambridge: CUP, 1992.

Bose, Sugata, *A Hundred Horizons: The Indian Ocean in the Age of Global Empire*, Cambridge and London: Harvard University Press, 2006.

Buck-Morss, Susan, *Hegel, Haiti, and Universal History*, Pittsburgh: University of Pittsburgh Press, 2009.

Burrows, Bernard, *Footnotes in the Sand: The Gulf in Transition, 1953–1958*. Salisbury: Michael Russell, 1990.

Busch, Briton Cooper, *Britain and the Persian Gulf, 1894–1914*, Berkeley and Los Angeles: University of California Press, 1967.

Chatty, Dawn, 'Rituals of Royalty and the Elaboration of Ceremony in Oman: View from the Edge', *International Journal of Middle East Studies*, Vol. 41, 2009.

Cleveland, William, *The Making of an Arab Nationalist: Ottomanism and Arabism in the Life and Thought of Sati' Al-Husri*, Princeton, NJ: Princeton University Press, 1971.

Darwin, John, *The Empire Project: The Rise and Fall of the British World-System, 1830–1970*, Cambridge: CUP, 2009.

Deffarge, Claude and Troeller, Gordian, 'Secret War Number Eleven', *Atlas*, Vol. 5, No.18, November 1969.

Dirlik, Arif, 'Mao Zedong and "Chinese Marxism", in Makdisi, Casarino and Karl (eds.), *Marxism Beyond Marxism*, New York and London: Routledge, 1996.

Dubois, Laurent, *A Colony of Citizens: Revolutions and Slave Emancipation in the French Caribbean, 1787–1804*, Chapel Hill: University of North Carolina Press, 2004.

Eagleton, Terry, *After Theory*, London: Penguin, 2004.

Ehteshami, A. and Hinnebusch, R., *Syria and Iran: Middle Powers in a Penetrated Regional System*, London: Routledge, 1997.

Eickelman, Dale, 'Kings and People: Oman's State Consultative Council', *Middle East Journal*, Vol.38, No.1, Winter 1984.

——'From Theocracy to Monarchy: Authority and Legitimacy in Inner Oman', *International Journal of Middle East Studies*, Vol.17, No.1, 1985.

Elkins, Caroline, *Imperial Reckoning: the Untold Story of Britain's Gulag in Kenya*, New York: Owl Books, Henry Holt and Company, 2005.

Fagen, Richard, *The Transformation of Political Culture in Cuba*, Stanford: Stanford University Press, 1969.

Fanon, Franz, *The Wretched of the Earth*, London: Penguin, 2001.

Fayad, Ali, '*Harb al-Sha'ab fi Oman, wa Yantasir al-'Hufa*, Beirut: Al-Itihad al-'Aam Lil Kutab Wal Sahafyeen al-Filastinyeen, 1975.

Freedman, Robert O, *Soviet Policy Towards the Middle East Since 1970*, New York: Praeger Publishers, 1978.

Furet, François, *Interpreting the French Revolution*, Cambridge: CUP, 1981.

Gause, F. Gregory' III, *Oil Monarchies: Domestic and Security Challenges in the Arab Gulf States*, New York: Council on Foreign Relations Press, 1994.

Geraghty, Tony, *Who Dares Wins: The Story of the SAS, 1950–1992*, London: Abacus, 2002.

Gerber, Haim, *Islam, Guerrilla War, and Revolution: A Study in Comparative Social History*, Boulder and London: Lynne Rienner, 1998.

Ghubash, Hussein, *Oman—The Islamic Democratic Tradition*, London: Routledge, 2006.

Giap, Vo Nguyen, *The Military Art of People's War: Selected Writings of General Vo Nguyen Giap*, New York; London: Monthly Review Press, 1970.

Goldfrank, Walter. 'Theories of Revolution and Revolution Without Theory: The Case of Mexico', *Theory and Society*, Vol.7, No.1/2, 1979.

Goldstone, Jack, 'Towards a Fourth Generation of Revolutionary Theory', *Annual Review of Political Science*, Vol.4, June 2001.

Grosrichard, Alan, *The Sultan's Court: European Fantasies of the East*, London: Verso, 1998.

Guha, Ranajit, 'The Prose of Counter-Insurgency', in *Subaltern Studies II: Writings on South Asian History and Society*, Delhi: Oxford University Press, 1983.

Haikal, Mohammad, *The Sphinx and the Commissar: The Rise and Fall of Soviet Influence in the Middle East*, London: Harper and Row, 1978.

——*Madafi' Ayatullah: Qisat Iran Wal Thawra*, Al-Tub'a al-Thalitha, Dar Al-Shurooq, 1983.

Halliday, Fred, *Revolution and Foreign Policy: The Case of South Yemen, 1967–1987*, Cambridge: Cambridge University Press, 1990.

——*Arabia Without Sultans*, London: Saqi Books, 1999.

Handman, Max, 'The Bureaucratic Culture Pattern and Political Revolutions', *American Journal of Sociology*, Vol. XXXIX, No. 3, November 1933.

Harik, Ilyia, 'The Origins of the Arab State System,' in Luciani, Giacomo (ed.), *The Arab State*, London: Routledge, 1990.

Hawley, Donald, *Oman and its Renaissance*, London: Stacey International, 1984.

Haynes, Mike and Wolfreys, Jim, *History and Revolution: Refuting Revisionism*, London: Verso, 2007.

Hazareesingh, Sudhir, 'Republicanism, War and Democracy: The *Ligue Du Midi* in France's War against Prussia, 1870–1871', *French History*, Vol.17, No.1.

—— 'Vincent Wright and the Jacobin Legacy in Historical and Theoretical Perspectives' in Hazareesingh (ed.), *The Jacobin Legacy in Modern France: Essays in Honour of Vincent Wright*, Oxford: Oxford University Press, 2002.

Hejlawi, Nour el Din bin-Al 'Habeeb, *Ta'thir al Fikr al Nas'iri 'ala al-Khaleej al-'Arabi, 1952–1971*, Beirut: Markaz Dirasat al-Wih'da al-'Arabiyya, 2003.

Herb, Michael, *All in the Family: Absolutism, Revolution and Democracy in the Middle Eastern Monarchies*, Albany NY: SUNY Press, 1999.

Hilal, Ali al-Dein, 'Ta'tawur Al-Ideologiyya al Rasmiya fi Misr: Al-Dimuqratiya wal Ishtirakya', *Misr: Min al-Thawra ila al-Rida*, Beirut: Dar al-Tali'a, 1981.

Hobbes, Thomas, *Leviathan*, Cambridge and Indianapolis: Hackett Publishing, 1994.

Ho Chi Minh, 'The Path Which Led me to Leninism', Ho Chi Minh Internet Archive (<marxists.org>) 2003.

Hourani, Albert, *Arabic Thought in the Liberal Age, 1798–1939*, Cambridge: Cambridge University Press, 2002.

Ibn Khaldun, *Al-Muqadima*, Beirut: Dar al-Jeel, n.d.

Ibn Ruzayq, Humayd, *History of the Imams and Seyyids of Oman*, New York: Burt Franklin Publishers, n.d.

Ibrahim, Sonallah, *Warda*, Third Edition, Cairo: Dar al-Mustakbal al-Arabi, 2002.

Al-Ikri, Abdel Nabi, *Al-Tanthimat al-Yassariya fil Jazeera wal Khaleej al 'Arabi*, Beirut: Dar al-Kunouz al-Adabyya, 2003.

Ismail, Tareq Y, *The Arab Left*. Syracuse, New York: Syracuse University Press, 1976.

—— *The Communist Movement in the Arab World*, London: Routledge Curzon, 2005.

Jamangar, Mohammad Jafar, *Bahran Zufar Va Regime Pahlavi*, Tehran: Mouassasat Mutalaat, 2004.

Janzen, Jorg, *Nomads in the Sultanate of Oman: Tradition and Development in Dhofa*, Boulder, Colorado: Westview Press, 1986.

Joffe, George. 'Concepts of Sovereignty in the Gulf Region', in Schofield, Richard, *Territorial Foundation of the Gulf States*, London: UCL Press, 1994.

Joyce, Miriam. *Kuwait, 1945–1996: An Anglo-American Perspective*, London: Frank Cass, 1998.

Kaiksow, Sarah, 'Subjectivity and Imperial Masculinity: A British Soldier in Dhofar (1968–1970)', in *The Journal of Middle East Women's Studies*, Spring 2008.

Karam, Fouad, *Thawrat Thufar Sira'a bayn al-Shuyuiya wal Islam*, Beirut: Isdarat Fouad Karam, n.d.

Kazziha, Walid, *Revolutionary Transformation in the Arab World: Habash and his Comrades from Nationalism to Communism*, London: Croom Helm, 1979.

Kechichian, J., *Oman and the World: the Emergence of an Independent Foreign Policy*, Santa Monica: Rand, 1995.

Kelly, J.B., *Britain and the Persian Gulf 1795–1880*, Oxford: Clarendon Press, 1968.

——'Hadramhaut, Oman, Dhofar: The Experience of Revolution', *Middle East Studies*, Vol.12, No.2, 1976.

Kerr, Malcolm, *The Arab Cold War, 1958–1964*, London: OUP, 1965.

Khalidi, Walid, 'Political Trends in the Fertile Crescent', in Laquere, Walter (ed.). *The Middle East in Transition: Studies in Contemporary History*, New York: Praeger.

Kiernan, V.G., 'Foreign Mercenaries and Absolute Monarchy', *Past and Present*. No.11, April 1957.

Kostiner, Joseph (ed.), *Middle East Monarchies: The Challenge of Modernity*, Boulder: Lynne Rienner, 2000.

Lackner, Helen, *P.D.R. Yemen: Outpost of Socialist Development in Arabia*, London: Ithaca Press, 1985.

Landen, R.G., *Oman Since 1856: Disruptive Modernization in a Traditional Arab Society*, Princeton, New Jersey: Princeton University Press, 1967.

Lawson, Fred, *Constructing International Relations in the Arab World*, Stanford: Stanford University Press, 2006.

Lin Biao, *Long Live the Victory of People's War!* Peking: Foreign Languages Press, 1965.

Lorimer, J.G., *Gazetteer of the Persian Gulf, 'Oman, and Central Arabia*, Dublin: Irish Academic Press, 1986.

Louis, Wm. Roger, *Ends of British Imperialism: The Scramble for Empire, Suez and Decolonization* (Second Edition), London: I.B. Tauris, 2006.

Luthi, Lorenz, *The Sino-Soviet Split: Cold War in the Communist World*, Princeton: Princeton University Press, 2008.

Al-Mdairis, Falah, *al-Mujtama' al-Madani wal 'Haraka al-Wat'aniya fil Kuwait* ['Civil Society and the National Movement in Kuwait'], Kuwait: Dar Qirtas, 2000.

——*Al Tawajuhat al Marxia al Kuwaitia.* Kuwait: Dar Qirtas lil Nashr, 2003.

Mamdani, Mahmoud, *Citizen and Subject: Contemporary Africa and the Legacy of Late Colonialism*, Princeton: Princeton University Press, 1996.

Mann, Michael, *The Trucial Oman Scouts: The Story of a Bedouin Force*, Wilby, Norwich: Michael Russell Publishing, 1994.

Mao Zedong, *On Practice and Contradiction*, London: Verso, 2007.

Marcuse, Herbert, *Reason and Revolution, Hegel and the Rise of Social Theory*, Boston: Beacon Press, 1968.

Massad, Joseph. *Colonial Effects: The Making of National Identity in Jordan*, New York: Columbia University Press, 1998.

Miller, John (ed.), *Absolutism in Seventeenth Century Europe*, New York: Palgrave Macmillan, 1990.

Montesquieu, *The Spirit of the Laws*, Cambridge: CUP, 1989.

Morris, Jan, *Sultan in Oman*, London: Sickle Moon Books, 2002.

Nabulsi, Karma, *Traditions of War: Occupation, Resistance and the Law*, Oxford: Oxford University Press, 2005.

Al-Nafisi, Abdallah, *Tathmeen al-Sira' fi Thufar, 1965–1975*, Beirut: Dar al-Nihaya, 1976.

Al-Naqeeb, Khaldoun H, *Society and State in the Gulf and Arab Peninsula: A Different Perspective*, London: Routledge, 1990.

Newsinger, J., 'Jebel Akhdar and Dhofar: Footnote to Empire', *Race and Class*, Vol.39, No.3, 1998.

Onley, James, *The Arabian Frontier of the British Raj: Merchants, Rulers, and the British in the Nineteenth Century Gulf*, Oxford: OUP, 2008.

Owtram, Francis, *A Modern History of Oman*, London: I.B. Tauris, 2004.

Panaspornprasit, Chookiat, *US–Kuwaiti Relations, 1961–1962*, London: Routledge, 2005.

Panikkar, K.N., *Against Lord and State: Religion and Peasant Uprisings in Malabar, 1836–1921*, Delhi: OUP, 1989.

Parker, David (ed.), *Ideology, Absolutism, and the English Revolution: Debates of the British Communist Historians, 1940–1956*, London: Lawrence and Wishart, 2008.

Peterson, J.E., *Oman in the Twentieth Century: Political Foundations of an Emerging State*, London: Croom Helm, 1978.

——'Oman's Diverse Society: Southern Oman', *Middle East Journal*, Vol.58, No.2, Spring 2004.

—— *Oman's Insurgencies: The Sultanate's Struggle For Supremacy*, London: Saqi Books, 2007.

Philips, Wendell, *Unknown Oman*, New York: David McKay, 1966.

Pimlot, J., 'The British Army: The Dhofar Campaign, 1970–1975', in Becket, I. and Pimlot, J (eds.), *Armed Forces and Modern Counterinsurgency*, London: St Martin's Press, 1985.

Plekhanov, Sergey, *A Reformer on the Throne: Sultan Qaboos bin Said*, London: Trident Press, 2004.

Podeh, Elie and Winckler, Onn (eds.), *Rethinking Nasserism: Revolution and Historical Memory in Modern Egypt*, Gainesville, FL: University Press of Florida, 2004.

Price, D.L., *Oman: Insurgency and Development*, London: Institute for the Study of Conflict, 1975.

——'Oman: A Communist Defeat', *Spectator*, 7 February 1976.

Priestland, David, *The Red Flag: Communism and the Making of the Modern World*, London: Allen Lane, 2009.

Primakov, Yevgeny, *Russia and the Arabs: Behind the Scenes in the Middle East from the Cold War to the Present*, New York: Basic Books, 2009.

Provence, Michael, *The Great Syrian Revolt and the Rise of Arab Nationalism*, Austin: University of Texas Press, 2005.

Al-Qassab, Basima, 'Laila Fakhro, Mama Huda: An Takuna Mualiman Qadiran ala al-Jura'a', *Al Waqt* (Bahrain), Issue No.682, 3 January 2008.

Al-Qassimi, Sultan, *The Myth of Arab Piracy in the Gulf*, London: Routledge, 1988.

—— *Sard al-That*, Beirut: Al-Mu'asasa Al-Arabiya lil Dirasat wal Nashr, 2009.

Rabi, Uzi, *The Emergence of States in a Tribal Society*, Brighton: Sussex Academic Press, 2006.

Al-Rayyes, Riad, 'Hikayat al-Sultan wal 'Aqeed wal Malik', *Al-Nahar*, 7 March 1975.

—— *Thufar: Al-Sira' al-Siyassi Wal Askari Fil Khaleej al-Arabi, 1970–1976*, Beirut: Riad el-Rayyes Books, 2002.

Riphenburg, Carol, *Oman: Political Development in a Changing World*, London: Praeger, 1998.

Robin, Corey, *Fear: The History of a Political Idea*, Oxford and New York: Oxford University Press, 2004.

Said, Edward, *The World, the Text and the Critic*, Cambridge: Harvard University Press, 1983.

—— *Culture and Imperialism*. New York: Vintage, 1993.

—— *Reflections on Exile and Other Essays*, Cambridge: Harvard University Press, 2000.

Al-Salimi, Abdullah Ibn Humaid, *Tuhfat al A'yan bi-Sirat Ahl 'Uman*, Part 2, Cairo: Al-Matba'a al-Salafiya, 1334/1928.

Al-Salimi, Mohammad bin Abdullah (Abu Bashir), *Nahdat al-A'yan Bi-'Hurriyat 'Oman*, Cairo: Dar al-Kitab al-'Arabi, 1961.

Sayigh, Yezid, *Armed Struggle and the Search for a State: The Palestinian National Movement*, Oxford: Clarendon Press, 1999.

Al-Sayyed Saleem, Mohammad, *Al Ta'hlil al-Siyassi al-Nassiri: Dirasa fil 'Akaaed wal Siyassa al-Kharijiya*, Beirut: Markaz Dirasat al-Wih'da al-'Arabiyya, 1983.

Scott, Joan, 'Gender: A Useful Category of Historical Analysis', *The American Historical Review*, Vol.91, No.5, December 1986.

Scott, J.C., *Domination and the Arts of Resistance: Hidden Transcripts*, New Haven and London: Yale University Press, 1990.

—— *The Art of Not Being Governed: An Anarchist History of Upland Southeast Asia*, New Haven and London: Yale University Press, 2009.

Seif, Said; Saad, Talal, 'Interview on the Political Situation in Oman and Dhofar', *New Left Review*, I/66, March–April 1971.

Shichor, Yitzhak, *The Middle East in China's Foreign Policy, 1949–1977*, Cambridge: CUP, 2008.

Sinha, Mrinalini, *Colonial Masculinity: The 'Manly Englishman' and the 'Effeminate Bengali' in The Late Nineteenth Century*, Manchester: Manchester University Press, 1995.

Skeet, Ian, *Muscat and Oman: The End of an Era*, London: Faber and Faber, 1974.

—— *Oman: Politics and Development*, Basingstoke: MacMillan, 1992.

Skinner, Quentin, *Liberty Before Liberalism*, Cambridge: Cambridge University Press, 1998.

Skocpol, Theda, *States and Social Revolutions: A Comparative Analysis of France, Russia, and China*, Cambridge: Cambridge University Press, 1979.

Al-Tabuki, Salim., 'Tribal Structures in South Oman', *Arabian Studies*, Vol.6, 1982.

Tackett, Timothy, *Becoming a Revolutionary: the Deputies of the French National Assembly and the Emergence of a Revolutionary Culture*, Princeton: Princeton University Press, 1996.

Teschke, Benno, *The Myth of 1648*, London: Verso, 2003.

Thompson, Robert, *Defeating Communist Insurgency: Experiences From Malaya and Vietnam*, London: Chato and Windus, 1966.

Tilly, Charles, *European Revolutions, 1492–1992*, Oxford: Blackwell, 1995.

Trabulsi, Fawwaz, 'The Liberation of Dhufar', *MERIP Reports*, No.6, January 1972.

—— *Thufar: Shahada min Zaman al-Thawra*, Beirut: Riad el-Rayyes Books, 2004.

Tripp, Charles, *A History of Iraq*, second edition, Cambridge: CUP, 2000.

Ubaidli, Ahmad, 'Ikhtilafat 'Hawl Jabhat Tahrir Thufar Wa Rabitat al-Talaba', *Al-Waqt*, 28 March 2010.

Valeri, Marc, *Oman: Politics and Society in the Qaboos State*, London: Hurst and Company, 2009.

Vassiliev, Alexei, *Russian Policy in the Middle East: From Messianism to Pragmatism*, Reading: Ithaca Press, 1993.

—— *The History of Saudi Arabia*, London: Saqi Books, 1999.

Ward, Kerry, *Networks of Empire: Forced Migration in the Durch East India Company*, Cambridge: CUP, 2009.

Weber, Max. *The Theory of Social and Economic Organisation*, New York: The Free Press of Glencoe, 1947.

Wilkinson, J.C., *Water and Tribal Settlement in South-East Arabia: A Study of the Aflāj of Oman*, Oxford: Clarendon Press, 1977.

—— *The Imamate Tradition of Oman*, Cambridge: Cambridge University Press, 1987.

Williams, Raymond, *Keywords: A Vocabulary of Culture and Society*, Glasgow: Fontana/Croom Helm, 1976.

Wolf, Eric, *Peasant Wars of the Twentieth Century*, New York: Harper Torchbooks, 1973.

Woodward, Michelle, 'Between Orientalist Clichés and Images of Modernisation: Photographic Practice in the Late Ottoman Era', *History of Photography*, Winter 2003, Vol.27, No.4.

Young, Robert, *Postcolonialism, An Historical Introduction*, Oxford: Blackwell, 2001.

Yu, George T., *China's African Policy: Study of Tanzania*, New York: Praeger, 1975.

Zahlan, Rosemarie, *The Making of the Modern Gulf States: Kuwait, Bahrain, Qatar, the United Arab Emirates and Oman*, Reading: Ithaca Press, 1998.

Index

Printed and bound by CPI Group (UK) Ltd, Croydon, CR0 4YY